The Complete Alabama Fisherman

by Mike Bolton

SEACOAST PUBLISHING INC.

Birmingham, Alabama

To my wonderful wife, Beth, whose patience and unselfishness made this book possible
and
to my little man, Cory. May the wonderful smell of outboard exhaust on a crisp fall morning
be the only thing you ever want to stick up your nose.

Bolton, Mike
The Complete Alabama Fisherman
Layout by Chris Roberts
Maps by Beth Bolton and Mary Shryock
Saltwater chapters by Tom Bailey

To order copies:
Seacoast Publishing Inc.
110 12th St. North
Birmingham, AL 35203
(205) 250-8016
$18.95

ISBN: 1-878561-46-4

Printed in the United States of America.

Table of Contents

Alabama: America's Best Fishing

Get a map of the United States and lay it before you. Other than Alabama, count the states that you imagine have the potential to give up 16-pound bass, 4-pound bream, 8-pound spotted bass, 10-pound smallmouth bass, 4-pound crappie, 55-pound striped bass and 80-pound catfish, not to mention 60-pound grouper, 100-pound tarpon, 75-pound Amberjack, 30-pound Red Snapper, 12-pound Speckled Trout and 55-pound King Mackerel.

Make the list of states with fishing diversified enough which you can catch a rainbow trout on a flyrod and five minutes later catch a 30-pound striped bass (at Smith Lake), or drop a minnow and catch largemouth bass, smallmouth bass, five species of catfish, sauger, white crappie, black crappie, drum, skipjack herring, five species of sunfish, striped bass, white bass and hybrid bass (at Wheeler Lake) or catch a 5-pound bass on one cast and a 10-pound redfish on the next (in the Mobile Delta).

Can fishing in any state compare with Alabama's? I honestly believe not. California has given up enormous largemouth bass, but the state has never seen a 4-pound bream or a 4-pound crappie. Texas has given up its share of big bass in recent years, but smallmouth bass don't exist there. Nor has the Lone Star state ever given up a 4-pound bream or a 4-pound crappie.

Georgia? It gave up the world record largemouth 57 years ago, but hasn't come close since. Almost every state fishing record in Alabama betters Georgia's. Florida you say? Lots of big bass, but not the first 4-pound crappie. Smallmouth bass and spotted bass can't be found in that state.

Check out the state record bass in each of the 50 states. The state record for 44 of those states wouldn't make the list of the 20 largest bass ever caught in Alabama. More than 75 percent of the states have never given up a bass larger than 9 pounds.

Study the nation's 60 largest metropolitan areas. Can anywhere compare with 55th-ranked Birmingham? The state's largest city is less than 100 miles from Weiss Lake, the crappie capital of the world; Lake Guntersville, the lake the pros call the nation's best bass lake; Smith Lake, home of five consecutive world record spotted bass; Lake Martin, which has given up a 51-pound striped bass in the 80's, Lake Pickwick, which gave up a IGFA line-class world record smallmouth bass in 1989; Aliceville and Gainesville lakes, which gave up one 16-pound bass and two 14-pound bass in less than a month in 1989; and Wheeler Lake, which gave up two 70-pound-plus and one 80-pound-plus blue cat in 19 days in 1988.

That doesn't include other public water in a 2-hour drive, water such as Wilson Lake, the Warrior River, Demopolis Lake, Holt Reservoir, Inland Lake, Lake Jordan, Lay Lake, Lake Logan Martin, Lake Mitchell, Lake Neely Henry, Oliver Reservoir, Lake Purdy, Lake Harris, Lake Thurlow, Lake Tuscaloosa, the Warrior Reservoir in Eutaw and Yates Reservoir.

That adds up to 26 bodies of water and more than a quarter-million acres of excellent fishing anglers in most states would kill for.

The lifelong Alabama resident fishermen may take that for granted, but the transplanted Alabama angler doesn't. One has to only look at nearby Southern cities such as Louisville, where an angler's best bet is the nearby filthy Ohio River, or Atlanta, where the angler's best close bet is overcrowded Lake Lanier, to see what Alabama has to offer.

In 1988, while serving as the outdoor writer for *The Birmingham News*, I was fortunate enough to wade the Little Cahaba River with my flyrod and catch a 2-pound bream, catch and release more than 60 largemouth bass caught on topwater in one day on Lake Guntersville, catch a 5-pound smallmouth in Wheeler Lake, catch a 25-pound striped bass from Lake Martin, catch and release 123 hybrid bass in one day below Wilson Dam, catch a 50-fish limit of slab crappie on Weiss Lake, hang into and lose a largemouth in a private lake that would have likely topped 12 pounds and land a 55-pound grouper and 60-pound amberjack - all in a 67-day period.

That's the kind of fishing Alabama has to offer.

I hope *The Complete Alabama Fisherman* will give Alabama's anglers — from the beginning perch jerker to the accomplished bass angler — a better insight into fishing in Alabama and greatly increase his fishing chances in a state where his fishing chances are already tremendous.

To call putting together *The Complete Alabama Fisherman* work is stretching the truth a bit. Being able to fish, in a 3-year period, every lake in Alabama with more than 50 of the state's best fishermen was nothing but pure joy.

The long nights at the typewriter transferring those tape-recorded conversations into the written word was as close to work as it got, but those long nights also served to rekindle the wonderful memories of Vienna sausage dinners in rain-filled boats, hours on the water with wonderful people and the stories of the big one that got away.

**Good fishing,
Mike Bolton**

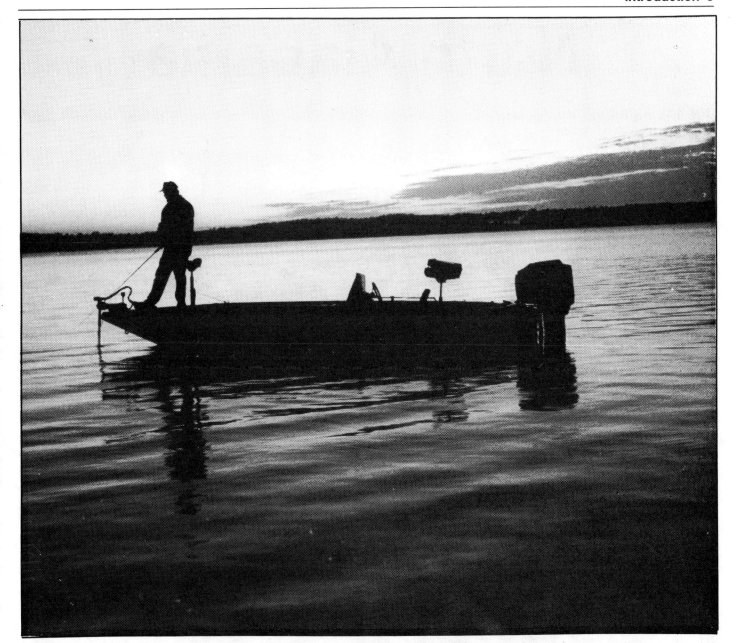

About Author Mike Bolton

Mike Bolton is a lifelong Alabama resident who has spent thousands of hours on Alabama's lakes and rivers and may be the only angler in the state to have caught fish from every one of the 25 largest lakes in the state. As outdoor writer for *The Birmingham News*, Bolton has been fortunate enough to fish with and observe the techniques of the best anglers on each lake. It was with those contacts he was able to put together this unique book.

Bolton has fished and hunted extensively abroad, as well as in Alabama. He has hunted whitewing doves in the foothills of the Sierra Madres in Mexico, has hunted elk and mule deer in Colorado and has caught a 38-pound salmon on his flyrod in Alaska.

Bolton attended Birmingham's Huffman High School for three years before graduating from Hewitt-Trussville High School in 1974. He attended the University of Alabama and worked in the UA Athletic Department from 1976-1980, a period in which the Crimson Tide won two national championships in football.

Bolton has been editor of *Bama Magazine*, worked as a sportswriter for *The Tuscaloosa News*, *The Alabama Journal*, *The Southeast Sun* and *The Birmingham News*, and was managing editor of the *Enterprise Ledger*.

Mike is married to the former Elizabeth Shryock, of Tampa, and they have a son and daughter. They live in Argo in St. Clair County.

North Alabama

The 12 counties in North Alabama provide fishermen with thousands of acres of prime fishing waters.

The mainstream reservoirs on the Tennessee River provide more than 182,000 acres of water. Smaller reservoirs, such as those found in the Bear Creek watershed, provide the opportunity to fish in lakes which are not as large as the mainstream reservoirs. Several streams offer the solitude of wading and float fishing. Farm ponds and fee-charging fishing lakes, including two state-owned lakes, round out the opportunities for angling enjoyment.

Reservoirs

The mainstream reservoirs of the Tennessee River – Guntersville, Wheeler, Wilson and Pickwick – provide excellent fishing for thousands of north Alabama anglers each year. Crowds of fishermen can be found on these lakes in early spring when crappie are concentrated around submerged treetops and stumps. Many fishermen use live minnows for bait on cane poles as did their fathers and grandfathers. Other fishermen prefer rods, reels and fish small plastic jigs.

Bream fishing is most productive on all these impoundments during the spring when the bream are bedding in shallow waters and during summer mayfly hatches. Fishing under trees heavily laden with mayflies, or willowflies as they are called locally, can result in large catches of bream as well as bass and catfish.

The best fishing for channel catfish usually occurs in the late spring when catfish are spawning. Catfish like to spawn in holes under rocks, so fishermen frequently fish along steep rocky banks or rip-rap. They fish baits such as gobs of live worms or chicken liver along the edges of the rocks. Although most of the catfish caught from these reservoirs weigh less than 10 pounds, some large ones are

present. A commercial fisherman caught a 106-pound blue catfish in Guntersville Reservoir in 1977 and the state rod-and-reel record fell three times in 19 days below Lake Guntersville Dam in 1988. That record eventually ended up at 82 pounds.

Flathead catfish larger than 50 pounds are caught occasionally.

Saltwater striped bass, and in recent years hybrid striped bass, have been stocked by the Fisheries Section of the Game and Fish Division to establish an additional sport fishery for the fishermen of Alabama. In the past two decades, more than 3 million saltwater and hybrid striped bass have been stocked in Guntersville, Wheeler and Wilson reservoirs. Catches in the reservoirs are sporadic, but the tailwaters have produced some excellent catches during the spring and fall.

White bass are popular game fish in these reservoirs. Fishermen harvest them most frequently by fishing the "jumps" during the summer when white bass break water chasing shad. Trolling or fishing under lights at night is also an effective technique.

Largemouth and smallmouth bass are present in the Tennessee River reservoirs. Largemouth bass fishing is good in all four reservoirs. Thanks to record catches in the BASS Alabama Invitational in recent years, Lake Guntersville has become well-known nationwide as one of the nation's top bass fishing lakes.

Wilson reservoir probably produces the largest average size largemouths in fishermen's creels.

Smallmouth bass fishing is confined primarily to the lower end of Wheeler Reservoir, Wilson Reservoir and Pickwick Reservoir. Some of the most popular smallmouth fishing occurs at night during the summer. Fishermen casting spinner baits or jigs often have excellent catches.

Any of the larger cities along the river (Quad-cities, Decatur,

District fisheries office: Decatur (353-2634)

● Denotes free launch area

Fishing opportunities in North Alabama

Huntsville, Guntersville and Scottsboro) provide accommodations and restaurants. Boat launching ramps are numerous on these reservoirs.

Tailwaters

The tailwater areas below Guntersville, Wheeler and Wilson Dams offer some of the most exciting fishing in the Tennessee Valley. These dams serve as barriers to upstream migrations of fish. Consequently, large concentrations of fish seasonally congregate below the dams. Because of these concentrations, harvests are usually excellent. TVA records over a seven-year period indicate that fishing trips in these tailwater areas averaged 198,426 fishing trips per year. These areas provide the greatest diversity of fishing available in the state. Although the majority of tailwater fishermen pursues largemouth bass, smallmouth bass, sauger, catfish and saltwater striped bass, they can expect to catch any of the approximately 20 species of game fish present.

The type of fishing found in tailwater areas is seasonal. During the winter, sauger are abundant and are sought by many fishermen braving the elements. Walleye are also present but not as abundant as sauger.

In the spring after the spawning runs of sauger has tapered off, crappie, white and yellow bass are caught in large numbers. Saltwater striped bass and hybrid striped bass start hitting in late spring and continue until fall. Largemouth bass also are often caught below the dams in the spring. The smallmouth bass fishing below Wheeler and Wilson Dams is often referred to as the best in the world. Spring and fall produce the best smallmouth fishing.

Catfish are readily caught below these dams. Live or cut baits fished on bottom catch the most fish, including blue, channel and flathead catfish. June is usually the month of choice for catfishing.

One should always exercise caution and basic common sense in tailwater areas. The Alabama Marine Police Division requires that each boater within 800 feet of hydroelectric dams and/or navigation locks must wear a Coast Guard approved life preserver.

Small impoundments and streams

Four small reservoirs, constructed by TVA on the Bear Creek wathershed, provide an opportunity for fishermen in the Franklin County area to have good fishing close to home.

The four lakes, ranging from 670 acres to 4,200, are controlled by the Bear Creek Authority. A BCA user permit must be obtained prior to swimming, fishing or boating. Camping areas are available at most of the lakes, and restaurants and motels are present in Russellville and Haleyville.

The Sipsey River, in the Bankhead National Forest, and Little River, above the fall at Highway 35 near Fort Payne, are excellent float fishing streams. Tributary streams to the Paint Rock River offer scenery and serenity to the wade fisherman.

All these streams provide beautiful scenery and super fishing for small bass and panfish.

Canoes and small flat-bottom boats are excellent vessels for floating the streams and fishing. Light spinning tackle with a four or six-pound test line is ideal.

Light spinners are preferred and will catch both bream and bass. Late spring is the most pleasant and productive season to float fish.

Central Alabama

Fishing in Central Alabama provides anglers with diverse warm water fishing experiences. No other similar size area in Alabama offers an angler a broader range of freshwater habitat. Located in this 11-county centralized region are reservoirs, tailwaters, small streams, swamps, ponds and one of the few unimpounded rivers left in the state.

Reservoirs

Twelve reservoirs are in this district. Each exceeds 500 acres.

Lake Jordan, a 6,800-acre reservoir, is the number one choice for many area fishermen. This Alabama Power Company reservoir is on the Coosa River a few miles north of Wetumpka. Largemouth and spotted bass fishing is best from March through May. This lake has relatively little shallow water, so most bass are caught along the shoreline from the mouths of creeks to the upper end of sloughs.

From February to April, crappie fishing is in full swing with fish commonly being caught in the three-quarter pound range. Preferred habitat for spawning crappie is submerged tree tops along steep banks.

After bass and crappie fishing slows down, catfishing begins to pick up with the summer months being the peak season. Trotlines are used to harvest most catfish. The bait is suspended to 20-foot depths.

Striped and hybrid striped bass have been stocked heavily in Lake Jordan. These fish have established a popular new fishery, with catches of stripers in the 5- to 10- pound range. These fighters are caught in the mouths of creeks during late spring, early summer and winter. Autumn brings on "jump fishing" where fishermen scan the lake with binoculars for the splash of white bass and stripers feeding on schooling shad, then rush to the feeding frenzy as quickly as possible casting spoons, spinners and medium-size jigs.

A unique feature of Lake Jordan is that it is impounded by two separate dams, Jordan Dam and the newer Walter Bouldin Dam. Bouldin Dam created a 1,000-acre embayment which is connected to Lake Jordan by a canal. The upstream end of this canal is a top spot on the lake.

For the fisherman wishing to catch a trophy largemouth, Lake Harding, also known as Bartlett's Ferry, is a good lake to fish. This area has produced several bass in the 13-pound range, with eight-pounders caught frequently. Lake Harding is primarily a river-run impoundment of the Chattahoochee River. The major backwater area is the Halawakee Creek arm; therefore, most of the fishing occurs here.

Besides the noted black bass fishing in Lake Harding, excellent catches of crappie are reported each spring. Hybrid striped bass have been stocked for several years and are commonly caught from most areas of the lake.

Two unique small reservoirs on the Tallapoosa River are Yates and Thurlow. Both reservoirs are famous for redears (shellcracker) in the one-pound range. Few public waters have trophy panfish, so these lakes are highly recommended to avid ultra-light tackle and fly fishermen. Live worms or small spinners fished along the shoreline during the summer months bring best results.

Jones Bluff Reservoir is between Montgomery and Selma on the Alabama River. Only a small amount of surface water extends beyond the original river banks in this river-run impoundment. Fishing this lake can be a real challenge because there is normally current flowing along the flooded river channel. A few creeks have been flooded along both banks and provide some backwater fishing. Black bass, at times, can be caught along sandbars, steep bluffs and in the creeks.

District fisheries office: Montgomery (261-3628)

● Denotes free launch area

Fishing opportunities in Central Alabama

A popular nighttime fishing experience during the heat of summer is "jug" fishing for catfish. Plastic bottles of all shapes and sizes are rigged at varying depths with shad pieces, minnows and freshwater clams. These jugs are scattered around the boat, and then the fishermen casually drift downstream and occasionally check the jugs with a flashlight. An actively moving jug means a fish is on the hook. Often a large catfish can take the jug completely under the surface, resurfacing several yards away, and adding to the excitement of this unique nighttime method of fishing.

Tailwaters

The most popular tailwater fishing for boaters in central Alabama is definitely below Mitchell Dam. In February, fishing begins with occasional catches of walleye and drum. March and April bring on fishing in earnest with spotted and largemouth bass, drum, catfish, white bass, and hybrid striped bass filling the creels.

The black bass are generally caught along the rocky river banks with live shad or artificial baits. Your best bet to catch the other species of fish is to anchor near the dam and fish with live or cut shad which can usually be dipped below the dam. Another popular live bait is the mayfly larvae, commonly called willow grubs. Be sure to take a variety of spoons, spinners and jigs in case the shad are not running.

The natural rocky habitat below Jordan dam has long been famous for its spotted bass. This area is good for catfish, drum, white bass and hybrid striped bass. Prime fishing time is from March through June. Small boats can be put in at a primitive ramp a few hundred yards below the dam on the east side. However, bank fishing is easy and there is plenty of parking area.

The tailwater below Walter Bouldin Dam is a large canal dug in clay material with only a few large rocks. Species caught in the prime fishing season are the same as in the Jordan Dam tailwater. Bank access on the west side is good with adequate parking. Larger boats can navigate this tailrace area. However, boat ramps are several miles away at Fort Toulouse and in Wetumpka.

For fishermen who want to catch a large striped bass, the tailwaters below Martin, Yates, and Thurlow Dams on the Tallapoosa River are prime striper areas. All of these tailraces have yielded fish in the 20- to 30-pound range. The state record of 55 pounds, in fact, was taken from this area several years ago, and nearly broken in 1983. May, June and July are the best fishing months, and the most popular baits are live shad, one-half to one-ounce buck tail jigs, large floating "Finnish minnow" lures. Although the three areas can be reached by boat, most of the fish are caught by bank fishermen.

The reported catches of smallmouth bass below Martin Dam and walleye, frequently caught below Thurlow Dam, further contribute to the uniqueness of this fishing area.

Fishermen in east-central Alabama also have excellent tailwater fishing. The area below Bartlett's Ferry Dam has developed into an excellent hybrid striper fishery in addition to the usual black bass and catfish catches. Fishing techniques here are similar to those of other areas; however, catfish are commonly caught on freshwater clams collected from shallow water areas along the banks and sandbars downstream.

Bank fishing access below Bartlett's Ferry Dam is nonexistent. However, boat access is excellent. A newly-renovated launching ramp is immediately below the dam on the Alabama side of the river.

Lucky are the fishermen who live in Phenix City; they are often able to catch their limit of hybrid stripers during an hour lunch break. A small dam, the Eagle-Phenix Dam, in downtown Phenix City has helped create some of the best urban fishing in the Southeastern United States.

Hybrids congregate in large numbers and provide some exciting fishing from March to early June. Only occasional high water will deter fishermen from lining the west bank in hopes of outfishing friends next to them. Jigs, floating plugs and live shad are favorite lures. If you are fishing and the water level is low with a slow current, then the "water is off." There is no electrical power being generated at upstream dams. Watch for rapidly rising water. Fishermen, occasionally, have spent the day stranded on a rock waiting for the water to "go off!"

The availability of excellent tailwater fishing in central Alabama means fishermen do not need an expensive boat and electronic equipment. A short drive in the family car can often place one in an area with the possibility of acquiring a full stringer of fish.

Rivers

Individuals who enjoy the solitude of floatfishing a free flowing stream or river should try the scenic Cahaba River. This small river is the only unimpounded major river left in Alabama.

Early in the spring several areas along the Cahaba produce excellent walleye fishing. During most of the year bass and catfish are the primary species sought. Access is relatively good. There are many bridge crossings; however, there are no ramps, so you will want to use a canoe or jon boat which you can slide up and down the banks. The beauty of the high bluffs and overhanging trees makes any trip on this river worthwhile.

Small Streams

Central Alabama contains hundreds of small streams ranging in width from six to more than 100 feet. Phenix City, Auburn, Opelika, Tallassee, Eclectic, Wetumpka, and Clanton, in the northern part of the district are located on or near the fall line. The fall line is a physiographic feature which sharply limits the range of certain species of fish. Above the fall line, many streams contain cobbles, boulders, and waterfalls of varying sizes. Below the fall line, streams typically have a sandy bottom, few rocks, and numerous large sandbars.

The fish in small streams are generally smaller than those in lakes and rivers; therefore, ultralight spinning tackle is ideal. Small lures are more productive and will take a wider assortment of species than larger lures. A small spinner (1/32 to 1/16 ounce) is probably the best all-around lure for creek fishing and small diameter line (1- to 4-pound test) is required to cast the small lures effectively.

Species commonly caught from small streams include longear sunfish (possibly the most beautiful of the sunfishes), bluegills, redbreast sunfish, spotted bass, largemouth bass and redeye bass. In the spring, walleye, white bass, striped bass and hybrid striped bass may enter small streams to spawn. Other species caught in creeks include black crappie, white crappie, green sunfish, rock bass, channel catfish, bullheads, suckers and carp. Halawakee, Osanippa, Wacoohee, Uchee and Little Uchee Creeks hold the distinction of being the only creeks in this area where shoal bass are known to occur. The shoal bass is in the process of being described as a new species. A unique fish, it grows to a relatively large size in small streams.

A few of the more impressive creeks (with regard to size, apparent number of fish and/or natural beauty) in the area are Autauga Creek (Autauga County), Bogue Chitto and Barron Creek (Dallas County), Sofkahatchee and Channahatchee Creek (Elmore County), Chewacla, Saugahatchee, and Little Uche Creek (Lee County), Big Swamp Creek (Lowndes County), Cubahatchee and Thobolocco Creek (Macon County), Catoma Creek (Montgomery County), Oakmulgee and Coffee Creek (Perry County), Watermelon and North Fork of Cowikee Creek (Russell County).

The lower portion of some of the larger creeks in the area can be float-fished from a canoe or flat-bottom boat. Boat launch sites on small streams are few, crude, and generally on private property; consequently, the best way to gain access to a floatable creek is to slide a canoe or light boat in at a bridge crossing on a public road.

Swamps

There are numerous swamps in Central Alabama, particularly in Macon, Bullock and Lowndes Counties. Even the Pea and Conecuh Rivers in Bullock County are mostly swamp habitat. Although swamps are probably the most overlooked fishing habitat, the fishing in them can be fantastic, especially when the water is low and the fish are concentrated.

Bluegill, bass, warmouth, bowfin, longear sunfish, chain pickerel and redfin pickerel are common in swamps and oxbows. People fishing in them should take along a can of mosquito repellant and exercise extreme caution to avoid being bitten by a cottonmouth.

Wading a small stream or swamp is a delightful way to fish. One of the best features of fishing a creek or swamp is the solitude - rarely do you encounter another fisherman in a day's fishing. To avoid trespassing on private property when fishing small streams or swamps, you should ask yourself, "Can this stream be floated by a regular canoe under average flow conditions?" If the answer is "no," then the adjacent landowner's permission is required before wading the stream. If "yes," then the stream can be waded without the landowner's permission. You would, however, need the landowner's permission to leave the stream and walk along the bank.

Ponds

Fishermen surveys have indicated that 20 to 33 percent of all fishing trips in Alabama are to private ponds. This represents approximately three million fisherman-trips annually.

There are many reasons why pond fishing is so popular with people of all ages. Ponds are often only a short distance from home. They are convenient for people who like to fish after work, and they are perfect for rural youngsters who are too young to drive.

Most trophy largemouth bass and bream come from properly managed ponds. Montgomery County alone has more than 3,000 ponds, so there are plenty of opportunities for pond fishing. However, the vast majority of ponds are privately owned, so the owner's permission must be obtained prior to fishing. Also, many ponds are open to the public for a small fee. These ponds usually can be found by asking at country stores or by contacting county extension agents.

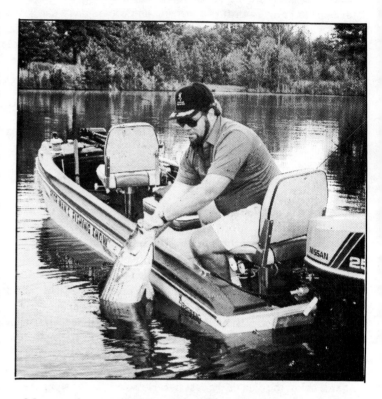

Most pond owners will not allow the use of minnows as bait, so be prepared to bass fish with artificial lures. Help prevent overharvesting the pond by keeping only a small number of bass. To insure a successful trip, take along some live crickets. This is a favorite bluegill morsel. Redworms and mealworms are popular for both bluegills and redears.

Accommodations

Motels, restaurants, bait shops, and outboard motor dealers can be found in several cities evenly distributed across the area. Montgomery is centrally located and has a wide variety of accommodations for fishermen headed for the Alabama and the Tallapoosa Rivers. Selma is ideally located in the western end of the area and is ideal for fishermen interested in fishing the Cahaba River and its tributaries of the lower section of Jones Bluff Reservoir. Accommodations are available in the Auburn-Opelika area for fishermen interested in the Tallapoosa River impoundments and the tributaries on Lake Harding on the Chattahoochee River. Phenix City, located on the banks of the Chattahoochee, has several motels, restaurants and bait shops available for anglers fishing local reservoirs, tailwaters and streams.

Boat launching access varies from excellent to poor in this portion of the state. Alabama Power Company and the U.S. Army Corps of Engineers have maps available for the major reservoirs in these counties. These maps show public access areas and other points of interest.

Access to smaller reservoirs, streams and swamps can be located on county highway maps. These maps are available from the Alabama Highway Department.

West Alabama

If you are a fisherman who enjoys angling in a variety of waters, then the fishing in west-central Alabama will delight you.

This 12-county region is blessed with an abundance of resources including large reservoirs, major rivers, scenic streams and creeks, swamp and backwater areas, and small impoundments such as watershed lakes and farm ponds. Each of these areas offers a unique type of fishing to the sportsman.

Perhaps the best known and the oldest impoundments in west Alabama are the waters of the Black Warrior River Basin. The second largest river system in Alabama, the Black Warrior contains more than 52,000 surface acres of water. Tributaries of the Warrior system include the Sipsey Fork, Mulberry Fork, and Locust Fork. The most widely sought fish is the largemouth bass. However, striped bass, hybrid bass, catfish, spotted bass, bluegill and crappie are popular favorites as well.

The Warrior River system has approximately 25 access areas along its length. Numerous private ramps are available to fishermen for a nominal launching fee. This river system includes the Bankhead, Holt, Oliver, and Warrior reservoirs as well as part of Demopolis Reservoir.

The first signs of mild weather in February usually bring the fisherman out of winter hibernation, with March and April the most productive bass and crappie months. During this time, fish are found near heavy cover such as log jams and weed beds, so spinnerbaits, plugs, and plastic worms are the best producers.

Lewis Smith Lake is a scenic reservoir on the Sipsey Fork of the Black Warrior drainage system. This reservoir is appealing with its beautifully wooded and steep rocky shoreline. Fishermen from all over the world have come here seeking the elusive and hard fighting

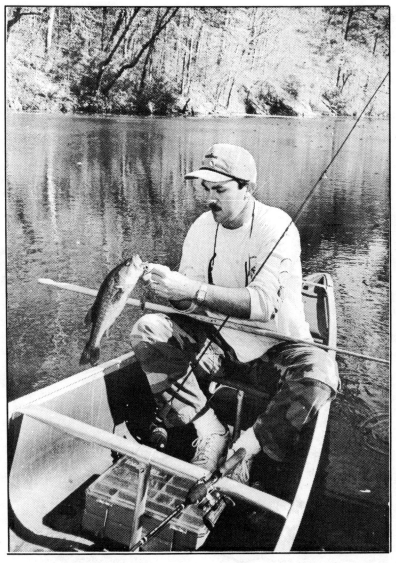

Alabama spotted bass.

Five previous consecutive world records have been caught here. Largemouth and spotted bass fishing is best during February, March, April and May. Plastic worms and deep diving plugs are the most popular baits. White bass, bluegill, and crappie are other popular species commonly caught in Smith Lake.

Because of its deep, clear water, Smith Lake's late spring and summer bass fishing is best for night owls. Many fishermen catch their limits of bass and crappie at night fishing around lighted piers and near underwater structures, such as bridges or pilings.

Smith Lake has also developed into one of the nation's best lakes for saltwater striped bass. The stripe were introduced in Smith Lake as 3-inch fingerlings in 1983 and by the summer of 1989, fish in the 32-pound range were being caught.

In addition, a tailwater fishery has been established for rainbow trout through the efforts of the Fisheries Section of the Game and Fish Division.

Lake Tuscaloosa, a 5,885-acre reservoir just north of Tuscaloosa, was created by the impounding of the North River in 1969. Largemouth bass, spotted bass, crappie, and bream are the most highly sought sportfish. Trophy bass in the 5- to 10-pound category are regularly caught by bass fishermen with a few going more than 10 pounds. Lake Tuscaloosa has received large numbers of Florida bass fingerlings as part of a five-year stocking plan that began in 1984.

More than 900,000 striped bass and hybrid striped bass have been stocked into Lake Tuscaloosa to establish a fishery for these species. Hybrid stripers are commonly caught in the tailwaters below the dam. Spoons and jigs are the most popular baits.

In addition, more than 115,000 walleye have been stocked there

Fishing opportunities in West Alabama

District fisheries office: Northport (339-5716)

● Denotes free launch area

since 1970. These fish are deep-water inhabitants and the best time to catch them is in the dead of winter using minnows fished just off the bottom.

West-central Alabama is the site of two of the state's newer reservoirs. Gainesville Reservoir (7,200 acres) was impounded in 1978 and Aliceville Reservoir (8,300 acres) was completed in 1980. These lock and dam reservoirs on the Tombigbee River link the Tennessee and Tombigbee Rivers to provide a shortcut for river traffic between the Tennessee Valley and the Gulf of Mexico.

Both reservoirs were built with the fisheman in mind. They contain large areas of standing timber which provide excellent habitat for many game fish species. Cut-offs were constructed at several locations to keep bend ways open and avoid disturbance by barge traffic. Fourteen public boat ramps are available.

Fishing on both reservoirs is good for largemouth bass, bream, crappie and catfish. The Fisheries Section has stocked both reservoirs with Florida largemouth bass and trophy bass fishing is excellent.

The Gainesville Reservoir shoreline is completely within Alabama. Aliceville Reservoir lies on the Alabama-Mississippi border. Alabama fishing licenses may be used on Aliceville as far as river mile 312.

Both lakes shook up Alabama fishermen early in 1989 when they produced two 14-pounders and one 16-pound largemouth. Ten-pound-plus largemouth have been common in recent years.

Excellent access is provided for shore fishermen to the tailraces of both reservoirs. Tailraces yield many catfish and concentrate striped bass and hybrid bass.

In the 12 counties, more than 19,000 acres of private ponds have been stocked by the Fisheries Section. Ponds are good producers of bass, bream and catfish. Many can be fished merely by obtaining permission from the owner.

State-owned lakes

There are five state-owned public fishing lakes in west-central Alabama which are intensively managed by the Fisheries Section. They are Bibb County Lake, Fayette County Lake, Lamar County Lake, Marion County Lake and Walker County Lake. In addition, Lake Lurleen in Tuscaloosa County is managed by the State Parks Division with assistance from Fisheries Section personnel. All these lakes provide excellent fishing for bass, bream and catfish.

Accommodations

If you are interested in visiting west Alabama to fish, Tuscaloosa is centrally located to most of the reservoirs and lakes and offers the sportsman a variety of accommodations at affordable prices. In the Smith Lake area, Jasper and Cullman are only a few minutes from the lake and have several conveniently located motels. Camping is available at Lake Lurleen State Park.

East-Central Alabama

The fisherman doesn't have to search long to find a good place to wet his hook within the 13 counties of east-central Alabama.

From the mainstream impoundments of the Coosa and Tallapoosa Rivers to the cascading streams of the lower Appalachian Mountains, a wide spectrum of fishing is available which offers something for everyone. Whether you're a high-tech bass fisherman with all the latest electronic fishing gadgets, or a stream fisherman equipped with an assortment of flies and spinners, you can find desirable fishing in this region.

Reservoir Fishing

Much of the fishing in east central Alabama is provided by the five reservoirs on the Coosa River ranging from sprawling Weiss Lake near the Alabama-Georgia border to Lake Mitchell in Coosa County. Between Weiss Lake and Lake Mitchell are Neely Henry, Logan Martin, and Lay Lake reservoirs.

Weiss Lake is a 30,200-

acre reservoir which has received national publicity for its outstanding crappie fishing. Many out-of-state anglers flock to the lake to catch a mess of the "slab" sized crappie. Spring crappie season begins in February with the peak of the season arriving between March 15 and April 15, depending upon seasonal trends. The crappie are found in creek channels and deep holes during the late winter and early spring. As the water temperature begins to warm, the crappie begin to congregate along the banks around whatever cover is available. In the spring crappie can be caught on 1/8-ounce chartreuse grubs, and later in the summer fishermen use minnows when fishing from lighted piers.

Spring bass fishing usually begins in early April. Jig-and-pigs, and spinnerbaits fished near weed beds are recommended lures.

Crank baits, thrown around rocks, road beds and creek channels, produce healthy stringers of largemouth bass. As water temperatures warm, most bass fishermen change to plastic worms and crank baits fished around deep points and and creek channels. Another good tactic is fishing around boat docks and piers in the early morning and late afternoon.

A good depth-finder is important when fishing Weiss Lake because shallow water, stumps and rock outcroppings are common. Also, prospective fishermen should pay close attention to weather forecasts because breezy weather can cause boating problems on this flat, open-water reservoir.

Lay Lake is one of the favorite Coosa River Reservoirs among fishermen, according to a recent statewide angler survey. It is within easy driving distance from the metropolitan areas of Birmingham and Montgomery. Typical of many of the Coosa impoundments, the most sought after species in Lay Lake are crappie and bass. The state record crappie for several years was a 4-pound, 5-ounce giant taken from Lay by Frank Gilliam of Birmingham. This lake has many areas with standing timber which provide excellent crappie habitat. The crappie season extends from late winter into May. Standard crappie bait includes small jigs and minnows. Depth is the critical factor for putting fish in the boat. Early in the year fish deep and then try shallower water as the fish move near shore to spawn. It would be wise to check current fishing conditions with a local marina operator at the time of your fishing trip.

Bass fishermen on Lay Lake can expect a mixture of largemouth and spotted bass in their catch. In the spring, spinnerbaits are favorite lures for "buzzin" grass and weed beds that line much of the main body of the lake.

Weedbeds are also productive in the spring as the bass move into

● Denotes free launch area

Fishing opportunities
in East Central Alabama

shallow water during spawning season. In the winter, large bass can be caught in the vicinity of the Gaston Steam Plant due to the heated discharge warming the river. Although not quite as well known as Weiss and Lay Lakes, the other Coosa River Reservoirs of Neely Henry, Logan Martin and Mitchell offer a variety of fishing. In addition to crappie and largemouth bass, the white bass fishing can be excellent in the spring as the white bass begin moving up the feeder creeks. Fishing the "jumps" is popular on Logan Martin in the summer months when the white bass surface in large schools and feed on shad.

West Point Reservoir is the only impoundment of the Chattahoochee River within the boundaries of east central Alabama. Approximately 3,285 acres are in Alabama and the remaining 22,708 acres are in Georgia. Remember that an Alabama fishing license is valid only on that portion of West Point Reservoir south of the Highway 109 bridge. A minimum harvestable length limit of 16 inches on largemouth bass was implemented on April 20, 1983, to effectively control the gizzard shad population and enhance all sport fishing on the lake. Bass fishing continues to be good on the lake, although most of the bass caught will have to be released. Crappie and hybrid fishing is excellent.

Tallapoosa River reservoirs in the area include 10,660-acre Harris Reservoir in Randolph County and Lake Martin (39,000 acres) near Alexander City.

Harris Reservoir was impounded in October 1982, and good population of largemouth bass, spotted bass and crappie are present. One 13-pound Florida largemouth was caught from the lake in 1988.

Harris also received a stocking of hybrid striped bass.

Catfishing is also good. The Fisheries Section stocked 125,000 channel catfish in 1983 to supplement the spawn of the native channel and flathead catfish.

Some overnight accommodations are available in Wedowee. Suitable boat ramps are limited on Harris Reservoir. Numerous road-ends are available for launching; however, it can be difficult to launch a boat at some of these sites because of the gentle incline.

Lake Martin is one of the most scenic lakes in Alabama and a fishing trip to its clear waters, set amid rolling pine-covered hills, can be a memorable experience. The lake is noted for its abundance of spotted bass. A recent creel survey confirmed that 30 percent of the yearly harvest of fish from the lake were spotted bass followed by the largemouth bass at 15 percent. Much of Lake Martin is excellent spotted bass habitat with its rocky points and steeply sloping banks.

Crappie comprise about 25 percent of the total catch in pounds of fish per year from Lake Martin. The prime months are February through May; however, there are many crappie caught during the summer months by night fishing. A lantern or a floating crappie light, a bucket of minnows, and a rod and reel are all you need to take advantage of this technique. Fishing near creek mouths in 15 to 25 feet of water is often productive.

Lake Martin is also known for large saltwater striped bass . The most productive area for stripers has been the headwaters of the lake in the vicinity of Erwin Shoals. The prime time has been late March and April when the rockfish move upstream and attempt to spawn. Many 30-pound-plus fish have been caught in this area. Live shad are recommended as bait.

Large stripers also have been caught by fishing shad in 20- to 40-feet of water just above the dam. The Kowaliga Bridge area continues to be a good spot for striped bass in the summer months. Techniques include night fishing with big shad near the old bridge pilings or trolling through this area with large diving plugs.

Lake Purdy is a 1,050-acre water storage rservoir located southeast of Birmingham just off Highway 119. Crappie fishing begins the last of February and continues through April. Bream fishing picks up in mid-April and hefty stringers of bluegills and shellcrackers are common. Bass fishing is best in the spring and in the fall when the draw-down begins.

No special permit is required to fish Lake Purdy. However, no private boats are allowed and only outboards of 10 horsepower or less or trolling motors can be used on rental boats.

Tailwater Fishing

East Central Alabama has some of the finest tailwater fishing in the state. Perhaps the best known area is the tailwater below Logan Martin Dam. This area has something to offer everyone; from the bank fishermen to the saltwater striped bass and hybrid striped bass angler. Depending upon the season, everything from catfish and drum to crappie, white bass, and spotted bass can be caught here.

The big news in recent years has been the several state record hybrid striped bass which have been caught in these turbulent waters. In the spring of 1983, the record was broken three times when fish were harvested in the 17- and 18-pound class. The 18.7 pound hybrid caught by James Hamilton near Childersburg on the Coosa River was the record from 1983 until beaten in 1989.

The hybrids are caught generally within several hundred yards of the turbine discharges. Most anglers anchor and cast Sassy Shads or grub jigs in either white, chartreuse, or yellow. Be prepared to quick release your anchor because a large hybrid can make several long powerful runs and you may need to move downriver with him to wear him down. The best months for hybrids are during March through early May when they are concentrated in the waters below the dam.

The Logan Martin tailwater has also yielded some trophy saltwater striped bass of 20 pounds or larger. Catches have been reported of up to 40 pounds.

Techniques are similar to hybrid striped bass fishing although striped bass seem to congregate farther below the dam. The area near the first island below the dam and the gas line crossings can be productive sites.

White bass and crappie action usually begins in late winter and early spring while catfish activity peaks in May and June. Largemouth and spotted bass are caught by anglers floating downriver and casting among the trees lining both banks.

The tailwater below Neely Henry Dam is a favorite fishing hole for many fishermen.

It is similar in many respects to the Logan Martin tailwater. Fishermen can be observed below Neely Henry with hefty stringers of white bass and crappie in the spring and excellent catfish harvests in late spring and early summer.

Large concentrations of saltwater striped bass occur in April and May, although fishing pressure is still light on them. The area on the east bank across from the old lock approach, and on the west bank, below the lock approach, are good areas.

Fishing rivers
and streams

For the angler desiring to float a scenic river or wade a remote stream, numerous opportunities are available in east-central Alabama. The Tallapoosa River is still floatable at times even though the new Harris Reservoir Dam has produced erratic river levels and flows downstream. Good catches of spotted bass have been made in the river since Harris Reservoir was impounded, but float fishing conditions are unpredictable and depend upon the power generation schedule at the dam. The stretch of the river below Horseshoe Bend to the headwaters of Lake Martin has continued to yield some nice stringers of spotted bass, but be prepared to do some boat dragging if the water is low at Harris Dam.

Hatchett Creek should not be overlooked when you are planning a float fishing trip. This scenic creek in Coosa County is aesthetically appealing and has a healthy population of spotted bass. The creek can be floated below the U.S. 231 bridge to Lake Mitchell, and there are several bridge crossings which provide access sites. The stretch from the new U.S. 280 bridge to U.S. 231 bridge is floatable in the spring and is quite remote. Fishing can be good in this section, but you should allow two days to make the trip. White bass fishing is outstanding from the middle of March to early April when the bass make a spawning run up the creek. The best section to fish is in the vicinity of the Highway 29 bridge in Coosa County.

For the wading fisherman, there is a wealth of small streams from which to choose. Many contain the spunky redeye bass. The Talladega National Forest has many excellent streams where a person can fish all day without seeing another fisherman.

Equipped with ultralight spinning gear or a light fly rod, the angler can get into some fast action on these redeye bass streams. Shoal and Little Shoal Creeks near Heflin are good streams and are easily accessible.

Farther south near Cheaha State Park, Salt, Hillabee and Horse Creeks are teeming with redeye bass. The Forest Service has an excellent map of Talladega National Forest which can be obtained by writing the Forest Supervisor, 1765 Highland Avenue, Montgomery 36107. Other suitable streams can be located by consulting U.S. Geological Survey topographical maps or county highway maps.

Southeast Alabama

The Wiregrass area, named for the wiry, stiff grass that grows there, includes Barbour, Butler, Coffee, Covington, Crenshaw, Dale, Geneva, Henry, Houston and Pike Counties.

The area is unusual in that except for having what many consider the state's top lake (Lake Eufaula), it lacks the large number of rivers and streams similar to those found in other parts of the state.

River and stream fishing

Major streams in Southwest Alabama are the Chattahoochee River, Choctawhatchee River, Pea River, Conecuh River, and the upper reaches of the Yellow River. Actually, the area from Columbia Lock and Dam to the Florida line is the only portion of the Chattahoochee River in this part of the state which is not impounded.

Except for the Chattahoochee River, streams are relatively shallow with mostly sandy bottoms. Bank fishing is limited and generally confined to highway rights-of-way at bridge crossings. One area on the Pea River which produces good bank fishing

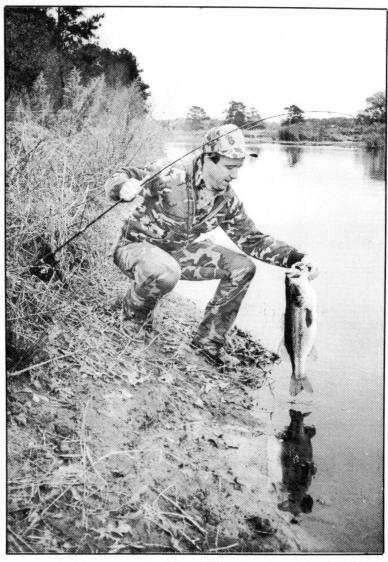

is below the power dam at Elba (access can be found on the Kinston highway). Another good spot is below Point A Dam on the Conecuh river near Andalusia. The principal species taken below these dams are bluegills, catfish and suckers. Fishing is best in the spring.

Float fishing is one of the more enjoyable and successful ways to fish these rivers. A small boat can be launched either from access areas or from the rights-of-way at bridge crossings. Before starting your trip, check county road maps to determine the distance between put-in and take-out points. Allow an hour for each mile of stream traveled. As mentioned before, the streams are relatively shallow and, during dry months, it is impossible to use an outboard motor to travel upstream.

For this reason, it is best to use two vehicles for a float fishing trip - one at the put-in point and one at the take-out point. The headwaters of these rivers should be avoided because they are narrow and contain many fallen trees.

Fishing is best in the spring and fall, although good fishing can be found the year round, depending upon river conditions. Bluegill and redear (shellcracker) fishermen usually have the best luck fishing in slow-moving eddy water with the usual assortment of worms, crickets and small spinner baits. Bass fishermen experience the most success when fishing crankbaits or spinner baits around tops of submerged trees, stumps, or log jams. Jigs and small lures can be effective in the pools below rapids and log jams. Bass fishing is best in the early morning and late afternoon along the shady side of the river.

Some areas of these rivers are swift in the spring, making it impossible to fish them effectively while floating. To overcome this, most fishermen use a small outboard motor (an electric trolling motor is not strong enough) to hold position in the current long enough to fish each area before moving downstream. Normally, two people will fish together, taking turns operating the motor. Good strings of largemouth bass are taken out of sunken tree tops and from around submerged logs by fishing this method. Diving lures, such as Bombers, Hellbenders and Balsa "B's," are commonly used.

Many people try their luck at catfishing and are often successful on these rivers. Set lines and bush hooks, as well as trotlines, usually are the best methods. Cut bait, liver, and small salamanders take the most catfish.

There are several beaver ponds near the Choctawhatchee River and many of them are accessible. These areas produce good bream

District fisheries office: Enterprise (347-9467)

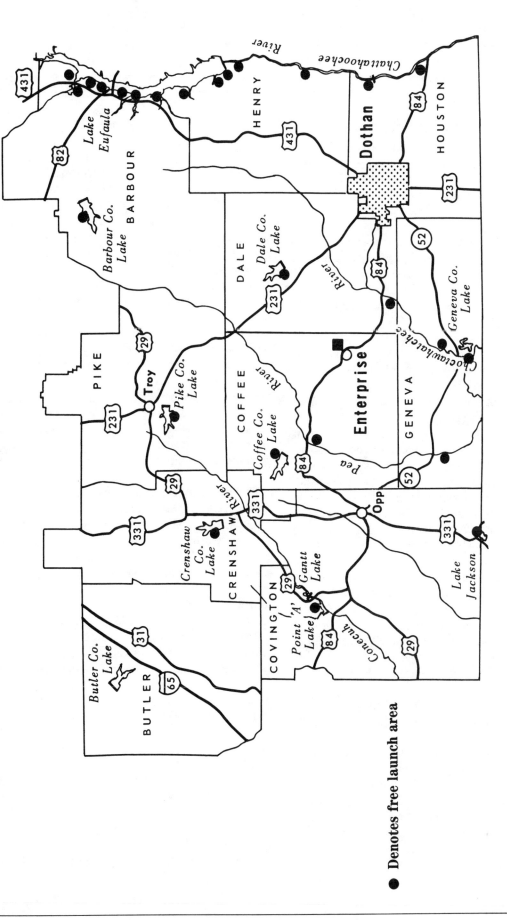

● Denotes free launch area

Fishing opportunities in the Wiregrass

and bass fishing in the spring, especially after they have been flooded by the river. Wading or using small aluminum boats is best for fishing. One important thing to remember is that landowner permission is required to fish beaver ponds on private property.

In addition to the fishing in the Wiregrass area, you will enjoy scenery seldom seen elsewhere. You are likely to see many of nature's creatures such as deer, turkeys, ducks, owls, hawks, river otters, beavers and alligators.

Reservoir fishing

The Wiregrass area has several large impoundments. The most popular is Lake Eufaula. This beautiful lake, with its 45,000 acres of diversified fishing water, is nationally known for its largemouth bass fishing. It is on the Chattahoochee River. The dam is approximately 11 miles east of Abbeville. The lake extends 85 miles upstream to Phenix City.

Bass fishing is generally good all year, but the better catches are made during late winter and spring months when there are large numbers of bass along the banks and are easy to find.

The most popular lures at this time are spinnerbaits, buzzbaits and deep-diving crankbaits. As the water begins to warm, plastic worms become more effective.

After most of the spawning activity has subsided, the bass tend to migrate to the creek and river channels. The better areas appear to be outside bends which have water from 10 to 15 feet deep along the ledges dropping off into the deeper channels. Plastic worms are the favorite lures but many people also like to troll deep-diving crankbaits in these areas.

Bass make a short migration back to the shoreline and up the creeks during the fall when the water begins to cool. Top-water fishing is probably at its best during this period. As the water cools further, the bass migrate to the deeper water of the river channel. They remain in the deeper water until the latter part of January, when they begin moving into the many "flats" found on the lake.

The "flats" are areas generally four to five feet deep containing a fair amount of cover. Yellow/white or chartreuse/white spinnerbaits are productive in these areas. From the "flats" the bass move back to the shoreline and up the creeks looking for bedding areas.

The preceeding paragraphs provide a general description of what occurs in the lake. There is no intention to imply that all of the bass follow these migrations. You can catch bass up the creeks, along the shoreline, and in the channels any time of the year. The large catches, however, are made by following these migrations.

In addition to the bass fishing, Lake Eufaula generally has good to excellent crappie fishing.

The best time to catch these fish is from late fall through the spring. Most fishermen prefer cane poles and small minnows. Good catches can also be made by using small white jigs.

Most of the crappie are taken near submerged tree tops and other cover. If you are unfamiliar with the lake, ask one of the area bait dealers who will gladly direct you to a likely spot.

In the early 80's, the Fisheries Section of the Alabama Game and Fish Division, in cooperation with the U.S. Army Corps of Engineers and the Georgia Game and Fish Commission, placed 56 fish attractors in Lake Eufaula. These attractors were made by placing cedar trees at various locations in the lake. These areas are marked with regulatory buoys. The location of these buoys are shown on the maps of Lake Eufaula in this book.

There is virtually unlimited access to the waters of Lake Eufaula with boat launching ramps in every well-known area. There are ample motel accommodations, restaurants and bait houses in the city of Eufaula at the water's edge.

Columbia Reservoir is directly downstream from Lake Eufaula. A river-run impoundment, it contains approximately 1,600 surface acres of water. Access to this reservoir is limited. However, there is a good ramp approximately one mile below Walter F. George Lock and Dam and one at Omusee Creek near Columbia.

Good catches of largemouth bass, hybrid striped bass, crappie, white bass, bream and channel catfish are made each spring. The largemouth bass fishing generally is good most of the year, but it takes several trips to locate the most productive spots.

Gantt Lake, a lesser known reservoir of the Wiregrass, is a 1,600-acre impoundment on the Conecuh River near Andalusia. The lake offers fair-to-good fishing for largemouth bass and crappie, but the favorite species of fishermen is the shellcracker (redear). Good strings of these panfish are taken during March and April when the shellcrackers are bedding. Most of the fish are caught in the shallow, upper end of the lake around the many cypress trees, stick-ups and aquatic weeds. Earthworms are used to take ice chests full of shellcrackers which commonly average half a pound.

The spring months are the best times to fish the lake for bass and crappie. The grass beds and stump rows in the sloughs near the dam provide the best bass fishing. Six-inch purple or black plastic worms or long, floating or diving minnow plugs are the most effective lures. Chartreuse crankbaits also will produce well. During the summer the bass go deep and usually are caught around the old river channel with plastic worms. Some are taken by trolling with deep-diving crankbaits.

Crappie fishing is best in Cottle Creek or along the steep banks of the main lake where the old river channel approaches the shoreline. Night fishing around lighted piers is productive.

Use of live minnows is by far the best way to fill a stringer. Boat ramps are available at Dunn's Bridge off County Road 43 or at Clearview Campground on Highway 29 North. Several privately owned fee ramps exist and directions can be obtained from local citizens.

Lodging and food can be found in Andalusia.

Point A is an impoundment of the Conecuh River just below Gantt Lake. As at Gantt, the most sought species in this 600-acre reservoir are largemouth bass, crappie and shellcracker.

The best fishing is generally found in March, April and May. The sloughs around Covington County Park, the FOP Lodge, and the Mallette Creek area provide the best bass fishing.

The same lures and methods which produce on Gantt also will work here.

Good catches of crappie are taken on minnows in the Patsaliga arm and along the deep banks of the lake proper.Shellcrackers can be caught on earthworms in most of the shallow sloughs by fishing the stickups and grassbeds.

A good boat ramp is available at Covington County Park, on the northwestern side of the lake.

Restaurants and motels are available in Andalusia.

Tailwaters

Hybrid striped bass fishing is good during the spring and fall. The best area to fish is the tailwater immediately below Walter F. George Lock and Dam. The best time to fish for the hybrids is when the hydroelectric turbines are operating. Large white jigs, spoons and live shad are the best baits. However, good catches of hybrids have been made using crayfish and/or shrimp.

Another well-known area for hybrid striped bass fishing is the tailwaters of Columbia Lock and Dam. During the early spring hundreds of fishermen flock to this area to catch hybrid stripers, one of the best fighting fish in the Chattahoochee River. There are two main areas to fish. One is from the bank on the Alabama side immediately below the dam. This area is lined with riprap and the fishermen stand on these rocks while casting into the swift, swirling water which flows over a marl bottom, lined with bigger rocks. White and yellow jigs are the best lures. The jig should be retrieved as slowly as possible, but kept just off the bottom to prevent hang-ups.

The other area is on the Georgia side of the river. However, one needs a boat. The boat should be anchored at the edge of the swift water between the end of the lock wall and the boat ramp. The favorite method of fishing here is to use live shad, the bigger the better. The shad should be hooked from the bottom of the jaw up through the hard area of the nostrils. Fish the shad as close to the bottom as possible.

Catches of eight and nine pound hybrids are common here and you usually experience little trouble catching the limit, once you have mastered the technique used by the local fishermen.

Lake Jackson

Lake Jackson is on the Alabama-Florida line in Florala. This is a shallow, bowl-shaped natural lake filled with aquatic vegetation. The most sought after species is the largemouth bass. The water is clear and fishing is difficult for most anglers. Those anglers willing to put in the time and effort are often rewarded with that once-in-a-lifetime trophy, however. Ten-pound-plus fish are taken each year. Most of the larger bass are caught in and around the mats of aquatic weeds. The best time to land a bragging-size bass is during the spring spawning season. The spawning beds and the large fish near them can be spotted easily in the clear water. A live shiner is usually cast into the bed and allowed to stay until the fish takes it. Heavy tackle is usually in order since the bass will most assuredly become entangled in the vegetation.

During summer, most anglers prefer to fish the lake at night. This is almost a necessity because of the clarity of the water and the heavy use of the lake by skiers. The lure of choice is a 10-inch black plastic worm rigged weedless.

Lake Jackson also offers good fishing for chain pickerel and crappie. Most of the pickerel are caught around the weedbeds by casting brightly colored crankbaits or spoons. Live minnows are the preferred bait for crappie. These panfish are taken around the weedbeds during the spring and in the deeper holes in the summer.

Private lakes and ponds

Because this area is primarily agriculture-oriented, literally thousands of private lakes and ponds dot the landscape. Many of these private lakes are open for a fee. To locate these lakes, contact the district fisheries office in Enterprise (see the phone number on the map in this section), or call the local county agent's office.

Southwest Alabama

Southwest Alabama can be described as an outdoor lover's paradise. The vast areas of waterways and woodlands in this region provide many opportunities to enjoy an outdoor experience.

This area includes Baldwin, Choctaw, Clarke, Conecuh, Escambia, Mobile, Monroe, Washington and Wilcox Counties.

The Alabama and Tombigbee Rivers, the main tributaries of the Mobile Bay drainage system, flow through this area and provide the foundation for some of the finest fishing in Alabama. The Mobile Bay system drains 43,560 square miles of land and includes portions of Mississippi and Georgia as well as a major portion of Alabama. This system empties into the Gulf of Mexico by way of the Mobile Delta, a major fishing area in Southwest Alabama.

In addition to those waters associated with the Mobile Bay drainage, there are waters in the Escatawpa River system, the Perdido River system, and the Conecuh River system which also provide good fishing opportunities.

outstanding features of this reservoir is that fish can be caught during the spring flooding season. Normal spring lake level fluctuations do not flood boat ramps or vast areas in the flood plain.

Lake Claiborne is a 5,850 acre reservoir below Miller's Ferry and is the last reservoir in the Alabama chain. Claiborne is smaller and more of a river-run impoundment than Miller's Ferry.

In addition to excellent fishing in these reservoirs, the tailwaters below both provide fishing excitement. Many species of fish tend to congregate below dams. There are also a number of oxbow lakes on the lower Alabama which offer good fishing.

The major sport fish in the Alabama River system are largemouth bass, crappie, bream, and catfish. Spotted bass occur here and a good striped bass fishery is developing due to an intensive stocking program by the Game and Fish Division.

Overall, spring and fall are the most productive fishing seasons on the Alabama system. Largemouth bass fishing begins in later winter and continues to be good until early summer. After a midsummer lull, bass fishing picks up again in the fall. Plastic worms, deep diving lures, and crank baits are effective.

Alabama River System

The Alabama River system, one of the two major tributaries of the Mobile Bay Drainage, has two large reservoirs and many miles of river in this area. The reservoirs are Lake Dannelly (Miller's Ferry) and Lake Claiborne.

Miller's Ferry is a 22,000-acre reservoir built by the U.S. Army Corps of Engineers in Wilcox and Dallas Counties. This reservoir provides excellent fishing and is one of Alabama's best kept fishing secrets.

Noted as both a haven for big crappie and bass, this lake has 516 miles of shoreline and an abundance of structure, deep channels, shallow flats, sand bars and flooded standing timber. One of the

Spring crappie fishing peaks at spawning time, which occurs when the water temperature is approximately 60 degrees F. During spawning, crappie can be found close to the bank in four- to eight-feet of water. Otherwise, they are most likely found associated with submerged brush and trees.

Striped bass will congregate below dams in the spring. In the summer stripers can be found in channels near the mouths of streams where cool water empties into the river. They also can be found in schools suspended in midwater in open river and reservoir areas. Shad are a favored food item for stripers. Fishing around schools of

District fisheries office: Spanish Fort (626-5153)

● Denotes free launch area

Fishing opportunities in Southwest Alabama

shad is often successful. Striper baits include live shad and bluegills, jigs, and large shad-like lures.

Tombigbee River System

The Tombigbee River, the other major tributary of the Mobile Bay drainage system, enters this area at the north end of Choctaw County. Coffeeville Lake, a river-run reservoir of 8,800 acres, is on this river. This lake provides good fishing for largemouth bass, especially in the spring and fall. Populations of crappie, bream and catfish inhabit this reservoir and provide a good sport fishery. Occasionally striped bass are caught, and as the stocking program of the Game and Fish Division continues, the striped bass fishery should improve.

The tailwater below Coffeeville Lock and Dam provides a good fishery for crappie, bass, bream and an excellent fishery for catfish.

As you move downstream, oxbow lakes and tributaries provide excellent fishing for crappie, bream and largemouth bass. Some of the more popular lakes are Three Rivers Lake, Fishing Lake and Bates Lake, all near McIntosh.

Mobile Delta

The Mobile Delta is formed by the confluence of the Alabama and Tombigbee Rivers in Clarke County. This river delta, the second largest delta system in the United States, is approximately 40 miles long and 10 miles wide. It consists of an intricate network of rivers, creeks, bayous, lakes, marsh and bays, which eventually empty into Mobile Bay. The Mobile Delta is the upper end of an estuarine system which is the basis for important sport and commercial fisheries.

The lower quarter of the delta consists of shallow bays, bayous and river channels bordered by wetland plants and few trees. The upper three quarters of the delta consists of deeper lakes and rivers bordered by tupical bottomland hardwoods. Most of the delta is undeveloped and is in a near-pristine state. The Mobile Delta is one of the most important ecological areas in Alabama.

By definition, a river delta is rich in natural fertility. As the river slows, the suspended and dissolved nutrients acquired from the 43,560 square miles of drainage area are assimilated by the delta system before being passed on to the marine environment.

Fish production in the Mobile Delta is high. In addition to the common freshwater species, the lower delta serves as a nursery ground for numerous marine fish and shellfish. A seasonal influx of desirable adult marine sport fish such as speckled trout, sheepshead and redfish also occurs. This invasion of marine species enhances an already good sport fishery in the Mobile Delta.

Sportfish in the delta include largemouth bass, bluegill, redear sunfish, crappie, warmouth, catfish, pickerel, yellow bass, white bass, striped bass, alligator gar, and mullet. The major fishing seasons are spring and fall.

Largemouth bass are abundant in the Mobile Delta. There are not as many large bass caught in the delta as are harvested in upstate impoundments. However, no other area in Alabama can match the delta in number of bass per acres of water. Bass fishing in the upper delta is best in deep lakes and dead river runs. These areas have plenty of cover for bass, such as submerged logs, brush tops, and drop-offs. The shallow bays and bayous of the lower delta provide good bass structures including grass beds, pilings, drainage cuts and old duck blinds. All the popular bass baits are effective. Live shrimp are an excellent bass bait in the lower delta.

Bream fishing is also good in the Mobile Delta. The shallow bays of the lower delta and the deeper oxbows of the upper delta produce heavy stringers of redear (shellcrackers), bluegill, and warmouth (goggle eye).

Crappie are more numerous in the deeper lakes of the upper delta than in the shallow bays of the lower delta. Favorite crappie fishing areas include Miflin Lake, Negro Basin, Tensaw Lake, Fishing Lake and David Lake. Many other areas in the delta also provide good crappie fishing.

The lower Mobile Delta and other tidal streams in Mobile and Baldwin Counties offer an extra bonus in the fall. From September through January speckled trout, redfish, and flounder enter the mouths of rivers and streams and add to the excellent freshwater fishing.

Big Creek Lake

Big Creek Lake is a 3,600-acre public water supply reservoir for the City of Mobile. This reservoir is on the Escatawpa River System which flows into Mississippi. Big Creek Lake, in west Mobile County, has great fishing, especially for largemouth bass, crappie and hybrid striped bass. The water in the lake is generally clear because of the wooded drainage area and low fertility. Water as deep as 90 feet can be found here, a phenomenon unusual in south Alabama.

Threadfin shad were stocked into the lake by the Game and Fish Division and have benefitted the crappie, largemouth bass and hybrid striped bass populations by providing more forage fish. Shad school near the surface during early morning and late afternoon hours of summer when the wind is calm. Excellent catches of hybrid stripes and largemouth bass can be made near shad schools.

Shelby lakes

The Shelby Lakes are natural freshwater lakes in Gulf State Park in Gulf Shores. The unusual situation of freshwater lakes within view of the Gulf of Mexico provides some unusual fishing opportunities for park visitors.

Lake Shelby is the largest in a chain of three contiguous lakes which cover a total of 829 acres. The water in these lakes has tannic acid stain typical of many aquatic systems in south Alabama. These lakes are relatively shallow with water rarely deeper than eight feet. There are a few holes which drop off to 20 feet. Although the bottom contour is rather constant, a depth finder will enable the angler to find some desirable bottom structure.

The sportfishes available in the Shelby system include Florida largemouth bass, channel and blue catfish, bluegill, shellcracker, crappie and redfish. Since Florida bass were first introduced into Lake Shelby in the early 1970's, the lake has gained a reputation of being a trophy bass lake. Although large numbers of bass were killed in this lake as a result of salt water intrusion from Hurricane Frederic in 1979, more Florida bass were stocked and a healthy population of largemouth is again present in the lake.

Channel and blue catfish are periodically stocked into Lake Shelby and are an important facet of the sport fishery. These fish seem to thrive in the slightly saline water, and their taste is unsurpassed by river or farm-raised catfish. A good fishing method for catfish is drifting and bottom fishing with dead shrimp. Other common catfish baits are also productive.

Bream fishing is best in the canals which connect the three lakes, especially near submerged brush and grass and reed beds which line much of the shoreline. Shellcracker fishing is particularly good in Lake Shelby.

Redfish, or red drum, were introduced naturally into this sytem by Hurricane Frederic. These naturally stocked fish grew so fast and created such a desirable fishery, that more fingerlings have been stocked by the Game and Fish Division. This marine species which often occurs in the mouths and lower reaches of rivers is an aggressive fighter which can be taken on live, cut, or artificial bait.

Spring and fall are the best fishing season for the Shelby system; however, summertime angling can also be productive.

Small streams
and ponds

Some of the better small streams are the Escatawpa River in Mobile County, the Styx River and the Blackwater River in Baldwin County, Murder Creek and Sepulga River in Conecuh and Escambia Counties, and Pine Barren Creek in Wilcox County. Most of these slow-moving and sand-bottom streams support populations of largemouth bass, spotted bass, longear sunfish, bluegill, warmouth, chain pickerel and catfish.

Stream fishing is generally best during the summer and early fall.

Many private ponds are present in southwest Alabama. These ponds are stocked with redear sunfish, bluegills, and largemouth bass and provide many fishing trips for local fishermen. In many cases permission of the pond owner is all that is required for an enjoyable fishing trip.

Access and
accommodations

One of the nicest things about fishing the public waters of Southwest Alabama is the ease of access to the waterways and accommodations available to the fishermen.

On the Alabama River system, Miller's Ferry has 16 public boat ramps built by the Corps of Engineers. In addition to these, the Parks Division of the Department of Conservation operates Roland Cooper State Park on the lake which provides boat launching as well as other amenities such as golf, tennis, swimming, camping and cabins. The towns of Camden and Selma have motel accomodations, restaurants and tackle shops for anglers traveling to Miller's Ferry.

Between Miller's Ferry Dam and Claiborne Dam, nine public boat ramps provide access to fishing. Restaurant facilities can be found in Monroeville, Frisco City and Uriah. Motel accommodations are available in Monroeville.

There are five public access areas in the Coffeeville Reservoir on the Tombigbee River. Lodging and restaurant facilities can be found in Grove Hill and Jackson. Jackson also is a good access area for fishing the Tombigbee River below Coffeeville Dam.

There are numerous fishing camps in the Mobile Delta which provide launch facilities, fishing supplies and lodging. These camps are accessible from Alabama Highway 225 on the east side, U.S. 43 on the west, and Battleship Parkway (U.S. 90) on the south. Motel accommodations and restaurants are available in the Bay Minette, Spanish Fort and Mobile areas. Delta maps can be found in this book.

Big Creek Lake is only 20 minutes west of Mobile and ample facilities are available for travelers. Two fishing camps on the lake provide the only access. Fishing supplies and topographical maps can be purchased at these camps.

Gulf Shores, as a tourist center, provides an abundance of accommodations for visitors to the Shelby Lakes. Gulf State Park, in which these lakes are located, has motel, cabin and camping facilities.

Guntersville Lake

Weeds, grass, moss, milfoil, hydrilla. Call it what you like, but the aquatic vegetation in Guntersville Lake has turned the Tennessee Valley Authority reservoir into what may be the nation's top bass fishing lake.

The ever-growing vegetation scattered from one end of this lake to the other is an excellent hatchery for bass and bream. It offers a safe haven for the smaller fry of both species to grow and become good fish. It does the same for minnows and shad. The result is an excellent food chain and terrific numbers of good fish.

The amount of grass in the lake either complicates or uncomplicates fishing here, depending on how you look at it. It uncomplicates things for many because it is the dominant structure in the lake and limits the number of patterns, or "tricks", needed to fish it well. Unlike a lake which may have a river-like upper end full of rocks and a ledge-filled lower end full of timber, Guntersville Lake offers a consistent makeup throughout its length. Wide water with grass is standard from one end to the other. A pattern that is working upriver is most likely working downriver, too.

For the competitive angler, the amount of grass tends to compli-

cate things. It is possible to catch so many fish in so many places, it's difficult to force yourself to stop catching good fish and move elsewhere in search of bigger fish.

The incredible catches during the BASS Alabama Invitational held on the lake in 1987, 1988 and 1989 drew nationwide attention to Guntersville Lake. BASS records for numbers of fish caught and poundage were shattered in 1988 and again in 1989, prompting the *Washington Post* to call the lake "...the best bass lake in America."

Most BASS pros readily agree. Former BASSMASTER Classic winner Jack Chancellor reported that he and his partner caught more than 200 bass in one day during the 1987 tournament.

Only the lake's lower end is featured in this section. It is here that the lake's better fishermen concentrate and where the top finishers in the BASS Alabama Invitational through the years have caught their fish.

It is recommended that a Guntersville Lake map such as the one produced by Carto-Craft Map Co. be purchased and studied when reviewing this lake. The thousands of sandbars and underwater islands are easily pinpointed on these maps.

Guntersville Lake Fact Sheet

Location, length, acreage

Lake Guntersville is Alabama's largest reservoir. The 69,100 acre Tennessee River impoundment is in Marshall and Jackson counties in Alabama, as well as Marion County in Tennessee. It is bordered upstream by Hales Bar and downstream by Wheeler Lake.

The lake begins at Guntersville Dam 11 miles northeast of Guntersville and stretches 82.1 miles to Hales Bar Dam. A total of 24,450 square miles drain into the lake.

Impoundment

Construction of Lake Guntersville Dam began Dec. 4, 1935, and discharge and normal flow of the river began Jan. 27, 1939.

Lake Guntersville Dam

Lake Guntersville Lock and Dam is 3,979 feet wide and constructed of 295,700 cubic yards of concrete and 4,600 tons of reinforcing steel. It has 18 40-foot-by-40 foot flood gates.

A total of 1,800 men worked 7.4 million hours building the facility. Three men lost their lives during the building process. The dam has four hydraulic turbines and four generators.

Stocking history

Florida-strain largemouth

1977-81	74,000
1984-1991	150,338
1992	136,221
1993	169,150
1994	76,410

Major and secondary creeks

On the lake's lower end, Lake Guntersville is fed by many wide creeks. Honeycomb Creek is the closest to the dam, while Brown's Creek, the widest water on the lower end, is above it. Spring Creek is a major water supplier, as is Town Creek. South Sauty Creek also is a wide creek with good water flow.

Lake configuration

The impoundment of the Tennessee River by Guntersville Lake Dam caused the river to spill its banks to a great degree and the lake boasts miles and miles of wide water and creeks.

Types of fish

Guntersville Lake has largemouth bass, a limited number of smallmouth bass, spotted bass, white crappie, black crappie, bluegill, shellcracker, longear sunfish, green sunfish, blue catfish, channel catfish, flathead catfish, bullhead catfish, sauger, hybrid bass and white bass. Rough fish include spotted gar, longnose gar, freshwater drum, carp, and buffalo. Baitfish include skipjack herring, gizzard shad, threadfin shad, yellowtail shad and various species of minnows. A recent discovery on the lake was wild river shiners.

Spring bass fishing
GUNTERSVILLE DAM TO U.S. 431 BRIDGE

Fish on this lake relate to aquatic vegetation. That's no one's secret. There are a number of fish on this lake that bury themselves in the weeds no deeper than 11 feet and stay there all summer and winter.

The angler who knows the location of grass-ridden deep humps and old creek channels in this end of the lake can start his year off right and put some big fish in the boat before most anglers get on the lake for the first time of the year. A jig-and-pig fished in the dead grass on these humps and along these channels usually will produce quality bass starting in late February. A 1/2-ounce orange/brown jig with a black pork frog trailer makes an excellent slow bait for these fish.

A depthfinder is needed to locate these areas. First, find areas you want to try by locating them on maps in this book. Then, ride the area in your boat and pinpoint them with a depthfinder. Use marker buoys to mark the spot.

A jig-and-pig worked slowly through the dormant grass is the key to catches of big fish.

Another pattern also works well during this time. In late February and early March, the water temperature is still low, but the fish are able to detect patches of warmer water and will move to them. This lake is full of riprap around bridges, culverts and banks and the large rocks used to prevent erosion absorb heat and radiate warmth into the nearby water. The water surface temperature next to this riprap will sometimes be three or four degrees warmer than surrounding water and that makes a big difference this time of the year.

A jig-and-pig fished in this riprap early in the spring often results in not only numbers of fish, but quality fish as well.

When mid-March arrives and there are three or four days of continuous sunshine, get ready for some good bass fishing. Those three or four days of sunshine will warm the water into the mid- to high-50s and that's warm enough to get out the Rat-L-Traps and start fishing the milfoil.

The best color of Rat-L-Trap this time of the year is a matter of debate. It takes an awful lot of rain to stain this lake and it is normally in pretty good shape in the spring. A chartreuse combination may be needed in a Rat-L-Trap on the rare occasions the lake is muddy, but a gold, white, chrome or a chrome with a blue or black back will work under normal conditions.

The key to fishing this bait, or any bait around the milfoil on the lake, is occasionally allowing it to drop and tick the weedtops on the retrieve. The reason for that is simple. Fish can tell this bait is coming toward them, but the weeds tend to disorient them to a small degree. Ticking the weed tops seems to help them find the bait much easier.

Bass are beginning to think spawn this time of the year and they will be in the milfoil in shallow water in the back of pockets on the main river or the back of creeks. This shallow (3 to 5 feet) water may be only two degrees warmer than water 30 yards away, but it makes a major difference.

April means bass are thinking hard about the spawn and topwater fishing becomes feasible. It's often still chilly this time of the year and the bass are like you and I in that they enjoy the feel of the sun on their backs. They will be close to the water surface. Stumps and the fringes of milfoil will hold bass this time of the year and buzzbaits, rats, frogs, Nip-I-Didees and other topwater baits will result in vicious strikes.

This is also the time of the year for those who like to fish spinnerbaits, but spinnerbaits usually take a backseat to Rat-L-Traps on this lake. The Rat-L-Traps cover more water quickly. Spinnerbaits are an excellent bait on this lake, nevertheless.

There are several key areas to concentrate on this end of the lake in the spring. Brown's Creek is a tremendous spring area with large expanses of stump-filled flat water, humps, and a winding creek channel.

Another key area is the what locals call "The Islands," the series of islands northeast of the U.S. 431 bridge. The area is full of small islands, humps, stumps and channels that concentrate bass.

Honeycomb Creek produces numbers of spring fish, but is an area most of the better anglers have marked off of their maps because the number of fish caught there doesn't justify the amount of time needed to catch them.

U.S. 431 BRIDGE
TO SOUTH SAUTY MARINA

The spring pattern above U.S. 431 bridge is basically the same pattern the lake's better anglers use below the bridge.

Shallow, grass-filled pockets are normally the areas of choice for springtime fishing, while humps on the main river come a close second. Anywhere 12 to 15 feet of water suddenly rises to 4 to 5 feet will hold fish this time of the year.

The grass will be dormant in the early spring and this is the time of year that experience on the lake really comes into play. The pockets and humps that held fish the spring before will hold fish this time of year, even though the grass they want may not yet be growing or visible.

There are several ares to concentrate on and several areas to avoid during this period.

Town Creek is one of those areas you need to consider first. The stumpy flats, winding creek channel, humps and milfoil make for excellent spring habitat.

The very back of Town Creek, back where it narrows, offers excellent fishing with jig-and-pigs in February.

The Claysville area, known to some fishermen as Siebold Branch, has everything you need for spring fishing, including stumpy flats, islands, winding creek channels and grass. It, too, is a key area.

The flats on both sides of the river from Town Creek to South Sauty Creek also offer good spring bass fishing in spots. Pay special attention to the sloughs in the back of these flats. These also are key areas for bass during the spring.

South Sauty Creek is another key area. The creek is filled with stump patches, a winding creek channel and plenty of flats covered in milfoil.

It should be noted that just because parts of this creek don't have milfoil, that doesn't mean it shouldn't be fished. Most areas without milfoil have underwater stumps that hold bass.

One would think that due to the amount of fish turned loose in Spring Creek following bass tournaments that it would be an excellent place to fish.

(More than 5,200 bass were turned loose there in just a three-day period during the 1989 BASS Alabama Invitational) It just doesn't work that way, however.

The creek just doesn't hold fish that well for some reason. The only exception to that being the far back area past the bridge. This area has some shallow water and boathouses and plays home to some spawning fish, but it is by no means an area to concentrate.

Hot-weather bass fishing
GUNTERSVILLE DAM TO SOUTH SAUTY CREEK

Like on all Alabama lakes, summer bass fishing on Lake Guntersville means the angler must move to deeper water.

Don Snider, winner of the 1988 Alabama Invitational on the lake, has made everyone sit up and take notice of his pattern of fishing crankbaits on the river dropoffs during the summer months. It is a pattern that is becoming more and more popular on the lake.

It isn't difficult to fish this pattern. The angler should parallel his boat to the bank in 25 feet of water on a ledge or creek channel that has 10 or 12 feet of water, as well as hydrilla or stumps. He should then cast his lure as close to the ledge as he can without becoming entangled in the milfoil, then crank it down at a speed that allows him to slightly bump the stumps or hydrilla.

The entire area should be worked in all directions to locate fish. These fish will usually be schooled in tight around the structure, with schools rarely being in a stretch longer than 20 yards.

Once the fish are located, the angler should back his boat off and position it in deeper water where the fish-holding area can be fished vertically, rather than horizontally.

The bass will be in different water depths depending on the time of the summer, so the type of crankbait may need to be adjusted. A pearl or white Mann's 20-Plus or a Maxi-R Rebel with a black or blue back are both effective when the fish are deep. When the fish are closer to the bank, a Mann's 15-Plus or Mini-R Rebel is needed.

Another pattern is strong in summer months when the fish are buried deep in the grass. Lake Guntersville's milfoil normally only grows into water 10 feet deep or less; but there, hydrilla has begun to take over in many places. Unlike milfoil, which is stringy and can entangle hooks easily, hydrilla is crisper, much like lettuce. Lures that hang in hydrilla often pull free easily.

Hydrilla is different in another respect, too. It has a long, thin stem that sometimes grows 12-feet-tall in summer months. It also has a broad leaf that forms a canopy. This is perfect habitat for summer bass not only because it is in deep water, but also because the large leaves block out much of the sunlight. As you probably know, bass have no eyelids, nor do their pupils constrict. Their only method of controlling the light in their eyes is moving into shade.

The canopy formed by hydrilla often holds numbers of bass and good bass, but it would seem tough to get to them under these leaves. Not so. A one-ounce lead-head bass jig with no trailer can be flipped into these areas and the heavy jig will punch its way through the hydrilla. It should be allowed to hit bottom then jigged. A heavy jigging spoon would seem a natural for this situation, but its open hook hangs in the hydrilla too often.

Another strong pattern during this time is flipping the piers. Permanent piers with wood pilings in deep water are best. These piers offer shade and cooler water bass need during this time and the bass gather under them in numbers. A 1/2-ounce black bass jig on 12-pound line is an excellent bait for flippin' these piers.

It should be noted that the piers are non-productive during overcast days. When there's cloud cover, the bass leave the piers and roam.

Many smaller bass stay in the milfoil throughout the summer, but they are tough to get to during most hours. Rats and frogs can be used in the milfoil during summer months, but only in the early morning and late afternoon when bright sunlight is not present. On overcast days, they can be used all day.

These patterns work up and down the river during the summer months. Although there are some summer fish in the creeks with deeper water, the better anglers concentrate on the main river. This is the area that receives the current and the water flow makes both the shad and bass active.

Cool and
cold weather fishing
GUNTERSVILLE DAM TO SOUTH SAUTY CREEK.

The are four seasons in the year, but Guntersville Lake really has only two fishing seasons. The spring and fall fishing is very much alike, as is the summer and winter fishing.

The cooling temperatures of October once again send the bait fish seeking shallow water and the bass follow. The major difference in fishing the lake in fall is the milfoil will be out of the water good and it will still be alive.

Buzzbaits become an excellent bait at this time. A black buzzbait thrown into the thinner, outer edges of the grass will evoke some exciting strikes. Rats and frogs will do the same.

You'll find bass in the grass on the main river channel, in the pockets and in the creeks during this time. Brown's Creek, Spring Creek, Town Creek and South Sauty Creek are excellent fall fishing spots.

When winter arrives, the bass once again drop into the deeper water, much like they did in summer. Jig-and-pigs and worms become the bait of choice at that point.

Other types of fishing
BREAM FISHING

For the same reasons this lake offers tremendous bass fishing, it also offers excellent bream fishing. The thousands of acres of aquatic vegetation and stumpy flats are excellent habitat for bream to not only spawn, but to hide and become big fish.

Bream fishing is tremendous during the spring. The larger bream head for the weedless pockets, sloughs and flats that have gravel or sand bottoms and lay their eggs. The areas are often covered with submerged stumps and the angler must plan on losing some tackle, but the gains are worth the losses. Guntersville Lake's spawning bream are usually good size, ranging from 1/2 to 3/4 of a pound. Tackle needed for this type of fishing is basic. A spincast reel allows longer casts which decreases the chances of spooking the fish. A small foam float, 4- or 6-pound test line, a single bb shot, a long-shanked bream hook and a cricket make a perfect combination.

A cane pole or fiberglass pole also will work at this time, but because of the opportunity to scare fish while pole fishing and the low cost of a spincast outfit, the spincast tackle is the way to go.

The first full moon in May usually will find bream hard on the bed in Guntersville Lake, and some species will spawn on the full moon every month throughout the summer.

Guntersville Lake's mayfly hatches are unpredictable, but they are regular throughout the summer months. The hatches send bream to the bank. Anything that hangs over the water from piers to bushes will concentrate bream during this time. The bream gather waiting for a bug to hit the water so it can become a tasty meal.

The same rig used for spring bream fishing can be used for this type of fishing. An especially fun way to fish forbream at this time is a flyrod. A mayfly imitation will sometimes produce 200 or more bream a day around boathouses and piers.

Bream fishing is much better on this lake during the summer than it is on most lakes in Alabama. The reason is the bream stay relatively shallow under the milfoil. A milfoil-covered hump that has an opening in the grass patch will produce large numbers of fish.

A spincast may be used at this time, but the opportunity for hanging the hook in the grass is great. A fiberglass pole or cane pole is much better at this time because it allows a worm or cricket to be gingerly placed on target.

Bream will stay in the milfoil until late fall when they drop into deeper water and become almost impossible to locate and catch.

Lake Guntersville's best fishing spots

1. Underwater hump.
2. Mouth of Honeycomb Creek. Good summer fishing.
3. Underwater hump.
4. Sandbars and humps. Covered with milfoil. Next to deep water. Good spring and fall fishing.
5. The Islands. Stumps and milfoil. Spring and fall fishing.
6. Underwater hump in Brown's Creek.
7. Winding creek channel in Brown's Creek.
8. Good milfoil patch. East of 69 bridge.
9. Underwater roadbed. Good in spring and fall.
10. Underwater depression. Good in spring. Surrounded to the north by stumps.
11. Stumpy flats all the way to back of the creek. Good spring fishing.
12. Riprap around U.S. 431 bridge. Good in early spring.
13. Mouth of Spring Creek. Good year-round. Good dropoffs.
14. Humps with milfoil.
15. Winding creek channel. Good interstate area to back of creek in spring.
16. Riprap around bridge. Good in spring.
17. Good spawning area. Boathouses and piers.
18. Henry Island. Good underwater island covered with milfoil.
19. Sandbars with stumps and milfoil.
20. Mouth of Short Creek. Good summer fishing area.
21. Claysville area. Lots of humps, stumps, islands, sandbars. Key area in spring and fall.
22. Town Creek. Lots of milfoil and hydrilla-covered humps adjacent to deep water.
23. Sharp bend in creek channel in Town Creek. Known as the Red Bank area. Good spring area.
24. Stump and milfoil-covered humps in Town Creek.
25. Stump patches in back of Town Creek. Spring and fall.
26. Bridge riprap. Good in spring.
27. Excellent flippin' area in back of Town Creek in January and February.
28. Good humps with stumps and milfoil.
29. Same as 28.
30. Mouth of Mill Creek. Good hump adjacent to shallow water.
31. Bridge pilings and riprap. Good in spring.
32. Stump patches with milfoil. Good in spring.
33. Murphy Hill area. Winding creek channel leading out of main river. Excellent year-round fishing.
34. Pine Island. Underwater island splits main river channel. Milfoil one end to other. Excellent year-round fishing.
35. Stump-filled slough. Good spring and fall.
36. Stump-covered sandbars.
37. Mouth of Preston Creek. Stumps and milfoil.
38. Highway 79 bridge pilings. Good spring fishing around riprap.
39. West finger of Preston Creek. Stumps in shallow water. Good in spring.
40. Islands. Deep water on north side; shallow water on south side. Good year-round.
41. Long, underwater island. Lots of milfoil. Good year-round.
42. Underwater humps. Lots of milfoil and stumps.
43. Bridge pilings and riprap.
44. Sharp drop as creek goes under bridge. Good spring and fall fishing area.
45. Winding creek channel. Locate with depthfinder. Excellent travel area in spring and fall.
46. Milfoil patches.
47. Shallow slough filled with stumps and milfoil.

Lake Guntersville

Guntersville
Dam

Sunrise Marine

Honeycomb
Creek

Snug Harbor
Marina

Guntersville
Boat Mart

Beech Creek
Fish Camp

Brown's
Creek

Guntersville Dam to U.S. 431 Bridge

Lake Guntersville

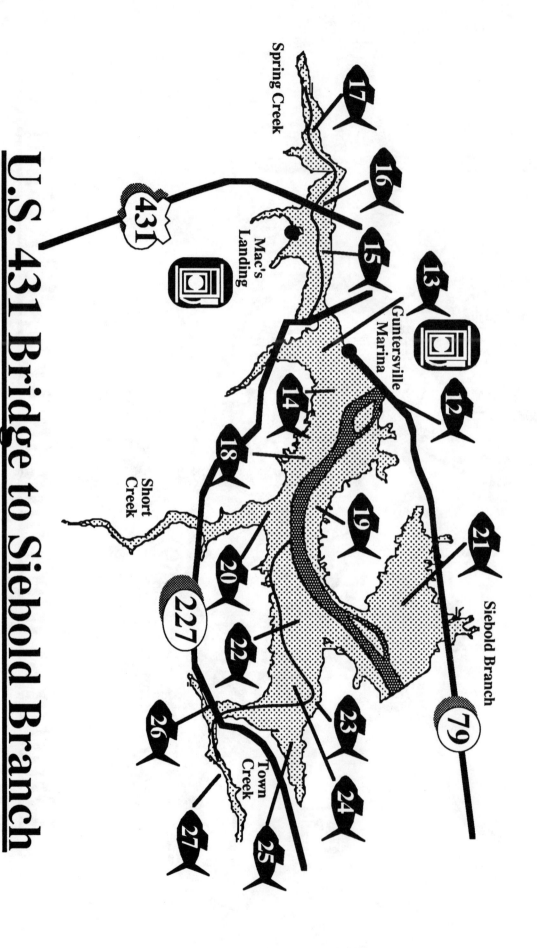

U.S. 431 Bridge to Siebold Branch

Lake Guntersville

Siebold Branch to Mink Creek

Wheeler Lake

The second-largest lake in Alabama, Wheeler Lake offers north Alabama some of the most diversified trophy fishing of any lake in North America. This lake has given up 10-pound smallmouth bass, 10-pound largemouth bass, 3-pound crappie, an 84-pound blue catfish (state record), a 38-pound striped bass and a 7-pound 6-ounce spotted gar (world line-class record).

Even if record-pushing fish aren't your bag, this massive lake is bound to have some type of fishing that you will enjoy.

Largemouth and smallmouth bass, catfish, crappie and sauger have long been staples of this lake, and the addition of striped bass and hybrid bass in the past two decades have enhanced the fishery even more.

A whopping 3.4 million hybrids have been placed in the lake since 1975.

An additional 633,000 striped bass also have been stocked.

On this lake, you cast your bait and take your chances.

It's not unusual for an angler fishing a curly-tail grub to catch as many as seven different species in a day's time.

Spring bass fishing
WHEELER DAM TO FOX CREEK

You will find little debate among anglers that the lower end of Wheeler Lake offers the best spring fishing.

The location of Second Creek, First Creek, Elk River, grass-filled Spring Creek and the numbers of tiny, shallow, structure-filled cuts on this end of the lake make it hard to compete with early in the year when spawning is on the mind of bass.

Both First Creek and Second Creek have the type of structure that make for excellent spring fishing. Sandbars, cuts with brush, rocky banks and points and flats dot the length of both creeks. Each creek also has some grass in its upper end. Second Creek has two roadbeds which produce bass in spring, and year round as well.

The cuts on the main river are havens for big springtime bass. There is just a smattering of grass in these cuts, but they are filled with blowdown timber, man-made brush piles and other wood structure. Many also have sand and pea gravel bottoms which bass love for spawning.

Wheeler Lake Fact Sheet

Location, length, acreage

Wheeler Lake is one of four Tennessee Valley Authority impoundments on the Tennessee River in Alabama and is the state's second largest lake, only slightly smaller than sister lake Lake Guntersville. The lake is bordered on the west by Wilson Lake and to the east by Lake Guntersville. Wheeler Lake begins at Wheeler Dam in Lauderdale and Lawrence counties and stretches 74.1 nautical miles to Guntersville Dam in Marshall County. Wheeler Lake consists of 68,300 surface acres and has 899 miles of shoreline. A total of 29,590 square miles drain into the lake.

Impoundment

Work began on Wheeler Lock and Dam January 21, 1933. The reservoir began to fill on Oct. 3, 1936.

Wheeler Dam

The concrete portion of Wheeler Dam is 2,773 feet wide and constructed of 548,000 cubic yards of concrete and 8,500 tons of reinforcing steel. It sits 72 feet high at its highest point. The navigation lock is 60 feet wide and 320 feet long and constructed of 121,000 cubic yards of concrete. The dam has 8 hydraulic turbines and 8 generators. A total of 5,500 workers were used to complete the project, which cost more than $48 million. Seven workers died during construction.

Stocking history

Florida-strain
1981-83	70,039
1990	68,200
1992	137,772
1993	60,400
1994	30,200

Hybrids
1979-84	1,627,501
1985	694,198
1986	310,200
1987	362,300
1988	136,700
1989	277,000
1990	323,600
1991	104,073
1992	204,239
1993	222,235
1994	206,107

Striped bass
1973-80	441,243
1981	192,440
1991	61,100
1992	136,759
1993	456,648
1994	89,140

Configuration

Like all Tennessee River impoundments, Wheeler Lake is a wide body of water with a somewhat limited number of incoming big creeks and a constantly changing river channel.

Major and secondary creeks

Besides the Tennessee River, Wheeler Lake has several large creeks and one large river which supply it with water. Second Creek, First Creek, Spring Creek, The Elk River, Coxey Creek, Poplar Creek, Mallard Creek and Fox Creek are water suppliers on the lower end, while Baker's Creek, Round Island Creek, Betty Branch, Dry Branch, Flint Creek, Piney Creek, Beaverdam Creek, Limestone Creek, Cotaco Creek, Barren Fork Creek, Indian Creek and Huntsville Spring Branch are creeks upriver, but below U.S. 231. The area between Wheeler Dam and U.S. 231 is the most fished part of the lake. Everything above that point is basically run-of-the-river.

Types of fish

Wheeler Lake has largemouth bass, smallmouth bass, spotted bass, white crappie, black crappie, bluegill, shellcracker, longear sunfish, green sunfish, blue catfish, channel catfish, flathead catfish, bullhead catfish, sauger, hybrid bass and white bass. Rough fish include spotted gar, longnose gar, freshwater drum, carp, and buffalo. Baitfish include skipjack herring, gizzard shad, threadfin shad, yellowtail shad and various species of minnows.

The Elk River also offers good spring fishing. The hundreds of tiny cuts sit adjacent to a stump-lined channel. Wash-in brush, blowdown timber and logjams can be found up and down this river.

Spring Creek somehow got the grass that much of the rest of this end of the lake missed. It also has a series of ditches, ledges, islands and other structure conducive to spring fishing.

Mallard Creek and Fox Creek are two more creeks on the lower end of the lake, although both are upriver a bit from the concentration of good spring fishing locations mentioned before. Many anglers start fishing on the lower end and, because of such good spring fishing there, never get this far upriver. Fishing both creeks, and especially Fox Creek, will not be a mistake if you decide to give fishing up that way a try.

During the pre-spawn period, which most anglers agree begins approximately Feb. 15, anglers should keep in mind that the bass find themselves in a predicament. They are ready to start feeding in anticipation of the spawn, but the water temperature still has their metabolism low and they aren't close to being the voracious feeders they'll be two months from then.

In other words, these fish can't catch a spinnerbait or crankbait ripped by them. The angler should fish accordingly.

A 1/2-ounce brown jig-and-pig with a chartreuse pork-frog trailer makes for a good, slow, visible bait in water that is almost always stained this time of the year. This bait is heavy enough to fall rapidly following the cast and it drops from ledges and other structure quickly into deeper water. That is important this time of the year when the bass are coming out of deeper water.

Another bait that works well is the spinnerbait because its speed can be easily controlled. A white or chartreuse/white spinnerbait with large nickel blades is preferred because it can be easily seen and because, by design, it must be fished slow.

It should be tipped with a white or chartreuse pork frog. The pork frog serves several purposes. First, it gives the lure added weight so it can be cast a great distance. Two, it gives a natural feel and taste when the fish hits the hook. Some fishermen also argue it makes the spinnerbait more weedless.

A 1/2-ounce or 3/4-ounce spinnerbait is best because it drops into deeper water quickly.

Once the water temperature rises and the fish move shallow, switch to a 1/4-ounce or 3/8-ounce spinnerbait. You want a lighter bait then that won't fall quickly and hang up in structure.

Some anglers also use a worm at this time, but most anglers agree jig-and-pigs and spinnerbaits catch more and better fish this time of year.

Once the water warms and the fish begin perodic forays onto the ledges and into the mouths of creeks in search of food, the faster baits can be used. A 1/4-ounce spinnerbait is still tough to beat, but a medium-running crankbait such as a Mann's 10-plus or a Rat-L-Trap is also good.

Once the fish are in water three feet or less and thinking spawn, or chasing shad in shallow water, buzzbaits, floating lizards, stickbaits and shallow-running crankbaits such as Rapalas are key.

There's not many reasons to do a lot of traveling on this lake during the spring. An angler can decide on fishing First Creek, Second Creek, the cuts on the main river channel, etc., and simply set up shop there for the day. If he fishes that area properly, he'll catch enough fish that moving won't enter his mind.

This author has set on the first secondary point on the right bank entering First Creek in April and caught and released a double limit of bass in less than an hour.

It's also possible to sit in Fox Creek all day with a spinnerbait and buzzbait anytime during the spring.

Fox Creek to U.S. 31 Bridge

When you move into this section of the lake, you'll find a much different lake than you found on the lower end. This area is made up of wide water flats with water depth that varies from 1 to six feet outside of the main channel. What anglers call "dropoffs" in this section may only be a 1-foot ledge, but this 1-foot ledge will still hold fish.

This area is full of islands, as well as flats with sprinklings of milfoil, and to a lesser degree, hydrilla.

Two spring baits are a must in this area - spinnerbaits and Rat-L-Traps. Just as on Wheeler's sister lake, Lake Guntersville, the milfoil will be submerged this time of the year and ripping a Rat-L-Trap across the top of it can be deadly. It was using this pattern in March of 1989 that Muscle Shoals angler Paul Cantrell and a partner caught and released 212 bass during a single-day bass tournament.

It's not possible to pinpoint any single area in this portion of the lake that offers good fishing. The presence of the milfoil and hydrilla make it possible for any spot to hold fish. Anglers should use common sense, however, and fish the deeper weeds early and progess to the shallow water as spawning time approaches.

Once the fish move shallow and the growth of the weeds increases, it will become necessary to switch from a Rat-L-Trap to a spinnerbait. Leave the pork trailer off the bait in this instance because you need the lightest bait possible. Go with a 1/4-ounce chartreuse spinnerbait and concentrate on the shallow water closest to the islands that have grass.

Unfortunately, that's like telling someone in Alabama to deer hunt near pine trees. It doesn't narrow it down much, but that's where you'll find fish.

U.S. 31 Bridge to U.S. 231

Once the angler goes east (upriver) of the U.S. 31 Bridge, he'll encounter a brief stretch of flats similar to those in the middle section, then he'll find a lake that narrows and is river-like the rest of the way to Guntersville Dam. This well-defined river channel has small ledges on both sides throughout its length.

Flint Creek, Piney Creek, Limestone Creek, Beaverdam Creek, Cotaco Creek, Barren Fork Creek, Indian Creek and Huntsville Spring Branch offer decent spring fishing.

These creeks have adequate water depth and enough stumps for good spawning grounds. These creeks have some grass, but not enough to be much of a factor in patterning fish to grass.

Due to the fact some of these creeks are the only shallow water in

the area, they are the only places capable of confining spring baitfish. Bass are forced to go into the areas.

Another factor that make these areas worth trying is the fact most of the creeks have small mouths which are easy to cover, especially before and after the spawn. Bass traveling to and from the creeks to deep water are funneled into a tiny area. An angler can fish these areas thoroughly and he can't help catching fish.

During the pre-spawn period, when bass are leaving the channel and coming into the creeks, jig-and-pigs, big-bladed spinnerbaits and Carolina-rigged lizards can be effective in the creek mouths.

Following the spawn, when the bass are forced back to deep water by the water temperature, faster baits such as Sassy Shads, Rat-L-Traps and medium-running crankbaits will do the trick.

When the bass are up in the creeks, the traditional spring baits - buzzbaits, spinnerbaits, lizards and twitch baits - will work.

Hot weather bass fishing
Wheeler Dam to Fox Creek

Once the spring spawn is over, the bass will resume the heavy feeding pattern they abandoned during the spawn and slowly move to deeper water. When the water surface temperature reaches the mid 70's, it's safe to assume you'll no longer find quality fish in water less than 8 feet deep.

Between the time the bass quit spawning and the time they head for deeper water, they are making up for lost time in the eating department. The mouths of the creeks are good places to find these transistion fish. A chrome or white Rat-L-Trap, or even a worm or spinnerbait, fished on the primary and secondary points can result in tremendous catches.

Once you don't find the quality fish shallow anymore, it's a safe bet they have gone off the ledges to find a summer home on deep bars, underwater humps and islands, dropoffs, deep rocky banks and long, deep points. It's not uncommon for these fish to be 30 feet deep before the summer is over.

Fishing during this time is tough, especially for the angler who lacks patience. He's probably not going to catch numbers of fish as he did during the spring, and instead of moving regularly in hopes of finding great fishing, he needs to fish key areas slowly and thoroughly.

Several baits will work during this period. The angler with an arm enough to hack it may find success with a pearl-colored Mann's 30-Plus crankbait, but few anglers have the gusto to battle the sun and a deep-diving crankbait all day.

One way around that, if you're not tournament fishing, is to troll a Mann's 30-Plus or Hellbender over the humps and bars in this part of the lake. One of the lake's better anglers does this with a three-rod setup and keeps a marker buoy close by his side. When there is a hookup, he throws the buoy to the spot, reels in the fish, then switches rods.

He first throws a jigging spoon he already had rigged to the spot, and if that doesn't work, he throws a pre-rigged Do-Nothing Worm. One of those rigs usually results in another fish or two and they are usually good fish. It's not unusual for bass to school in tight schools this time of the year and multiple catches from one spot aren't uncommon.

Another pattern that works well is locating bass on the deep, rocky, stumpy points with a depthfinder, then attacking them with a jigging spoon. Not many anglers stop to think about it, but unlike most other lures, a spoon can mimick an injured baitfish and do it over and over again in the same spot. This often triggers an angry strike from a fish that isn't interested in hitting a bait, or even a fish that is leery of what he's seeing and knows something isn't right. The spoon will catch fish this time of the year that worms, crankbaits and spinnerbaits won't catch.

It takes little more than your eyes and a depthfinder to locate summer fish on this end of the lake. Any long, sloping point that goes into deep water is likely to be good, as is any sudden change in the bottom. The underwater islands in the main river channel between the Elk River and Spring Creek is an excellent place to start.

FOX CREEK TO U.S. 31 BRIDGE

Unlike on the lake's lower and upper ends, the shade and cover provided by the acres of milfoil and hydrilla in this area delays the movement of bass into the deep river channel during the summer. While you may find bass on deep structure in early summer on the lake's upper and lower sections, it's possible you may catch them on buzzbaits and other topwater lures here on the same day.

The grass provides shade which holds the water temperature lower longer, and provides cover for the baitfish. This growing grass also produces oxygen during the critcal time of the year when the water needs oxygen.

Getting the bass to leave is akin to making somebody leave the air-conditioned den during the summer to go sit in the backyard.

The baits you used here during the spring will catch fish into the summer as long as the bass are holding in the grass. As the water temperature rises, the bass will eventually be forced to go to deep water at least for part of the day. That exit from the grass will begin earlier and earlier each day during the summer. However - except during an unusually hot July or August - the bass will come back to to the grass sometime during the evening or night.

Almost any summer morning at daybreak, or summer evening at dusk, it's possible to throw a Nip-I-Didee, Crazy Shad or Devil's Horse on the fringe of this grass facing the channel and catch bass. On rainy, overcast days, it's sometimes possible to catch fish that way all day long.

The ability to catch bass shallow throughout the summer on this lake will be in direct contrast to some other lakes in the state, such as grass-filled Lay Lake. The reason for that is Wheeler Lake's slightly lower water surface temperature.

There's two reasons for that minor water temperature difference. First, Lay Lake and some other grass-filled lakes are further south and are a degree or so warmer because of it. Second, Wheeler Lake is a navigable waterway and Lay Lake isn't. The dams and locks on the Tennessee River move much more water during the summer than does the Coosa River. Moving water is more difficult to heat than still water.

Back to Wheeler Lake. During dog days, once the sun clears the treeline, the better anglers switch to plastic worms and Carolina-rigged lizards and fish the ledges adjacent to the grass. To do this, the boat should be positioned in the deep water at least 25 yards into the main channel and the cast made onto the ledge. The retrieve should

bring the worm across the ledge and eventually allow it to fall in the channel.

Many strikes come when the worm "falls off the table." Why? Because the schooling bass will often chase shad onto the ledge, then retreat to deep water and suspend themselves a few feet below the ledge out of view. The shad will swim back toward the deep water and once they exit the ledge, they have their last surprise.

U.S. 31 BRIDGE TO U.S. 231 BRIDGE

Because of the well-defined, deep river channel, this part of the lake offers good summer fishing for the angler who understands river and ledge patterns.

The ledges are scattered with blowdowns and other debris, and summer ledge fishing can be excellent.

The bass are forced to suspend in the deep water in this area during the summer. The baitfish attempt to get as close as possible to the deep water without giving up their lifesaving structure, meaning they usually end up on stump rows, brush piles and other such debris on the edge of the ledge.

There are two ways to go about enticing these fish to bite. The most tiring and difficult is to spend the day fishing parallel to the ledges with deep-diving crankbaits. This is a tough pattern to fish during the summer heat, but it can be effective and can produce big fish. The angler should first locate the fish with a depthfinder, then drop a marker buoy. He should then make a long cast well past the schooling fish and using his judgement, make the retrieve fast enough so the lure runs right over the top of the fish.

Another pattern that works well is locating the stumps and other structure on the edge of the ledge and fishing for the bass running up on the ledge to feed. Locating this structure can be time consuming, but running the boat along the ledge will show this structure on the depthfinder. Another way to locate the structure is by positioning your boat in open water and watching for the tell-tale signs of bass knocking shad out of the water. It's a safe bet that wherever there's a sign of feeding activity, some type of structure can be found nearby on the ledge.

Once this structure is located, several baits can be used. Two of the best are a 3-inch pearl-colored Prissy Shad or a white bucktail jig fished on 6-pound test line with a spinning outfit. These shad imitations should be cast onto the ledge and hopped back to the boat. Once they fall off the ledge, allow either to fall and make the hops, or jigging motion, more pronounced as to allow them to cover both deep and shallow water.

Plastic worms and small crankbaits such as a Bagley's DB2 also will work.

This is also the area on Wheeler Lake in which flippin' can be productive during the summer. Pig-and-jigs or lizards flipped into structure on the deeper ledges and onto stumpy points will also produce bass.

Cool and cold
weather bass fishing
WHEELER DAM TO FOX CREEK

The bass you found in summer won't be far away from that same location during the fall and winter. The bass will move into shallower water during the fall in search for food on which to fatten up for the winter, but not the shallow water in which you found them during the spring.

Bass holding on long, deep points during the summer will use that point as a roadway on which to move back and forth to less deep water. It's no secret that the baitfish use this pathway, too.

For the bass who find summer homes on underwater islands or sandbars, the fish will move up to the uppermost point of this structure in search of food. If food isn't available, they'll move onto ledges or in the mouths of creeks.

Several patterns can be used to catch these fish. A Carolina-rigged worm is one bait that works well, especially when the water temperature drops below 72 degrees. A jig-and-pig also works well during this time, and on onto the cold of the winter.

A semi-jigged Rat-L-Trap, its speed of retrieve determined by the water temperature, also works well, especially coming down the points.

Early in the fall, a 3-inch pearl curly tail grub fished on stumpy points will produce bass if you can keep the crappie and hybrids off of it.

The better anglers stay out of the creeks during this time, even though it's possible to catch some bass on the ledges of the creeks that have deep channels.

Keep in mind that the bass arc finicky during this time. A change in color of a lure, or adding a shorter worm to a Carolina rig, can bring strikes in areas where you couldn't buy a strike before.

Why? Who knows. That's why they call it fishing instead of catching.

Fox Creek to U.S. 31 Bridge

Because this area is so full of shallow grass, it isn't a very good place to fish for bass during the fall and winter, especially during the colder months. The dying grass robs the water of oxygen and fish can't survive for long in the area.

The better anglers elect to fish the upper or lower ends of the lake where the water is deep enough to thwart grass.

U.S. 31 Bridge to U.S. 231 Bridge

During the fall and winter, the patterns for catching bass don't change much from those used during the summer.

The fish still make the deep-water channel home, but during the fall will use the ledges more to feed on, especially when the winter feeding frenzy starts. Fishing on the deep points also gets a little better during the fall.

During the winter, fishing is tough in this area. Bass suspended in a channel during the winter are almost impossible to get to except with jigging spoons and lipless crankbaits. Go hunting instead.

Other types of fishing
Spring smallmouth fishing

This lake takes a backseat to Pickwick Lake when it comes to smallmouth fishing. But Wheeler Lake can offer some might good smallmouth fishing in the spring.

Few anglers will argue that the lower end of the lake is not the best area for smallmouth fishing, and or that the spring is the best season.

The deep, sloping rocky banks next to deep water in First Creek, Second Creek and the mouth of Elk River offer the best spring smallie fishing, with a Jumping Minnow the primary bait.

Wheeler Lake's best fishing spots

1. Mouth of Second Creek. Good drop-off from 5 feet to 45 feet. Good largemouth and smallmouth area year round.

2. Excellent point. Good spring in pre-spawn.

3. Good fishing around pilings and rip-rap on U.S. 72 bridge.

4. Good point for spring bass fishing.

5. Underwater ditch. Good spring fishing.

6. Underwater road bed.

7. Rocky cuts. Good for spring fishing.

8. Mouth of First Creek. Good year-round fishing.

9. Good bank for spring and summer fishing. Full of treetops.

10. Good spring bass.

11. Island in First Creek. Good spring fishing.

12. Good spring point.

13. Good crankbait area in spring.

14. Excellent points on south bank for spring fishing.

15. Excellent point for year-round fishing.

16. Island in mouth of Elk River. Good spring fishing.

17. Excellent bank for year-round fishing. Cuts, logjams, blow-downs, etc.

18. U.S. 72 bridge pilings and rip-rap. Good spring and summer. Good crappie fishing at night in summer.

19. Good cut. Good spring fishing.

20. Bank filled with logjams. Good buzzbait area in spring. Good flippin' area in summer.

21. Bend in channel. Good ledge fishing in spring, summer and fall.

22. Good spinnerbait and shallow-running crankbait in spring and early summer.

23. Underwater islands. Good summer fishing for all species.

24. Oxbow-shaped underwater island. Good summer fishing area for all species.

25. Mouth of Spring Creek. Good schooling area for largemouth in summer and fall.

26. Island in Spring Creek. In shallow water next to deep water. Excellent spring fishing.

27. Islands in Spring Creek. Good spring fishing.

28. Good buzzbait fishing in back of Spring Creek.

29. Good cuts. Good spring fishing.

30. Underwater island in main river channel. Good summer area, especially when current is moving.

31. Excellent spring cuts.

32. Coxey Creek. Good spring fishing.

33. Point in mouth of Mallard Creek. Good year-round fishing.

34. Island in Mallard Creek. Good spring fishing.

35. Bridge pilings and rip-rap around bridge. Good crappie fishing in spring and summer.

36. Mouth of Fox Creek. Good year-round fishing.

37. Shallow island in back of Fox Creek. Good spring fishing with spinnerbaits.

38. Excellent point. Good year-round fishing up and down point.

39. Good spring flats. Milfoil and hydrilla.

40. Island. Good spring fishing.

41. Series of small islands. Good spring fishing.

42. Island. Good spring fishing.

43. Islands. Good spring fishing.

44. Sandbars with stumps. Tremendous spring fishing for largemouth and smallmouth.

45. Underwater island that splits main river channel. Good summer and winter fishing.

46. Underwater islands in mouth of Baker's Creek. Good year-round fishing.

47. Mouth of Baker's Creek. Good year-round fishing.

48. Long underwater ditch leading from bank to main river channel. Tremendous for bass year round. Bass travel up and down from shallow to deep water in this ditch.

49. Keller Bridge. Good crappie fishing in summer.

50. Mouth of Flint Creek. Good year-round fishing.

51. Bridge pilings in Flint Creek. Good in spring for bass. Summer crappie fishing at night.

52. I-65 bridge pilings. Summer fishing at night for crappie.

53. Narrow mouth of Piney Creek. Good funnel area for bass pre- and post-spawn.

54. Good bank for spinnerbaits in spring.

55. The Bayou. Good spring spinnerbait and buzzbait.

56. Lily Pond. Good spring area with floating lizard.

57. Mouth of Barren Fork. Good funnel area for spring bass.

58. Cotaco Creek. Numerous world-record gar caught here. Good spring fishing for bass.

Wheeler Lake

Wheeler Dam to Fox Creek

Wheeler Lake

Elk River

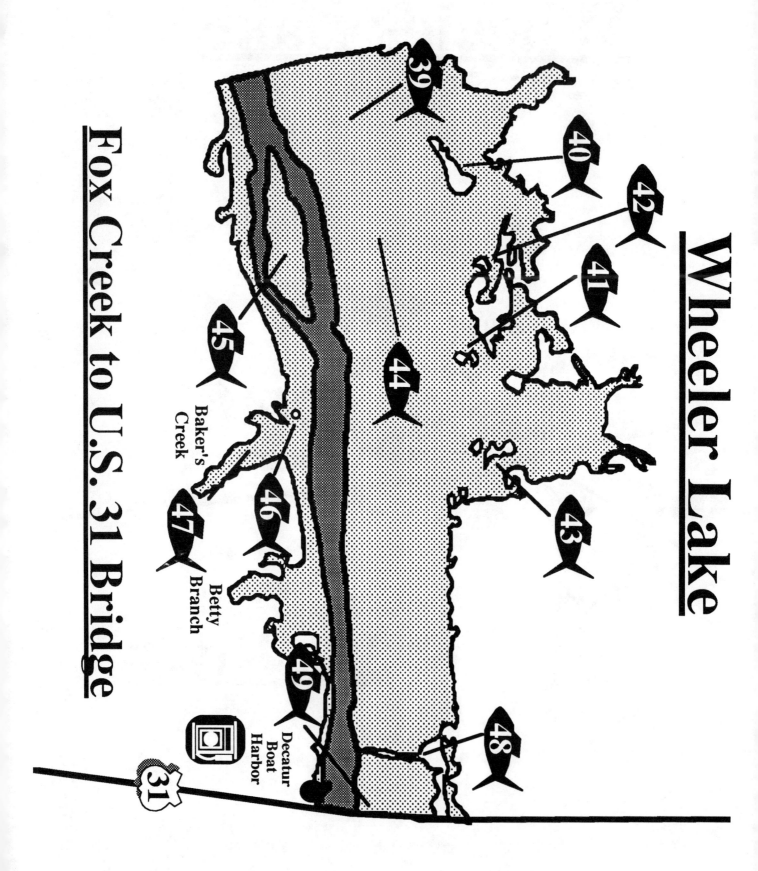

Wheeler Lake

Fox Creek to U.S. 31 Bridge

Baker's Creek

Betty Branch

Decatur Boat Harbor

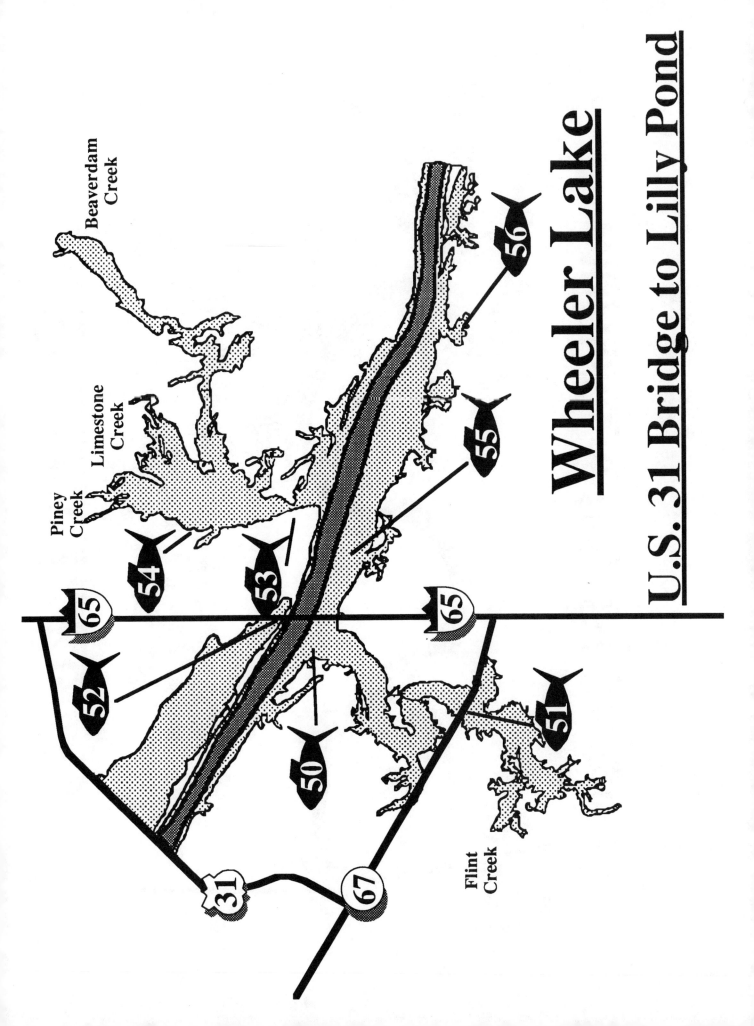

Wheeler Lake

U.S. 31 Bridge to Lilly Pond

Wheeler Lake

Lily Pond to U.S. 231 Bridge

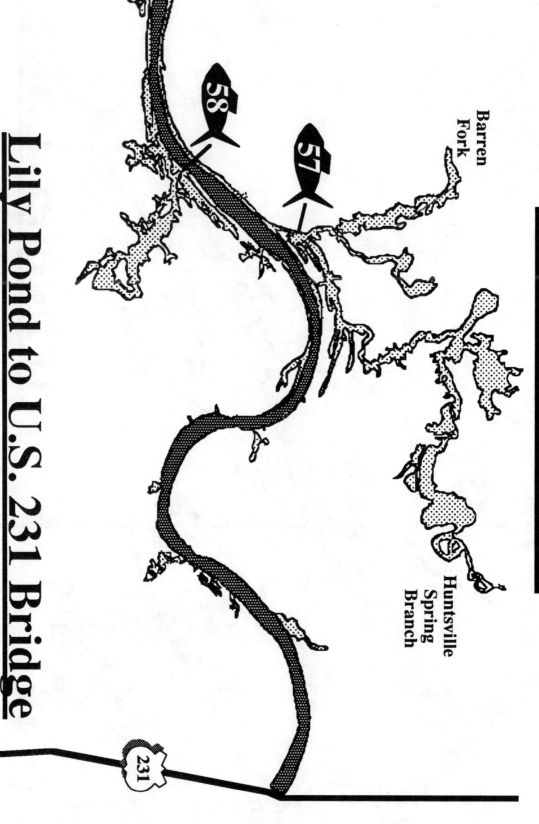

Barren
Fork

Huntsville
Spring
Branch

58

57

231

Wilson Lake

Because it's a 15,930 acre lake wedged between 68,300-acre Wheeler Lake and 47,500-acre Pickwick Lake, "tiny" Wilson Lake doesn't always get the respect it deserves.

This tremendous fish producer may be old, but it's by no means feeble. It's probably the most varied fishery in Alabama and it annually produces excellent catches of largemouth bass, smallmouth bass and spotted bass, not to mention crappie, catfish, stripe, hybrid, white bass, sauger and rough species.

Two of the current state records have come from this body of water, both former world records. One of those catches, the 10-pound, 8-ounce smallmouth caught in 1950, was a world record for several decades.

Spring bass fishing

As is the case in all of the Tennessee River impoundments in Alabama, Wilson Lake has its share of aquatic vegetation. The presence of non-native species of weeds such as Eurasion milfoil and hydrilla, coupled with a variety of native species of grass, makes Wilson Lake a first-class spring bass fishery.

February and begin feeding heavily in anticipation for the spawning period, a time in which many of them do not eat.

This spawning period can be described as a human walking up a flight of stairs and coming back down. The bass begin in the deep water and step themselves up into more shallow water as the water temperature allows.

Once the preferred water temperature is available, usually around 68 degrees, the bass will spawn in shallow water, then begin their journey back down the steps. By summer, the bass will be back at the bottom of the steps where they were in winter.

Most Wilson Lake bass will be found in the deep water of the main channel in early February, but soon start moving toward the banks, pausing briefly at different levels on different types of structure. Two key areas during this time are the underwater islands in the mouth of Big Nance Creek and in the mouth of Town Creek. These islands allow the bass to move up and down as the weather does its early spring flip-flops. A Carolina-rigged lizard or plastic worm, a 5/8-ounce brown jig with a black frog pork trailer or a shad-colored crankbait such as a Bagley's DB3 will take the fish off these islands in early spring.

The lake lacks the numbers of large, wide creeks that its Tennessee River neighbors Wheeler Lake, Pickwick Lake and Lake Guntersville enjoy, but the hundreds of small, grass-filled pockets off the main river channel offer spring spawning grounds for bass that are actually easier to fish than creeks.

If you're a spring creek fisherman, don't fret, however. Wilson Lake has a few creeks that can keep you busy. Town Creek, Blue Water Creek, McCernan Creek and Shoal Creek offer excellent spring fishing.

The basics of the spring ritual for bass is no different here than it is on any other lake in Alabama. The bass begin leaving their deep-water winter homes at the first sign of warming water in late

Once the water temperature is right, the fish will move off the islands and up into Big Nance Creek and Town Creek. These creeks are perfect for spring bass because they have both deep and shallow water, as well as humps, logjams, piers, brush and grass-filled cuts.

Several baits will work during this time. A 1/2-ounce chartreuse/white spinnerbait with a chartreuse pork frog trailer is probably the most effective bait because of its ability to cover so much water.

Wilson Lake Fact Sheet

Location, length, acreage

Wilson Lake is one of four Tennesee Valley Authority Reservoirs on the Tennessee River in Alabama. It is bordered to the east by Wheeler Lake and to the west by Pickwick Lake. Wilson Lake begins at Wilson Dam near Florence in Lauderdale and Colbert counties and stretches 15.5 river miles to Wheeler Dam in Lauderdale and Lawrence counties.

Wilson Lake consists of 15,930 surface acres and has 150 miles of shoreline. A total of 30,750 square miles drain into the lake.

Impoundment

Work started on Wilson Dam on April 14, 1918 under orders of the United States War Department. The dam was completed on April 24, 1924. The power generation units were placed in service on Sept. 12, 1925.

Wilson Dam

Wilsom Dam was acquired by the Tennessee Valley Authority from the War Department on May 18, 1933. The concrete portion of the dam and spillway is 4,535 feet wide and constructed of 1.2 million cubic yards of concrete. It sits 137 feet high at its highest point.

The dam has 18 hydraulic turbines and 18 generators. The Wilson Lake project cost more than $48 million.

Stocking history

Florida-strain largemouth	
1986-88	92,800
1990	16,000
1992	29,596
1993	49,500
1994	35,150

Hybrid bass	
1977-84	520,887
1985	159,000
1986	159,000
1987	95,600
1988	31,700
1989	61,700
1990	79,700
1991	79,727
1992	80,300
1993	79,736
1994	80,664

Configuration

Wilson Lake is a short, wide, stubby lake. Its main river channel isn't well defined.

Because of the lake's width, it's susceptible to high winds.

Major and secondary creeks

Wilson Lake is fed by several major creeks. Shoal Creek, on the lake's lower end, is the largest water supplier. McCernan Creek, also on the lower end, is also a major creek. Six-Mile Creek and Four-Mile Creek are lesser water suppliers on the lower half.

Town Creek is the large water supplier on the upper end, while Big Nance Creek and Blue Water Creek are smaller water inlets.

Types of fish

Wilson lake has largemouth bass, smallmouth bass, spotted bass, white crappie, black crappie, bluegill, shellcracker, longear, green sunfish, blue catfish, channel catfish, flathead catfish, bullhead catfish, sauger, hybrid bass and white bass. Rough fish include spotted gar, longnose gar, freshwater drum, carp, buffalo and skipjack herring.

Baitfish present include gizzard shad, threadfin shad, yellowtail shad and various species of minnows.

As said before, the hundreds of cuts and sloughs along the main river channel hold the majority of the spring bass, however. The bass are able to stage themselves out of deep water and onto the ledges before moving into the pockets.

A jig-and-pig or deep-diving crankbait is needed when the bass are still suspended on the ledges. Once the fish move up on the ledges and begin to make their move into the pockets, a spinnerbait is the key. Use a 1/2-ounce bait early and allow it to fall into the channel as part of the retrieve. Once the bass are up on the ledges to stay, switch to a lighter 1/4-ounce bait.

Once the bass are in the pockets, the topwater angler may switch to his favorite kind of baits. Buzzbaits, jerk baits and floating lizards will work on the grass fringes, as well as up in the grass.

These same patterns will work in Shoal Creek and McCernan Creek. Both have grass-filled cuts full of spring bass.

Hot weather bass fishing

Once the spawn is over, the bass will hang in the grass in the cuts and creeks until the increasingly warm water temperature (usually 80-plus degrees) forces them to escape to deeper, cooler water.

This exit to deeper water will not be a sudden movement, for the bass will fight to stay in the grass as long as possible. They like it there. The fish will be in the grass at daybreak early in the summer and may stay there until 10 a.m., but the increasing summer heat will force the bass to leave the weeds earlier and earlier each day until,

eventually, they'll be gone.

That's only in theory, of course. It actually may be possible to find some bass in this grass all summer, but these will almost never be quality bass. By mid-June, the water temperature will have forced most large bass to deeper water.

During this period that the fish are in the grass, several patterns will work. A buzzbait will usually work throughout the period the bass are in the grass, but the last few weeks the bass are in the weeds, the grass may be too thick for a buzzbait. Flippin' will be needed then. A 3/4-ounce brown jig with a black pork frog will be strong enough to poke through most of the grass you'll find on Wilson Lake.

While some of the smaller bass will be fooling with the grass during the summer, the true quality bass will be deep on structure in the main river channel. The main river channel area is full of underwater islands and sandbars, many covered with brushpiles and stumps.

Some of those areas anglers should key on are the constantly changing humps and sandbars below Wheeler Dam, the series of underwater ridges and ledges near the mouth of Blue Water Creek, the major underwater island out from the mouth of Town Creek, the series of large islands and sandbars in the middle of the lake, the sandbar out from the mouth of McCernan Creek and the two large humps above Wilson Dam. It is from these deep underwater areas that better anglers catch most of the best summertime bass.

Several patterns will catch these fish. If you're fishing for fun and not in a tournament, Mann's 20-Plus or 30-Plus deep diving crankbaits trolled over these humps will catch fish. This is a tremendous pattern for big fish when the water is being pulled through both dams. It will also work at night.

Other lures that will work include Carolina-rigged plastic worms, deep-diving crankbaits, jig-and-pigs with a pork frog trailers and last, but surely not least, jigging spoons.

The jigging spoon is a well-kept secret of many of the lake's top tournament anglers who fish in summer. Once a school of summer-time bass is located with a depthfinder, a Mann's Mann-0-Lure or other similar jigging spoon should be dropped directly on top of the fish. The spoon should then be lifted 18 inches in a medium-speed motion, then allowed to fall with a fluttering motion. Most strikes will take place when the lure is on the fall. Be forearmed. The strikes are violent. Have the rod steady in your hands and the drag set properly.

Quality fish are rarely found in the creeks during the hot summer months, so the angler looking for big bass should stay in the deep water in the main river channel.

If you're just looking for fish large enough to claim you caught some, plenty of small bass can be found in the creeks, however. The angler looking to just catch a fish or two of any size can find some success by fishing worms in the brush around piers and on the ledges of the deeper creeks, especially at night.

The only exception to avoiding the creeks during the summer to catch big fish is the cool-water spring in Blue Water Creek. This spring, which emits cool water in the summer and warm water during the winter, will hold quality fish - of all species - year round.

This spring can easily be located with the use of a surface temperature gauge.

Cool and cold weather bass fishing

Because of the unusual situation on this lake of some water being deeper on some banks than it is 50 yards out from the banks, the cuts and the mouth of cuts adjacent to that deep water offers good fishing during the fall.

Grass-filled cuts next to deep water means the bass have easy access to both deep and shallow water as the fall weather does its inevitable flip-flops. Keep in mind that the bass are schooling and feeding heavily at this time to store fat for the winter and that shad are their No. 1 food.

Two of the key baits at this time are shad look-a-likes - Sassy Shads and Rat-L-Traps. Early during the fall, when the bass are on the ledges and running up on the ledges in the mouths of the cuts to feed, either of the baits can take numbers of quality fish. A pearl white 3-inch Sassy Shad fished on spinning tackle and 8-pound test line should be against the law this time of the year. Some anglers catch 50 and 60 bass a day with this pattern when they hit it right. A chrome or pearl Rat-L-Trap will give similar results.

Several other baits will work well during this period, too. A white spinnerbait fished on the fringes of the grass and in the mouth of the cuts is a prime producer after the fish exit the channel and begin staying on the ledges. This bait covers a lot of territory quickly and tends to produce more quality fish than other lures.

The more the water temperature cools, the slower a bait must be. Many of the better spinnerbait anglers force themselves to slow

down by using larger blades, while other anglers switch to naturally slower baits such as jig-and-pigs and worms.

These worms and jig-and-pigs fished on the fringes of the grass and in ditches and creek channels in the cuts, as well as the mouth of the cuts, will sometimes produce fish through the late fall and winter, especially during mild winters like this area saw in 1987 and 1988.

During normal winter patterns, however, the falling water temperature will force the quality bass into warmer, deeper water.

The sandbars, islands, humps and other structure over 12 feet deep will concentrate these winter fish and a good rule of thumb is to look for them in the same place you found them in July and August.

Jig-and-Pigs and worms are the only bait that give you much chance at these bass during the winter and even then, it's not that good a chance.

A few other types of bass fishing

TAILRACE FISHING

It may not be an exaggeration to say Wilson Lake's upper end, the tailrace below Wheeler Dam, may offer the best tailrace fishing in the U.S.

Nowhere else in Alabama can an angler have a more varied catch of large fish. It was in this tailrace on September 30, 1988, that this author and Birmingham's Nolen Shivers had a day of fishing like many anglers only dream of. By lunchtime, the two of us caught and released 23 smallmouth between four and six pounds. Eleven of those fish topped five pounds, including the largest, a 6-pound, 2-ounce beauty.

Included in that day's catch were a 6-pound largemouth, a 16-pound catfish, numerous smaller cats, some 10-pound-plus drum and several crappie.

It's almost impossible to find a negative in fishing this tailrace. Unlike many tailraces in Alabama, this one doesn't have a single underwater obstacle that poses a boating hazard. There is uniform depth of 12 feet for at least a half-mile or more below it.

And because this is a navigable waterway, there will be periodic water flow through the dam even during the worst of droughts. Fishing is always best when this water is moving.

This tailrace produces fish year-round, too. During the summer of 1989, anglers caught nice stringers of smallmouth throughout the summer there. You don't go there fishing for just one species, either. It's possible to spend a day fishing and end up with a catch of largemouth bass, smallmouth bass, Kentucky spotted bass, white bass, yellow bass, hybrid bass, striped bass, white crappie, black crappie, sauger, five species of catfish, skipjack herring, drum and on and on.

There is easy access to the tailrace from several areas, most notably John Hill's Fisherman's Resort in Big Nance Creek.

If this area does have a negative, it's that bad weather can make the area treacherous. A good storm and a west wind can make it extremely dangerous. Keep that in mind when you see weather approaching.

An angler has a wide array of ways to catch these tailrace fish. Most anglers opt for live bait fishing, choosing to scoop their bait free of charge with a dip net or cast net along the walls of the dam and powerhouse. Threadfin shad, gizzard shad and yellowtail minnows are the favorites.

Other anglers choose to fish with plastic grubs, imitation minnows such as Red's Prissy Shads, live worms, minnows (for crappie) or cut baits.

An angler may anchor in the swift current or run his boat up to the head of the dam, cut the motor and drift fish.

The fall run of smallmouth to the dam is something an angler can't afford to miss. Starting in mid-September, the larger smallmouth make a run at the dam to feed on the millions of minnows and shad that gather around the concrete walls. The fish are in a feeding frenzy, stuffing themselves in anticipation for the winter. The good news is that at no other time and on no other lake will you see so many quality smallmouth schooling in such a confined space.

Although the angler will try to convince himself it can't possibly matter, light line is a must here. Eight-pound test on a spinning reel is needed, as well as a No. 2 or No. 4 (depending on the size of the shad being used) pattern 84 Eagle Claw hook. A No. 5 or 6 split shot should be placed 18 inches above the bait.

The angler runs his boat within 50 yards of the turbines (water must be moving), cuts the motor and fishes as he drifts. The shad should be cast gently and reeled just fast enough to keep the hook from grabbing bottom.

A hookup in this swift water, coupled with the fact smallmouth will often make dazzling 5-foot jumps out of the water, is nice.

These fish begin close to the dam in early October and will slowly move further and further downriver as winter approaches. By the end of December, they may be as much as a mile below the dam.

SMALLMOUTH FISHING

Any time an angler is bass fishing on this lake, he's a threat to tear into a smallmouth bass. Smallmouth often share the same water (rocky points and banks, gravel bottom) as the Kentucky spots that are found on this lake.

An angler can do things to increase his chances of catching smallmouth, however.

The smallmouth have a strong liking for smaller baits, most notably white grubs and 4-inch worms.

The areas around and including Four-Mile Creek and Six-Mile Creek and the Wheeler Dam tailrace are prime smallmouth locations and novice smallmouth anglers should direct their attention to those places.

During the spring, the angler should locate rocky points and banks and fish them with grubs. Any cuts that have red clay banks will likely hold some smallmouth, too.

During the summer, the smallmouth gather on the deep islands, particularly the underwater humps closest to the dam. Slider worms, grubs and an occasional crankbait will take the smallmouth then, especially when water is being pulled.

Some anglers prefer to fish for smallmouth at night during the summer and numbers of fish, rather than large fish, can be caught then. A small, white spinnerbait fished along the rocky points and banks will produce.

During the fall, there isn't a reason to fish for smallmouth except below Wheeler Dam. This is when the quality fish come forth.

Wilson Lake's best fishing spots

1. Grass-filled cuts on right bank above Wilson Dam. Good fishing area in spring.
2. Underwater islands. Good fishing in summer and winter for all species. Especially good in summer for bass when water is being pulled.
3. Mouth of McCernan Creek. Good year-round fishing. Next to deep water and underwater island.
4. Back of McCernan Creek. Excellent spring spawning area. Lots of grass-filled cuts.
5. Excellents cuts on left bank of dam. Good spring and fall.
6. Excellent slough. Grass, points and piers. Good spring and fall.
7. Good spring cuts.
8. Mouth of Shoal Creek. Good year-round fishing. Shallow-water adjacent to deep water.
9. Cuts up right bank of Shoal Creek. Good except in winter.
10. U.S. 43 bridge pilings. Good for spring bass and crappie. Good summer crappie fishing at night. Good rip-rap banks.
11. Edgewater Beach slough. Shallow slough. Full of grass. Good spring fishing for topwater.
12. Good deepwater slough. Good spring and summer.
13. Good cuts in upper end of Shoal Creeks. Excellent spring fishing with jig-and-pig.
14 to 20 -- Underwater Island.
21. Excellent, grass-filled pockets.
22. Six-mile Creek. Good spring fishing.
23. Key point. Pay attention here. One of the best fish producers on the lake. Good year-round.
24. Four-Mile Creek. Good spring and fall fishing.
25. Another key point. Good year-round fishing.
26. Excellent grass-filled cuts. Good spring and fall.
27. Huge underwater island in mouth of Town Creek. Good year-round fishing. Lots of brushpiles and stumps.
28. Excellent grass-filled cuts.
29. Mouth of Town Creek. Good year-round fishing.
30. Foster's Mill Bridge pilings. Good spring fishing area.
31. Steep-cut bank. Good fishing in spring.
32. Mouth of Blue Water Creek. Good year-round fishing.
33. Location of underwater spring. Excellent spot for all species in summer and winter.
34. Logjams. Good flipping area.
35. Hog Island. Next to deep water on all sides. Good stopover point before and after spring spawn. Backside holds good bass when water is moving through dam.
36. Tailrace. Excellent year-round fishing.
37. Good rock piles. Good topwater area in spring. Backside holds fish when water is being pulled.

Wilson Lake

Shoal Creek

Emerald Beach Marina

72

43

Six Mile Creek

Four Mile Creek

McCernan Creek

Wilson Dam to Four Mile Creek

Wilson Lake

Blue
Water
Creek

Town
Creek

Fisherman's
Resort

Big
Nance
Creek

Four-Mile Creek to Wheeler Dam

Pickwick Lake

I f trophy smallmouth fishing is your bag, few places in Alabama are better than Pickwick Lake. This 47,500-acre Tennessee Valley Authority impoundment is unquestionably trophy smallmouth headquarters in Alabama.

But never doubt this lake is full of other trophy fish, too. No less than three state records - sauger, muskellunge and paddlefish - came from this reservoir. This lake also gave up one world record in January, 1988. On that date, Mt. Olive's Terrell Nail set a new standard for the 17-pound class world record with his 8-pound, 6-ounce smallmouth.

Spring bass fishing

ABOVE NATCHEZ TRACE BRIDGE

The deep points on the main river begin to release their bass in late February as the water temperature begins a slight rise. These cold-blooded bass are sluggish and a long way away from chasing a swift bait. Gravel bars, rocks and sandy points are staging areas during this time. These areas, usually in 12 to 15 feet of water on both sides of the main river channel, are easily located with a depthfinder. Those with stumps, brush and logjams are especially productive.

A 1/2-ounce black/brown jig-and-pig with a black pork frog trailer makes an excellent early season bait because it drops quickly and can be retrieved slowly. Small grub-type baits also are excellent at this time. A small white or smoke-colored grub fished slowly on light line is especially strong. Feathered crappie jigs and horsehair jigs are also effective.

As the water warms, quicker baits such as 1/4-ounce spinnerbaits become more productive because they cover more water. The warming water allows the bass more movement and they will begin to chase faster baits. A chartreuse/white spinnerbait tipped with a white curly-tail jig body works well.

The warm waters of late March and April eventually will send the bass into the shoals looking for spawning areas. This area has few creeks and most of the bass are forced to look for stump and brush-filled pockets off the main river channel.

Shallow-running crankbaits such as Rapalas, plastic worms and Carolina-rigged lizards become the best baits in the shallow water. All handle brush well and produce fish.

The Little River side of Seven Mile Island is one of the first areas to warm in spring and it plays host to numbers of shallow-water fish. The area between Coffee Slough and Woodland Stumps offers spring fishing as good as most anglers will ever see. Coffee Slough has a well-defined creek channel, plenty of stumps and several springs that feed it. Woodland Stumps is across from the steam plant and receives some warm water.

It is also full of stumps and brush.

This area does have a few small creeks that are worth a look at this time. Spring Creek and Sinking Creek offer relatively poor fishing, but Little Cypress Creek, Little Bear Creek, Dry Creek and Cane Creek do boast some spring fish worth trying. Cane Creek offers the best spring fishing.

While the spinnerbaits don't work that well in the shoals, they are effective in the creeks.

Pickwick Lake Fact Sheet

Location, length, acreage

Pickwick Lake is in northwest Alabama with approximately 75 percent of the lake in Alabama and 25 percent in Tennessee and Mississippi. It is the only lake in Alabama that flows through three states. The lake also is unusual in that it flows north for much of its 49-mile length. Pickwick is a major link in the chain of lakes that allows river traffic from the north to connect with the Gulf of Mexico.

Configuration

Pickwick Lake is somewhat narrow in its upper end widening below Natchez Trace bridge. It lacks the extremely wide water of its sister lakes Wheeler, Wilson and Guntersville.

Major and secondary creeks

Pickwick Lake isn't blessed with incoming creeks. Little Cypress Creek, Spring Creek, Little Bear Creek, Dry Creek, Sinking Creek, Cane Creek, Mul-

berry Creek and Beck Creek are relatively small creeks on the upper end above Natchez Trace bridge.

Below the bridge, the creeks are larger, but still few in number. Colbert Creek, Bluff Creek and Brush Creek are small inlets just below the bridge. Both Second Creek and Bear Creek are wide creeks with good water flow. Indian Creek, Short Creek, Panther Creek and Yellow Creek are smaller creeks on the lower end.

Types of fish

Pickwick Lake has largemouth bass, smallmouth bass, spotted bass, white crappie, black crappie, bluegill, shellcracker, longear sunfish, green sunfish, blue catfish, channel catfish, flathead catfish, bullhead catfish, sauger, hybrid bass and white bass. Rough fish include spotted gar, longnose gar, freshwater drum, carp, and buffalo. Baitfish include skipjack herring, gizzard shad, threadfin shad, yellowtail shad and various species of minnows.

Spring bass fishing

BELOW NATCHEZ TRACE BRIDGE

The lower section of Pickwick Lake has many more gravel bars, sandbars, dropoffs, rocks, rock ledges, ridges, ditches - and most noticeably - fewer creeks than the section above Natchez Trace Bridge. The bass making their move out of deep water have no trouble finding structure on which to stage during their route to shallow water. These irregularities in the bottom are easy to locate with a depthfinder and it's for that reason that most anglers find pre-spawn fishing much easier in this area of the lake.

The most simple method of fishing these pre-spawn bass is to ride with the depthfinder on and drop marker buoys whenever a piece of irregular bottom shows fish. The angler can then pull his boat in deeper water and cast to the buoy, thus lessening his chances of spooking the fish.

Once again, water temperature determines the bait. Spoons, such as a Mann's Mann-O-Lure or a Krocodile, are the best shot at trophy fish. The lure should be cast well past the buoy and slowly hopped back to the boat. A jig-and-pig will work just as well as long as the angler has the patience to allow the bait to sink to the bottom before beginning his retrieve.

Once the water temperature moves up, faster baits such as spinner-baits and deep-diving crankbaits are best. These baits cover much more territory and greatly increase the odds of a catch.

Once spawning time arrives, fish in this area are somewhat hard-pressed to find suitable habitat for spawning and many anglers believe many are forced to spawn in deeper water than they'd prefer. Cuts, pockets, sloughs and small branches hold most of the spawning fish, especially between Natchez Trace Bridge and Bear Creek.

Once past Bear Creek, things get somewhat better. Bear Creek itself is a major body of water that plays host to much spawning activity, as does Second Creek. Indian Creek, Panther Creek and the cuts on both banks just inside the mouth of Yellow Creek also hold

some spawning fish.

The flatter banks on the lower end allow something the upper end doesn't have - lots of grass. This makes excellent spring fishing when the fish are shallow. Shallow-running crankbaits, grubs and topwater baits such as Bang-O-Lures and Nip-I-Didees work well on the grass fringes, while spinnerbaits, floating worms, rats, frogs and buzzbaits work well in the grass. Most of the grass is on the north banks.

Hot weather bass fishing

ABOVE NATCHEZ TRACE BRIDGE

Following the spawn, the bass slip out of the shallow water and gather on the backside of the points in an attempt to escape the current and rest. Spawning is hard on the fish and most will be in bad shape for up to three weeks. These fish are non-aggressive at this time.

Once they recover, their appetite returns and they become voracious feeders. Plastic worms and medium-running crankbaits thrown on the backside of points, especially when the water is running, result in some of the most vicious strike's you'll encounter.

The glaring June sun eventually will drive these fish deep on the points where they will stay until fall. These deep fish are much more difficult to locate and catch than they were a month before. Worms and deep-diving crankbaits become the choice lures at this time, with worms producing the most fish and crankbaits the larger fish.

A Mann's 20-Plus or a Bagley's DB-3 is the choice of the better anglers. Crawfish-colored baits are best in clear water, with the Tennessee Shad color running a close second. Worms are a matter of choice. Pumpkinseed and appleseed are popular.

The dropoffs and points below Seven Mile Island to Natchez Trace Bridge will all hold fish during the summer months. Fishing is better in the morning and afternoon hours.

Below Natchez Trace Bridge

The multitude of irregular bottom structure below Natchez Trace bridge makes this the area to fish during summer months. This area was full of islands before the Tennessee River was impounded, but time has taken its toll. The islands have eroded leaving rough underwater humps, bars and rock outcroppings. Many of these islands are covered with mussels. These areas are on the north side of the main channel and easily located with the depthfinder. All make for perfect bass habitat during the summer months.

These mounds can be found in 8 to 20 feet of water, so fishing can be good no matter the temperature or weather. The mounds in the shallow water will hold fish in early summer, overcast days and often during the morning and evening hours on hot days. The deeper mounds hold fish during July and August.

A good topo map of the area before the lake was impounded is beneficial. Lakes Illustrated makes a good map which shows these irregularities.

It's sometimes possible to pull up on one of these spots and ambush schooling fish, catching 20 or more without moving the boat.

Carolina-rigged worms, Texas-rigged worms, grubs and spoons will work on these fish, but light line is a must.

Cool and cold weather bass fishing

Above Natchez Trace Bridge

Bass anglers fishing this area during the cooler months usually experience an increase in catches of spotted and smallmouth bass regradless of the fact that isn't what they're fishing for.

The weather plays a major role in largemouth fishing in the fall. If the weather stays warm (as it did in 1987 and 1988 until Christmas), the bass will hold tight to deep points. This enables them a good route in which they dash to shallow water to chase baitfish, or to deeper water when a front approaches.

Crankbaits and spinnerbaits are key in this situation. A crawfish or shad-colored Bagley's DB-3 or Mann's 20-Plus is probably the best bet, followed by a 1/2-ounce or 3/4-ounce spinnerbait. The heavier spinnerbait is needed because of the deeper water. The spinnerbait, either chartreuse and white or solid white, should be outfitted with a No. 5 nickel blade and tipped with a white pork chunk.

Grubs are a good bait for those who enjoy fishing light spinning tackle. A white 1/4-ounce grub is hard to beat, especially when the fish are finicky and longing for smaller baits.

On the occasions of a cold fall and winter like Alabama had in 1989, the pattern is much different. The bass move much deeper and are much less active. Slower baits such as jigging spoons, grubs, Do-Nothing Worms and jig-and-pigs are needed.

Ledges and humps with structure and in 15 to 25 feet of water are prime locations to look for largemouth bass during the colder periods. The underwater island in the mouth of Dry Creek is one of the better locations. Buck Island, the underwater island near the mouth of Little Bear Creek is another. The upriver point of Seven Mile Island will hold some winter fish, as will the north ledges next

to the channel across from Mulberry Creek.

Below Natchez Trace Bridge

The same irregular areas that offered good summer fishing also offers good fall and winter fishing. The mounds and bars in 12 feet of water or less hold the fish during September, October and early November under normal conditions, as does the many ditches and roadbeds in the area. Although there is a limited number of incoming creeks, the mouths also will hold fall fish.

Grubs, worms and crankbaits are the baits of choice during the fall.

Areas to concentrate on include the road beds leading from the bank to the main channel (No. 5, No. 9, No. 18, No. 22 and No. 35 on the map), the series of underwater islands on the north bank below Panther Creek, the rough bars on the south bank east of the mouth of Bear Creek, and the numerous bars and humps on the north bank stretching from Second Creek to Natchez Trace Bridge.

During the colder months of December and January, grubs fished on the deeper humps in the same areas will produce some of the lake's better bass.

Other Types of Fishing

Smallmouth fishing

It's possible that you'll catch smallmouth bass when bass fishing any time of the year on Pickwick Lake, but an angler can greatly increase his chances by purposely fishing for them. Fishing baits and different areas will significantly increase those odds.

Smallmouth need clean, fast-moving water and rocks to thrive and the river channel dropoffs, rocky ledges, deep rocky banks and gravel-covered bars on Pickwick Lake offer that.

The rocky ledges on the river side of the area close to the head of Seven Mile Island is an area to concentrate on for smallmouth year round because it offers suitable habitat in both deep and shallow water. Other key areas are the rocky dropoffs along the north edge of the original river channel and the mussel-covered humps near the channel.

Cigar-shaped topwater baits such as Nip-I-Didees and Jumping Minnows are excellent for smallies in spring, but much of the rest of the year grubs are needed. A 3-inch smoke-colored Mr. Twister grub with a 1/8 to 3/8 lead head will catch smallmouths most months of the year.

Since rocky dropffs are needed for the best summertime fishing and the rocks aren't visible, many inexperienced anglers have trouble with summer smallmouth fishing. Smallmouth will suspend on these rocky areas in 10 to 40 feet of water, with the bigger fish being deeper. A good rule of thumb is that anywhere up to 18 feet of water falls off in the river channel is likely to be rocky, thus likely to be holding smallmouth.

The good summer smallie angler needs a lot of time to fish and a lot of trial-and-error before he can become good at summer fishing. Some of the better anglers have no trouble catching summer smallmouth, however.

Fall fishing for smallmouths can be excellent, especially in the downriver section. Smallmouth will move somewhat shallower during this time and situate on humps and rocks. Spoons become the top bait then, with grubs a close second.

Early winter is good as many smaller fish move to the eddy areas behind points.

Live baits such as shiners and yellowtails are good at this time because it's the type baitfish they are feeding on. The live bait should be hooked through the lips with a 2/0 hook and a bb shot placed 12 inches above the bait. Spinning tackle should be used to cast the bait into the eddies.

Pickwick Lake's best fishing spots

1. Mouth of Yellow Creek. Summertime schooling area for bass. Smoke grubs and Sassy Shads.

2. Cuts in Yellow Creek. Excellent spring spawning area for largemouth, smallmouth and crappie.

3. Excellent point.

4. Shallow sandbars. Good in spring.

5. Underwater roadbed leading from shallow to deep water. Good year round.

6. Underwater island.

7. Panther Creek. Both shallow and deep water.. Good year round.

8. Cedar Fork. Good in spring.

9. Underwater road bed leading from shallow water to deep water. Good year round.

10. Whetstone Branch. Cuts offer good spring fishing. Point good year round.

11. Excellent point leading into Short Creek.

12. Shallow sandbars. Excellent spring area for smallmouth.

13. Mouth of Indian Creek. Excellent year round.

14. Excellent cuts and points. Cuts in spring. Points year round.

15. Excellent crappie area in spring.

16. Good smallmouth fishing in spring. Grubs and Sassy Shad.

17. Underwater road bed leading from bank to channel.

18. Underwater road bed leading from bank to channel.

19. Underwater road bed.

20. Underwater island.

21. Underwater island.

22. Underwater road bed.

23. Underwater road bed.

24. Underwater island next to main channel. Good in summer.

25. Underwater ditch out from mouth of slough. Best in summer.

26. Underwater islands and dropoffs. Good staging area in spring. Holds good summer fish.

27. Underwater island. Good year round.

28. Underwater hump in middle of large flats.

29. Underwater road bed.

30. Man-made underwater brush piles. Someone has placed brushpiles in row, using telephone poles on the bank as markers. Each brush pile lines up with pole.

31. Underwater road bed.

32. Underwater road bed.

33. Well-defined creek channel. Key area for spring bass.

34. Tremendous crappie fishing in spring. Underwater islands.

35. Mouth of Second Creek. Good year round.

36. Points in Second Creek mouth. Good year round, best in spring.

37. Second Creek. Shallow grass. Good in spring for largemouth.

38. Underwater road bed.

39. Underwater island splits main channel. Good summer and winter.

40. Fantastic spring fishing for smallmouth and largemouth. Hundreds of sandbars with grass.

41 to 43. Underwater island.

44. Shallow, grass-covered sandbars.

45. Underwater island.

46. Good smallmouth area year round.

47. Colbert Creek. Good spinnerbait area spring, early summer.

48. Natchez Trace Bridge pilings. Good year round fishing. Old road bed can be found upriver on right bank right above bridge.

49. Good rock rows. Runs parallel to bank for 50 yards. Tremendous area year round for largemouth and smallmouth.

50. Koger Island. Good spring and summer fishing.

51. Stumpy ledge next to main river channel. Excellent early summer spot.

52. Long sandbars parallel to bank. Good smallmouth area in spring and summer.

53. Woodland stumps. Underwater sandbars. Good spring area for largemouth and smallmouth. Good buzzbait area.

54. Cane Creek. Good warm water in winter, cool in summer. Excellent for largemouth, smallmouth, hybrids and stripes. Gave up one 38-pound stripe in summer of 1988.

55. Excellent catfish area in summer. Twenty-pound-plus cats here common.

56. Pipeline area. Good in spring-summer around pipeline.

57. Good underwater island that splits flow of main river channel. Good summer fishing.

58. Little river side. Good year round. Lots of small islands.

59. Big river side. Good year round.

60. Buck Island. Good year round.

61. Underwater rock rows. Excellent spring fishing for smallmouth and largemouth.

62. Underwater rock row.

63. Little Bear Creek. Good spring and summer fishing with deep water. Lots of stumps.

64. Coffee Slough. Good spring fishing in flats, good year round fishing in channel.

65. Points at mouth of Spring Creek. Summer schooling area.

66. Back of Spring Creek. Good spring fishing.

67. Head of Seven Mile Island. Good year-round fishing with grubs and worms.

68. Cypress Creek mouth. Good year round.

69. Cypress Creek. Good to bridge. Lots of stumps. Good spring and summer.

70. Main River Bridge riprap. Good topwater area all spring, early mornings in summer.

71. Rocky gravel bank with stumps. Good smallmouth area.

72. Stump rows.

73. Jackson Island. Good year-round fishing. Good escape area from current behind island year round.

Labels: Tennessee, Alabama, Yellow Creek, Cedar Fork, Panther Creek, Whetstone Branch, Short Creek, Indian Creek
Bottom: "Ala./Tenn. Line to Bear Creek"

Pickwick Lake

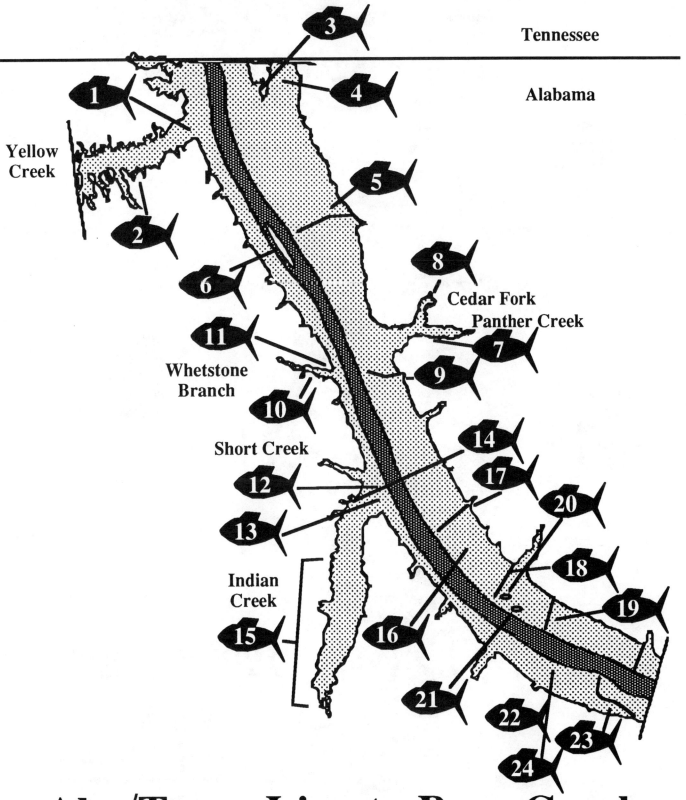

Ala./Tenn. Line to Bear Creek

Pickwick Lake

Second Creek

Threet Marina

Eastport Dock

Mill Creek
Boat Dock

Aurora Springs
Boat Dock

Mill
Creek

Bear Creek
and
Second Creek

Pickwick Lake

Colbert Creek

Natchez Trace Parkway

Mulberry Creek

Cane Creek

Bear Creek to Cane Creek

Pickwick Lake

Cane Creek
to Wilson Dam

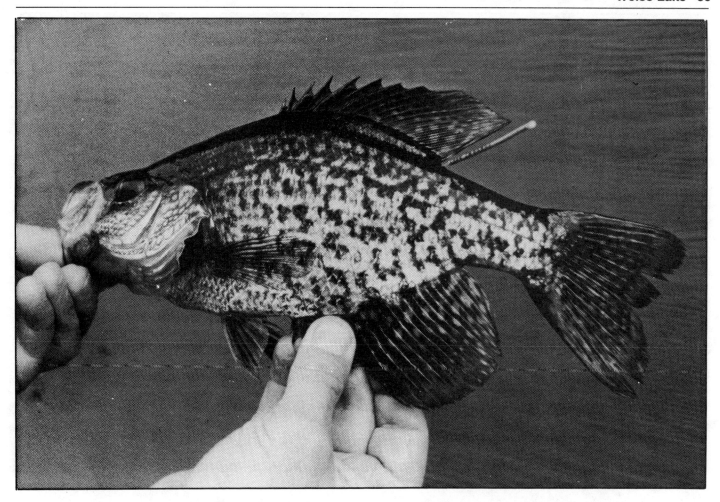

Weiss Lake

"Crappie Capital of the World" is a self-appointed title, the result of the creative minds of former Bay Springs Marina owners Kenneth and Cathy Mackey, who spent many hours promoting Weiss Lake as the world's best crappie fishing hole.

Not many lakes in the world have cried foul over this lake's boastful claim, however.

This northeast Alabama reservoir annually entertains crappie fishermen from not only Alabama, but from across the U.S. as well.

Very few crappie fishermen have ever left disappointed.

The lake is full of papermouths.

Surprisingly, and unknown to many across the U.S., the lake is without question one of Alabama's finest bass fishing reservoirs, too.

The conditions that provide for excellent crappie fishing are also conducive to an excellent bass fishery.

Here is a look at what makes Weiss Lake the "Crappie Capital of the World," and at the lake that can give you a run for your money at bass fishing, too.

Spring Bass Fishing
Georgia state line
to Cedar Bluff Bridge

When the first warm rays of spring sunshine come to Weiss Lake, no section of water heats up faster or becomes more desirable to bass earlier than the area from Cedar Bluff Bridge to the Alabama-Georgia line.

This shallow, dingy water absorbs heat rather than reflecting it, and as a result, it woos the bass out of the river channel earlier than other locations on the lake.

The area lacks the structure that can be found elsewhere on the lake, so shallow water pocket fishing becomes necessary. The northest banks of coves, sloughs and islands receive the most sunlight in early spring, warm up the quickest and get fish first.

Some of the best areas for this early spring fishing is Cowan Creek and around Godfrey's Island. The main thing to look for to hold fish this time of the year is exposed brush. Due to minimum structure, locating exposed brush pile will just about guarantee fish. Another

Weiss Lake Fact Sheet

Location, length, acreage

Weiss Lake is one of six Alabama Power Company reservoirs on the Coosa River. Weiss Lake is wedged between the Georgia state line to the east and Lake Neely Henry to the southwest.

Weiss Lake begins at the Georgia line and extends 34 nautical miles to the Weiss Dam powerhouse in Cherokee County. It should be noted that Weiss Dam and the Weiss Dam powerhouse are separate units. The Weiss Lake Park Music Campground sits almost perfectly as the lake's mid-point.

Weiss Lake consists of 30,200 acres and offers 447 miles of shoreline. A total of 5,273 square miles drain into the lake.

Full pool is 564.0 feet.

Impoundment

Construction began on Weiss Lake Dam July 31, 1958. The dam and powerhouse were placed in service June 5, 1961.

Weiss Lake Dam

The concrete portion of Weiss Lake Dam is 392 feet wide and is constructed of 142,000 cubic yards of concrete. It rises 85.5 feet at its highest point.

The powerhouse, separate from the dam on a separate reservoir, has three hydraulic turbines capable of passing 3.9 million gallons of water per minute. The dam also has three alternating current generators capable of annually producing 215.5 million kilowatt hours of electricity.

Each of the dam's five spillway gates is capable of passing 12.6 million gallons of water per minute during flooding conditions. The dam's cost to date is $38.6 million.

Stocking history

Florida-strain largemouth	
1981-90	358,802
1991	10,778
1992	39,030
1993	60,400
1994	30,200

Striped bass	
1972	275
1974	20,000
1980	21,560
1985	30,000
1986	59,700

Configuration

Weiss Lake is the only one of the six Coosa River reservoirs which overflows the banks of the original river channel to any degree in its upper end.

The lake boasts plenty of open water flats which cover what was once fertile farmland. The lake boasts a multitude of structure including standing timber, old road beds, collapsed bridges, creek channels and old home foundations.

Major and secondary creeks

Weiss Lake is blessed with an abundance of creeks and rivers which dump water along its length.

The Coosa River, the Chattooga River and Little River are the main water suppliers, but Mud Creek, Ballplay Creek, Three Mile Creek, two Spring Creeks, Cowan Creek, Yellow Creek, Big Nose Creek and Little Nose Creek do their share.

Kanady Branch, Sharp Branch, Muddy Branch and Bay Springs are lesser water suppliers.

Types of fish

Weiss Lake is nationally famous for its white and black crappie populations, but the lake also features popular species such as largemouth bass, spotted bass, white bass, hybrid bass, saltwater stripe, channel catfish, flathead catfish, blue catfish, longear sunfish, redear sunfish and bluegill.

The lake also has several species of gar, drum and carp.

As for baitfish, gizzard shad, threadfin shad and several species of minnows are present.

---

key fish-holding bit of structure is isolated stumps. Bass tend to gather around these isolated stumps rather than clumps of stumps. Gravel points and gravel bars are a key third area.

A jig-and-pig is the bait to use before the water reaches the 53 to 55-degree range. A brown/orange with a brown pork frog is best in the continuously dingy water.

This slow bait works equally well in the brush and stumps. A surprise bait the better anglers use once the water passes the 55-degree mark is a shallow-running lipped crankbait such as the Rapala of Pogo Shad. These work well with a slow retrieve over and around the stumps.

Of course, the spinnerbait is the lure most use effectively here this time of the year. A 1/2-ounce chartreuse or chartreuse and white spinnerbait with a larger blade works well in the stained water. When the water begins to clear, drop down to a 3/8 or 1/4-ounce spinnerbait and a No. 5 or 6 blade. When the water gets a little warmer, a Lunker Lure also will work well.

Godfrey's Island, Cowan Creek, Spring Creek, James' Branch and Pruett's Island are they key spawning areas where the bass eventually end up at the height of the spawn.

Also pay close attention to boathouses, docks and piers in any of these creeks.

Almost all have man-made brush piles around them. These brushpiles will concentrate baitfish and will attract bass on the way to the spawning grounds.

CEDAR BLUFF BRIDGE TO U.S. 411 BRIDGE

During spring months, an estimated 75 percent of the lake's bass fishing takes place between the U.S. 411 Bridge and the Cedar Bluff Bridge and for good reason - lots of bass.

The Chattooga River, Little River, Big Nose Creek and Little Nose Creek all feed this portion of the lake and provide excellent spawning areas.

The cutoff area between Yellow Creek and Little River is the prime bass area this time of year. This area offers approximately 1,000 to 1,500 acres of shallow water full of stumps, rocks, road beds and humps. This water offers excellent structure, as well as the ability to warm fast. Those are always two key ingredients in good springtime bass fishing on any reservoir.

Little River, the back of Big Nose Creek and the back of Little Nose Creeks are key areas in the spring.

Avoid Yellow Creek. It's much too deep to provide consistently good spring fishing.

Big brush piles and individual stumps are the structure you're looking for. Sandy banks and pea gravel banks are key fishing areas, too. Avoid muddy, silty bottoms and banks because bass avoid them.

The bass will stage themselves this time of the year, moving from the main river channel, to the structure adjacent to it, to the structure in the creek mouths and then into the creek flats to spawn. Although crankbaits, and, later, spinnerbaits, are key baits, never underestimate the ability of an old bait - the Snagless Sally - in these conditions.

THE POWER HOUSE LAKE

Although the powerhouse lake is technically a portion of Weiss Lake, it is literally a separate reservoir from Weiss Lake connected by a 1 1/4-mile man-made canal. The power house lake is part of an unusual situation on Weiss Lake in that unlike any other Coosa River reservoir, the dam and power generating facilities are separate units more than 1 3/4 miles apart.

Anglers may choose to launch their boats at several ramps on the power house lake, or they may travel from the main portion of Weiss Lake by boat under the U.S. 411 bridge, taking the 1 1/4-mile man-made canal until it dumps into the smaller reservoir. This canal linking the two reservoirs is deep and safe to navigate. The shallow lake, like the rest of Weiss Lake, is full of structure including road beds, stumps, islands and old home sites. The lake is dishpan in configuration and lacks steep drop-offs on its banks, but deep water can be found in the originak river channel.

With the water normally being down in the early spring, the key to good fishing here is positioning your boat in five feet of water and casting into 18 inches to 3 feet of water with jig-and-pigs, spinnerbaits or shallow-running crankbaits. All three baits can be ultrasuccessful catching bass from this structure this time of the year.

The makeup of this small reservoir provides an excellent spawning area. The area near the power house offers deep water adjacent to shallow water ledges full of stump rows. This is an excellent spawning area.

Although the power house lake offers good spring fishing, much better spring fishing can be found on other portions of Weiss Lake. The power house lake offers its best fishing in the summer and fall.

Hot weather bass fishing

GEORGIA STATE LINE TO CEDAR BLUFF BRIDGE

If you wish to be a good summer bass fisherman on this end of Weiss Lake, it wouldn't be a bad idea for you to spend the winter fishing here.

The low water level at winter pool reveals a lake that many summer-only anglers don't know exists. Stumps, logjams, and other such structure can be found all along the original river channel and it's in this structure that you'll find bass during the hot-weather months of May, June, July and August.

Pay close attention to the map of this area that accompanies this book. It shows the location of a great many the stumps, timber, roadbeds and other bass-holding structure adjacent to the river channel. These are the areas that you need to fish during the summer.

The stump rows above Pruett's Island, the sharp bend in the river between Dead Boy Branch and Water House Creek and the sharp bend in the river between Poole's Ferry and Ballpark Creek are among the best areas.

This structure on ledges should be fished as you would any other ledges on the Coosa Chain. For those who don't know the location of the original river channel well, use your depthfinder to locate it and drop marker buoys. Position your boat in the river channel and cast to the structure on the ledges. Stick with medium running

crankbaits, spinnerbaits with a pork frog or a jig-and-pig with a pork frog until the water temperature reaches 70 degrees. At that point, switch to plastic worms, jig-and-pigs with a plastic worm trailer, or an artificial minnow such as a Red's Prissy Shad.

Other areas to look for are the causeways of any incoming creek, such as the rip-rap laden entrance to Cowan Creek. Fish these areas with a crankbait first, and if you're sure there's fish there, come back with a plastic worm or a jig-and-pig. A buzzbait will often work in these areas at daylight and dark.

CEDAR BLUFF BRIDGE TO U.S. 411 BRIDGE

The middle section of Weiss Lake provides hot weather ledge fishing much like you'll find on most reservoirs in Alabama. The bass exit the creeks following the spawn and are forced to seek water temperatures much more tolerable than the shallow water offers. The deep water in the original river channel is just what the doctor ordered.

Although it might not be evident to the casual observer, the bass don't gather in random locations along the channel. There's rhyme and reason to their madness. They must continue to eat and they'll concentrate in areas with the structure that holds shad.

Finding these aren't that difficult. The major bends in the river tend to grab floating logs and form a jam, creating excellent sructure immediately adjacent deep water like the bass like. Look at the map and you'll see these major bends.

Another area with good structure piled on it is the deep water mouths of inlets such as Big Nose Creek, Little Nose Creek, Yellow Creek, Little River and the entrance to Bay Springs.

Texas-rigged worms, small crankbaits, spoons and Prissy Shads all seem to work well.

Texas-rigged plastic worms are the No. 1 bait most anglers uses this time of the year in this structure, but it's not the No. 1 bait the better fishermen use. The worm's major drawback is that it's not a good bait to "hunt" fish with. It's time-consuming to use. If you're a fisherman out there for leisure, the worm's okay to locate fish with. If you're trying to catch numbers of fish, it isn't.

Use a crankbait first. You'll either locate bass or structure with it. Once the bass or the structure has been located, switch to a worm.

THE POWER HOUSE LAKE

With so many open flats to cover in the power house lake, the best bass anglers on the lake often choose to attack the area in summer months with the Do-Nothing worm.

The Do-Nothing Worm, made famous by Phenix City's Jack Chancellor in winning the 1985 BASSMASTER'S Classic, is nothing more than an adaptation of the South Carolina-rigged worm. The worm hook is attached to a 3 to 5-foot leader, and then a swivel is added. A 3/4-ounce to 1-ounce bullet worm lead is then added to the line coming from the fishing rod, a bead is added and this is then attached to the swivel. This results in a weight that will drag bottom, but the worm is allowed to float. The hook in the worm is left exposed. The Do-Nothing worm works well in the open, deep water found in many areas of the power house lake. Many of these open areas have small humps which hold fish and the Do-Nothing worm is tailor-made for these areas.

Other summer areas to watch are the shallow flats next to the main river channel above the powerhouse lake. Bass suspend in the deep water and rush to the ledge to chase bait fish. Texas-rigged plastic worms, Prissy Shads and small, shad-colored crankbaits work well in these areas.

Cool and cold weather bass fishing

GEORGIA STATE LINE TO CEDAR BLUFF BRIDGE

Due to the vast expanses of shallow water, this end of Weiss Lake isn't your best area to find cool and cold-weather bass. The bass will move out of the main river channel back into the structure nearby when fall arrives, but as it gets colder, the bass become harder and harder to locate.

One reason for this difficulty is apparently the bass' movement into the headwaters of many creeks. During the dead of winter, many crappie anglers show surprise at catching bass in the headwaters of Cowan and Ballpark Creek.

These bass gather around the areas with incoming waters. Whether they gather there to chase sluggish shad or whether they find water a few degrees warmer isn't known.

Other areas that hold cold-water bass are the bridge pilings in Spring Creek and Cowan Creek. Bass gather around these piling and can be taken by crankbaits, jig-and-pigs or spoons.

CEDAR BLUFF BRIDGE TO U.S. 411 BRIDGE

From approximately Sept. 15 until the water surface temperature reaches 55 degrees, small, vibrating, shallow-running, lipped crankbaits such as the Killer B1, the Pogo Shad, Little N or Rapala are bass slayers in the cut-off area between Yellow Creek and Little River.

Bass seek the security that wood offers when the water turns cool. As mentioned before, this shallow-water area is innudated with stump rows, roadbeds and humps.

For those who don't like fishing shallow-running crankbaits, spinnerbaits, worms and jig-and-pigs also work.

THE POWER HOUSE LAKE

You'll have to look long and hard to find better fall fishing on Weiss Lake than you'll find on the power house lake. This reservoir is where the water comes from to pass through the generators in the powerhouse and the result is many hours of much-needed moving current. That translates into superb fishing.Bass sometimes school by the hundreds on brush-laden roadbeds and humps, ends of roadbeds and steep ledges in this area when the current is moving. Do-Nothing Worms and crankbaits are the primary baits.

When winter hits and the water surface temperature drops below 48 degrees, Texas-rigged worms and jig-and-pigs will take bass from the same roadbeds and humps.

Other types of fishing

CRAPPIE FISHING

Weiss Lake is known as the Crappie Capital of the World and for good reason. The tremendous amount of crappie in the lake draws large numbers of crappie fishermen from not only Alabama, but Georgia, Tennessee, Kentucky, Indiana, and Ohio as well. A liberal limit of 50 crappie per angler and a very real chance of catching that many fish team up to make Weiss Lake a crappie fisherman's delight.

Because of several recent years of drought and the tremendous amount of crappie fishing pressure on the lake, fishing isn't as good as it was in the lake's heyday in the early 1970's, but a beautiful weekend during the spring will always result in the lake being full of anglers chasing crappie.

It's no secret that spawning crappie are easy to catch as they move up into shallow water, so the lake gets its most pressure then. The area around Godfrey's Island is the perfect spring location because it offers vast acres of perfect spawning territory, as well as water that warms up much quicker than on other portions of the lake.

Any area with water from 18 inches to 5-feet-deep that has stumps, trees, brush or piers is likely to hold crappie during the spring. A long cane pole or a graphite pole such as a B'n' M pole outfitted with light line, a small split shot, a small wire hook and a cork or bobber work well enough for most fishermen. The rig should be baited with a small chartreuse jig or live minnow.

The cut-off area, Little River and the Chattooga River also offer excellent spring crappie fishing using the same methods. The power house lake generally has too much current to be conducive to excellent spring crappie fishing, but the area around Pine Cone Marina and Budweiser slough often produce good spring crappie. A good rule of thumb is that any slough on the lake which has a sandy or rock bottom and is void of current is a threat to hold spring crappie.

Unfortunately for most anglers, the best time they have to fish is the summer and the summer isn't the best time to fish for crappie on Weiss Lake. The best method for summer crappie fishing is the tedious pattern of bumping live minnows on the bottom of the main river channel. This can be accomplished by using light line, a small wire hook and a 1 1/2-ounce weight.

If you fish areas with good structure such as stump rows and brush, you'll find fish, but you'll also lose a lot of rigging. One of the best rigs for this summer pattern is a light spinning outfit rigged with 6-pound test. At the end of the line, attach a three-way swivel. From the bottom eye, hang approximately 36 inches of 2-pound test line. A 1 1/2-ounce lead weight attached to the 2-pound test line works well, but a cheaper weight (consider that you'll lose a lot of weights) is a spark plug. Garages and service stations usually have plenty of old spark plugs they'll give away. The electrode can be pushed down to form a loop you can attach the line to.

From the remaining eye of the swivel, attach approximately 18 inches of six-pound line and a light wire hook. Bait the hook with a live minnow.

If the weight (the spark plug) hangs on brush while bumping bottom, the 2-pound test line breaks easily and you don't lose the entire rig. If the hook hangs up, the wire hook will usually straighten with a steady pull.

You can make several weight rigs from spark plugs ahead in your spare time. Simply bend the electrodes, attach the 36-inch piece of 2-pound test, and add a snap swivel to the end. Wrap the line around the spark plug and secure it with a piece of tape for easy storage.

Another summer pattern that works well and allows the angler to escape the summertime heat is fishing at night with lights. Many anglers choose to use a Coleman lantern, but a sealed beam headlight attached to a styrofoam block is a better rig because its easier and safer.

Anchor your boat near or atop bridge pilings, road beds with brush, humps with brush, treetops or brush piles and be patient with this type of fishing. Let the light draw in the baitfish and the crappie will follow.

The area between Cedar Bluff Bridge to the Leesburg Bridge offers the best summer fishing. Little River, Chattooga River and Yellow River are all full of the type structure needed for good summer crappie fishing.

When fall and winter arrives, it's time to move back to the ledges in 10-17 feet of water with the bottom bumping rig. The Little River area offers the best fall and winter fishing.

When bumping bottom in both the summer and winter, outline a stretch of the river channel by dropping marker buoys. This is critical. Being five feet off off the channel can put you out of the picture.

Weiss Lake's best fishing spots

1. Excellent bass and crappie sloughs January and February. Good fishing when water is up.

2. Standing trees in back of slough. Good for crappie and bass in spring when water is up in slough. Use topwater or spinnerbaits for bass.

3. Ballpark Creek. Accessible when water is low elsewhere in area. Good spring crappie fishing. Bass use the mouth to escape current in the spring.

4. Standing bushes. Good when water is up in spring.

5. Mud Creek. Excellent bass and crappie area when this creek has water in spring.

6. Standing trees in back of mud creek. Buzz topwater bass in spring and summer.

7. Standing trees in shallow water.

8. Underwater roadbed. Old Pooles Ferry Road.

9. Small islands near Poole's Ferry. Topwater at night in summer, spinnerbaits in spring for bass.

10. Stump patch off of northeast end of Godfrey's Island. Holds late spring crappie and bass.

11. Godfrey's Island. Excellent cover and brush. March to May bass and crappie.

12. Standing timber. Good flipping.

13. Sandbar where main river channel splits. Good logjams and brush on top. Excellent when water is off at night in summer.

14. Stump rows.

15. Dead Boy Branch. Expanses of shallow water, rocks, stumps and man-made brush piles. Excellent fishing in spring for bass, crappie and white bass.

16. Riverside Slough. Closest access to Godfrey Island. Fish escape current in mouth in spring when boat traffic is slow.

17. Underwater road bed.

18. Stump rows.

19. Underwater road bed.

20. Extended stump row adjacent main river channel. Excellent for schooling summer bass.

21. Underwater road bed.

22. Spring Creek. Lots of shallow water in spring. Good crappie and bass fishing above and below bridge. Mouth an excellent spot for bass in late fall and winter.

23. County Bridge in Spring Creek. Excellent dropoffs both side of bridge. Both dropoffs full of brush and stumps.

24. Back of Spring Creek. Acres of shallow water stumps. Excellent bass fishing in spring with buzzbaits and other topwater lures. Also good spawning area for crappi.e.

25. Cowan Creek. Excellent spring fishing for crappie and bass. Susceptible to high winds in March.

26. Bridge in Cowan Creek. Good bass fishing around pilings in spring and fall. Good crappie fishing at night in late spring and summer.

27. Yancey's Bend. Excellent area early spring and winter. Bass bunch up on stumps, brush and logjams in river bend.

28. Dead End Bridge Slough. River channel makes its first bend directly out of the mouth of slough and good fishing begins there. In the slough itself, shallow water slough behind Alabama Queen restaurant offers good bass and crappie fishing in spring. Boathouses produce numbers of big fish.

29. Old home foundations. Use depthfinder to locate.

30. Underwater road bed.

31. Stump patch.

32 and 33. Old home foundations.

34. Cedar Bluff Bridge. Points offer schooling June to September.

35 to 37. Underwater road bed.

38. Island in mouth of Little River. Very good drop on north side of island. Stumps and cedar brush tops placed here by Weiss Lake crappie guides. Good for crappie in early winter, bass in fall and summer. Many Weiss Lake bass tournaments have been won here.

39. Underwater road bed.

40. Old home foundations. Locate with depthfinder.

41. Defined drop in Little River. Good bass fishing in this drop during the summer.

42. Meeting of the Chattooga River and Little River. Island offers deep water on three sides. Schooling bass in summer and fall; crappie in late fall and early winter.

43. Sailboat Club. Well-defined river ledge; stumps and brush.

44. The Hogback. Stretch of riverbank that shallows up to 3 feet. Spring crappie on minnows or chartreuse jigs, summer bass on worms or crankbait.

45. Gaylesville Bridge. Excellent summer schooling for bass. Good dropoffs, good concrete pilings where old Gaylesville Bridge was located.

46. Cornwall's Furnace. Historical landmark. Made cannonballs here during war between the Americans and Yankees. Shallow stumps directly across from furnace. Excellent for early spring crappie fishing.

47. Chattooga River. Beautiful fishing on scenic river where Deliverance with Burt Reynolds was filmed. Once you cross silted in place where No. 47 is located, you can go all the way to Triana, Ga.

48. J.R.'s Marina slough. Store has good sandwiches if you aren't catching fish.

49. Levee area, 600 yards long. Sandbags were placed here before river was impounded to keep river in the channel. Sandbag wall still remains. During the summer and fall, cast deep running crankbaits until schooling fish are located.

50. Back end of North Spring Creek. Excellent creek channel usually holds first bass in winter. Jig-and-pigs, worms and shallow and medium running crankbaits are good here in winter. During the summer, grass produces good fish.

51. Wolf Creek meets Little River. Excellent spotted bass area in early spring. Clear water here means light line.

52. Stump patch in Black Mallard Cove. Good topwater for bass at night in summer. Good spinnerbait area in spring. Some spring crappie also caught here.

53. Intersections of underwater roadbeds.

54. Old home sites due south of Hog Island.

55. Stump patch.

56. Stump patch directly south of Hog Island.

57. Underwater road bed.

58. Stump patch.

59. Underwater road bed. Lots of brushtops placed on top. Summer and fall for bass.

60. Underwater road bed.

61. Stump patch. Danger area.

62. The Hat. Little River meets the Coosa River. Big sandbar offers excellent crappie fishing in spring, excellent schooling bass in summer.

63. Old home foundations.

64. Intersection of underwater road beds.

65. Stump patch.

66. Little Nose Creek.

67. Stump patches.

68. Big Nose Creek.

69. Old railroad trestle collapsed in mouth of Yellow Creek. Good schooling area for bass in summer. Excellent crappie fishing at night during summer.

70. Good sandbar in Yellow Creek runs up to 12 feet deep. Good for bass with worm or crankbait. Topwater bait good early in morning during summer. Look for seagulls diving into shad.

71. Yellow Creek falls dumps into lake here. Good early spring fishing for bass. Nearby bridge offers some of best crappie fishing at night during summer.

72. The tower area. Good schooling fish in area during summer. Texas-rigged red or blue worm best.

73. Stump patch.

74. Mouth of Crazy Woman Slough. Point on downstream side full of brush and stumps. Excellent summer, fall and winter. Excellent for bass and crappie.

75. Underwater road bed in back of Crazy Woman Slough.

76. Stump patch in back of Crazy Woman Slough.

77. Bay Springs. Most bass and crappie tournaments are held here, so area gets re-stocked about twice a week.

78. Pockets with brush and shallow-water stumps. Rat-L-Trap and spinnerbait year round for bass.

79. O'Neal's Point. Bass in late spring, summer and fall.

80. The Canal. Connects Power House Lake with Weiss Lake. Can be productive for spots.

81. Mouth of canal. Schooling hole for bass in summer and fall.

82. Shallow water with stumpy banks. Spring fishing for bass or crappie. Good cane pole area for crappie. Rat-L-Trap for bass in spring. Spinnerbait for bass in fall.

83. Underwater road bed.

84. Underwater hump. Underwater road beds intersect here. Also old home foundations on hump. Medium-running crankbait or worm is best in summer for schooling fish.

85. Underwater road bed.

86. Underwater hump. Underwater road beds intersect; old home foundations on top of hump. Good for schooling bass in summer.

87. Powerhouse area. Wing walls hold big bass.

88. Underwater road bed.

89. Underwater hump adjacent Pine Cone Marina. Schooling for spring bass.

90. Stump-lined underwater island. Plastic worms for summer and winter bass.

91. Stumps in back of Cedar Point Slough. Crappie, bass in spring.

Cedar Bluff Marina

James Branch

Trotter Branch

Pruett's Island

Cotton Patch

Cedar Bluff Bridge

Brown's Grocery

Pruett's Fish Camp

Cowan Creek

Spring Creek

Weiss Lake

Trotter Branch to Cedar Bluff Bridge

Weiss Lake

Chattooga River

North Spring Creek

Spearman's

68

J.R.'s Marina

Wolf Creek

Big Oak Campground

Little River

Match to B

A

A

Chattooga River and Little River

Weiss Lake

Cedar Bluff Bridge
to
U.S. 411 Bridge

Bay Springs Marina

Big Nose Creek

Little Nose Creek

Chestnut Rec area

Yellow Creek

Driftwood Campground

Hog Island

Match to A

411

273

69

Weiss Lake

Powerhouse Lake

Budweiser Slough

Lack's

Pine Cone Marina

Weiss Dam Powerhouse

411

80

81

82

83

84

86

87

88

89

90

91

Lake Neely Henry

Few places in Alabama can a businessman in his suit and tie walk out of the office for lunch and in a matter of minutes be catching fish. Lake Neely Henry, which winds through downtown Gadsden, offers that rare opportunity.

Lake Neely Henry is something of a well-kept secret among those who know the lake. It offers excellent bass fishing, but its downstream neighbor Lake Logan Martin receives the majority of the bass fishing publicity and the resulting pressure. It's crappie fishing is top-notch, but crappie anglers from around the U.S. flock to upstream neighbor Weiss Lake.

Lake Neely Henry offers the best of both worlds without the fanfare.

Spring bass fishing

WEISS DAM TO GADSDEN BRIDGES

The upper end of Lake Neely Henry, which offers such poor fishing during the summer months, offers just the opposite during the spring.

During the spring, this end of the lake consistently gives up larger fish than any portion of the lake any time of the year.

Numerous pockets and small feeder creeks enter the main river channel all along the upper section. Most of these pockets and creeks have stump rows running the length of their original channels.

Cove Creek, Henley Creek, Ballplay Creek and Turkeytown Creek offer excellent spring bass fishing, but no small pocket should be passed up because almost all have pretty good amounts of water and can be productive.

Early in the morning and late in the evening, bass move into these creeks to feed along small ledges supporting stump rows. But as on

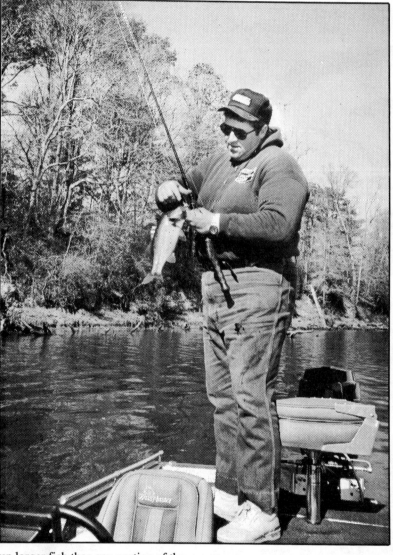

all creeks on the Coosa chain, remembered that action in creeks is best when current is moving in the river. The best possible situation is when water is moving out of the creeks.

The creeks fill when Weiss Dam generates power and empty whenever Weiss Dam ceases generating power, or when Neely Henry Dam is moving water and Weiss Dam is not.

Traditional spring baits such as spinnerbaits, buzzbaits and jig-and-pigs work well in these areas.

GADSDEN BRIDGES TO SOUTHSIDE BRIDGE

If an angler likes topwater action, or if he enjoys spinnerbait fishing, Lake Neely Henry's middle section offers the spring grass beds that make this type of fishing so productive.

Minnesota Bend, the lake's most pronounced bend, is full of grass beds during spring. A lot of small pockets also can be found on this river section and they, too, are full of grass beds during the spring. These small pockets are the spring bedding area for bass.

For those who don't like topwater or spinnerbait action, this area offers a few alternatives.

The eastern side of Minnesota Bend offers a good rocky bank which provides excellent fishing for spotted bass. A brown jig-and-pig, tipped with a black Josh's pork frog, is often murder when water is being pulled through the area.

Night fishermen have success in this area in late spring by throwing the same bait.

There's action for the crankbait fisherman, too. Spring bass often school in the flats when water is being pulled and gold or shad-colored, blue-back Rat-L-Traps often catch large stringers of fish.

Lake Neely Henry Fact Sheet

Location, length, acreage

Lake Neely Henry is one of six Alabama Power Company reservoirs on the Coosa River. Lake Neely Henry is wedged between Weiss Lake to the north and Lake Logan Martin to the south.

Lake Neely Henry begins at Weiss Dam in Cherokee County and stretches 77.6 miles to Neel Henry Dam in Calhoun and St. Clair counties.

Lake Neely Henry consists of 11,200 acres and offers 339 miles of shoreline. A total of 6,600 square miles drain into the lake.

Full pool is 508.0 feet.

Impoundment

Construction began on Neely Henry Dam on Aug. 1, 1962, and it was placed into service on June 2, 1966.

Neely Henry Lake Dam

The concrete portion of Neely Henry Dam is 605 feet wide and constructed from 1.3 million cubic yards of concrete. It sits 104 high at its highest point.

The dam has three hydraulic turbines each capable of discharging 4.1 million gallons of water per minute.

The dam also has three alternating-current generators capable of producing 210.7 million kilowatt hours of electricity annually.

Each of the dam's six spillway gates are capabale of passing 7.6 million gallons of water per minute during flooding situations.

Stocking history

Florida Largemouth
1981-89	153,562
1990	10,555
1991	22,446
1992	22,240
1993	22,240

Striped bass
1972-84	191,955
1985	55,000
1992	45,110

Hybrid bass
1982-85	279,407
1986	59,031
1988	60,752
1989	44,940
1990	56,100
1991	22,084
1993	33,806

Configuration

Lake Neely Henry is like the other five Coosa River reservoirs in that its upper end is nothing more than a river.

But once you pass the Gadsden bridges, Lake Neely Henry becomes a reservoir more like those that southern anglers are accustomed to. The river overflows it banks and covers thousands of acres of what was once prime farmland. Standing timber, old roads, collapsed bridges, creeks channels and other good fishing habitat can be found underneath the water and it offers excellent fish habitat.

Major and secondary creeks

Lake Neely Henry is fed by numerous creeks. Cove Creek is a moderate size creek above the Gadsden bridges, while Big Will's Creek is a major water supplier just south of downtown Gadsden. Honey Creek feeds the area near Minnesota Bend. The next major creek - Big Canoe Creek - is on the lake's lower end, as is Broughton Springs, Green Creek, Beaver Creek, Shoal Creek, Ottery Creek and Bridge Creek.

Types of fish

Lake Neely Henry features popular species such as largemouth bass, spotted bass, white bass, hybrid bass, saltwater stripe, white and black crappie, channel catfish, flathead catfish, blue catfish, longear sunfish, redear sunfish and bluegill. The lake also has several species of gar, drum and carp. As for baitfish, gizzard shad, threadfin shad and several species of minnows are present.

SOUTHSIDE BRIDGE TO NEELY HENRY DAM

The lower third of Lake Neely Henry boasts the large feeder creeks which supply the backwater of the lake.

Canoe Creek is by far the largest and most productive because it offers almost everything any angler could want, including spawning areas, boat docks, rocky banks, stump rows and grass beds.

One of the most effective methods of fishing Canoe Creek during the early spring is using a crawfish-colored crankbait, a worm or brown jig-and-pig to work the deep banks where fish have begun schooling prior to spawn.

The back of Canoe Creek past Canoe Creek Marina offers grass beds and stumps and either spinnerbaits or flippin' a jig-and-pig can be productive.

Beaver Creek can be fished the same way as Canoe Creek and although it lacks numbers of fish, it often produces big fish in the spring.

Shoal Creek offers a road bed across its mouth and this road bed traditionally holds spotted bass in spring. A Do-Nothing Worm fished atop the road bed will produce fish.

Rocky banks extend back into Shoal Creek and these banks hold spotted bass. Crawfish-colored crankbaits and brown jig-and-pigs should be worked along the banks.

A large number of downed trees and brush extend to the back of the creek and offer good cover for pre-spawn largemouths. Worms and jig-and-pigs are effective.

Bridge Creek also has a road bed in its mouth. Rocky banks, timber and deep water can be found in this creek.

Hot weather bass fishing

WEISS DAM TO GADSDEN BRIDGES

The upper portions of Lake Neely Henry, cursed by its river-like makeup and its lack of major, cool-running creeks, generally offers poor bass fishing during the summer months.

The Coosa River doesn't overflow its original banks in the upper portion of the river and the result is a lack of ledges that provide such good summer fishing elsewhere on the lake.

The mouths of Henley Creek, Cove Creek, Ballplay Creek and Turkeytown Creek offer the best opportunity to catch summer bass, but these fews spots are well known and receive extreme fishing pressure during the summer. Bass anglers find limited success by tossing deep-running crankbaits, worms or jig-and-pigs in the areas.

Other patterns offer limited success, too. On the occasions when water is being generated, shad tend to congregate in the small river cuts and river bends where logjams have formed. Bass will occasionally slip into these areas for an easy meal. Worms or imitation shad such as a Sassy Shad or Red's Prissy Shad will sometimes evoke a strike.

Another semi-productive area during summer months when water is moving is fishing the rocky and debris-strewn banks directly below the Weiss Dam powerhouse. Largmouth and spots gather there to chase shad. Imitation shad and shallow-running crankbaits are the best baits there.

Although the upper end of Lake Neely Henry offers poor summer fishing, never doubt the fish are there. Fish finders will show definite schools of bass suspended in the main river channel on hot summer days. Many anglers fish for them with jigging spoons, but that fishing is too tough and too erratic when much better fishing is so close by.

GADSDEN BRIDGES TO SOUTHSIDE BRIDGE

As much as summer fishing is poor in the upper reaches of Lake Neely Henry, it is great in the middle portion. The area is full of ledges, ditches, cuts, riprap and log jams that offer excellent cover for summer bass.

If sheer numbers of bass excite you, this portion of Lake Neely Henry offers probably the best summertime fishing in Alabama. It is possible to catch 75 to 100 keeper-size bass per day during 90-degree temperatures by fishing the ledges.

In fishing the summer ledge pattern, anglers should use their depthfinders to locate the orginal river channel's western bank. It is at this point that 18 to 20 feet of water will be adjacent to a ledge with 7 to 9 feet of water. This ledge is full of stump rows the length of the western bank from the Gadsden bridges to approximately four miles south of Southside Bridge.

Marker buoys should be dropped along this ledge to allow the river channel and stump rows to be located.

During the summer, bass school and suspend in the deep water offered by the original river channel. Whenever a hunger pang hits, they dash onto the ledge to pursue shad that find refuge in the stump rows.

Plastic worms fished on a light spinning outfit offers the most deadly weapon, but shad-colored crankbaits are a close second.

Almost all of the fish caught by this method will be tournament-measurable fish 12 inches or longer. This pattern rarely gives up fish three pounds or larger, however.

The second most productive method - and probably the most exciting - is fishing the same area with topwater lures shortly after daybreak. Buzzbaits, chuggers and stickbaits will be effective until the sun clears the treeline.

Big Will's Creek is one of the few creeks on the lake to have enough influx of springs to make a difference in water temperatures.

Its cooler waters during the hotter part of summer naturally draw fish. Worms and crankbaits work well throughout its length.

This area continually gives up big fish during summer.

SOUTHSIDE BRIDGE TO NEELY HENRY DAM

Approximately four miles of river south of Southside Bridge offer the ledges like mentioned above and they, too, offer excellent fishing. They should be fished exactly as you would fish the ledges in the middle portion of the lake.

The most widely used and most successful summer pattern for bass fishing in the lower section is fishing the creek channel in Canoe Creek, however.

Large, thick, standing timber runs approximately four miles into

the creek along the original creek channel and this creek channel is well-defined and easy to find. The lake's better summer fishermen use the trolling motor to ride the deepest portion of the creek channel while casting deep-diving crankbaits and worms to the timber that lines both sides of the original creek channel.

The summer months offer lots of schooling activity in these areas.

The mouth of Big Canoe Creek is full of stump rows and worms or deep-diving crankbaits will take an occasional fish there. Canoe Creek also hosts a large number of boat houses and piers. Anglers may find success by flipping a jig-and-pig into the Christmas trees and other brush placed around many of the structures. A worm skipped under the structures will take bass, too.

These same patterns will work in the other major creeks on the lower end such as Beaver Creek, Shoal Creek and Ottery Creek, but Big Canoe Creek offers the best fishing by far.

Cool and cold weather bass fishing

WEISS DAM TO GADSDEN BRIDGES

The small feeder creeks in Lake Neely Henry's upper end are excellent spots for cool and cold-weather fishing as bass move into the stump rows in 10 to 15 feet of water.

The timber along the original creek channel was cut off to stump level (2- to 3-feet high) with chainsaws before the lake was impounded and what remains is stump rows running the length of most of the original creek channels.

Plastic worms, slider worms and jig-and-pigs all seem to work in these areas equally well.

The warm-water discharge at the Alabama Power Co. Steam Plant attracts all species of fish during cool and cold months, but the location is nobody's secret and fish there receive extreme pressure.

Bass fishermen find success by fishing crankbaits such as medium-depth, lipped crankbaits or Rat-L-Traps in open water, or worms or jigs and pigs along the banks.

Some anglers choose to fish the main river channel in winter by using their depthfinders to find schools of fish and then using jig-and-pigs and spoons to catch them.

But the main river channel normally stays dingy during winter months, which forces bass into the feeder creeks. That's one of the main reasons the feeder creeks in the upper end offer such good fishing during winter months.

These creeks will muddy during strong rains, but clear quickly and bass fishing quickly turns good again.

GADSDEN BRIDGES TO SOUTHSIDE BRIDGE

The middle portion of Lake Neely Henry offers poor winter fishing because of the lack of creeks that run into it.

Big Will's Creek offers only fair winter fishing in the middle portion.

SOUTHSIDE BRIDGE TO NEELY HENRY DAM

The number of large feeder creeks which dump into Lake Neely Henry's lower third during cool and cold months offer excellent bass fishing.

One of the key areas is Beaver Creek which offers not only deep water next to stump rows, but three road beds and a flooded homesite as well.

The road beds and home sites traditionally hold numerous large bass during the cool and cold months. Jig-and-pigs and slow-fished worms work best on and around the old road beds.

The next best winter fishing area in the lower third is Big Canoe Creek. This creek offers stump row-lined creek channels and deep-brush throughout its length.

A road bed which runs through the mouth of the slough above Shoal Creek, extends through the mouth of Shoal Creek, crosses the river and into the slough on the east bank. It offers excellent winter fishing.

Bridge Creek also has a road bed across its mouth and it will, too, hold winter bass.

Other types of fishing along Neely Henry

CRAPPIE FISHING

Only a dam separates Lake Neely Henry from the Crappie Capital of the World, Weiss Lake, and it doesn't take a rocket scientist to know a major difference between the two lakes is publicity.

Studies by the state have shown that Weiss Lake has an unexplainably large number of crappie for an Alabama reservoir and admittedly, Lake Neely can't boast that. But what the powers-that-be on Weiss Lake don't want you to know is that when it comes to big fish, studies show Lake Neely Henry has the edge.

While crappie fishermen from around the U.S. flock just upstream to Weiss Lake, Lake Neely Henry regulars sit back and enjoy their own little secret.

Lake Neely Henry lacks numbers of large, wide creeks, so a few creeks are left with the burden of handling the spring crappie spawn. Shoal Creek, Big Will's Creek, Canoe Creek and Beaver Creek bear the brunt of the spawn which means fish are concentrated and easy to catch.

Crappie will begin leaving the main river channel in late February and early March and will use the creek channels as their route to shallow water. These spring crappie will first hold in the stumps along the ledges awaiting the 68-degree water temperature in which they prefer to spawn.

The fish won't be tight on structure, so catching them can be relatively easy. Drift fishing is the best pattern. Either spincast or spinning tackle - the more rods the merrier - should be used.

First, tie either a pearl-white or chartreuse jig to 8-pound test line on as many poles as you have or feel that you can handle.

Second, using the trolling motor and not using fishing rods, make a run parallel to the creek ledge as close as possible to where it drops in the river channel. Make a mental note of the shallowest water you located and remember exactly where it was.

Next, start in the main creek channel and drop your lines two feet deeper than the average water depth you found along the ledge. Using the trolling motor on medium speed, run the boat along the path you took before. The speed of the boat should pull the jigs above the ledge and prevent them from becoming entangled. You may have to experiment some.

When you come to a hump or other obstacle that you found on the preliminary trip, switch the trolling motor to high and this should lift the jigs high enough to avoid entanglement. Switch back to medium speed when you clear the obstacle.

This type of fishing is a two-person pattern with one running the trolling motor and the other reeling in fish. When only one person is available, he will need fewer rods and will have to steer the boat into the creek channel to remove the fish to keep the other lines from dragging bottom.

Another pattern that works well is to use a live minnow with a float and bobber stop. Several bobber stops are available on the market ranging from small rubber beads to nylon string which can be tied onto your line. A bobber stop comes with a float that has hole completely through it and this float runs up and down your line freely, stopping only at the bobber stop.

It is possible to set the stop at any depth and this stop can be wound up inside the reel. The float hangs down against the hook when casting, thus making casting is easy. When the bait hits the water, it sinks, pulling the line through the float. The line stops when the bobber stop hits the top of the float, putting the bait at the correct depth.

When the water temperature hits the 68-degree range, usually in mid-April, the crappie will move from the ledges and head to the banks. Any structure from blowdown timber to a single stick stuck in the bottom will hold fish.

Many anglers choose to use spincast or spinning tackle with jigs or minnows, but a long, telescoping fiberglass pole is much more effective. The crappie will be holding tight at this time and getting the bait right next to them is important. A fiberglass "cane" pole allows you to do that.

Following the spawning period, the crappie will return to the ledges where they were during the pre-spawn period and they can be caught with the same pre-spawn patterns. They will stay there until the warm water temperatures force them deep.

Summer fishing for crappie is much more difficult than spring fishing because the crappie are deep. Many crappie will stay in the creek channels year round, but the better crappie move out to the river channel during the summer and take up residence in the logjams and brushpiles found on the inside bends of the original river channel.

One of the more productive patterns at this time is pretty much a secret among the better fishermen.

They use a 1/4-ounce curly-tail jig and rig it weedless Texas-style, just as you would a plastic worm. This allows the jig to be jigged in the logjams and brush.

A depthfinder is a must for fishing for Lake Neely Henry crappie any time of year other than spring. During the summer months, the depthfinder is needed to locate the structure in the river bends. If that structure isn't showing fish along with it, don't spend much time trying to fish it. Look elsewhere.

During the fall, you're likely to find crappie anywhere on this lake. Some move into the creek channels and suspend in the middle of the channel. Those fish are difficult to catch.

Other crappie move into the mouths of the many ditches that run from the ledge of the original river channel to shallow water. These ditches were dug before the lake was impounded as drainage and irrigation ditches.

The crappie you'll find here are easier to catch.

Use the depthfinder to locate both the mouth of the ditches and the fish in them. They can be caught by drift fishing live minnows or jigs.

During the winter months, the crappie will move back to deep water, usually 20 feet or more. They pile up in the outside bends of river ledges and can be caught with jigs or minnows.

Lake Neely Henry's best fishing spots

1. Hokes Bluff Island. Stump rows on both ends. Produces lots of big fish with current moving. Worms or crankbait in spring, Rat-L-Trap or worm in summer.

2. Mouth of Cove Creek. Deep crankbaits or worms in summer.

3. Stumps rows run the length of right bank going in. Spinnerbaits in springtime.

4. Boat docks and piers on left bank going in. Lots of brush in water around them. Good most of year.

5. Small ledge in mouth of Henley Creek. Deep water and well-defined creek channel. Hot weather crankbait or worm.

6. Weed beds in Henley Creek. Spinnerbaits in spring.

7. Scattered stumps in mouth of Henley Creek. Shallow-running crankbait or spinnerbait in spring. Worm in summer.

8. Warm-water discharge of Alabama Power Company steam plant. Fantastic cold weather fishing. Little Georges, spoons, shad-colored crankbait in winter.

9. Old furnace pond or old Conservation Lake. Excellent spring spawning area. Shallow water and weed beds. Buzzbaits and spinnerbaits.

10. Riprap banks from Goodyear plant to Gadsden Bridges, both banks. Spring and fall fishing area for spots and largemouth. Buzzbaits, worms, jig-and-pigs and crawfish-colored crankbaits.

11. Bridge pilings. Fish suspend in this area during summer months. Grubs and light line.

12. Pockets. Spinnerbaits or flippin' in spring or winter.

13. Mouth of junior college slough. Deep crankbaits and worms in summer.

14. Grass beds in junior college slough. Spring spawning area. Spinnerbaits and buzzbaits in spring.

15. Mouth of Big Will's Creek. Cold-water creek. Hot weather patterns such as deep crankbaits or worms.

16. Highway 411 Bridge and riprap under it. Good spring and fall fishing.

17. Big Will's Creek original creek channel. Spring and hot-summer months.

18. Boat docks and piers in Big Wills Creek. Lots of brush around and under them. Worms or jig-and-pigs.

19. Grass beds and multi-channels. Good spring and summer areas. Spinnerbaits in spring. Worms in June, July and August.

20. Waax radio tower area. Excellent summer and fall schooling area. Rat-L-Traps, Little Georges and medium-diving crankbaits.

21. Grass beds and flats in cut. Fish both with spinnerbaits in spring.

22. Sand pits. Sand was once pumped from this area causing mini-ponds and lakes. Although fairly deep water, a super area for big spotted bass in spring.

23. Keeling's Island. Standing timber around island produces lot of schooling activity during summer. Crankbaits and worms.

24. Mouth of Honey Creek. Stump rows gives up summertime bass. Grass beds hold spring bass.

25. Back of Honey Creek. Boat docks in fall hold fish around brush.

26. Large grass beds in Minnesota Bend. Spring spinnerbaits and buzzbaits.

27. Rocky banks in Minnesota Bend. Lots of schooling activity from spotted bass during summer and early fall.

28. Stump rows in Minnesota Bend. Good spinnerbait fishing on summer nights and in early fall.

29. Cuts and small feeder creeks. Good summertime fishing in mouths in summer with crankbaits.

30. Grass beds. Good spring fishing with spinnerbaits and buzzbaits.

31. More sand pits. Surrounded by grass beds and stump rows. Good fall fishing.

32. Pockets. Spring fishing in back of pockets with spinnerbaits and buzzbaits, summer and fall fishing in stump rows in mouths with worm or jig-and-pig.

33. Bridge area. Fish suspend around pilings in summer and into fall. Crankbaits, grubs and jigging spoons.

34. Best ledge fishing begins. Use depthfinder to find original creek channel. Stump rows run length of original channel on both sides, but west bank is best. Great summer fishing with worms or crankbaits along ledge for four miles south.

35. Marked standing timber running length of original channel to Neely Henry Dam. Well-marked and fishy-looking, but surprisingly gives up few fish. Standing timber is best.

36. Ledge fishing continues this far.

37. Broughton Springs. Prime spring fishing area. Grass beds and boat docks. Spinnerbaits and buzzbaits.

38. Mouth of Broughton Springs. Good summertime area as fish school. Worms and crankbaits.

39. Excellent summer ledge fishing area with worms and crankbaits.

40. Cooper's Branch. Good spring spawning area. A few weed beds, but mostly pea gravel. Spinnerbaits and worms.

41. Standing timber in Canoe Creek stretches one mile from the mouth up the right bank. Crankbaits in spring through fall.

42. Weed beds and piers in Canoe Creek stretch to the bridge. Buzzbaits and spinnerbaits in the weeds in spring, worms and jig-and-pigs in pier brush in summer, fall and winter.

43. Above bridge. Good fall and winter fishing area. Jig-and-pig or worm.

44. Road bed. Runs parallel to east bank between Broughton Springs and Green Creek. Good winter schooling area with worm or jig-and-pig.

45. Standing timber. Good schooling area in summer or fall.

Worms or crankbaits.

46. Road bed. Crosses Green Creek. Good winter jig-and-pig.

47. Green Creek. Impossible to cross under bridge, however. Must launch behind bridge with small boat. Good spring bedding area. Spinnerbaits or buzzbaits.

48. Mouth of Beaver Creek. Stump rows. Good in summer with crankbaits. Fish school there in spring, too.

49. Road bed. Crosses mouth of Beaver Creek, makes sharp turn east and crosses main channel. Good in summer with worms or crankbaits. Roadbed section in main channel occasionally good in winter with jig-and-pig.

50. Another road bed in Beaver Creek. Crosses middle of creek and parallels west bank before exiting out of cut. Do-Nothing worms in summer, jig-and-pigs in winter.

51. Another road bed in Beaver Creek. Crosses small slough. Same as above.

52. Big fish area. Jigs and worms in spring and in winter.

53. Another road bed. Crosses Beaver Creek. Same as No. 50.

54. Road bed. Crosses cut. Same as No. 50.

55. Road bed. Crosses cut above Shoal Creek and then crosses Shoal Creek, hangs a sharp left across main channel and enters feeder creek on east bank. Same as No. 50.

56. Road bed crossing Ottery Creek. Fish same as No. 50.

57. Road bed crossing Ottery Creek and passing directly under bridge. Fish same as No. 50.

58. Good spring spawning area for spotted bass. Spinnerbaits.

59. Mouth of feeder creek. Good standing timber in mouth. Good summer and fall schooling area. Crankbaits and worms.

60. Road bed crosses cut in feeder creek. Fish same as No. 50.

61. Deep-water pockets full of logjams. Good in late spring until water warms and fish move to ledges. Worms, jig-and-pigs and crankbaits.

62. Road bed in mouth of Bridge Creek. Excellent schooling area for white bass, hybrids and spotted bass.

63. Rip-rap around dam. Excellent topwater area in spring; swim a weightless worm around dam in hot summer.

Temperature Preferences for Alabama's Most Popular Fish

°F °F

80

Bullheads 78°
Channel Cats 78°

White Bass 76°

75 Bluegill 75°

Largemouth 73°

Striped Bass 72°

Crappie 71°

70 Smallmouth 70°

Walleye 69°

Yellow Perch 68°

Muskellunge 67°

Lake Neely Henry

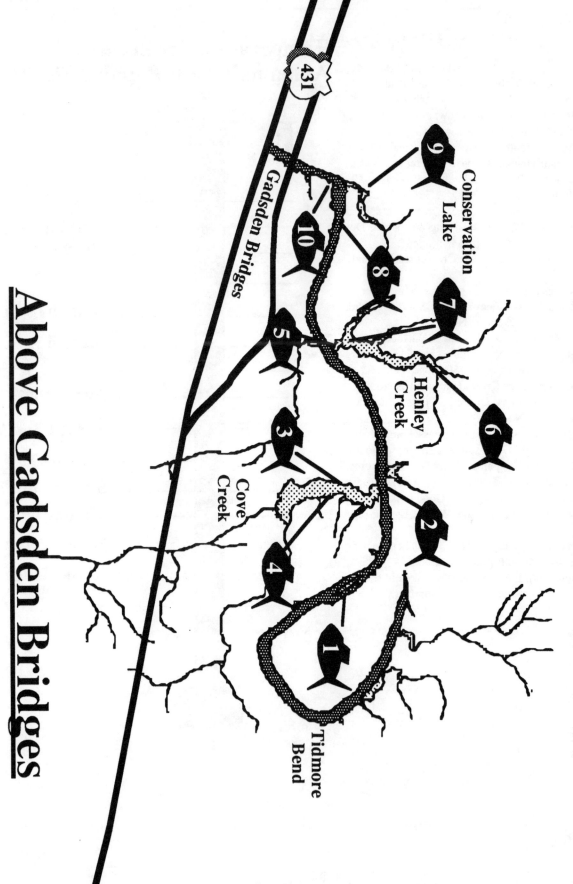

Tidmore Bend

Cove Creek

Henley Creek

Conservation Lake

Gadsden Bridges

431

Above Gadsden Bridges

Lake Neely Henry

Honey Creek

Minnesota Bend

Keeling's Island

Junior College Slough

Big Will's Creek

Rainbow Marina

431

759

411

77

Gadsden Bridges
to
Southside Bridge

11 12 13 14 15 16 17 18 19 20 21 22 23 24 25 26 27 28 29 30 31 32 33

Lake
Neely Henry

77

34

411

Buck's
Boats

35

Canoe
Creek
Marina

43

Big
Canoe
Creek

36

37

40

39

41

Broughton
Springs

38

Canoe Creek
Campground

42

Permeter Creek

Southside Bridge
to
Big Canoe Creek

24

77

Lake Neely Henry

Green Creek

Beaver Creek

Shoal Creek

Lakeshore Marina

Ottery Creek

Bridge Creek

Neely Henry Dam

Big Canoe Creek to Neely Henry Dam

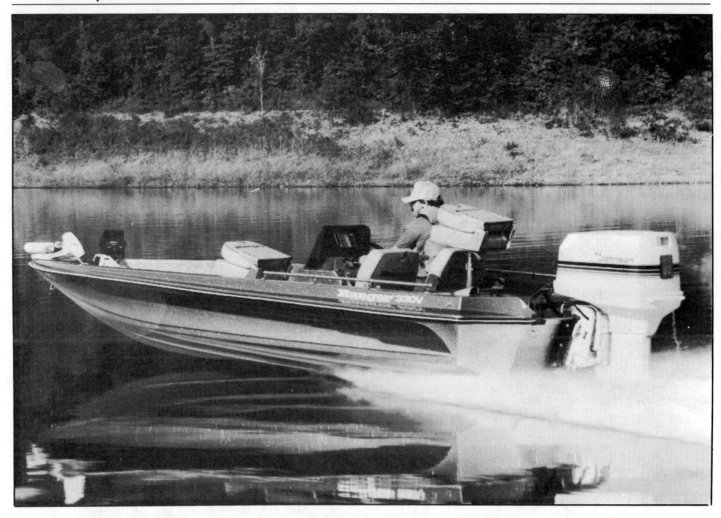

Lake Logan Martin

L ake Logan Martin is living proof that a major reservoir receiving extreme pressure from major urban areas can produce excellent fishing.

Lake Logan Martin is near the top of the list of the state's most fished lakes, yet many anglers will argue it offers bass fishing as good as any lake in the state. It's large population of better-than-average spotted bass, a large population of largemouths, incredible numbers of catfish and excellent fishing for hybrids, stripes and bream makes Logan Martin a near-perfect lake for the urban-based fisherman.

Spring bass fishing
NEELY HENRY DAM TO I-20 BRIDGE

Spring fishing in the upper portion of Logan Martin is feast or famine depending on whether rain supplies the water to fill the creeks and accompanying flats.

If the rain comes, spring fishing in these areas can be excellent.

Keep in mind the cool-water creeks such as Ohatchee Creek and

Acker Creek will be too cool for spawning during the spring and anglers should seek warm areas such as Alligator Creek, Broken Arrow Creek and Blue Springs.

These areas are full of stumps, weed beds and flats - the type areas bass bed in.

Other good areas that many anglers overlook are the stump rows in the main river channel. Fish that aren't quite on bed or coming off the bed will hold in these areas. Slow-crawling a spinnerbait through these stump rows will produce fish.

I-20 BRIDGE TO STEMLEY BRIDGE

Unlike the upper portion of Logan Martin, which is really nothing more than a river, the mid-section from the I-20 bridge south to Stemley Bridge is a full-fledged reservoir full of creeks and flats that make excellent spring spawning areas.

Some of the most notable areas are Seddon Creek, Fish Creek, much of Choccolocco Creek, Poorhouse Creek and Stemley Cove.

When warm weather approaches after the long winter, the small male bass are the first to seek these areas while the females will hold

Lake Logan Martin Fact Sheet

Location, length, acreage

Logan Martin is one of six Alabama Power Co. reservoirs on the Coosa River. The 15,263-acre reservoir, sandwiched between Weiss Lake to the north and Lay Lake to the south, draws much fishing pressure from Birmingham, Anniston, Talladega and surrounding areas.

The popular fishing lake begins at Neely Henry Dam in Calhoun County and stretches 48.5 nautical miles to Logan Martin Dam in Talladega and St. Clair counties. The lake boasts 275 miles of shoreline. The Interstate 20 bridges sit almost perfectly as the lake's halfway point. A total of 7,700 square miles drain into the lake.

Full pool is 465.0 feet.

Impoundment

Construction began on Logan Martin Dam July 18, 1960 and the dam was placed in service Aug. 10, 1964.

Logan Martin Dam

Logan Martin Dam is 612 feet wide and constructed of 180,000 cubic yards of concrete. It is 97 feet high at its highest point.

The dam has three hydraulic turbines, each capable of passing 4,488,000 gallons of water per minute. The dam also has three alternating current generators capable of annually producing 400.2 million Kilowatt hours of electricity.

Each of the dam's six spillway gates are capable of passing 12.6 million gallons of water per minute during flood conditions.

Stocking history

Florida-strain largemouth

1981-88	132,626
1989	60,970
1992	30,520
1993	30,520
1994	71,040

Striped bass

1972-83	407,873
1984	75,200
1985	98,400
1986	70,800
1987	92,000
1988	76,300
1989	76,800
1990	76,300
1991	76,616
1992	76,989
1993	80,798
1994	19,791

Hybrids

1976-86	875,262
1987	94,500
1988	45,800
1989	30,000
1990	30,500
1991	30,823
1992	30,520
1993	30,745

Configuration

Lake Logan Martin's upper-end is a typical Coosa River reservoir as the the upper 16 3/4 miles varying only slightly from the original river channel.

But from that point downstream, the reservoir widens dramatically as sloughs, pockets, flats and incoming creeks dot the landscape as far as Logan Martin Dam.

Major and secondary creeks

Besides the Coosa River, Lake Logan Martin is fed by several creeks. Choccolocco Creek, Clear Creek, Poorhouse Creek and Rabbit Branch - all creeks on the lake's lower half - are the most prominent and most widely fished.

Cropwell Creek (Town and Country, Big Bull and Aqualand Marina area) and Seddon Creek are smaller, but widely fished creeks also found in the lake's middle section.

In the area above I-20 bridge, Ohatchee Creek, Cane Creek, Acker Creek, Alligator Creek, Arrow Creek and Blue Eye Creek not only feed the lake, but offer good fishing as well.

Types of fish

The lake features popular species such as largemouth bass, spotted bass, white bass, hybrid bass, saltwater stripe, white and black crappie, channel catfish, flathead catfish, blue catfish, longear sunfish, redear sunfish and bluegill.

The lake also has several species of gar, drum and carp.

As for baitfish, gizzard shad, threadfin shad and several species of minnows are present.

---

in the main river channel or creek channels.

Two or three days of warm weather will normally warm up the shallow water enough to spur the male bass into their first aggressive feeding of the calendar year. Worms, jig-and-pigs and occasionally a shallow-running crankbait or Rat-L-Trap will draw strikes.

The warming eventually stretches toward the creek mouths. The main river is always the final area to warm. After water warms to approximately 68 degrees, the big females laden with eggs move in to spawn. Poorhouse Creek and Choccolocco Creek are the best spring fishing areas in the mid-section because the larger female bass are relatively easy to find. The top pattern for this April through May fishing is to use jig-and-pigs to fish the piers and docks where these large females like to find the brush tops that homeowners have placed there.

Another key spring bass area is the junction of the original river channel and Choccolocco Creek. A large underwater island surrounded by brush is located there and bass ready to spawn or in the spawn gather there.

STEMLEY BRIDGE TO LOGAN MARTIN DAM

Like the middle section of the lake, the lower area also boasts flats and incoming creeks that offer fine spring fishing.

Top spring spawning areas include the Redstone area south of Powell's campground, the sunken roadbeds and flats in the red barn area, much of Clear Creek, the upper end of Rabbit Branch, Burn's Slough, the first large pocket on the east bank above Logan Martin Dam and the riprap along the dam itself.

The bass during this period like to move up to feed on flat sandbars and warming pea gravel banks in 5 feet of water or less. These areas almost always have a little stained water during these times so shallow-running crankbaits like Bill Norman's chartreuse baits or chartreuse Rat-L-Traps work well. These are the areas that spring bass first move into.

The water on the main river is normally a little cool during this period so fishing isn't good on main river points, but secondary points will often hold larger fish because they are warmer. The secondary points with the most exposure to the spring sun will almost always hold the most fish. This is the northwest side of the lake. Following the spring spawn, the bass will situate in 8 to 12 feet of water on humps or stump rows and that's one of the main reasons this area is considered so poor for those who like to fish the banks.

Literally hundreds, maybe thousands of brushpiles, have been placed in this area by tournament fishermen and almost every point or underwater hump has at least one or two on it.

There are two April and May patterns which consistently take fish off of these locations. The best is a spinnerbait with a No. 5 or No. 6 willow-leaf blade slow-crawled through these brushtops and tree tops. Most people consider these good crappie locations and they are, but after the water warms past 69 or 70 degrees, the crappie move off to the channels and the bass move in.

For those who don't like spinnerbait fishing, a jig-and-pig will work just as well in these areas but it doesn't cover ground as quickly.

Another excellent spring fishing area is the old U.S. 231 roadbed through the Cropwell Creek area. The Harmon Lake and Avondale Lake beds also are good. All of these areas should be fished with willow-leaf spinnerbaits or jig-and-pigs.

If you're looking for the perfect spring bass fishing situation, two or three days of bright sunshine the week before a full moon will make fishing as good as it gets on Logan Martin.

Hot and warm weather fishing

NEELY HENRY DAM TO I-20 BRIDGE

Although less popular as a fishing spot, the upper reaches of Lake Logan Martin offer excellent hot weather fishing.

Several hot weather patterns will work, but it is important to remember that for these patterns to be successful, current is a must for day fishing and a lack of current is a must for night fishing.

One of the most effective methods is known as "fishing the cuts," the cuts being the tiny sloughs and pockets that sprout from the river bends.

Every single cut along this length of the river has stump rows in its mouth and offers the perfect place for shad to escape the currents when power is being generated.

Naturally, with shad being in these cuts, bass are sure to follow. Shallow-running crankbaits or plastic worms are effective and when conditions are right, as many as 15 or 20 bass will come from a single cut.

Another popular summer pattern in the upper end is fishing the cool-water creeks. Cane and Acker Creeks, as well as the back of Ohatchee Creek, are spring fed and will often be as much as 10 degrees cooler when the mercury hits 80 degrees elsewhere. Naturally, bass bunch up there.

It was in Acker Creek, near the Calhoun County Highway 73 bridge, that well-known Birmingham-area tournament anglers Don Bland and Paul Chapple put together one of the largest tournament stringers in state history.

While fishing the Sheriff's Boy's Ranch Charity Tournament during the late 70's, the pair weighed in a 20-fish, 52.4-pound stringer after culling another 20 wish weighing more than 30 pounds.

These creeks all have stumps in mid-channel and bass congregate at the base of the stumps and down in their roots. Slow-moving lures such as a Snagless Sally or jig and pig should be pulled on bottom and bounced over these stumps and roots.

Another lure that works well early and late in the day is a Lunker Lure. The bass are much more active in these creeks because of the cooler temperatures and will attack a noisy topwater bait.

It is important to understand two important things about fishing

cool-water creeks in this area:

A. Bass are most active when water is being pulled through Logan Martin Dam - not when it is being pushed through Neely Henry Dam - and the water level in the creeks is falling.

B. It is possible to be caught sitting in too shallow water if you keep your boat in these creeks too long while the creek level is diminishing.

The third pattern - a late summer pattern that works well at night - is fishing the rock shoals in the main river channel with spinnerbaits. Every year during August, September and October, shad migrate to Neely Henry Dam for the fall and the bass follow.

The area between the dam and Cane Creek offers the best fishing. A spinnerbait, tipped with a contrasting-color pork frog to make it more visible and more buoyant, and slow-crawled in 5 feet of water, can produce tremendous bass during this time of the year.

This area is full of boulders including a cofferdam, which is a dam that diverted the water flow while Neely Henry Dam was being built, and a fish trap, a rock formation in a V-shape that Indians once used.

An interesting note is that the river, from the CSX Transportation railroad trestle to Neely Henry Dam, is almost solid with rocks and on summer nights, bass could be anywhere in the area.

I-20 BRIDGE TO STEMLEY BRIDGE

Take special note of the map of the middle portion of Logan Martin. This map shows the original river channel (dark area) and where the water overflowed the channel to create the lake.

It is important to know that when impoundement preparations were being made, trees along the river channel that would be covered with water fell to the chainsaw.

Many stumps remain in rows down both sides of the main channel for the length of the river.

Hot weather patterns in this area are much like the area above it in that you need current and stumps to be successful.

Just as in the upriver areas, fishing the cuts can be productive, but the cuts in this area have two stark differences. Not only are they much larger, they also boast ledges at their mouths. It is common to find 8 feet of water in the cut itself and then 25 feet at the mouth.

This is where an understanding of ledge fishing is important. Baitfish will hole up in these cuts to get out of the current and the bass will follow. They will suspend in anywhere from 5 to 15 feet of water.

Spinnerbaits, worms, or jig-and-pigs, thrown into the mouths and pulled toward deeper water, will most often provoke a strike.

It was in this section of river on July 9, 1988, that Leeds' Rex Posey and Ron Robinson, fishing an all-night tournament out of Aqualand Marina, weighed in a 10-fish stringer of spotted bass that weighed 36-pounds, 8-ounces. Four of the spots weighed 20 pounds.

All of those fish fell to spinnerbaits using this pattern.

It is also important to remember that bass in these areas are not always active and failure to draw an immediate strike is not necessarily a sign that no fish are there. If fish are showing on the fish locator, it may take patience to cast until the lure is dragged right across a fish's face or body before a strike comes.

Another hot weather pattern that works in the mid-lake area is fishing the back end of Choccolocco Creek from the Alabama 77 bridge to the the Jackson Shoals area. This area is often referred to as the Rushing Springs area. A cold-water spring near Jackson Shoals causes cooler water as far west as the Alabama 77 bridge and makes good hot-weather fishing.

This area boasts plenty of structure and shallow-running crankbaits or spinnerbaits work best.

Just as in the creeks in the upriver area, Choccolocco Creek should be falling to be most productive. It is also important to note that numerous large stumps are just below the surface between the Alabama 77 bridge and Jackson Shoals. Extreme caution is needed in navigating that area.

Another hot weather method that works well is using electric red plastic worms to fish the shady piers and boathouses. Baitfish are attracted to Christmas trees and brush placed at the end of piers and docks, and the smaller bass feed in these areas at dawn and again at sunset.

In bright sunlight, bass will position themselves underneath these structures to avoid the rays. Bass usually avoid floating structures and choose permanent docks, boathouses and piers because they not only offer shade, but the pilings offer structure as well. Expect to find the bigger bass hovering near the most centrally located, most hard to get to poles.

Smaller bass often can be caught on the fringes and around outside poles.

STEMLEY BRIDGE TO LOGAN MARTIN DAM

The lower third of Logan Martin is probably the most productive portion simply because it has more water. Prime fishing areas are Cropwell Creek (Town and Country, Big Bull, Aqualand, Pine Harbor area), Rabbit Branch and Clear Creek.

Many top anglers also believe this portion has a larger concentration of spotted bass.

The plastic worm is the primary summertime weapon here. Motor oil, pumpkinseed and electric red are consistently the most productive colors.

Any irregularity on the bottom such as a hump, hole, sunken roadbed, etc., as long as it has some structure such as a brush top or stump row, will likely hold summer fish.

Deep stump rows can be found in the mouth of almost all incoming creeks and the lake's most serious fishermen often shine during June, July and August as they run deep-diving, big-lipped crankbaits through these areas in 12 to 15 feet of water.

They crank these big baits down so they bump brush tops, rocks, stumps and cause a commotion.

These baits also churn up sediment as they bump structure and many anglers think the bass believe they are attacking a crawfish, one of their favorite foods.

A pattern that works in this area for the anglers not necessarily hunting the biggest fish is flippin' or casting worms or jigs around and under pier pilings.

Cool and cold weather fishing

NEELY HENRY DAM TO I-20 BRIDGE

The most productive winter pattern in this area is one that many anglers have refused to believe until they see for themselves.

This pattern works best from October to February when the lake is full and Alabama Power Company is forced to open floodgates and turbines.

What happens is this: The swift water forces the shad, which cannot buck the current, to head for the banks to seek refuge in the nooks and crannies, logjams and other structure to escape the current. Naturally, the bass will flock to these areas for an easy meal.

An angler can position his boat in this swift water and use his trolling motor to keep his boat facing the onrushing water.

While drifting backwards, he can cast a 1/2-ounce or 1-ounce spinnerbait or jig-and-pig against the bank and, while keeping a tight line, let the lure wash down in the current.

The key to this pattern is that there must be an abundance of water coming through Neely Henry Dam.

The shad will school behind the large boulders in the middle of the creek and will do so in moderate current. It takes extreme current to force them to the banks.

Anglers should note that many times each little nook and cranny can have several bass in it, so if you catch several fish, crank the big motor and go upstream and drift back over the exact area.

Do not continue drifting downstream because you have already located the fish.

A pattern that works when there is no current is flippin'.

The stump rows in the mouths of the creeks and cuts, stump rows in the mid-channel of warm creeks and the logjams in the river's bend are all excellent areas.

I-20 BRIDGE TO STEMLEY BRIDGE

Although several winter patterns will work in this section of the lake, the most notable is sunken roadbed fishing because it is there that bass gather and can be found the easiest.

Several sunken roadbeds can be found in the mouth of Choccolocco Creek and Poorhouse Creek. Bass will school in these areas during December and January. Jig-and-pigs dragged across the roadbeds and dropped down the sides will catch fish for the patient fisherman.

Several of the lake's better fishermen use hair jigs on a spinning outfit because this not only produces numerous spotted bass, it is possible to catch crappie at the same time.

During the fall, bass fishing often becomes erratic as the fish turn on and off for no apparent reason.

During the early fall, the fish are gorging themselves, but as the first cold fronts come in, they'll turn on and off at a moment's notice. In the early fall, when the fish are schooling and chasing shad, shallow-running crankbaits, Rat-L-Traps and Rattlin' Spots are best for checking out where the fish are.

The bass will almost never be found in the back of creeks, sloughs or pockets during this time. The bass will always be close to the river off points or flats.

One of the best-kept secrets among top anglers during this time is the use of spinnerbaits. A small, double-bladed, 1/4-ounce, white spinnerbait thrown into the schooling fish and retrieved slowly is absolute murder.

STEMLEY BRIDGE TO LOGAN MARTIN DAM

Fall fishing in the lower end is good when bass can be found, but many anglers have difficulty finding them because of wide expanses of water and greatly varying depths.

The quickest pattern is locating schooling bass because they like to bunch up on the main river points. Grubs or an imitation shad such as a Sassy Shad or Red's Prissy Shad work wonderfully. Unfortunately, this pattern works only when current is moving and anglers may find current only on certain days.

Winter bass fishing in the lower end is poor and many anglers crappie fish instead. But with the water down during winter pool, it gives the angler an excellent opportunity to see structure he normally doesn't get to see.

Other types of fishing

STRIPE AND HYBRID FISHING

The introduction of hybrid and saltwater striped bass into Logan Martin has opened up a new world for many anglers. For many fishermen, the hybrid or striped bass - not the black bass - has become the largest freshwater fish they've ever caught. The sheer numbers of hybrids (1.04 million) and stripes (897,373) stocked in this lake in recent years have livened up many an angler's otherwise dull fishing life.

Summertime stripe and hybrid fishing has caught on like wildfire in recent years on Logan Martin and for good reason. The fish are plentiful when other species are not.

The secrets to good summertime fishing are healthy live shad and locating cool-water springs. Threadfin shad, which make excellent stripe bait, live for only a few minutes in a common minnow bucket. They must have a round baitbucket (they'll pile up in the corner of a square bucket and die from lack of oxygen) and the baitbucket must have aerated and flowing water.

The second gadget needed to do the job correctly is a water temperature gauge, and not a surface temperature gauge like many boats are equipped with. This gauge must be attached to a cable so it may be lowered into the lake in varying depths to find thermoclines.

Threadfin shad are easily caught a cast net as they school by the thousands in the mouths of sloughs and creeks. The appear as a large dark cloud.

Finding a thermal refuge in which to fish these live shad is the key to successful fishing. Cool-water springs such as those located in Choccolocco, Ohatchee and Cane creeks attract hybrid and stripe and offer the best fishing.

Hybrids are less susceptible to the heat and light than stripes and are more easily caught in these areas. Stripe tend to move in the later afternoon period as the temperature cools and the sun drops.

Open-face reels equipped with 14- to 17-pound test line are best and the live bait can be hung beneath a float. Water in the 72- to 76-degree range is where the big stripe are normally found. An angler can expect to catch his share of small hybrids before catching a big hybrid or stripe, however.

Hybrid and stripe also can be found chasing shad in shallow water flats during the summer and winter.

Hybrids and stripes will be found in the same creeks in the spring where they are found in the summer, but water temperatures are not nearly as critical. These fish seem to have a dislike for lively bait during this period and cut baits (threadfin shad with their heads cut off) work better than live shad.

Almost any bend in the creek that has rocky banks will have stripes and hybrids schooling on them during this time of year.

Although many stripe and hybrid stay in the same creeks to enjoy the warm water that springs emit in December through February, a great number move into Cropwell Creek near the Pine Harbor, Aqualand and Harmon Island areas.

Many anglers watch for gulls chasing the shad to give away the location of hybrids and stripes. Topwater lures such as Boy Howdees and Bang-O-Lures or shallow-running crankbaits such as Little Georges, Rat-L-Traps and Rattlin' Spots will catch these fish.

The extreme upper end of the lake in the Neely Henry Dam tailrace offers the easiest fishing for hybrids. Unlike the Logan Martin Dam tailrace, the area below Neely Henry Dam is smooth and void of dangerous rocks and boulders. When the dam is moving water, an angler needs only to run his boat up to the dam, kill the motor and drift backwards while bumping a Prissy Shad or Bolden's Firehouse Spoon along the bottom.

Another popular method is anchoring outside of the swift water and casting a pearl-colored, 3-inch Prissy Shad with a 1/4-ounce or 1/2-ounce lead head into the swirls. The best time for either of these patterns starts when the dogwoods bloom and extends into the fall.

The hybrids along the banks in the tailrace will often feed on topwater, especily when the water has just been turned on or off. Boy Howdees or Crazy Shads will catch these fish.

CRAPPIE FISHING

Lake Logan Martin has a limited number of serious crappie fishermen, but the lake annually produces a number of trophy-size fish. Leed's Willard Isbell is proof of that. Isbell, who crappie fishes on the lake year-round, has caught two 4-pounders, several 3-pounders and a large number of 2-pounders from the lake.

Like all lakes, spring crappie fishing is best because the fish move shallow and are accessible to more fishermen. When the water warms for the first time of the year, both species of fish begin looking for shallow water in sloughs and creeks that have blowdowns, stickups and logjams in which to spawn.

The water color in these areas can vary drastically from year to year, so the jig fisherman should vary his baits accordingly. Chartreuse, lime green, and orange bodies with red heads work well when the water is dingy, while pearl, white and smoke colors work well when the water is clear.

Fiberglass crappie poles such as those made by B&M Poles is the choice of the better crappie fishermen because they allow the angler to stay a distance away while jigging a jig or minnow tight against the crappie holding structure.

Many anglers don't like losing the tackle that is lost fishing this method and choose rather to fish submerged structure with a float and jig or a float and minnow. Piers with brush around them are prime areas for this type fishing. A float and jig can be an effective method. The angler should cast the rig well past the structure, then "pop" the float back to the boat over the structure. This popping draws the attention of fish and the float holds the jig out of the structure where it won't become entangled.

Rabbit Branch, the Town and Country area and Choccolocco Creek are the lake's best areas for spring crappie fishing.

Once the spawn is over, the whites and blacks split into different areas. It should be noted that the white and black crappie on this lake segregate with the whites being oriented to deep-water points and blacks oriented to deep-water rocks and stumps. The white's tend to weigh more, but the lake has produced several black crappie in the 3-pound range. These crappie will move to water 7 to 12 feet deep until late June or early July. The better crappie fishermen bump bottom for the fish at this time, using a minnow on a bottom-bumping rig outfitted with a 1/2-ounce to 1-ounce weight.

Summer fishing for crappie is almost non-existent on the lake, but these fish can be caught during this time. These summer crappie move to river ledges in water up to 25 feet deep. The river ledges between Town and Country and Stemley Bridge are excellent for summer crappie fishing as are the ledges between Town and Country and Clear Creek. The Mouths of big creeks all along the lake also hold summer crappie

Logan Martin's best fishing spots

1. Large boulders remaining from cofferdam use to divert water-flow when Neely Henry Dam was being built. Good bass fishing with spinnerbaits on summer nights when no current is flowing.

2. Railroad trestle. Good summer bass fishing day or night with spinnerbaits slow-crawled around pilings. Plenty of rocks and rock shoals in the area. Good with either current flowing or off. Train going over will scare you to death, however.

3. Rock rows on the western shore in the river bend. Lots of large boulders. Good spring and fall bass fishing when bass chase shad that school there. Best fished with jigs, spinnerbaits or worms when no current is flowing.

4. Rock banks. Good drift-fishing area during the winter for spinnerbait fishing for bass.

5. Ohatchee Creek. Excellent cool water creek. Good summertime fishing for all species.

6. Cane Creek. Also an excellent cool water creek for all species.

7. Acker Creek. Excellent spring spawning area for bass. A Snagless Sally works well in warming months. Also an excellent flipping area for bass during the winter.

8. Old Indian fish trap. Boulders placed in main channel in V-shape. Good spinnerbait fishing early morning or late evening during hot weather months. Best when current is off. Located approximately 1/2-mile above Alligator Creek.

9. Alligator Creek. Excellent spring spawning area.

10. River cuts. Good hot weather fish as shad gather in cuts to escape currents. Crankbaits or worms.

11. Rocky banks adjacent to deep water. Good crankbait area spring, summer and fall.

12. Broken Arrow Creek. Good spring shallow fishing area back in the creek when water is falling. Lots of stumps and roots. Spinnerbait fishing.

13. Excellent spring spawning areas. Worms or Lunker Lures.

14. Location of old dam, now partially collapsed. Sits about three to five feet underwater at full pool. Worms or jigs year round.

15. Thick stump rows adjacent main channel. Good year-round fishing with worms and jigs with no current flowing.

16. Blue Spring Creek. Excellent spring spawning area. A long string of thick stump rows run northeast from the mouth of the creek halfway to the back. Spinnerbaits, jigs and worms.

17. Railroad trestle. Summer fishing is good around pilings and rocky banks with crankbaits and spinnerbaits with current on or off.

18. Highway 78 bridge. Good warm-weather crappie fishing area at night with lights. A rocky point from eastern bank juts under the bridge and offers occasional good bass fishing.

19. Pipeline crossing. Large rocks dumped into seven feet of water. Good summertime bass fishing with worms. Also excellent trotline or jug fishing area.

20. Stump rows, adjacent to old river channel. Good bass fishing area year round with worms or jig-and-pigs.

21. One of very few weed beds in upper end. Small islands with weed beds on top and around them. Spring topwater area. Caution: shallow area that doesn't always appear shallow. Can be dangerous.

22. Good ledge fishing area. Water dips from eight feet to 25 feet. Lots of stumps in the area.

23. Seddon Creek. Good spring spawning area.

24. Powerline tower island. Rocky. Good spring area for several species as rocks catching sunlight warm surrounding area.

25. Underwater hump. Good summer bass fishing with crankbaits and worms when current is moving.

26. Fallen trees and man-made fish attractors in mouth of the slough.

27. Old Lock No. 5, now partially collapsed. Concrete wall and rubble running from north bank clear into the channel. Good worm or jig-and-pig fishing year round.

28. Logjams and fallen trees on southern bank of river bend. Spinnerbaits, jig-and-pigs and worms. Summer, fall and winter.

29. Mouth of Choccolocco creek where old river channel and old creek channel meet. Several humps and rises. Spring and summer worm, crankbait or spinnerbait area.

30. Good point with fallen trees and brush tops. Good worm or spinnerbait area.

31. Large, warm underwater spring. Good fishing for bass, stripe and crappie in winter.

32. Highway 77 bridge to Jackson Shoals. Late summer or early fall area. Shallow water. Lunker Lures or other top water when creek is falling.

33. Old roadbed in Poorhouse Creek. Excellent winter fishing area for bass and crappie using spin outfits with hair jigs.

34. Back of Poorhouse Creek. Excellent spring spawning area for bass and crappie.

35. Old Stemley Bridge Road, a sunken roadbed. Excellent hair jig fishing on roadbed sides for winter crappie and bass. During spring and fall, fish the top of roadbed with crankbait or worm when there is current.

36. Hump known as "stripe heaven." Stripe and hybrid often school here by hundreds during the summer. Topwater baits or Little Georges, Rat-L-Traps, etc. Lower edge of hump is also surrounded by fallen tree tops and is good bass area year round.

37. Shallow spring fishing area. Bass school here often chasing shad.

38. Excellent summer stripe fishing area. Shallow sandbar. Little Georges or topwater baits when the fish are chasing shad.

39. Red Barn area. Sunken roadbed not shown any map crosses area. Good spawning area, too.

40. Rocky bank leading to deep water. Good trolling area in spring. Worms and jig-and-pigs in winter.

41. More rocky banks. Worms and jig and pigs in summer and winter.

42. Old U.S. 231 roadbed running north-south in the Cropwell Creek area. Well-known hotspot. Fish roadbed dropoffs in summer.

43. Old Avondale Lake, now underwater. Fish lake with spinnerbaits during summer.

44. Old Harmon Lake Dam. Fish area with spinnerbaits during summer.

45. Flagpole hump. Good area for various species. Good night fishing for crappie and stripe. Lots of brush placed in area. Good early morning jig-and-pig fishing for bass.

46. Brush tops and fallen trees. Crappie and bass.

47. Hump loaded with brushtops. Fish for summer bass at night with spinnerbaits and jig-and-pigs.

48. Deep, rocky bank in river's bend. Night fishing for bass with spinnerbaits.

49. Old homes flooded when Logan Martin impounded. Rubble and foundations still stand. Good spring and early summer spinnerbait, worm or jig area.

50. Rocky point. Good spring point with crankbaits or worms. Good summer night point on spinnerbaits.

51. Rocky point. Same as above.

52. Road bed crossing Clear Creek. Excellent winter crappie fishing.

53. Clear Creek Causeway. Summer night fishing with spinnerbaits and worms.

54. Rocky point. Worms and crankbaits in spring, worms, jigs and slow-crawled spinnerbaits in summer.

55. Deep pit area. Good summertime hole for bass, crappie.

56. Excellent spring spawning flats.

57. Underwater rubble from dam. Lunker lures and other topwater in spring.

58. Deepwater ledge. Jigs, worms in winter, crankbaits in summer.

59. Upper end of Rabbit Branch. Excellent spring spawning area.

60. Rabbit Branch Causeway. Fish summertime bass with spinnerbaits at night.

61. Above water islands. Fish summertime bass with spinnerbaits at night.

62. Causeway. Fish summertime bass with spinnerbaits at night.

63. River points. Good nighttime spinnerbait fishing.

64. Rocky banks falling into deep water. Good trolling area with deep-diving crankbaits.

65. Burn's Slough. Excellent spring spawning area.

66. Rubble left by house that was flooded by impoundment.

67. Good spring spawn area.

68. Underwater pit. Good summer and winter bass spot, good summer stripe location.

69. Good points for summer nightfishing with worms, jigs and spinnerbaits.

70. Riprap above the dam. March through April, crankbaits or worms.

71. Logan Martin tailrace area. Excellent stripe and hybrid fishing.

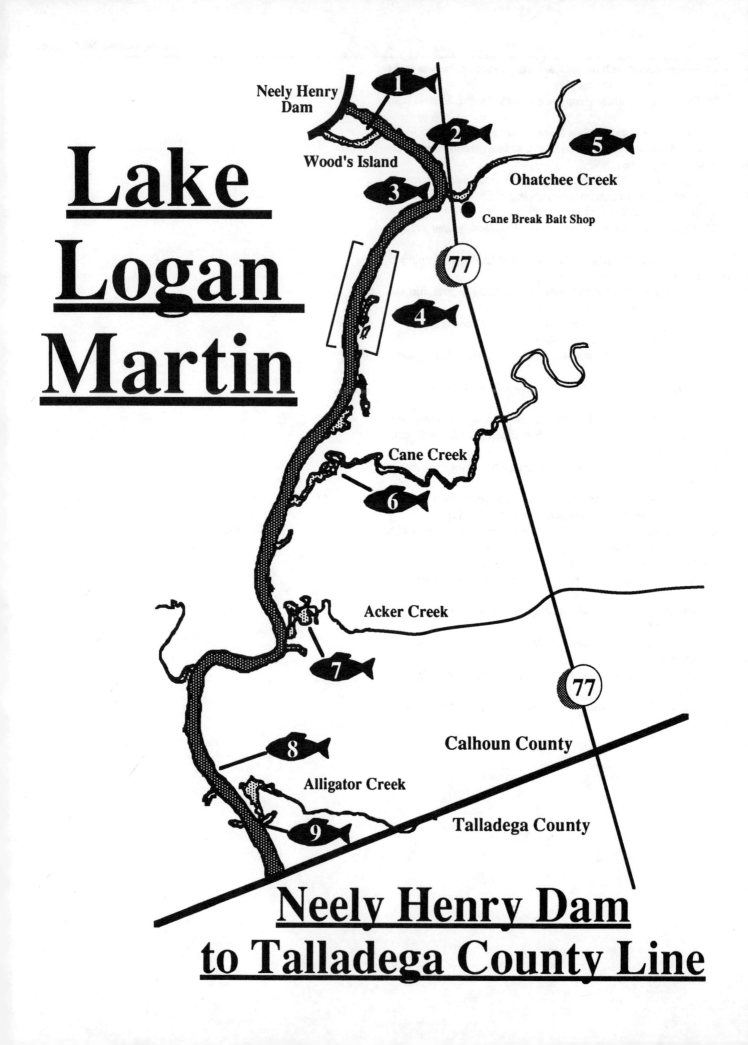

Lake Logan Martin

Neely Henry Dam

Wood's Island

Ohatchee Creek

Cane Break Bait Shop

77

Cane Creek

Acker Creek

Calhoun County

Alligator Creek

Talladega County

Neely Henry Dam to Talladega County Line

Lake Logan Martin

Kiker's Marina

Broken Arrow Creek

Clear Springs Marina

78

Hwy. 78 Boat Dock

Buckner's Landing

Uncle Eddie's Grocery

20

Talladega Co. Line to I-20 Bridge

Lake Logan Martin

I-20 bridge
to
Stemley Bridge

Stemley Bridge

Joe's Fish Camp

Maguire's Park

Poorhouse Creek

Riverside Marina

Choccolocco Creek

20

20

22 23 24 25 26 27 28 29 30 31 32 33 34

Big Bull Campground

Aqualand Marina

Town and Country

Shelter Cove Marina

Pine Harbor

Surfside 6

Stemley Bridge

St. Clair Shores

Camp General Lee

Rabbit Branch Marina

Surfside Marina

231

Frankie's Marina

Clear Creek Harbor

Clear Creek

Alpine Bay Marina

Logan Martin
Stemley Bridge
to
Logan Martin Dam

Logan Martin Dam

Lay Lake

As one of the oldest lakes in Alabama, Lay Lake had become somewhat stagnated by the mid-60's, but reimpoundment of the lake flooded an additional 6,000 acres of farmland and timber and virtually created a new lake. The lake immediately became a haven for bass and crappie, and despite the fact it receives tremendous fishing pressure, that excellent fishing is carrying on into the 1990's. The lake is as fine a lake as you'll find so near a major metropolitan area.

The introduction of more than 750,000 striped bass and 625,000 hybrids in the past 20 years has helped bass fishing on the lake. Not only has it taken some of the fishing pressure off the bass, the stripes and hybrids have kept the large, sickly shad in check and kept a constant hatch of small shad in the lake. This translates into tons of bass food.

The Logan Martim Dam tailrace at the head of Lay Lake has become the state's top spot for hybrid bass fishing. Catches of limits of hybrids in the 6-, 7-, and 8-pound range almost year round are foregone conclusions for most of the better tailrace anglers.

The state has stocked more than 123,000 Florida-strain large-

mouth in the lake in recent years and that has helped bass fishing. The miles of grass beds that can be found in this lake is a plus, too, for they tend to hold bass shallow where they are accessible to more fishermen.

Spring bass fishing

LOGAN MARTIN DAM TO U.S. 280

The upper end of Lay Lake offers few flat, sandy areas which bass can use to spawn, but that doesn't mean spring bass fishing can't be excellent there.

When there is current in the river, pre-spawn bass tend to gather along the river banks underneath the hundreds of willow trees along the banks, or just inside cuts or behind logjams. A lack of current is rarely a problem in the spring months as the turbines and/or floodgates are working overtime to accommodate spring flooding.

An angler should position his boat in the swift current near either bank and use the trolling motor to keep his boat headed upriver. With

Lay Lake Fact Sheet

Location, length and size

Lay Lake is one of six Alabama Power Company reservoirs on the Coosa River. Lay Lake is between Lake Logan Martin, to the north, and Lake Mitchell, to the south.

Lay Lake begins at Lake Logan Martin Dam and stretches 47 nautical miles to Lay Lake Dam. Lakeshore Marina sits almost perfectly at the lake's mid-point. The river channel is the boundry for four counties: Shelby, Chilton, Talladega and Coosa. The lake has 12,000 acres and 289 miles of shoreline. It drains 9,087 square miles.

Impoundment

Lay Lake was first impounded in 1914, and in 1968 it was redeveloped and the size of the lake nearly doubled. The lake rose 14 feet as a result of the re-impoundment.

Lay Lake Dam

Lay Dam is near Clanton where it straddles the Chilton and Coosa county line. Construction on the original dam began in 1910 and was completed in 1914. The dam was redeveloped beginning August 31, 1964 and was completed Feb. 24, 1967. The cost after redevelopment was $36.4 million dollars. The dam is 2,260 feet wide and 129 feet high and is constructed of 343,985 cubic yards of concrete. The dam has 26 30-foot-by-17-feet spillway gates capable of passing 2.8 million gallons of water per minute each in flooding situations. The dam has six hydraulic turbines and alternating current generators capable of producing 581.4 million kilowatt-hours of electricity annually. Like all Alabama Power Company dams, Lay Dam does not have a warning buzzer to announce water passage.

Configuration

The 14-foot rise in the water level when Lay Lake Dam became functional wasn't enough for the river to greatly overflow its banks in the upper half. Anglers must travel 23 miles below Logan Martin Dam before finding signs of water escaping the original river channel to any degree.

Stocking history

Florida-strain largemouth

1983-91	290,604
1992	24,000
1993	27,363
1994	24,000

Hybrid bass

1976-86	482,595
1987	70,800
1988	36,000
1989	36,100
1990	36,000
1991	36,000
1992	36,062
1993	36,098
1994	36,078

Striped bass

1969-76	140,990
1977	24,150
1978	50,390
1979	42,600
1982	68,119
1983	66,480
1984	60,300
1985	74,400
1986	31,900
1987	76,800
1988	54,200
1989	59,990
1990	60,100
1991	59,989
1992	59,968
1993	63,684

Once past that point, Lay Lake becomes a reservoir like most southern anglers are accustomed to. The river overflows it banks and covers thousands of acres of what was once prime farmland. Standing timber, old roads, collapsed bridges, creeks channels, railroad beds and collapsed railroad trestles can be found underneath the water and they offer excellent fish habitat.

Major and secondary creeks

Lay Lake is blessed with an abundance of large and medium-size creeks, as well as branches, which dump water into it all along its length.

Kelley Creek, Beaunit Creek (some maps show this as Flipper Creek), Locust Creek, Talladega Creek and Tallaseehatchee Creek empty in the upper third, as do Bailey Branch and Deer Lick Branch.

Yellowleaf Creek, Dry Branch, Bulley Creek, Beeswax Creek, Cedar Creek, Sulphur Creek and Peckerwood Creek are all major creeks in the middle portion of the lake.

Hay Spring Branch, Pope Branch, Sally Branch, Mud Branch, Flat Branch and Kelley Branch also dump water in Lay Lake's middle section, but to a lesser degree.

The lake's lower third boasts Spring Creek, Blue Springs Creek, Waxahatchee Creek and Paint Creek as major water suppliers. Reed Creek, Coagie Creek, Camp Branch, Sawmill Branch, Chalybeate Creek, Little Tom Creek, Slaughter Creek, School Branch, Wash Creek, Crawford Branch and Mill Creek are smaller arteries supplying water.

Types of fish

Lay Lake features all of the fish found in other reservoirs in the Coosa Chain including largemouth bass, spotted bass, white bass, hybrid bass, saltwater striped bass, both crappie species, channel catfish, flathead catfish, blue catfish, longear sunfish, redear sunfish and bluegill.

The lake also has several species of drum and carp.

Baitfish-wise, gizzard shad, threadfin shad and several species of minnows can be found.

---

his boat drifting backward, a spinnerbait pitched underneath these overlapping willow trees will sometimes produce tremendous stringers of spotted bass.

Fishing this pattern can be tricky in that it takes a knack to properly place the spinnerbait upriver of a willow tree and then allow it to drift with the current under the tree all the while the boat is drifting backward at a different speed.

This pattern also can be tricky in that the angler may fish a quarter-mile stretch of bank and not get a bite and then get 10 strikes in the next 50 yards. The pre-spawn bass tend to school and a number of strikes may come in a short distance. When that happens, crank the big motor, run upstream and fish the productive area again and again.

Also remember that these bass are against the bank in the small eddys to escape current. Rarely will you find one further than five feet from the bank. Once your lure is five feet from the bank, crank it in and cast again.

U.S. 280 TO OKOMO MARINA

During the early spring, largemouth bass and spotted bass segregate on this lake to a certain degree. The spots tend to gather on main river points and humps, while largemouth move to the secondary points inside sloughs and creeks. The spots aren't nearly as grass-oriented as the largemouth. It's not unusual to find 100 or more spots schooled up on these points in the pre-spawn stage.

Several baits can be productive at this time. The Carolina-rigged lizard has become this lake's No. 1 bait in recent years and for good reason. The slow bait has been catching tremendous numbers of fish. Jig-and-pigs, spinnerbaits and Texas-rigged worms also will work.

These fish will eventually move up into the shallow water of creeks, and they'll look for bottoms with sand or pea gravel. Beeswax Creek is a prime spring spawning area, as are the sloughs northwest of Beeswax on both sides of the river. Look for the large blacks in the thick matted grass during this time. They'll bury themselves in weeds that seems impossible for them to be in. Sometimes it becomes necessary to flip a jig in a 1-inch hole to get to them.

The normal spring baits - spinnerbaits, buzzbaits, worms, jig-and-pigs and twitch baits - can be productive in these shallow water areas.

OKOMO MARINA TO LAY DAM

Fishing in this area during the spring is basically the same as fishing the lake's middle section, the only difference being the lake's lower end lacks shallow ledges. Most spring fishing takes place on the points, humps and old roadbeds.

Spring Creek, Blue Springs, the back part of Waxahatchee Creek and Paint Creek are prime spring fishing spots. Paint Creek has about every type of structure imaginable for spring fishing.

Warm and hot weather bass fishing

LOGAN MARTIN DAM TO U.S. 280

The upper end of Lay Lake is much like the upper end of all of the lakes in the Coosa River chain in that it is nothing more than a river.

And like the upper ends of Weiss Lake, Lake Neely Henry, Lake Logan Martin, Lake Mitchell and Lake Jordan, this river-like upper end of Lay Lake can offer good summertime bass fishing at night.

One of the best-kept secrets among Lay Lake's bass fishermen is the art of night fishing the upper end during summer months. When Logan Martin Dam ceases generating power in the afternoons, the shad that have gathered below the dam lazily float down the river to gather in the creek mouths, around the islands and in the hundreds of logjams directly below the dam.

As a result, night fishing on Lay Lake's upper end is often tremendous. Spinnerbaits, worms, jig-and-pigs and even topwater lures offer superb fishing when the sun goes down.

A spinnerbait tipped with a pork frog is probably the best all around nightime bait because it can be fished in so many different ways and because it covers so much territory so quickly.

It can be thrown into the mouths of the large creeks, allowed to settle to the bottom and slowly retrieved through the stump rows and standing timber. It also can be fished in and around the stump rows that encircle the islands on the upper end, dragged across logjams or skipped underneath the willow trees that overhang the banks.

The worm or jig-and-pig can be fished in the same locations with much the same success, but neither are able to cover the territory as quickly as a spinnerbait and, as a result, are less productive.

Another exciting alternative is fishing topwater at night. Fishing the same areas with medium to slow topwater baits such as Jitterbugs, Hula Poppers and Nip-I-Diddees will sometimes produce when spinnerbaits, worms or jig-and-pigs won't.

During the day, the artificial shad such as a Sassy Shad or Red's Prissy Shad are unquestionably the kings of lures on Lay Lake's upper end. Anchored 30 yards from shore on either bank when the water is turned on, the angler can take a light spinning outfit and a pearl-colored Prissy Shad and often catch bass by the dozen.

An angler should cast the artificial shad upriver and allow it to drift downriver in the current. A bass running the banks in search of shad find this bait too tempting to pass up. The only problem with fishing this bait - that is if you consider it a problem - is the number of hybrid bass that will be caught in addition to largemouth bass.

Another lure that works well when the current is running during the daytime is a plunker-type topwater lure such as a Dalton Special with a trailing horsehair or bucktail jig. This lure combination, thrown into the eddies around the islands and logjams, often produces large numbers of smaller bass.

Unfortunately for the average angler who works for a living, Alabama Power Company rarely generates power on weekends during summer months. The weekend angler must opt to fish the upper-end ledges with Prissy Shads, worms or medium-running, pearl-colored crankbaits on weekends when no power is being generated. This type of fishing is average at best.

Although the upper end of Lay Lake offers several excellent cool-water creeks such as Kelley Creek, Beaunit Creek and Tallassee-hatchee Creek, these creeks surprisingly do not offer good summer bass fishing. Keeper-size bass are rarely found further than a quarter-mile from their mouths during hotter months.

U.S. 280 TO OKOMO MARINA

Once the bass angler finds himself south of the U.S. 280 bridge, he'll find three distinct changes in Lay Lake that will affect fishing.

One of the most notable changes is that the river widens and spills the banks of the original river channel, thus creating shallow ledges next to deep water.

Another noticeable difference is the number of large, wide creeks which pump fresh water into the lake.

The third, and maybe most important difference, is the grass beds.

No matter what type of structure a bass angler likes to fish, the middle section of Lay Lake offers it. There are ledges, humps, stump-row laden creek mouths, roadbeds and railroad beds, islands, cool-water creeks, collapsed bridges, rip-rap, weedbeds, piers and docks and a host of other fish-holding structure.

Just as the case on the five other reservoirs in the Coosa River chain, a summertime fisherman who wants to be successful on Lay Lake during the dog days of summer better have an understanding of ledge fishing.

Beginning where the river bends just south of Wilsonville and directly across from Heaslett's View, the good bass fishing ledges begin. Bass gather here by the dozens during hot summer months and these schooling bass are a fool for worms and crankbaits. They also will attack buzzbaits and Nip-I-Didees during the early-morning and evening hours.

Another productive ledge area is directly across from Sally Branch. This ledge is a strange one in that it sits at least 85 yards from the bank. A bass fisherman should use his depthfinder to find the ledge. He should then place his boat in 17 or 18 feet of water and cast into five feet of water with a worm. Such an incredible amount of structure rests on the bottom here that other lures will constantly stay hung up.

Another good ledge area is directly below that on the same side approximately a quarter-mile to the south.

Ledge fishermen will find good summertime fishing in the mouth of almost every creek or branch entering the middle section. Bully Creek, Dry Branch, Pope Branch, Beeswax Creek, Mud Branch, Flat Branch, Kelly Branch and Cedar Creek all boast humps and ledges where summer bass school.

The hot-weather bass fisherman in Lay Lake's middle section wouldn't be complete, however, without a good understanding of fishing weedbeds.

You can generally catch bass in these weeds year around, although the better fish move out by mid-summer. Spinnerbaits and buzzbaits early in the morning will take fish, as will flippin' worms and jigs.

Another hot-weather pattern that works is fishing around the large number of boat houses and piers in Bully Creek. Almost all of these piers and boathouses have Christmas trees and/or brush tops around them. Bass tend to hold in these brush piles on the shady side of the structures.

OKOMO MARINA TO LAY DAM

Current, if you can find it, is a key to river fishing on this end of the lake during the summer. Bass that are sluggish during the hot part of the summer spring to life when the water starts moving. Fish suspended on points, or even bass buried in the weed beds, can be affected by current. This current starts shad to moving and this is apparently what triggers the bass' feeding instincts.

Points, ledges and dropoffs hold the majority of these fish and crankbaits, worms and jigging spoons are needed to catch them. A good way to locate the better areas is to look at the bank and assume the points will come off into the water at the same angle. This gives mental picture of what's under the water. If the bank has a steep angle, the point probably goes deep into the water. If the bank has a sharp curve, the original river channel probably does, too. Look for these points and ledges that have some type of structure on them and you'll find summer bass.

Cool and cold weather bass fishing

LOGAN MARTIN DAM TO U.S. 280

Cool weather fishing in the upper end is much like spring fishing there in that bass tend to school along the banks underneath the overhanging willow trees when current is being generated.

Spinnerbaits can be used during the cooler months, but a crankbait such as a Fat Rap or Shad Rap will work equally well when the water has cooled.

Flippin' also works well at times in the upper end during winter months. Some bass will move into Kelley Creek, Beaunit Creek or Tallaseehatchee Creek for their warmer spring-fed waters and a jig-and-pig flipped along stump rows, trash or logjams will produce an occasional fish.

Flippin' also produces a few winter fish from the stump rows around Ratcliffe's Island, Buzzard Island and Prince's Island.

U.S. 280 TO OKOMO MARINA

In terms of numbers of fish and big fish, fall fishing on this section of the lake is as good as it gets. Granted, a lot of big fish are caught from this lake in spring, but spring bass have loving on their minds. Fall bass have feeding on their minds and are much easier to catch.

By the end of October, the feeding frenzy is usually well underway. These fall bass school heavily in the creeks and it's not unusual to find 50 or more bass schooled together. To make things even better, these bass can usually be caught in 10 feet of water or less.

Peckerwood Creek, Cedar Creek, Spring Creek, Beeswax Creek, Bully Creek, Dry Branch and Kahatchie Creek are good fall fishing creeks, with the first three being the best.

The fish school up on the ledges and points and the key to finding them is locating shad. This is normally easy as huge schools of shad can be seen roaming in the flats and creeks, their unmistakable small ripples giving them away. These shad don't always indicate bass are under them, but you can usually bet they are there. Largemouths rarely bust the top of the water when chasing shad like spotted bass do.

Once the schools of shad are located, the first bait to try is a fast-running lipless crankbait like a Rat-L-Trap or Hotspot. Shad-colored lures are good, but if the water has a little stain, a chartreuse bait might be needed.

Cast well past the school of shad and rip the lure through them.

Once the temperature dips below 68 degrees, the metabolism of the fish also drops. The fish that were so active a month before will be back out on the main river channel on points, humps and roadbeds. That's when the jig-and-pig becomes the top bait again.

OKOMO MARINA TO LAY DAM

The only difference in fall fishing in this area and the area above it is that it often becomes necessary to change lure colores due to water clarity. The clearer water in this area makes shad-colored and mirror-colored baits the best bet.

When using a worm, go with a pumpkinseed or june bug color.

Almost every creek on the lower end offers good fall fishing, with Blue Springs, Spring Creek and Waxahatchee Creek being best.

Other types of fishing

CRAPPIE FISHING

Although Lay Lake isn't well known as a crappie lake, studies show it boasts a crappie population as healthy as any Coosa River chain lake other than Weiss.

Spring is the best time for crappie fishing. The downed trees in the back of Kelley Creek offer spawning cover, as does the old bridge in Cedar Creek. Cedar Creek and Blue Springs Creek get some of the earliest warm water of the year, thus crappie spawn in these creeks earlier. Look for them around the standing timber around the banks. Curlytail 2-inch chartreuse grubs are best, with a 1/32-ounce or 1/8-ounce lead head. Use the 1/8-ounce to fish deep or when it's windy, and the 1/32 to fish shallow or on calm days. Plan on using 6-pound test line with spinning tackle for best results. Cast to the structure, allow the jig to sink to the desired depth, then begin the retrieve. If the jig hangs up, shorten the count before the retrieve. If it doesn't, go deeper. Strive to pull the jig just above the structure.

Crappie go deep in Lay Lake during the summer months. Night fishing is best. Plan to use lanterns and minnows around old bridges and railroad trestles in 15 to 20 feet of water. The old trestle in Sulphur branch, the old trestle in Peckerwood Creek and the second bridge in Cedar Creek are among the best areas holding summer crappie.

Fish can be found during the day in deep brushpiles. Always remember in summer months that crappie tend to seek shade and stay close to areas that hold shad. Also remember that crappie are always in or near deep water and always near structure.

January to March is the best crappie time on Lay Lake if you're looking for big crappie. Fish the same way as in summer, only deeper and slower. Cedar Creek and Beeswax Creek are always the best winter crappie areas. Fishing the main river channel from Beeswax Creek to Sulphur Branch can be productive, too.

STRIPE AND HYBRID FISHING

If catching big fish is your dream, you probably have no better opportunity in Alabama than fishing for stripe and hybrid in Lay Lake in the Logan Martin Dam tailrace. It is not uncommon for anglers to catch 25 fish a day with all of those fish topping five pounds each.

Unfortunately, fishing the Logan Martin Dam tailrace is among the most dangerous fishing in Alabama. Large boulders dot the area directly below Logan Martin Dam and, along with the incredibly swift current, an angler can find himself facing trouble in a split second. Anglers comtemplating fishing the area should first contact an angler experienced in tailrace fishing this area. Leed's Armond Ritch (699-1008) is probably the most helpful as he has taught literally hundreds of anglers to safely fish for hybrids and stripe there. He is a wonderful gentleman who welcomes your calls.

Artificial shad imitations are the best baits for this area. A popular pattern is to anchor in the quiet water to the right of the powerhouse (facing upriver) and let a Red's Prissy Shad or a Sassy Shad equipped with a lead head wash downstream on a tight line.

Another method that works well is to anchor directly in the swift water and cast the same lures behind the large visible boulders. Stripe and hybrid hide there out of the current while waiting on a shad crippled by the dam's turbines to wash by.

Fishing the tailrace is normally good year-round, but spring is best. A good rule of thumb is that when the dogwoods bloom, bring a big cooler.

Although it's possible to catch an occasional stripe in the tailrace, (it's almost impossible to land a 20-pound-plus fish in the swift current, however) stripe fishing further down Lay Lake is best. In late spring, these big stripes move from below the dam into the mouth of creeks. Kelley Creek, Talladega Creek and Beaunit Creeks are among the best. Live shad fished 15 to 20 feet deep offers the angler the best chance to hang into one of the big ones.

Once hot weather arrives, the stripe move up into the creeks seeking cooler water. Look for deep holes in the creeks. Stripe will gather there. Live shad floated above them with a cork produces the best fishing.

Once fall arrives, the stripes begin their migration out of the creeks into the main river channel and back up to the dam to feed for winter. Live shad fished in the creek mouths will once again catch them.

Fall is also the time hybrids begin surfacing to attack shad on topwater. Almost any white or shad-colored topwater bait that resembles an injured minnow, or a crankbait such as a Rat-L-Trap, will produce hybrids at this time.

The key to this type of fishing is watching for seagulls diving to feed on the shad schools. Hybrids will almost always be in the area. The mouths of Peckerwood and Spring Creek are especially good for schooling hybrids.

Hybrids can also be caught on topwater during the summer. Approximately 1/2-mile below Logan Martin Dam, the hybrids will attack topwater lures on the west bank of the river when power is first generated. The hybrid race upstream at the first inkling of current and think topwater lures are dead shad floating downstream. This type of fishing is popular with those afraid to get into the immediate tailrace area.

Lay Lake's best fishing spots

1. Boulder-strewn tailrace. The state's best fishing for big hybrids. When turbines are running, Sassy Shads thrown into swift current produce consistent stringers of hybrids 5 pounds or more. Summer and fall good; spring excellent.

2. Alabama Power Co. fishing platform. Enables anglers to fish tailrace without a boat. Good for hybrids, striped bass, catfish, drum and carp year round.

3. Steep muddy bank on west bank of river, west of first tiny island below the dam. You can often see shad trying to jump out of water here. Big stripe move in here during colder months. At least one 22-pounder has come from this spot.

4. For those who don't like to fish the swift tailrace, the water is more stable here. Hybrids swim along these banks to and from the dam when water is cut on or cut off. Topwater baits such as Boy Howdy's, Bang-O-Lures, etc. produce explosive action. Late spring, summer best. West bank always better than east bank.

5. Mouth of Kelly Creek. Good drop going into the mouth. Fish of all species congregate here. Excellent spotted bass, hybrid and crappie fishing.

6. Deep hole in Kelly Creek. Approximately 200 yards below big rock. Watch depthfinder. Live shad fished in deep hole produce big stripe, hybrids and spotted bass which gather in cool water. Creek temperature is at least 10 degrees cooler than main lake in July and August.

7. Big rock in Kelly Creek. Deep water between rock and right bank going in. Deep, cool pool holds big stripe, hybrids and spots in summer. Live shad fished below a cork is best.

8. Upper end of Ratcliffe's Island. Good stump rows and log jams. Upper end is best for flipping when current is off, spinnerbaits when current is on.

9. Overhanging willow trees along Ratcliffe Island's east bank. Good spinnerbait and buzzbait fishing in spring and fall.

10. Underwater rock pile 15 yards below railroad trestle. Thirty feet off of west bank. Spotted bass holder. Spinnerbaits.

11. Jetties and cuts on both sides.

12. Buzzard Island. Upper end good, lower end fair.

13. Mouth of Beaunit Creek. Temperature is 10 degrees cooler in July and August. Worms or Sassy Shad in mouth during summer months.

14. Sharp bend in Beaunit Creek. Twelve-foot hole 20 feet to right directly off point. Stripe and hybrid lay here awaiting shad traveling the creek.

15. Narrows in Beaunit Creek. Only five feet wide. When creek's flow reverses (current flows into creek) as a result of Logan Martin Dam generating power, hybrid go on a feeding binge here. Live shad is best.

16. Fork of Beaunit Creek (Railroad Lake) and Little Blue Creek. Excellent summer schooling area for spotted bass and hybrid. Worms for spots, live shad for hybrids.

17. Excellent stump rows, rock piles and ledge 22 yards from east bank adjacent to old powerhouse. Good spot schooling area. Worms in warmer months, jig-and-pig in cooler months. Live shad bumped on bottom will also produce hybrids when current is moving.

18. Mouth of Tallasseehatchee Creek. Real good with Sassy Shad or worm during late spring and summer.

19. Tallasseehatchee Creek. Good logjams and stump rows the whole length. Buzzbaits and spinnerbaits.

20. Prince's Island. Surrounded with stumps. Excellent flipping area when current is moving. Good year round.

21. Small, unnamed island. Good flipping area year round when current is moving.

22. River cuts. Mouths are good in summer with Sassy Shad or worm. Back of cuts early and late with buzzbaits or spinnerbaits.

23. Kahatchie Creek. Spring spawning area. Shallow. Weed beds in late spring and early summer. Spinnerbaits and buzzbaits.

24. Yellowleaf Creek. Mouth of creek good year round with worm, jig-and-pig. Weed beds in back of creek good early and late with spinnerbaits and buzzbaits in late spring.

25. Wilsonville Steam Plant discharge.

26. Standing timber around Bullock's Islands adjacent to Three Island Shoals. Good largemouth fishing with spinnerbaits or worms.

27. Mouth of Hay Spring Branch. Occasionally holds hybrids. Some spring bass spawning in back area.

28. Cuts in river bend. Shad use this as an escape area when current is on. Use worm or crankbait in the mouths for bass that follow shad.

29. Beginning of excellent ledge fishing area. Bass school here in summer to chase shad up on ledge. Water is 8, 10 or 12 feet on ledge and falls off to 65 feet or more. Lots of rip-rap on west bank, too. Holds some spotted bass. Worms, crankbaits and jig-and-pig all work here.

30. End of ledge fishing area.

31. Mouth of Bulley Creek. Worms, crankbaits.

32. Back of Bulley Creek. Weedbeds back in creek in spring. Good early morning fishing with spinnerbaits, buzzbaits or floating worm.

33. Mouth of Pope Branch. Good hump in mouth with brush. Worms, jig-and-pigs.

34. Mouth of Beeswax Creek. Sassy Shad, smoked grubs.

35. Bridge in Beeswax Creek. Good rip-rap. Crankbaits, worms almost year round.

36. Creek channel in back of Beeswax Creek. Stump rows. Good flippin .

37. River ledge 100 yards out from mouth of Sally Branch. Drops from 6 feet to 18 feet. Covered in stumps and rocks. Hellbenders good, but you'll get hung up easily. Worms next best.

38. Hump in mouth of Mud Branch. Kimberly-Clarke Penthouse slough. Recognize by large house with golf course. Good hump 6 feet on top that falls to 30 feet on one side, 20 on the other. Covered in brush piles. Excellent jig-and-pig fishing.

39. Good ledge area. Worms and Sassy Shad year round. Big bass producer.

40. Road bed. Old Perkins Ferry Road. Worm, crankbait or smoked grub.

41. Hump in mouth of Flat Branch. Worm, year round. Sassy Shad or Smoked Grub spring and summer.

42. Dual points leading from Flat Branch out into river channel. Hump in mouth with a few stumps. Good summer schooling area for bass. Rat-L-Traps work well when fish are hitting shad on topwater. Sassy Shad; worms other times.

43. Back of Kelley Branch. Left bank has downed trees that hold good largemouth in spring.

44. Deep hole. Spots, hybrids, stripe and crappie can be found here from time-to-time. Site of old Fort Williams Ferry.

45. Mouth of Cedar Creek. Where creek channel meets river channel is good summeer schooling area for both bass and hybrids. Worm, Sassy Shad or smoked grub for bass, topwater plunkers for hybrid.

46. Island in Cedar Creek. Left of main creek channel. Underwater point southwest of visible point good with Sassy Shad, smoked grub and occasionally a crankbait.

47. Collapsed underwater bridge. Must find with depthfinder. Pilings, fallen timbers still remain. Big bass area in hot summer months with jig-and-pig.

48. Rip-rap in Cedar Creek under bridge near Cedar Creek Marina. Conservation Department shocked up more big bass here in tests than in any area of Lay Lake. Large crawfish population likely responsible.

49. Island in back of Cedar Creek surrounded by weedbeds. Floating worms work well.

50. More weedbeds, but a dangerous area if you stray out of creek channel. Good flippin', or with buzzbaits and spinnerbaits.

51. Standing timber begins here. Good flippin' area.

52. Tiny rocky points inside treeline off of main channel. Good with Sassy Shad, worm.

53. $600 point. Named that because that's where Nolan Shivers sat to win his first tournament ever. Downriver side of point extends into river. Excellent schooling area for bass year round.

54. Mouth of Sulphur Branch. Downriver point is where old railroad track hugged bank and turned into Sulphur Creek. Downriver point best. Old bed of railroad only six feet under water. Holds bass year round. Worm, shallow-running crankbait, jig-and-pig, Rat-L-Trap.

55. Remains of old railroad trestle. Fifty yards in creek from point.

56. Good weed beds. Some of Lay Lake's best bass have come from these beds. Flippin', worms, spinnerbaits, buzzbaits. Year round.

57. Same railroad bed mentioned above crosses mouths of small cuts.

58. Shelby Shores flats. Big, flat grassy area behind standing timber line. Early and late with buzzbaits often produces good fish. Low water over some humps. Danger area.

59. Mouth of Peckerwood Creek. Same railroad bed mentioned above crosses here. Remains of dynamited trestle are next to standing timber. Can be found with depthfinder. Good flippin', crankbaits and worms.

60. Peckerwood Creek. Treacherous running area. Standing timber near bend. Good with spinnerbaits and buzzbaits. Worms work well around piers and fallen trees.

61. Sunken railroad bed exits river adjacent Okomo Marina. Sign proclaiming "dangerous area" marks exit point. Good schooling point for bass year round. Sassy Shad, worms, Shad Raps and Rat-L-Traps work well.

62. Mouth of Spring Creek. Points on island offer good spotted bass fishing. Worms by far the best bait. Standing timber surrounds island. Buzzbaits and spinnerbaits work well.

63. Bridge area in back of Spring Creek. Rip rap under bridge always good for a few small bass. Worm, jig-and-pig or Sassy Shad.

64. Small humps in flats in Spring Creek. Must be located with depthfinder. Humps adjacent to deepwater is good schooling area.

65. Bridge crossing Kate's Branch. Good rip rap. Crankbait, jig-and-pig or worm.

66. Back of Kate's Branch. Loaded with stumps 3 to 8 feet under water. With Polarized glasses, you can usually see them. These stumps often hold bass. Worm or spinnerbait in day. Buzzbait early.

67. Good points at entrance to Blue Springs Creek. Good for spotted bass.

68. Blue Springs Creek. Good spring spawning area. Lots of standing timber which bass school around. Worm or Rat-L-Trap.

69. Ledge next to entrance to LaCoosa Marina. Standing timber has broken up and collapsed and is hard to see. Good schooling area for bass. Worms best.

70. The narrows. Some of the lake's best spotted bass fishing. Steep rocky banks next to 125 feet of water. Flippin', worms and jig-and-pigs on ledge.

71. Mouth to Waxahatchee Creek. Good fishing on points of river ledge with worms, crankbaits, smoked grubs.

72. Points of pockets. Good all the way up creek with spinnerbaits, buzzbaits or flippin'.

73. Paint Creek. Good cool creek in summer. Small island in mouth good with jig-and-pig. Clear water. When everything in state is muddy, this creek will be clear and holding fish. Deep water throughout its length. Worm is best along banks.

Lay Lake

Logan Martin Dam
to
U.S. 280

Kelly Creek

Logan Martin Dam

Ratcliff
Island

Glover's
Point

Seaboard Coast Line railroad

Little Blue Creek

Beaunit Creek

Locust Creek

280

Talladega Creek

Tallasseehatchee
Creek

Lay Lake

(145)

Dry Branch

25

26

Bullock's Island

32

Bulley Creek

29

27

Hay Spring Branch

36

Beeswax Creek

30

28

Chopper's
Beeswax Gro.

31

33

38

(28)

35

34

50

37

49

28

48

Sally Branch

39

40

Cedar Creek Marina

47

Flat Branch

41

42

46

43

45

Kelly Branch

44

51

53

52

57

Sulphur Branch

54

56

Okomo Marina

58

55

59

Yellowleaf Creek
to
Okomo Marina

60

Peckerwood Creek

Spring Creek
Fish Camp

Spring Creek

Kate Branch

Lacoosa Marina

Bozo'z Fish Camp

Blue
Springs
Creek

Reed Creek

Coagie Branch

Waxahatchee Creek

Camp Branch

Camp
Waxahatchee
Marina

Lay
Port
Marina

Sawmill Branch

Lay
Lake

Okomo Marina
to
Lay Dam

Pineview
Camp

Lay Lake Dam

Little Tom
Fish Camp

Paint Creek

Lake Mitchell

Lake Mitchell owes its existence to Alabama Power Co. It is one of six power company reservoirs on the Coosa River. Lay Lake is its northern neighbor, and Lake Jordan lies south.

With 147 miles of shoreline, Lake Mitchell offers a variety of bass fishing - as well as catfish, crappie and other species.

Spring bass fishing

LAY DAM TO COVE BRANCH

The effect moving water has on the quality of bass fishing has no better example than the upper end of Lake Mitchell. Spring, summer, fall or winter, the fishing is always better on this end of the lake when power is being generated by Lay Dam.

The reasons for this are simple. Besides the obvious increase of oxygen in the water, swift water forces baitfish from the security of vast expanses of open water. Unable to withstand the current, these baitfish rush to the banks where pockets, sloughs, logjams and other structure offer a haven from the current.

The bass, as well as other species such as stripe, hybrid and crappie, find the hemmed up baitfish easy pickings. This sends these fish to the banks in search of food, and there, they become easily accessible to fishermen.

During spring months, something slightly different happens, however. Heavy rains that normally come during February, March and April force dams across the state to open their floodgates. When that happens, largemouths and spots are forced to seek refuge behind structure just as the baitfish do.

For years, the opening of floodgates sent 90 percent of the bass anglers to the house for the week, but times have changed. The better bass fishermen now realize these conditions mean fishing suddenly

becomes excellent.

The pattern for these fish is simple. The outboard motor is used to put the boat as close to the dam as deemed safe (sometimes no closer than 1/4 mile) and the outboard is turned off. The trolling motor is then used to keep the boat pointed into the current and the boat drifts backward down the river.

The trolling motor, besides keeping the boat straight, also slows the boat's backward movement enough that whenever a pocket, creek mouth, slough or eddy is found, the fishermen can cast into that area.

It should also be noted that because of the trolling motor operator's struggle to keep the boat straight and because of the back-seat fisherman's position, this is one of the rare times the fisherman in the back of the boat has the best opportunity to catch fish.

Several baits work well for this pattern. A white spinnerbait with a single spin No. 5 nickel blade is the best bait in dingy water, but a chartreuse spinnerbait with a gold blade is needed in muddy water. A 1/2 ounce or 5/8 jig-and-pig tipped with a pork frog is close behind. A black on black jig-and-pig works best in dingy water while a brown on brown or brown on orange jig and pig works best when the water clears some. A dark-colored plastic worm also works well. Some anglers have had success with a crankbait, but the number of crankbaits lost doesn't justify using them. If you use crankbait, use a chartreuse bait when it's muddy and a shad-colored bait when the water is dingy.

The best time for this pattern is usually three days after the floodgates have been open. By that time, the water flow has sucked all of the muddy water out of the creeks and the water directly against the bank of the main river channel has also cleared some.

A straight-running bank with a few indentations or points tend to hold the most bass on this pattern. It should be noted that most strikes

Lake Mitchell Fact Sheet

Location, length, acreage

Lake Mitchell is one of six Alabama Power Co. reservoirs on the Coosa River. The 5,850-acre reservoir is sandwiched between Lay Lake, to the north, and Lake Jordan, to the south. The reservoir begins below Lay Lake Dam and stretches 14 nautical miles to Lake Mitchell Dam. The reservoir has 147 miles of shoreline. Walnut Creek sits almost perfectly at the lake's halway point.

Impoundment

Construction began on units 1, 2 and 3 of Mitchell Dam on July 1, 1921, and the dam was placed into service on August 15, 1923. A fourth power generator was installed in 1949.

Lake Mitchell Dam

Lake Mitchell Dam is 1,264 feet wide and constructed of 205,746 cubic yards of concrete. It sits 106 feet high at the highest point.

The dam has four hydraulic turbines capable of passing 2.1 million gallons of water per minute each. The dam also has four alternating current generators capable of producing 354.5 million kilowatt hours of electricity.

Each of the dam's 26 spillway gates are capable of passing 2.7 million gallons of water per minute during flooding conditions.

Configuration

Lake Mitchell's upper end configuration is long and thin

Stocking history

Florida Strained Largemouth

1983-91	78,475
1992	35,962
1993	11,700
1994	11,700

Striped bass

1969	3,000
1973	31,766
1974	30,000
1975	29,250
1980	29,200
1984	30,100

Hybrid bass

1982-88	274,816
1989	17,000
1990	23,400
1991	23,400
1992	12,524
1993	97,580
1994	23,400

with the river overflowing its banks only in a few locations the first eight miles below Lay Dam.

Downstream from that point, the reservoir widens dramatically and looks much more like a lake. Sloughs, pockets and incoming creeks dot the landscape to Lake Mitchell Dam.

Major and secondary creeks

Besides the Coosa River, Lake Mitchell is fed by several major and secondary creeks.

Yellow Leaf Creek, Dry Branch, McSwain Branch, Clay Creek, Mountain Branch, Cove Branch and Walnut Creek are main bodies of water entering the lake on the upper half. Yellow Leaf Creek is the upper end's largest artery and is fed by Page Creek.

Bird Creek, Hatchet Creek, Cargile Creek and Blue Creek are main creeks entering the bottom half of the reservoir.

Hatchet Creek is by far the reservoir's largest artery. Weogufka Creek, Noneless Creek, Fixico Creek, Swamp Creek and Rocky Branch feed Hatchet Creek.

Types of fish

The lake features popular species such as largemouth bass, spotted bass, white bass, hybrid bass, saltwater stripe, white and black crappie, channel catfish, flathead catfish, blue catfish, longear sunfish, redear sunfish and bluegill.

The lake also has several species of gar, drum and carp.

As for baitfish, gizzard shad, threadfin shad and several species of minnows are present.

---

come within two feet of the bank because it's directly against the bank that the bass find the best refuge. Once the bait is six to eight feet off the bank, it's time to reel in and re-cast.

The number of spotted bass that can be caught using this pattern can be shocking. Birmingham's Fred Bland, a master at this pattern, has caught 10-fish stringers of spotted bass weighing 35 or 45 pounds on numerous occasions.

Anglers often have a difficult time trying to keep up with their baits in the swift water and more than one has thrown up his hands in disgust. It takes patience to learn the pattern and practice is the best teacher. The angler who masters the pattern and suddenly catches 15 or more quality fish in a 100-yard stretch find their efforts worthwhile, however.

This pattern works all the way from below Lay Dam to Cove Creek. The back sides of Gilchrist and Ware Islands also hold fish on this pattern.

One other pattern will work when the floodgates are open. This is for those who don't like the idea of tackling the incredible swift water.

When the floodgates open, the first refuge many fish can find is Yellowleaf Creek and Cove Branch. These two incoming water sources act much like the logjams, points and cuts on the main river. Fish find calm water there.

These two locations - especially Yellowleaf Creek - are extremely

muddy and virtually worthless as fishing spots the first three days after the floodgates are released, but on the fourth day the mud is sucked out and bass by the hundreds can be found stacked up in the mouth.

Fred and Belinda Bland discovered this pattern by accident in a Forestdale Bass Masters tournament in 1974. With a dead trolling motor battery, the couple pulled into Yellowleaf Creek to switch batteries. They decided to make a few casts with plastic worms.

To make a long story short, they eventually caught 20 bass weighing 47 pounds, 13 ounces. Eleven of those fish were spots weighing more than 38 pounds. They found fish stacked up for 400 yards from the mouth of the creek toward the back.

The pattern will also work in Cove Branch, but doesn't work in Clay Creek for some reason.

For those who don't like getting on the lake when the flood gates are open, drifting the main river channel pattern will work when the floodgates are closed. Water must be moving through the dam, however. The diminished water flow that comes with the floodgates being closed also means diminished catches.

COVE BRANCH TO MITCHELL DAM

Unlike the river-like upper end of the lake, the lower end of Lake Mitchell offers not only wide expanses of water, but beautiful grass beds as well. Blue Creek, Walnut Creek and the public boat landing area at Higgins Ferry offer some of the prettiest and fishiest-looking grass you'll encounter on the Coosa River Chain.

The grass beds hold the majority of the spring bass and the angler should attack this end of the lake with that in mind. Several patterns will work in the grass this time of the year, the most notable being flippin' and buzzing the Sally.

The Snagless Sally has diminished in popularity in recent years, but only with finicky fishermen, not the fish. It is still an effective bait on the lower end of Lake Mitchell in spring and the lake's better bass fishermen use it religiously.

It should be noted that the Snagless Sally is a method that tends to catch numbers of fish while flippin' tends to catch larger fish.

A No. 4 black/yellow Sally with a green pork frog trailer is the No. 1 setup for this pattern. Besides being weedless, this bait also has the advantage of being lighter than other baits and doesn't scare the shallow-water fish when it lands at the end of the cast. This bait also rides the grass better than most spinnerbaits. The bait's only real drawback is its small hook. Larger fish tend to throw the bait on occasion.

For those who like to flip, this lower end of the lake is prime real estate. The area is full of grass beds in 3 to 5 feet of water. These grass beds will be matted and laid over in early spring and punching through them to get to fish is a tough chore. The lake's top anglers have solved that problem by switching to a full 1-ounce jig.

A jig of this weight will punch a hole through the thick grass and fall quickly. Black on black or black on brown jigs work best.

The angler who likes to flip should concentrate his efforts in the grass beds upriver from Higgins Ferry Public Launch, and from Higgins Ferry Public Launch downriver to the mouth of Blue Creek. The grass beds on the same side of the river as the launch tend to hold the better fish.

HATCHET CREEK

For all practical purposes, the Hatchet Creek area on Lake Mitchell is a lake in itself. The large creek carries nearly as much water as the remainder of the lake. Pennamotely, Weogufka and Hatchet Creek are a trio of major feeder creeks that supply water to the big body of water and a trio of creeks bass fishermen need to be aware of.

When the lake's better bass fishermen want to win a tournament in the spring, this is the area where you'll find them. There's plenty of spotted bass in this area, but the larger, tournament-winning largemouth bass are abundant here.

The sheer numbers of big largemouth, coupled with the fact the weedy water is dingy and moving almost every day, makes this a bass fisherman's delight.

The sight of terribly muddy water in this area often chases anglers away in the spring, but the backs of the three feeder creeks usually are much clearer and are full of 3-, 3 1/2- and 4-pound largemouths.

The successful tournament angler will usually start the tournament by running to points in this area and catch a limit of smaller spotted bass that will measure. These smaller spots will take worms and Sassy Shads readily. The tournament anglers then start looking for "kickers," or the larger largemouths in the backs of these creeks.

They do this by flipping a jig-and-pig or fishing a Snagless Sally. Most go with a black/brown jig-and-pig or white Sally with gold blades. A green frog pork chunk also makes a good trailer for some reason.

It should be noted that the above patterns are daytime patterns. The large influx of largemouth in the area don't seem to bite as well as night. The fishing is better out on the main river channel after dark.

Hot weather bass fishing

LAY DAM TO COVE BRANCH

Unfortunately for the working man, the quality of summer fishing on the upper end of Lake Mitchell depends on water flow, and water flow is non-existant on weekends when most people are able to fish. Alabama Power Company normally moves water through its turbines on the peak user days of Monday through Friday, but the lack of need for power on Saturdays and Sundays leaves the turbines off on those days.

The best pattern to use during those weekdays in the hot part of the summer surprisingly is the same pattern you should use during winter months.

With the current running, let your boat drift backward down the river while using the trolling motor to keep the front of the boat facing the current.

Instead of a spinnerbait or jig-and-pig that works there in the spring, a plastic worm is needed for summer fishing. A 6-inch blue worm is ideal for crystal clear water, while an electric red worm produces better in dingier water. Spinning tackle outfitted with 12-pound test line will complete the rig.

With the boat drifting backward at a slow pace, cast the worm directly against the bank and bring it slowly to the ledge and let it fall. Bass hold on these ledges and occasionally scoot up on the ledge to feed on shad, and they find the falling worm irresistable. Some anglers finds similar success on Sassy Shads or Prissy Shads, either white or pearl in color.

Approximately 90 percent of the anglers who use the lake can only do so when the water is off, however. Locating fish during this time is a much more difficult chore.

With the water off, the main river channel varies from 9 to 15 feet in depth, but an occasional hole 20 to 25 feet deep can be found and that is where summer bass will be holding. Several drops and waterfalls caused these holes in the river beds many years ago and the current has kept these holes from silting in.

A depthfinder is a must in locating these holes, but the effort is well worth the results. It is not uncommon to drift along and see the bottom plunge from 10 to 25 feet and see bass stacked on top of each other on the LCR. Worms or Sassy Shads will take these fish.

When the water is off, the smart angler attacks this portion of Lake Mitchell at night. The bass will leave these hard to find deep holes and chase shad onto the ledges near the banks and these fish are more accessible to the average fisherman. Worms and single blade spinnerbaits cast against the banks and slowly retrieved off the ledge will produce fish.

Cove Branch to Dam

Just like the upper end of of the lake, current is a must to have any real chance of catching bass on the lower end of Lake Mitchell. Summer bass suspend themselves between 20 and 35 feet in 50 to 80 feet of water and become downright tough to locate. Even if these fish are located, getting the bait down to them and enticing them to strike is a shot in the dark. If the current is off in the hot summer months, plan to fish the lake above Cove Branch.

If you find one of those rare instances where current is moving during the summer, don't hesitate to take advantage of it, however. Light spinning tackle, light line and pearl Prissy Shads or plastic worms fished off points and ledges adjacent to grass can offer good bass fishing.

Hatchet Creek

The lack of the deep water needed by bass in summer makes the area that was so good in spring just an average place to fish for bass during the hot summer months. The quality spotted bass get scarce in this area in the summer and the 12-inch or better largemouth aren't much more common. The larger fish move out of the area onto the ledges of the main river channel where they can find cooler water and baitfish.

This isn't to say an angler can't pull into this area and catch a limit of bass during the hottest part of August, but it will be rare. Don't waste your time here if you're looking for a good day of fishing. The numbers of bass and quality bass come from the main river channel this time of the year.

Cool and cold weather bass fishing

Lay Dam to Cove Branch

Starting in November, the bass in the upper end of Lake Mitchell begin a feeding frenzy to store fat for the long winter. Fortunately, fishing for these bass doesn't require that the water be moving, although moving water does provide better fishing.

Since the bass are feeding almost entirely on shad, a shad imitation bait such as a Sassy Shad, Red's Prissy Shad or 2 1/2-inch grub with a 1/4-ounce jig head is ideal. An angler needs only to rig a spinning reel with 8-pound line and the bait of his choice. Eight pound line is the perfect choice because it's thin enough not to scare fish, but strong enough to straighten a hook when the lure is hung up.

The angler needs only to go point-to-point or on the backside of islands to find bass feeding. The bait should be fished just as you would fish a worm. Cast it to shallow water, allow it to sink and hop it back to the boat.

A keen eye helps in locating where to fish. Any sign of shad activity or bass hitting shad on top of the water is a signal that fish are in the area.

The mouth of Mountain Branch is the Number One spot for this pattern this time of year.

This pattern will hold most of the late fall and, depending on the temperature, on into December or early January.

Cove Branch To Mitchell Dam

Once the stifling heat of August turns into crisper mornings and eventually into evenings that require a sweater, Lake Mitchell bass begin leaving their deep, rapidly cooling summer home to move into shallow, more tolerable water.

Every angler knows cover is a must for bass, and the lower end of Lake Mitchell offers the type shallow-water cover bass like most - grass. Besides cover, the grass offers protection from the sun, it produces oxygen (during its growing cycle) and is a natural magnet for baitfish that also are looking for cover. The bass can bury themselves deep in the grass and have every need met without moving more than a few yards.

Because of the amount of grass and the number of fish that can be found there in the fall, the lower end of Lake Mitchell is Lunker Lure heaven.

Before choosing your Lunker Lure, first check the water clarity. If the water is dingy as it normally is this time of year, use a chartreuse on white bait. If the water is clear, stick with a white bait.

This patterns works early and late in normal conditions, and all day if there are overcast skies.

As the weather turns colder, the lake's better anglers realize that the shallow grass can't hold bass forever. Not only does the water begin to get uncomfortably cool for the bass, the dying grass is also robbing the water of oxygen. The bass move out to the points and down the rock bluffs in 12 to 20 feet of water and a jig-and-pig becomes the weapon of choice at that point. Go with a black jig and brown pork frog trailer.

The fish at this time are beginning to fatten up for winter. Not only are they more active at this point, they also tend to be larger fish.

Hatchet Creek

The fish that make Hatchet Creek their home in the summer months stay there during the fall and are joined by numbers of fish that come out of the main channel. Most of these fish seek out the weed beds and flats because it is there that the baitfish are located this time of year.

Lunker Lures and spinnerbaits work well when the fish are feeding heavily in anticipation of winter. The good news is that some October and November days are dreary and overcast, meaning the fish stay shallow all day long.

The angler fishing this area in the fall should concentrate in Hatchet Creek because that not only has the deepest creek channel, but easy access to the main river channel as well. The upper reaches of other creeks in this area rarely produce numbers of fish or quality fish during the fall because there's no deep water nearby where the fish can escape during the sudden changes in pressure that always come this time of the year.

Other types of fishing

Hybrid fishing

Lake Mitchell was without hybrid bass until 1982 when the state stocked 65,616 there, but the stocking of more than 291,000 hybrids since 1982 has made Lake Mitchell a first-class hybrid fishery.

As is the case of all new species stocked into a reservoir, it took Lake Mitchell anglers awhile to get a pattern on these fish, but once they did, hybrid fishing quickly became a favorite pasttime of many.

The hybrids on this lake behave much like they do on the other lakes on the Coosa Chain. Spring sees these fish make artificial spawning runs (they can't reproduce) upriver to the tailrace and into various creeks and long sloughs.

Tailrace fishing is excellent usually about the time the dogwoods bloom. These hybrids get into the swift water below Lay Dam to feed on the shad that are sucked through the turbines and shreded into bite-size pieces. These hybrid are easily caught by using either artificial or live bait. Live bait fishermen anchor adjacent to boils and use bass rods outfitted with 20-pound test line to cast live willow grubs into the boils.

Artificial bait fishermen use the same fishing outfit with bucktail jigs or Sassy Shads cast into the boils.

This type of fishing can be exciting because the angler is just as likely to hang into a saltwater stripe, catfish, drum, carp or crappie.

For the angler who doesn't want to wrestle with the swift water in the tailrace, he can find the spring hybrids in various creeks on the lake. Cargile Creek, Blue Creek, the mouth of Hatchet Creek, Bee Branch in Hatchet Creek and Bird Creek are known for their influx of spring hybrid.

Anglers should locate baitfish in these areas to find hybrid. This can be done visually on days without wind, or with a depthfinder on windy days. These baitfish will gather on long points and humps. A Little George, Rat-L-Trap or a No. 266 Blue Fox spoon thrown well past the school of baitfish and jigged back to the boat will produce hybrid, small saltwater stripes and white bass.

Hybrid fishing gets tough during the summer months, but a few anglers have unlocked the pattern. These fish head back to the main river channel to suspend themselves on the ledges during the summer, but they make periodic feeding runs to the top of the ledges to eat. A jigging spoon works well on these fish.

The end of September usually signals the hybrids return to the creeks. They return to the same areas they used in the spring and can be caught using the same lures. These fall hybrids tend to school more this time of the year and feed a little more heavily, however.

Lake Mitchell's best fishing spots

1. Exposed rocks below dam. Dangerous navigating. Dumpster-size rocks. Spinnerbaits produce super spots at night in summer when water is off.
2. New bridge at LaVada's Camp. Sassy Shads or grubs around pilings in fall produce numbers of spotted bass.
3. Yellowleaf Creek. Good escape area for fish when current is swift. Fishing is excellent for 1/4-mile in creek.
4. Northern tip of Airplane Island, or Ware Island. Long string of rocks run out upper end and lower end. Dangerous navigating. Good spinnerbait fishing.
5. Lower end of Ware Island. Good area when current is moving.
6. Down river point of Mountain Branch. Stump piles in 7 to 15 feet of water. Fish schooling area.
7. Cove Branch. Bass school up in back of creek in spring and fall chasing shad.
8. Clay Creek. Far back as possible. Waterfall area holds spotted bass in spring and fall.
9. Big Rock Island. Fast current makes back of island a fish haven. Spots gather in numbers.
10. Mouth of Clay Creek. Upriver side has steep, sharp rock bank. Fish there in numbers or not at all.
11. Long grass bed 1/2-mile. Big spots on Lunker Lures in fall.
12. Excellent drifting bank when current is moving. From LaVada's Camp half mile downstream.
13. Excellent drifting bank when current is moving. From mouth of McSwain Bank to 1/4-mile downstream.
14. Great drifting bank when current is moving. Sheer rock bluffs.
15. Excellent drifting bank when current is moving in spring.
16. Excellent drifting bank when current is near Gilchrist Island.
17. Good sheer rock bluffs. Good spinnerbait fishing at night in spring, summer and fall.
18. Good grass beds above Walnut Creek.
19. Good pockets. Sassy Shads in spring and fall.
20. Good schooling area for hybrids and stripes.

21 to 28. Grass beds.
29. Good fishing point. Upriver point of Cargile Creek.
30. Good secondary point in Cargile Creek.
31. Good point in back of Cargile Creek.
32. Rocky Island in Cargile Creek.
33. Grass beds. Good spinnerbait area in summer.
34. Back of Cargile Creek. Excellent bass schooling in fall.
35 and 36. Grass beds.
37. Cuts. Excellent in spring, early summer and fall.
38. Grass beds on upriver point.
39. Back of Blue Creek. Good bluff fishing.
40. Grass beds.
41. Grass beds in "Y" Slough.
42. Grass beds on point between "Y" Slough and downriver pocket.
43. Grass beds on point.
44. Grass beds in Little "Y" Slough.
45. Grass beds in mouth of Hatchet Creek.
46. Grass beds in shallow water.
47. Good pockets and points.
48. Long cut. Good spring fishing.
49. Good pocket opposite mouth of Pennamotley Creek.
50. Good cut in a Penamotley Creek.
51. Right bank of Pennamotley. Full of cover.
52. Left Bank of Pennamotley. Same as 51.
53. Back of Pennamotley. Excellent schooling area in fall.
54. Last 300 yards of Bee Branch. Excellent cold weather and early spring fishing with worms and jig-and-pigs.
55 and 56. Weed beds.
57. Good point.
58. Good creek point in Weogufka Creek. Back of creek tremendous spring and early summer area.
59. Early spring area for flippin' or Snagless Sally.
60. Afixico Creek. Same as 59. March to May. Rough navigating.

Lake Mitchell

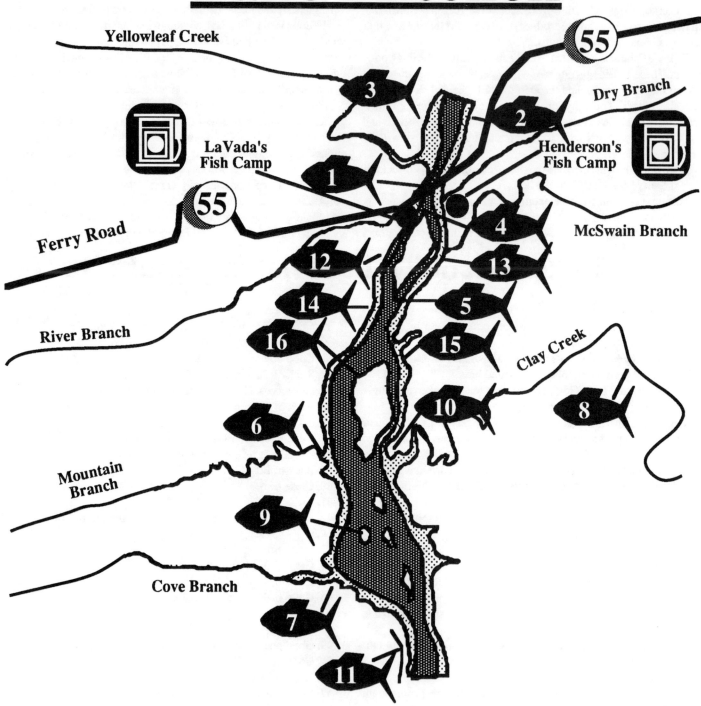

Yellowleaf Creek

55

Dry Branch

3

2

LaVada's
Fish Camp

Henderson's
Fish Camp

1

McSwain Branch

55

4

Ferry Road

12

13

14

5

River Branch

16

15

Clay Creek

10

8

6

Mountain
Branch

9

Cove Branch

7

11

Lay Dam to Cove Branch

Lake Mitchell

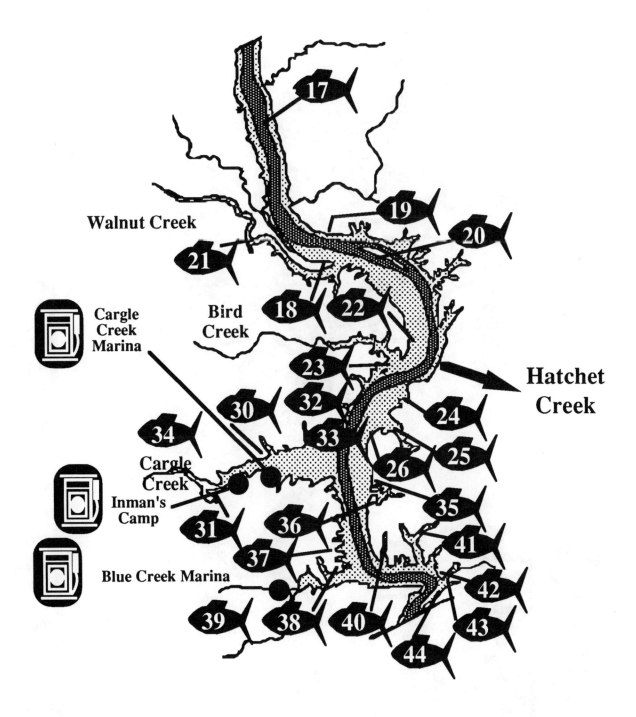

Cove Branch to Mitchell Dam

Weogufka Creek

Lake Mitchell

Fixico Creek

Noneless Creek

Barrett's Fish Camp

Bee Branch

Pennamotley Creek

Hatchet Creek

Lake Jordan

L ake Jordan is the smallest reservoir on the Coosa Chain, but its combination of deep and shallow water and its variety of structure make for an excellent fishery for largemouth bass, spotted bass, crappie, hybrid and catfish.

This is a lake all types of anglers can enjoy. Its large amount of shallow structure makes for excellent fishing for bank fishermen and anglers with a small aluminum boats without depthfinders, while its deeper water offers excellent fishing for the serious angler with the $15,000 rig.

Like all the Coosa River impounds, Lake Jordan has excellent spring bass fishing, but its fall bass fishing is equally good, many top anglers believe. It also offers excellent summer bass fishing at night.

The tailrace below Mitchell Dam offers excellent year round fishing for bass, hybrid, crappie and catfish, and thankfully lacks the big boulders and rocks that make tailrace fishing so dangerous in other tailraces on the Coosa River.

The lower end offers much wider water which makes for excellent spawning grounds.

Spring bass fishing

MITCHELL DAM TO BLACKWELL SLOUGH

The lack of large creeks and big sloughs for approximately three miles below Mitchell Dam makes for an unusual fishing situation on Lake Jordan, but a situation most anglers find favorable. The lack of escape areas on the upper end means fish are forced to gather on bank structure and on the stump-lined original channel. These are areas even the angler without a depthfinder has little trouble locating.

Just as on the upper end of sister lakes Lay and Mitchell, fishing the upper end of Lake Jordan offers some tremendous spring bass fishing opportunities. The rocks, stump rows, humps, rock piles, grass, standing timber and logjams along this stretch of the lake plays home to both spotted bass and largemouths. This visible structure holds numbers of fish.

It should first be noted that the area between Highway 22 bridge and Mitchell Dam offers an unusual current situation. This area lacks the dangerous boulders found below many dams, but it does

Lake Jordan Fact Sheet

Location, length, acreage

Lake Jordan is one of six Alabama Power Company reservoirs on the Coosa River. Lake Jordan sits below Lake Mitchell and eventually drains into the Alabama River.

Lake Jordan begins at Mitchell Dam in Chilton County and stretches 18.4 miles to Jordan Dam and Walter F. Bouldin Dam, both in Elmore County. Lake Jordan consists of 6,900 acres and offers 188 miles of shoreline. A total of 10,165 square miles drain into the lake.

Full pool is 252.0 feet.

Impoundment

Construction on Jordan Dam, which originally impounded the lake, began June 16, 1926. It was placed in service Dec. 31, 1928.^

Construction began on Walter Bouldin Dam Aug. 20, 1963 and the dam was placed in service July 27, 1967.

Walter Bouldin Dam collapsed Feb. 10, 1975. It was reconstructed and placed back in service Oct. 21, 1980.

Jordan Dam

The concrete portion of Jordan Dam is 2,066 wide and constructed of 389,000 cubic yards of concrete. It sits 125 feet high at its tallest point.

The dam has four hydraulic turbines capable of passing 2.2 million gallons of water per minute. The dam has four alternating current generators capable of producing 195.5 million kilowatts of electricity annually.

Each of the dam's larger spillway gates is capable of passing 3.5 million gallons of water per minute during flooding situations.

Stocking history

Florida-strain largemouth

1980-91	106,315
1992	13,600
1993	13,600
1994	13,600

Striped bass

1969	6,800
1973	36,466
1974	34,000
1975	69,000
1976	60,450
1977	62,550
1978	60,000
1979	70,070
1980	40,000

Hybrids

1981-86	428,902
1987	40,300
1988	33,200
1989	27,200
1990	27,200
1991	26,378
1992	27,200
1993	67,500
1994	27,200

Walter F. Bouldin Dam

The concrete portion of Walter F. Bouldin Dam is 228 feet wide and constructed of 210,000 cubic yards of concrete. It sits 120 feet high at its tallest point.

The dam has three hydraulic turbines capable of passing 4.3 million gallons of water per minute. The dam also has three alterating-current generators capable of producing 822 million kilowatt hours of electricity annually.

The dam is not equipped with spillway gates.

Configuration

Like the other reservoirs on the Coosa River, Lake Jordan's upper half is river-like with the lower half spreading out into a wide reservoir.

Major and secondary creeks

Besides the Coosa River, several major and secondary creeks contribute water to Lake Jordan.

Proctor Creek, Chestnut Creek, Pollis Creek, Pinchoulee Creek, Jake Creek, Welona Creek and Town Creek are water suppliers in the upper end, while Weoka Creek, Shoal Creek, Pinkston Creek and Sofkahatchee Creek are on the lower end.

Types of fish

Lake Jordan features popular species such as largemouth bass, spotted bass, white bass, hybrid bass, saltwater stripe, white and black crappie, channel catfish, flathead catfish, blue catfish, longear sunfish, redear sunfish and bluegill.

The lake also has several species of gar, drum and carp.

As for baitfish, gizzard shad, threadfin shad and several species of minnows are present.

---

have a large amount of reverse current, or backflow.

The water exiting the turbines of Mitchell Dam immediately swings to the east bank. The path of the original river channel in conjunction with some underwater rocks make a swirling motion and actually pushes current up the west bank. An angler can go down to the Highway 22 bridge, position his boat on the west bank and be pushed upstream to the dam while the current is going downstream.

This isn't a dangerous situation, but is noted because this west bank offers tremendous fishing when this happens. During the spring months, an angler can take a brown and orange 1/2-ounce jig with a No. 11 brown pork frog trailer and fish the jig-and-pig in this area. First, ride the current down the east bank with the boat pointed upstream approximately 25 yards off the bank while allowing the jig-and-pig to bounce down the underwater rocks on the east side of the boat. If this fails to produce fish, move to approximately 30 yards above the bridge, and use a white or white/charteuse 1/4-ounce spinnerbait with double gold willowleaf blades to fish the west bank as you float upstream. Again, position your boat 25 yards off the bank and fish between you and the west bank.

The tendency is to cast these baits in the eddy areas and that is fine, but expect to get strikes in water that doesn't look productive, too.

This area is relatively shallow 10 yards off the bank and there are underwater rocks that you can't see (too deep to be a boating hazard) that hold fish. Stay alert and fish the lure back to the boat.

This is a pattern that works best when power is being generated at Mitchell Dam and water is being passed through the turbines. It is not when for when the floodgates are open in heavy spring rains. Drifting down the banks will work to a degree when the current is off, but not nearly as well.

There are some occasions, such as when all turbines are running or a floodgate is open, that the current will be too swift for some boats. During this time, it's possible to pull your boat into a deep pocket, deep slough or in Chestnut Creek, Proctor Creek or Pollis Creek just far enough that a long cast will clear the mouth of the creek.

Current too swift for a boat to fight with its trolling motor is too swift for fish to fight for long and the fish in this area will be forced to seek refuge out of the current. Sometimes hundreds of bass will gather behind the primary point of a slough or narrow creek. Throw a Sassy Shad or a grub upstream as far as possible and allow it to bounce downstream on a tight line. This pattern will sometimes produce tremendous numbers of big spotted bass.

If the floodgates are open, that means the water is muddy and the fishing will be poor for several days. The swift muddy current will eventually suck the muddy water out of the three creeks in this area after a few days. Never miss the chance to fish the stain line where muddy water meets clear water in the creeks. Schools of bass following this line out of the creeks are easily catchable on Sassy Shads or Rat-L-Traps.

Except for the underwater rock pile under the overhead gas line and the underwater gas line (see map) downstream of the bridge, the rest of this area to Blackwell Slough offers only average spring fishing. Spinnerbaits, buzzbaits, stick baits and worms fished in the grass pockets along the stretch of river from the last gas line to Blackwell's Slough will produce some fish.

MITCHELL DAM TO BLACKWELL SLOUGH

If you were a stranger fishing Lake Jordan's upper end, then were to fish its middle section another day, it might not dawn on you that you were on the same lake.

The river-like upper end turns into wide water in the middle section and the patterns needed to fish the two areas are considerably different.

The middle section offers the wide, shallow water more conducive to the spring spawn, thus is an excellent spring fishing area.

Blackwell's Slough, as well as the Weoka Creek/Holiday Shores area across the lake, offers excellent spring fishing.

The bass will stage out of the deep water by moving up the many points. It's at this time that what may be the lake's best bait is needed. A chartreuse or lime-colored crankbait fished on these points in February will often produce large numbers of big fish.

Blackwell's Slough, fed by Hogbed Creek and Shoal Creek, has a tiny opening but expands into a big area. It is basically a lake itself. The bass move into this area in March and April. Points and sea walls will hold the fish at first, but they'll eventually move into the grass where spinnerbaits, buzzbaits and flippin' come into play.

Another key area is the three pockets below the mouth of Blackwell Slough. Due to the bend in the lake in this area, the current drives directly into all three of these sloughs. This forces thousands of shad into the back of the pockets and bass have a field day there. Plan to fish Rat-L-Traps, Sassy Shads and Little Georges.

The Holiday Shores/Weoka Creek area across the lake is another prime location for spring bass fishing.

The islands, piers and seawalls draw shad, and schooling bass feed on them. In Weoka Creek, buzzbaits work exceptionally well. Almost all of the points and sloughs will hold bass sometime during the spring.

BELOW BLACKWELL SLOUGH

Fishing the lake's lower end is almost identical to fishing the middle section during the spring. Spinnerbaits, lipless crankbaits, worms and Sassy Shads will take fish.

The only real difference is the presence of the canal. This man-made canal holds spring fish in its mouth and throughout its length.

Spring bass love the canal because it almost always has some type of water movement. The canal has several cuts, nooks and crannies and these areas hold fish, but so do the slick banks.

This is an excellent area for spinnerbaits, buzzbaits, Ratl-L-Traps and worms.

Many sloughs and pockets on the main river channel also offer good spring fishing. Many of these pockets have grass, as well as piers surrounded by brush.

Sofkahatchee Creek is one of the lake's top spring spawning areas. A plastic crawfish or lizard floated around grass is a deadly lure here.

The reservoir above Walter Bouldin Dam offers spotty spring fishing.

The road bed (see map) across the reservoir is a good location to try with jig-and-pigs or crankbaits when current is moving, as are the three underwater humps in the area.

Hot weather bass fishing

MITCHELL DAM TO BLACKWELL SLOUGH

Summer fishing during the day is poor except for early morning and late afternoon hours when worms and an occasional spinnerbait will take bass off ledges or points. Let the sun go down and it's a different story.

From May through November, night fishing can be excellent. A dark (black, brown or red) 1/2-ounce or 1/4-ounce spinnerbait with a dark pork frog trailer and a No. 5 nickel blade is the bait of choice for the better anglers.

The angler should position his boat 25 yards off the bank and cast the spinnerbait to the bank and retrieve it slowly back to the boat, always being alert for a sharp strike from one of the river's feisty spotted bass.

A black light and fluorescent line makes for improved fishing, allowing the angler to keep tabs on his line.

BLACKWELL SLOUGH AREA

Because Blackwell Slough is so shallow, the quality fish vacate in hot weather. The same pretty much holds true across the river at Weoka Creek, although it does have some deep water. Some bass will stay close to the grass in these areas all summer, but they are usually lesser bass. The larger fish move into the river channel area and gather on the deep points and ledges.

A worm, Sassy Shad or a deep-running crankbait can be used to take these deep fish. Water flow is a big advantage, although you won't see water flow as often as you like.

Night fishing is a good way to fish this area in July and August. The bass will move somewhat shallower at night, often gathering around lighted piers and seawalls. A good rule of thumb is to look for piers with some signs of fishing, such as rod holders, bass boats, etc. These piers normally will have some brush around them. If a pier has a diving board, avoid it.

BELOW BLACKWELL SLOUGH

Summer bass fishing in this area isn't that good. Worms or spinnerbaits fished on the river points early in the morning or late in the evening will produce both largemouth and spots, but rarely larger than two pounds. Fishing here is tough like it is on most other Alabama lakes.

Hot weather
bass fishing

The coming of fall means bass will be on a feeding binge in anticipation of winter. It's not unusual to see huge schools of shad scurrying in fear of their lives. It's a good rule of thumb that if you see shad jumping out of the water, they are being chased by largemouth. If you actually see the shad being hit on the surface, they're being chased by spotted bass.

If you can throw a Sassy Shad, a jig, a grub or lipless crankbait, you will catch fish on this lake during the fall.

Points, stickups, concrete sea walls, piers - just about anything irregular - will hold shad this time of year and bass won't be far behind. Sea walls and the stump rows along the original river channels are areas to concentrate on.

The easiest way to fish is "jump fishing," or watching for schooling shad and rushing to them. A pair of binoculars in the boat during this time of the year is a big plus.

When the cold of winter arrives, this area also offers good fishing, although baits must be slowed down considerably. Hair jigs, jig-and-pigs and worms on ledges, deep points and rocks are prime areas to look for.

Blackwell Slough area

This area that offered such good bass fishing in the spring does likewise when the bass return to shallow water again in the fall. This is an excellent area for willowleaf spinnerbait fishing.

The shad school heavily in the pockets and cuts on both sides of the river and the bass follow for an easy meal. Rat-L-Traps will work when shad are spotted.

The three pockets on the west bank below Blackwell Slough, the same pockets that produce such good catches in the spring, also concentrate shad and bass in the fall. Don't pass up these sloughs.

During the cold part of the winter, bass in this area will sometimes be found in surprisingly shallow water. Anytime there are several days of bright sunlight, the concrete sea walls will hold fish. These walls attract and hold heat and radiate it into the nearby water. Bass somehow know that and concentrate there.

If you were to tell friends you caught bass on spinnerbaits in five feet of water during January, they will probably snicker behind your back. Let 'em snicker.

Below Blackwell Slough

Once again, fall bass use the shallow water sloughs and pockets in these areas as a dead end street for trapping shad. Bass will travel in large schools this time of year in Sofkahatchee Creek and in the mouth of the canal and will be roaming in search of shad. The best method is to watch for signs of shad schooling on topwater and head to the area armed with Rat-L-Traps, Sassy Shads or Little Georges.

This area is also a wonderful place for night fishing in October and November. Spinnerbaits fished on the banks on grass fringes, sea walls, stump rows and other structure will sometimes result in true trophy bass.

Many of this lake's better fish come from this end of the lake at night in the fall.

Lake Jordan's best fishing spots

1. Rock outcropping on west bank below dam. Holds fish year round. Bass, hybrid, crappie.

2. Rock outcropping on east bank below dam. Same as No. 1.

3. West bank below dam and above bridge. Excellent year round fishing, but exceptionally good in spring. Rocks, blowdown timber, logjams.

4. East bank below dam. Same as No. 3.

5. Bridge pilings under Highway 22 bridge. Good year round fishing. Good crappie area at night in late spring and summer.

6. Long stump row on east bank. Old creek channel. Stumps run length of channel. Approximately 20 yards off bank. Good year round fishing.

7. Long stump row on west bank. Same as No. 6.

8. Large rock pile. Sits in middle of channel directly under overhead pipeline. Approximately 35 feet of water around rock pile. Rock pile comes up to 12 feet. Tremendous fall and winter gathering location for spotted bass.

9. Long stump row 40 yards off of bank. Runs along ledge of old river channel. Good year round fishing. Especially good in summer.

10. Underwater gas line. Signs mark spot. Rocks cover gas line. Gas flowing through pipe cools surrounding water in summer. Excellent bass fishing spot in July and August with jigging spoons, crankbaits or worms.

11. East bank. Excellent spinnerbait and worm fishing area year round.

12. Mouth of Chestnut Creek. Stumps on upper point, rocks on lower point. Good year round fishing.

13. Hole in first bend of creek. Five feet of water falls off into 13 feet of water. Good summer hole for hybrid and crappie. Some bass.

14. Mouth of Pollis Creek. Good year round fishing.

15. Mouth of Pinchoulee Creek. Good year round fishing.

16. Excellent stretch of bank on east side. Lots of stickups and stumps. Good in spring and fall with spinnerbaits, crankbaits and worms.

17. Double pocket. Holds lot of fish. Spots and largemouth. Good spring and fall.

18. Mouth of Welona Creek. Good summer and fall schooling area for bass and hybrid.

19. Excellent bank for night fishing with spinnerbait.

20. Same as No. 19.

21. Excellent spring spawning pocket. Good buzzbait area.

22. Good fall crankbait bank.

23. Excellent worm point year round.

24. Never pass up this point for bass fishing. Crankbaits, worms, jig-and-pigs and Sassy Shad.

25. Good spring and fall fishing bank. Exceptional in March and April. Lime-on-lime crankbaits, spinnerbaits, worms.

26. Same as No. 25.

27. Bridge pilings. Crappie fishing hotspot year round.

28. Spring fishing bank in Blackwell Slough. Grass. Good flippin' area. Buzzbaits and spinnerbaits.

29. Good worm bank in spring.

30. Super pocket. Water flow pushes right into pocket. Shad get trapped there and are easy prey for bass and hybrid. Best spring fishing cut on the lake.

31. Same as No. 30.

32. Same as No. 30.

33. Underwater hump in deep water. Excellent summer fishing. Stripe and bass schooling area.

34. Island. Bass and crappie fishing. Bass good around island, crappie under causeway.

35. Good fall schooling area for bass. Some spring fishing.

36. Same as No. 35.

37. Excellent point. Good year round.

38. Pockets and points. Late afternoon fishing with worms on points. Piers have brush. Overall good area.

39. Good pocket for spring fishing.

40. Spring fishing area. Shallow water. Rapalas and buzzbaits.

41. Sofkahatchee Creek. Points on left bank going into creek has stumps. Good spring area for bass and crappie.

42. Back of Sofkahatchee Creek. Excellent spring spawning area.

43. Good fall fishing area on points and in pockets for bass. Some stripe school in pockets, too.

44. Mouth of canal. Excellent area for hybrids and bass. Live shad for hybrids; Rat-L-Traps for bass.

45. Canal. Good worm, spinnerbait or jig-and-pig area in spring.

46. Walter Bouldin Dam powerhouse lake. Good March, April and May Sassy Shad fishing.

47. Underwater road bed. Excellent area for Shad Rap when water is being pulled.

48. Underwater island. Good fishing around island when water is being pulled.

49. Underwater island. Same as No. 48.

50. Underwater island. Same as No. 48.

Lake Jordan

Mitchell
Dam

Chestnut
Creek

Pollis
Creek

Pinchoulee
Creek

Mitchell Dam
to
Pinchoulee Creek

Lake Jordan

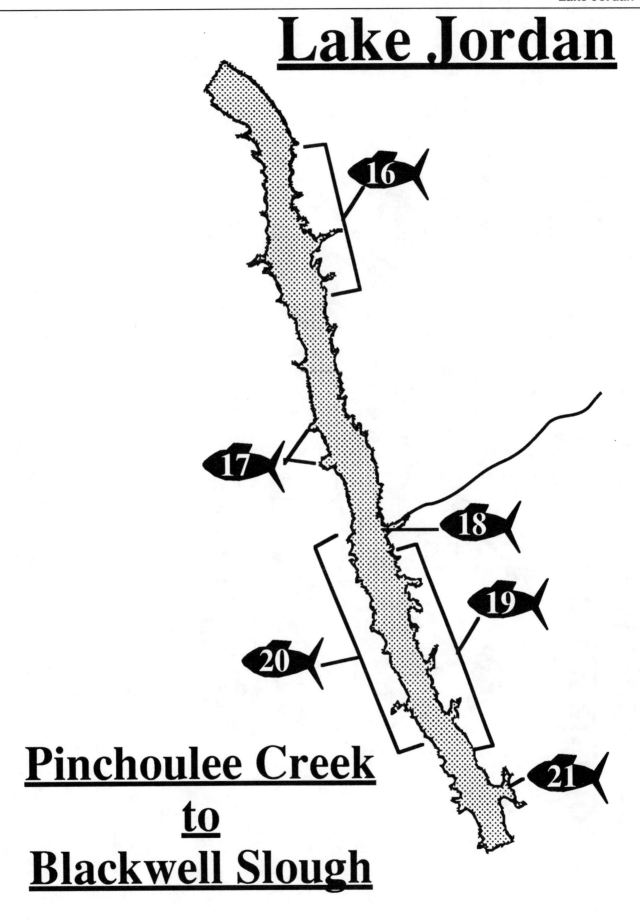

Pinchoulee Creek
to
Blackwell Slough

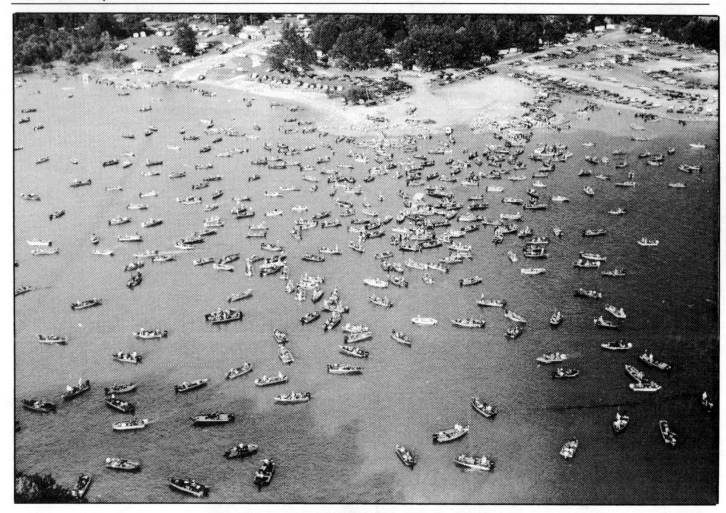

Smith Lake

There's a story that a scuba diver once went to the bottom of Smith Lake above the dam in search of an outboard motor that had fallen off a boat. Upon returning to the boat, the diver was asked if he had seen anything.

"No, I didn't," the diver said. "But the strangest thing happened. I could have sworn I smelled rice cooking." In other words, this lake is pretty deep.

If a poll were to be taken among Alabama's fishermen as to what Lake in Alabama is the most difficult to fish, Smith Lake would unquestionably get the majority of the votes.

Deep water and clear water are two situations which Alabama anglers aren't normally accustomed to and it shows when it's fish-catching time on this lake. It's not uncommon to find bass 40 feet deep in August, and there are times when striped bass can be located in 80 feet of water. For bass fishing in summer, nightime fishing is a must. When the stripes go that deep, you simply have to wait.

There's no better example of how difficult summer bass fishing is on this lake than the annual Anderson Boat's Classic. This annual tournament - the world's largest night bass tournament - is held in July or August every year. Despite the fact more than 9,000 anglers participated in the tournament from 1981 to 1988, fewer than 10 limits of bass were caught during that time. Only once has more than half the boats in the field managed to catch a single fish.

If you accept Smith Lake's challenge, forget what you know about shallow water fishing and plan to fish deep.

Spring bass fishing

ABOVE BIG BRIDGE

Simpson Creek offers the shallowest of all water in Smith Lake and as a result, it is the first water to warm as the lake shucks the bonds of winter. This is always the first location on the lake you can catch a fish on a spinnerbait when the new year rolls around.

If you are an angler that feels he must fish the banks, this is the only location and time of the year you can get by with that tactic on this lake. The shallow cuts, pockets and sloughs running off of Simpson Creek tend to hold large numbers of fish on the banksin spring.

Smith Lake Fact Sheet

Location, length, acreage

Lewis Smith Lake is an Alabama Power Company reservoir on the Sipsey Fork of the Black Warrior drainage system, in Walker, Cullman and Winston counties. It drains into the Bankhead Reservoir.

Smith Lake consists of 21,200 acres, but because of its extreme water depths, may hold more water than any lake in the state.

The lake has 500 miles of shoreline and 944 square miles drain into the lake. Full pool is 510.0 feet.

Impoundment

Construction began on Lewis Smith Dam on Nov. 25, 1957 and it was completed and placed in service nearly four years later on Sept. 5, 1961.

Lewis Smith Dam

Lewis Smith Dam is the largest earthern dam east of the Mississippi River. The rock-filled dam is 2,200 feet wide and constructed of 5.1 million cubic yards dirt and 55,000 cubic yards of concrete in its structures. The dam sits 300 feet high at its highest point.

The dam has two hydraulic turbines each capable of passing 2.5 million gallons of water per minute at full power. The dam's two alternating current generators are capable of produing 78,750 kilowatts of electricty each and 208.9 million kilowatt-hours of electricity annually.

Configuration

Smith Lake is a three fingered lake with the Sipsey River (Jasper side) making up the left fork, Rock Creek making up the middle fork and Ryan Creek (Cullman side) making up the right fork.

Stocking history

Florida-strain largemouth	
1981	20,000
1985	20,000
1986	43,700
1987	16,400
1990	21,200
1991	42,000
1992	42,400
1993	42,400

Striped bass	
1983-89	269,900
1990	42,700
1991	63,600
1992	66,500
1993	72,900
1994	66,100

Major and secondary creeks

Smith Lake is nothing more than a series of rivers and creeks. The Sipsey River makes up the lake's left fork, and it is fed by several small branches and creeks. Grindstone Creek, Mill Creek, Buck Branch, Bull Branch, Penitentiary Branch, Cooper Branch, Gillen Branch, Big Bear Branch, Little Bear Branch, Canup Branch, Butler Branch, Devil's Branch and Battle Creek are small water suppliers. Other than the Sipsey River itself, Brushy Creek is the main water supplier. It is fed by Chimney Branch, Burns Branch and Stear Branch. Rockhouse Creek, which is fed by Hoghouse Creek and Clear Creek, which is fed by Caney Fork and Coon Creek are other large Creeks above Duncan Bridge.

Duncan Creek, Dismal Creek, which is fed by Maple Branch and Little Dismal Creek, as well as Rockhouse Creek, are other water suppliers to the Sipsey River.

Rock Creek, the lake's middle fork, is fed by White Oak Creek and Crooked Creek - major water suppliers - and smaller creeks such as Cut-Off Branch, Panther Branch and Mill Branch. The right, or east fork is Ryan Creek, which has Simpson Creek as a major water supplier. Simpson Creek is fed by Reed Creek. Brushy Creek, Broglen Creek, Bate's Branch, Pigeon Roost Creek, Willoughby Creek, Spring Branch, Long Branch and Lick Creek are all water suppliers to Ryan Creek.

Types of fish

Smith Lake has an array of fish swimming in its deep waters. Spotted bass, largemouth bass, striped bass, white and black crappie, white bass, bluegills, redear sunfish, green sunfish, longear sunfish, redeye bass, rock bass, and warmouth are the most popular game fish caugh there. Smallmouth bass have been stocked there, but rarely show up. Rainbow trout have been stocked in the tailrace. Channel catfish and flathead catfish are present. Rough fish include freshwater drum, carp, spotted gar, longnose gar and redhorse suckers. The lake has a good supply of threadfin and gizzard shad, as well as minnows.

The large concentrations of smaller bass will be way back in the pockets in the bushes, while the larger bass will be in the deeper cuts where they have quick access to deep water.

These patterns will work for daytime fishing until about the second week of April. At that time, the better bass fishermen switch to night fishing.

BETWEEN BIG BRIDGE AND DUNCAN BRIDGE

Rock Creek, Crooked Creek and White Oak Creek offer good spring bass fishing in the lake's middle area. Crooked Creek offers both the numbers of fish and the larger fish, but that's nobody's secret and it receives the most spring fishing pressure.

White or white/chartreuse spinnerbaits with tandem blades (No. 7 willowleaf), a brown jig-and-pig with a black pork chunk and crankbaits are the best baits for this area.

Spinnerbaits and jigs should be thrown in 10 feet of water and worked down into 25 feet of water.

Another good pattern is casting a crankbait parallel to the broken rock banks on Rock Creek's upper end.

ABOVE DUNCAN BRIDGE

After the spring rains raise the water in Smith Lake, Brushy Creek, Rockhouse Creek and Hoghouse Creek have flippin' fish that are ready to be caught. The dingy water covers bushes and other structure on the banks and the bass gather there for their annual spawning ritual. A black/brown jig-and-pig with a pork frog trailer of a contrasting color flipped with 20-pound test into this structure will catch these fish.

Another pattern that works well is a big-bladed spinnerbait "buzzed" along the bluff walls in the area following the spawn. A chartreuse or chartreuse/lime Top Hog spinnerbait with a long twister tail worm trailer should be cast parallel to the bluff walls and retrieved quickly enough to "V" the water. This pattern will give up big spots and largemouths.

Hot weather bass fishing

ABOVE BIG BRIDGE

If night fishing or fishing deep isn't your forte, don't plan on fishing Smith Lake during the summer. Its clear, deep water makes daytime fishing almost impossible.

As early as June, temperatures force bass into 20-foot water. By the dog days of August, bass anglers regularly catch fish 35 feet deep.

A spinnerbait at night is the method most of the lake's best fishermen use to catch bass during the hot summer months. A chartreuse spinnerbait with a No. 11 green spotted pork rind or a black spinnerbait tipped with a No. 11 green pork frog are tops.

When the lake was first impounded, a great deal of timber in Ryan Creek and Simpson Creek was bulldozed and piled up into wide rows adjacent to the original creek channel. These trash piles still remain and they make excellent fish-holding habitat.

Most anglers have an urge to fish the banks during the hot summer months, but doing so on this end of Smith Lake is a waste of time.

Bass anglers should ignore the banks and pay close attention to their depthfinders in these creeks. Once 45 to 50 foot depths in the main body of water are located, the angler will know the boat is in proper position. This will allow him to fish the spinnerbait away from the boat in water 10 feet deep or deeper.

In June, throw the spinnerbait into 10 feet of water, allow it to settle to the bottom, then slow roll it through the debris on bottom to about the 30-foot level. A lot of big bass call these piles home during this time of the year, so don't be shy in continually throwing to the same area and fishing it hard.

In July and August, forget the 10-foot water and start throwing into 15 feet of water. Work the spinnerbait down to 40 feet of water before ending the retrieve.

Although these piles of debris offer some of the best fishing in this area this time of the year, don't overlook ledges and long points in the same areas. These deep points and ledges also hold quality fish on occasion. They should be fished in the same manner and with the same baits as the brush piles.

Between Big Bridge and Duncan Bridge

This area of the lake is known by several names, some of which are unprintable in a family-type book such as this one. This area, which offers unbelievably clear, deep water (315-plus in some locations) is sometimes known as the "well water," the "swimming pool" or the "gin bottle."

No matter the name, the bass fishing in the main body of water running from bridge to bridge is extremely tough during summer months. During the hot days of June, July and August, you will find bass 10 feet deeper here than any other location on the lake. If you're catching bass in 25 feet of water elsewhere on the lake, the bass in this area will be 35 feet deep.

So much for the bad news. The good news is that during the full moon of June, you'll find no better area on the lake that will produce 5-pound-plus spots. Surprisingly, some of these early-June spotted bass are late spawners and you'll find them full of eggs. Many anglers believe these fish bury themselves so deep (45 feet-plus) during winter months that they mess up their spawning times.

These spots normally gather around any of the long clay points located near steep bluffs. Jigging spoons, deep-diving crankbaits (20-plus), Rat-L-Traps or even spinnerbaits can be used to extract them.

After these spotted bass disappear from the area some time in June, the best bass anglers usually consider the area pretty much useless until late fall.

The exception to this rule of thumb is the Rock Creek area. Unlike the main body of water between the bridges, this creek offers excellent summer fishing. Of course, night fishing is the key.

Ledges and long-points are spread throughout the creek and offer the best bass-holding structure. Many anglers make the mistake of fishing too close to the bank and as a result, are usually sitting directly atop the fish.

Just like in the area above Big Bridge, use the depthfinder to put yourself in 45 to 50 feet of water and let your casts land 15 to 20 feet off the bank. Allow the spinnerbait to settle and bump the structure on a slow retrieve back to the boat.

Many of the banks will have extremely deep water immediately, but many times a rock pile or other structure juts 20 yards off the bank and this is the type of structure that produces good stringers of bass.

Above Duncan Bridge

Once again, finding the points and ledges away from the bank in deep water is the key to catching summer bass on the area of Smith Lake above Duncan Bridge.

The stretch of the Sipsey River from Duncan Bridge to the mouth of Brushy Creek offers the area that holds the most summertime bass. Just as in fishing other areas of the lake during summer, the angler should fish at night. He should back off of these points into deep water and cast into 10 to 15 feet of water and begin his retrieve with slow-rolled spinnerbaits. Casting any closer to the bank may result in an occasional small bass, but rarely produces a keeper fish.

Cool and cold weather bass fishing

Above Big Bridge

The cooler temperatures of October and the months that follow give Smith Lake anglers some relief from the heat, but more importantly, relief from the necessity of fishing strictly at night.

Both Ryan and Simpson Creek offer good daytime fishing this time of the year. Jig-and-pigs (flippin'), spinnerbaits, lunker lures and crankbaits all will put bass in the livewell, but the angler serious with his flippin' seems to fare the best.

Ryan Creek offers the best bass fishing of the two creeks, and anglers will find something rare for Smith Lake there this time of the year – water color.

Ryan Creek plays home to a large amount of stumps, brush and logs and other type structure flippers love. Ryan Creek won't produce large numbers of fish this time of the year, but hookups will result in a high percentage of quality fish. During fall night tournaments on the lake, it is not uncommon to see the creek filled with fishermen flippin' jig-and-pigs with great haste as they try to pull a big bass out before darkness falls.

The back end of Ryan Creek (above Speegle's Slough) is a good fall area for those who like to continue with their night fishing. Spinnerbaits fished in shallow water almost always produce fish.

The back end of Simpson Creek is a good bass area starting in late October. Jig-and-pigs flipped in debris in medium-depth water also produces good fish.

Between Big Bridge and Duncan Bridge

October at night is the angler's best opportunity to catch big fish in this area of Smith Lake. Bill Vines and Bruce Holcombe, two of the lake's best bass fishermen, have dominated fall tournament fishing on the lake by fishing their spinnerbaits in Rock Creek. The pair won the annual Misty Harbor Classic 6 of 8 years and did so by catching 30 or 40 keeper fish each time.

Start by fishing spinnerbaits in 10 feet of water and fish the baits to 25 feet of water. Long points with stumps are the best areas to fish, but the better tournament fishermen narrow down these areas by visiting the lake during the day and watching for schooling shad. The fish are schooling heavily during this time of the year and finding fish chasing shad is not a problem. The long points on which you find shad during the day is the points that will hold shad at night.

Above Duncan Bridge

For those who have found that fishing season doesn't necessarily end on Labor Day, fall and winter bass fishing on this area of the lake can be a pleasure. Better yet, night fishing isn't a must.

The blown-down timber above the dam offers good Lunker Lure fishing and other types of topwater action early in the fall. When November arrives, a surprisingly good pattern is ripping a spinnerbait parallel to the rock walls. For some unexplainable reason, the spots will leave a slow spinnerbait alone. Instead, a spinnerbait cranked fast enough to make the water "V" drives them crazy. Just as surprising, clear water seems to produce better than dingy water with this pattern.

Other types of fishing

Stripe Fishing

Never in Alabama has the introduction of a new species of fish into a lake had the impact of the introduction of the saltwater striped bass into Smith Lake.

The 3-inch fingerlings first placed in the lake in 1983 had transformed into 30-pound-plus monsters by the summer of 1989 and Smith Lake, considered by many to be the lake in Alabama to stay away from, was suddenly offering the most exciting new freshwater fishery in the state.

The deep, clear, cool, infertile water found in Smith Lake is a natural for the implanted saltwater striped bass. The deep standing timber also provides the type structure the fish needs to thrive.

Interestingly enough, although Smith Lake was probably the most natural location for the saltwater striped bass, it was the last Alabama lake to receive the fish. And for good reason.

The state kept the lake free of stripes and hybrids until 1983 as the basis for an experiment. While other reservoirs in the state were receiving the Atlantic Coast strain of striped bass, Smith Lake was stocked with the Gulf Coast strain of striped bass starting in 1983. The rapid-growing Gulf Coast strain was believed to be more tolerant of warm water and how it fared in Smith Lake would be a factor in the fish being introduced into other state lakes.

Lake Martin was a thriving striped bass fishery in 1987, but it didn't take long for Smith Lake to steal that thunder. By the summer of 1989, guides Dale Welch, Joe Traywick, Bill Vines and Bruce Holcombe (the two latter names well-known bass fishermen) had unlocked the secrets of fishing for the stripes and 15-pound to 20-pound fish were almost a daily occurrence.

Other fishermen began to bank on the practices these guides utilized and soon their techniques were common knowledge. Striped bass fishing on Smith Lake was off and running.

The introduction of the striped bass into Smith Lake meant many pluses for the lake. No. 1, it meant a new fishery for those lived in the vicinity. Smith Lake is full of bass, but the deep, clear water means tough bass fishing for most people not accustomed to that type of fishing.

No. 2, it meant an ecomomic plus for the Cullman area and the stores and marinas on the lake. Stripe fishing began to bring in a wave of new fishermen who had traditionally avoided the lake.

No. 3, and probably most importantly, it meant a boon to bass fishing. Not only did stripe fishing take some pressure off the bass, the striped bass themselves were a help. The tremendously large (too large for bass to eat) shad suddenly disappeared and fishermen were suddenly discovering the largest schools of small shad they had ever seen on the lake.

Biologists attributed this to the demise of the large, sickly shad that were in no condition to reproduce. The smaller, healthy shad that remained were suddenly back in the reproduction game.

Many bass fishermen cried foul over the introduction of the striped bass into the lake saying they were eating the bass, but the facts were that in 1989 it took more pounds to win a Smith Lake bass tournament than it had in the 10 years previous.

Catching Smith Lake's striped bass is either easy or difficult, depending on how you look at it. If you understand stripe fishing and have the right equipment, it can be a snap. If you're taking up stripe fishing from scratch, you may find it difficult.

Ideally, the stripe fisherman will have (1) a bait tank designed to keep shad alive, (2) numerous (up to six) stiff backboned rods with limber tips, (3) a wide-spooled reel with a clicker, (4) a boat with rod holders and (5) a graph depth recorder to locate fish. Those items make for a perfect setup, but stripe can be caught with other setups.

Stripe bass fishing on the lake is almost entirely done with live bait, so a live bait tank of some type is important. Some have had luck in keeping shad alive in boat live wells and in foam coolers, but the most successful fishermen are the ones who have bait tanks. These tanks can vary from a custom-made $400 rig, to a plastic drum with the top cut off.

Tanks should always be round (shad will pile up in a corner of a square tank and smother) and they should be white to reflect heat. An aerator is important, and a filter to remove scales and slime is nice if you keep the shad for a long day of fishing.

Another key consideration is the rod and reel. A custom-made striper rod is nice, but a bass rod with strong backbone (a flippin' stick, for example) will suffice. On the rod itself, measure 24 inches from the front of the reel to the front of the rod and mark this spot with a pice of white tape wrapped around the rod. You'll read later why this is important.

A wide-spool Ambassadeur with a clicker is the reel of choice of the better fishermen, but again, other reels will work. A baitcaster with the drag set lightly will do.

Because of the clear water, relatively light line (15 lb. to 20 lb. test) is needed. That may sound light for a 20-pound-plus fish, but almost every fish is caught in open water and landing one on a well-set drag isn't that difficult. (During the 1989 Hungry Fisherman tournament, one 25-pound striped bass was hooked and landed on 4-pound test line.)

A 4-foot leader of the same line is needed, as is a strong swivel, a 1-ounce or larger weight and a orange bead. Hooks vary between fishermen, but a 4/0 is probably the average.

Rig your outfit by placing a 1-ounce worm weight on the main line. Put the bead on next and then tie on the swivel. The bead keeps the worm weight from cutting the knot.

Tie on the leader and the hook next and you're ready to fish.

Shad can be hooked in several ways, but in one nostril and out the next works best. Another popular method is placing the hook through the throat and out the mouth, but a shad hooked in this manner doesn't live as long as one hooked through the nostrils.

Stripe need to be located with a depthfinder. When they are located, lower your bait right on top of them. This can be done by counting out line using the 24-inch mark you made on your rod. If the fish are 30 feet deep, for instance, subtract the 4-foot leader and pull your line out of the reel to the mark 13 times (26 feet) that will put your bait exactly at the 30-foot level.

If the stripe are shallow (20 feet or less) and they will be in the spring and fall, the presence of the boat will often spook the fish. This can be avoided by balloon fishing. In balloon fishing, you rig the same way except you tie a balloon (blown up to the size of a baseball) on to your line. Tie it the distance of the fish above the hook. (If the fish are 20 feet deep, tie it 20 feet above the hook). Allow the balloon to drift away from the boat and this will greatly increase your chance of hookups.

Another method the better stripe fishermen use in spring and fall is using at least one free line. A free line is nothing more than a hook tied to a main line with no other terminal tackle involved. The free line is let out 30 feet or more with the shad allowed to swim free. This is a good method if the stripe are staying deep and occasionally coming up to feed. This free-swimming shad may range from 30 feet of water to five feet and offers an enticing meal.

Another pattern that offers tremendously exciting fishing in the spring and fall is fishing a Redfin. This 1-foot-long artificial bait is deadly on stripes that feed on topwater and hell hath no fury like a 28-pound stripe exploding on a topwater bait.

Many of the lake's top guides keep a Redfin tied on a rod at all times and are ready to strike when the fish suddenly start hitting topwater. The striped bass in Smith Lake, like all striped bass, travel great distances and knowing where to look for them is important. The fish spend most of their lives in the deep water areas directly above the dam, but spring and fall will find them on the move.

During spring months, the stripe attempt to spawn even though it is impossible for them to do so. They will make long spawning runs as far as the shallow water in the back of Ryan Creek. The spring months will find these fish scattered throughout the shallow-water creeks all over the lake.

It should be noted that because striped bass are relatively new to the lake, the knowledge of their movements and whereabouts is limited.

Also, Smith Lake's deep water makes it very difficult to catch shad from the lake. By the summer of 1989, only two locations at the lake – Speegle's Marina and Big Bridge Marina – sold shad commercially. As a result, almost all stripe fishing originated out of those two marinas and the eastern end of the lake received almost all of the fishing pressure.

Biologists are convinced the Jasper side of the lake holds as good or better fish, but the lack of available shad forces a 20-mile or more run by river. The abundance of fish on the lake's eastern side just hasn't made this necessary yet.

The hump directly out of the mouth of Speegle's Slough, the shallow flats around Goat Island, Burr's Island and Miller's Flats and other relatively shallow water in the area have traditionally held the most spring fish. The fall months will see some fish make a less pronounced run to the same shallow-water areas.

During the hot summer months and the cold winter months, the deep water within five miles of the dam is where you're most likely to find the most fish. The rocky points in the lower end of Ryan Creek, the intersections of smaller creeks and Ryan Creek (such as Coon Creek and Lick Creek), the mouth of Rock Creek, the deep-water piers in Rock Creek and a host of other areas hold summer fish.

Smith Lake's best fishing spots

1. Upper end of Ryan Creek. Good colored water, stump rows, rocks. Good flippin' area spring and fall bass.

2. Southeast bank of Ryan Creek. Excellent night fishing for bass. May to July.

3. Goat Island. Good spinnerbait fishing in spring. Trophy spotted bass area.

4. Speegle's Slough, also known as Brushy Creek. Back end good for spinnerbait fishing for bass in spring. Excellent spring fishing area for crappie. Lots of brush.

5. Bailey Holler. Excellent crankbait fishing in February. Hungry Fisherman tournament won here on crankbait in February, 1988.

6. Upper end, Simpson Creek. Bass move here earlier in spring than any other location. Start with crankbaits early February, move to spinnerbaits early March.

7. Rocky bank between Calvert's Marina and Misty Harbor Marina. Good night fishing for bass in fall.

8. Cuts on north bank of Simpson Creek. Late spring spinnerbait area.

9. Miller's Flats. Good stripe fishing area. Fish school in this area much of year.

10. North slough, Miller's Flats. Spring fishing. Good spawning area for bass, crappie.

11. Northeast slough. Excellent schooling area for bass and stripe.

12. Mouth of Miller's Flats to castle. Good stripe fishing, summer months. Big stripe school at either end of wider water.

13. Adjacent to Calvert Island. Night fishing in hot summer months. Spinnerbaits.

14. Calvert's Slough. Spring, summer bass fishing. All bank fishing at night. Good schooling for bass and stripe.

15. Pigeon Roost Creek. Lot of rocks. Good summer bank fishing for bass. Night fishing.

16. Castle Rock area. Good stripe fishing area at night during summer months. Live shad.

17. Big Bridge. All columns will hold spotted bass or stripe at times.

18. East bank of Ryan Creek. Holds bass only in late spring. Fish rocky bluffs with buzzbaits and spinnerbaits. You'll find 315 feet of water here. Bass and stripe schooling area.

19. Back end of Willoughby Creek. Early spring fishing. Big rains dump lots of water into feeder creeks. Spots and largemouth school in mouths following big rains.

20. Coon Creek. Same as No. 19.

21. Good, rocky points. Standing bluffs. Winter fishing with light line and grubs, jigs.

22. Upper end Spring branch. Good run-in fishing where spring rains enter from feed creeks. Stripe school here in fall.

23. Lick Creek. Good run-in fishing in early spring with buzzbaits and spinnerbaits. Stripe school in the mouth of creek in the fall.

24. L.M. Smith Dam. Good stripe area in summer.

25. Feeder creeks on northeast bank. Late fall and winter bass schooling area. Lots of open water. Stripe school here in winter.

26. Mouth of Rock Creek. Big spot area in early summer with spinnerbait and jig. Bass and stripe school on up in creek.

27. Mouth of Little Crooked Creek. Good spot schooling area.

28. East Sipsey Fork. Good bass fishing year round from Little Crooked Creek to Bailey's. Points and a few ledges. Jig and pig February to March, good night fishing until fall with spinnerbait.

29. Mouths of White Oak and Crooked Creek, Bailey Bridge. Good year round fishing for crappie.

30. Crappie holes. Good spawning flats and brush.

31. Clay points in White Oak Creek. Good bass fishing with crankbaits in March. Also good spring spawning area for crappie.

32. Rock Creek. Good year round creek. Deep water for winter fishing with jig-and-pig. Good spring with spinnerbaits and crankbaits.

33. Underwater timber.

34. Underwater island.

35. Underwater island.

36. Dismal Creek. Trophy spot area mid-February to early spring. One of most underfished creeks in lake. Bass and stripe move from mouth of creek to upper end during spawn.

37. Deep water (225 feet) area from mouth of Dismal Creek to Duncan Bridge. A few points, a few ledges. Good night summer fishing for bass.

38. Bridge pilings, Duncan Bridge; try around pilings year round.

39. Schooling area for bass and stripe summer and fall.

40. Underwater island.

41. Clear Creek. Logjams and blowdowns in mouths of pockets. Buzzbaits and spinnerbaits in April and May.

42. Underwater timber in Butler Branch. Spring crappie.

43. Underwater island. Good schooling area for bass, stripes in schooling months.

44. Bluffs. Good fall fishing with buzzbaits and spinnerbaits.

45. Mouth of Big Bear and Little Bear Creek. Good night fishing in summer. Spinnerbaits, jig-and-pig.

46. Mouth of Brushy Creek. Good for a small bass or two at any time with spinnerbait of jig-and-pig.

47. Brushy Creek. Good year round. Spinnerbaits or flippin' early in year, buzzbaits early spring. Lots of willow bushes in area. Good crappie fishing.

48. Upper end Brushy Creek. Good fall of the year with spinnerbaits.

49. Yellow Creek. Flat creek with very little structure. Good early spring with spinnerbaits.

50. River points. Good at night in summer with worms or jig-and-pig.

51. Hoghouse Creek. Good fishing early spring with crankbaits and jig-and-pig.

52. Rockhouse Creek. Few fish, but an occasional big bass in late spring.

53. Sipsey River above Houston Recreation Area. Best crappie fishing on lake in spring. Blowdowns and treetops coming off banks.

Smith Lake

Ryan Creek above Big Bridge

Sipsey River

53

Rock House
Creek

50

49

52

Brushy
Creek

Hoghouse
Creek

47

51

Yellow Creek
Camp

Stear Branch

Big Bear Br.

45

46

Canup Branch

Little Bear Branch

43

42

41

Smith
Lake

44

Butler Branch

40

39

Coon
Creek

Devil's
Branch

Clear Creek

41

Clear
Creek
Marina

Huey's Marina

38

257

Duncan
Bridge

Above Duncan Bridge

Bankhead Reservoir

L ooking at the map, you may think the Bankhead Reservoir is nothing more than a stretch of river, but it has a lot of wide water off the original river channel. This wide, shallow water is full of structure that includes grass, brush, and blowdown timber.

The angler who has a particular pattern he likes to fish can find the type water in which to fish it in this lake.

Spring bass fishing

BELOW HOWTON'S CAMP

Much of the water on this reservoir's lower end is deep and clear, thus spring bass fishing is limited.

The bass, both spots and largemouth, begin their year deep in the main river channel, but begin stair-stepping themselves up on structure on the way to shallow water. Points are the main route for this migration.

Light line and small baits are the key to having any success on this end of the lake during the move. Tube-

type crappie jigs, deer hair jigs, 4-inch plastic grubs or 4-inch plastic worms are the best bait for this finesse fishing. Six- or 8-pound test line is needed.

The baits should be cast shallow, then gingerly hopped down into deeper water.

This pattern catches the majority of fish, but not the bigger ones. The bigger fish are usually taken by fishing a jig-and-pig in the brushtops just inside the main pockets. Keep in mind that northeast banks receive the most sunlight and heat the quickest. A water surface temperature gauge is critical.

For those wanting to fish for spotted bass, the deep river bluffs will hold the majority of them at this time. The spots school at this time and a limit of keeper-size fish is possible.

When spawning time arrives, the bass move into shallow water in the creeks and pockets. Spinnerbaits are impossible to beat at this time. A 1/4-ounce, lime-colored spinnerbait with a single No. 4 or No. 5 gold willowleaf blade is best. These spawning bass will gather in flat pockets amid blowdown timber to build their beds and spawn, and the spinnerbait works well there.

Topwater baits also will work where the brush and trash aren't too thick. Either a black/ gold Bang-O-Lure or a similarly colored jerk bait should be used.

These spring fish are spooky because of the clear, shallow water. An angler needs to back off and make long casts with a spinning outfit.

Yellow Creek is full of shallow cover that is excellent for spawning. It has a good water flow and lots of flow off the creek. Friley's Creek is much the same way. Both of these creeks are areas to concentrate on. Walker County Shoal Creek has lily pads and grass in the back which holds some good fish. White Oak Creek is much like Walker County Shoal Creek. Shoal Creek and Camp Creek offer only fair spring fishing. Short Creek has plenty of shallow water structure that holds spawning bass.

Many of the post-spawn bass will stay shallow in grass in four feet of water throughout the summer. A Red's Leapin' Lizard in plum or June bug colors flipped into the grass works wonderfully.

ABOVE HOWTON'S CAMP

The water above Howton's Camp is shallower and dingier than the water on the lower end of the lake. This allows the angler to fish patterns that take much less finesse. Most creeks off the main lake on this end are shallow and full of grass or lily pads. This makes for excellent spring fishing which most anglers find easy.

The bass start off deep in the channel, then in mid- or late-

Bankhead Reservoir Fact Sheet

Location, length, acreage

Bankhead Reservoir, better known to fishermen as the Warrior River, is in Tuscaloosa, Jefferson, Walker and Cullman counties. The 9,200-acre reservoir is sandwiched between Holt Reservoir to the south and Smith Lake to the North. The popular fishing lake begins at Bankhead Lock and Dam near Northport in Tuscaloosa County and stretches 77.8 miles to Lewis Smith Dam in Walker and Cullman counties. A total of 3,969 square miles drain into the reservoir.

Impoundment

The John Hollis Bankhead Lock and Dam was completed for navigation and flood control in 1916. Spillway rehabilitation was completed in 1970 with lock work completed in 1970 and 1975. On July 12, 1963, Alabama Power Co. completed power production facilities.

John Hollis Bankhead Dam

The John Hollis Lock and Dam was built for navigation and flood control by the U.S. Army Corps of Engineers in 1916, but it wasn't until 1963 that Alabama Power placed power production facilities at the dam. The Bankhead Hydroelectric Project is owned by Alabama Power while the dam and lock chamber are owned by the U.S. Government and operated by the Army Corps of Engineers.

The dam has a single hydraulic turbine and a single alternating current generator capable of producing 160 million kilowatt-hours of electricity annually.

Stocking history

Florida strain largemouth	
1981-87	50,720
1988	36,800
1989	15,500
1990	18,400
1991	18,400
1992	18,400
1993	18,400
1994	18,400

Hybrid bass	
1987-88	73,200
1989	8,400
1990	18,400
1991	18,400
1992	18,400
1993	18,400
1994	92,400

Lake configuration

The Bankhead Reservoir is river-like with no real wide pools, but does have many wide ledges and wide creeks.

Major and secondary creeks

Big Yellow Creek, Shoal Creek, Camp Creek, Little Camp Creek, Little Shoal Creek, White Oak Creek, Walker County Shoal Creek, Short Creek, Hurricane Creek, Valley Creek and Friley's Creek are all major water suppliers on the lower end of the Bankhead Reservoir below the largest water supplier, the Locust Fork of the Black Warrior River. Prescott Creek and Short Creek feed the Locust Fork.

Above the Locust Fork-Black Warrior River intersection, White Branch, Bluff Creek, Lost Creek, Baker Creek and Mosquito Creek are water suppliers.

Types of fish

The Bankhead Reservoir has a wide array of fish swimming in its waters. Spotted bass, largemouth bass, striped bass, white and black crappie, white bass, bluegills, redear sunfish, green sunfish, longear sunfish, redeye bass, rock bass and warmouth are the most popular game fish caught there. Channel catfish and flathead catfish also are present. Rough fish include freshwater drum, carp, spotted gar, longnose gar and redhorse suckers. The lake has a good supply of threadfin, gizzard shad, and minnows.

February begin their move toward the pockets and creeks. Points are their primary migration routes. A jig-and-pig or a single-bladed spinnerbait slow-rolled here is needed to catch these cold fish.

Once the bass are in shallow water, they begin seeking cover. Many anglers make the mistake of thinking bass want thick cover to spawn in, but that isn't the case. The bass need sunlight to penetrate the weeds to warm the water and hatch their eggs. That's why small isolated patches of grass or lily pads on this end hold more spring bass than thick patches. Thick, matted grass won't usually hold bass until after the spawn.

Try Rats, frogs, spinnerbaits, buzzbaits and jig-and-pigs in grass.

When the bass move onto the points Bluff Creek is a key spring area to focus. The logjams in the mouth hold fish coming and going from the creek. The brush and wood up in the creek hold spawning bass. Lost Creek is excellent and good anglers can usually catch a limit of fish in there in an hour or less in the spring.

Another area to concentrate on in spring is the section of river that stretches for at least a mile below the steam plant at Gorgas. There is always a radical change in water temperature below the steam plant and the bass gather there in numbers.

It, too, is a key area. The blowdowns along both banks hold fish. Kisner Slough, Miller's Slough and Richardson Slough all have fair spring fishing.

The little river area lacks the shallow water and pockets needed for good spring fishing and most good anglers stay out of it during the early part of the year.

Hot weather
bass fishing

BELOW HOWTON'S CAMP

Because of the deeper water, the lower end of the Bankhead Reservoir offers relatively good summer bass fishing. The mouths of the creeks, the rock-pile points and the sheer rock bluffs hold the majority of these hot weather bass.

Grubs, worms, or crankbaits can catch bass in this area during the summer. If you choose to grub fish, a blue or black Getzit works well. Worm fishermen need a blue or black 6-inch worm, and crankbait fishermen need a Mann's 15-Plus or Bagley's DB3. Black on silver foil works well in the crankbaits.

It is possible to catch some topwater bass early in the morning or late in the evening. Most gather on the rocky points and will fall to Jumping Minnows, Pop-R's, Nip-I-Didees, etc.

The mouths of the three pockets on the left side of the bank above the dam offer good summer fishing, as does the mouth of Yellow Creek and all the rocky points with cedar trees growing on them. Friley's Creek is excellent.

ABOVE HOWTON'S CAMP

This section of the lake can offer some good fishing during the spring months. The grass and lily pads in the area often grow in five or six feet of water and they put off oxygen, hold baitfish and offer shade. It's no secret these offerings attract bass. Summer fishing around this greenery is exciting, too. A 1/2 ounce white on white Lunker Lure with a white grub trailer works well in the grass, while spinnerbaits and jerk baits work on the fringes of the grass. It's also possible to flip this grass with a black jig-and-pig. Prescott Creek, which flows into the little river, and Lost Creek on the big river, are excellent areas for this type of fishing. Both creeks have good water depth, as well as a large amount of grass and lily pads.

Cool and cold weather fishing

BELOW HOWTON'S CAMP

By September, shad have started running heavily in the creeks and the bass move in in hot pursuit. Spinnerbaits are difficult to beat at this time. A double-bladed chartreuse/blue spinnerbait with a No. 3 gold in the front and a No. 5 gold in the back works best. Any grass-covered secondary point is likely to be holding bass at this time. The spinnerbait should be cast up to the bank and rolled slowly down the point.

Topwater prop baits work well in the fall, too. Nipi-I-Didees, Dalton Specials and Zara Spooks work good early and late and all day when there is a cloudy sky.

A 1/2-ounce lunker lure with a gold blade also works well. Yellow Creek, Walker County Shoal Creek and White Oak Creek are all good fall fishing areas. The mouth of Camp Creek with its grass-covered flats and blowdowns is also good.

ABOVE HOWTON'S CAMP

The fall fishing in this area is basically the same as in the area below it. Spinnerbaits fished in the pockets is the choice of the better fishermen, but Rat-L-Traps fished in the middle of schooling fish are good in that situation.

The blowdowns on the main river also will hold bass in the fall. Worms are excellent in this fallen wood.

Once winter arrives, the ledges off the mouth of creeks will hold large numbers of fish.

A black/blue jig-and-pig tipped with a No. 11 pork frog is the best bait for winter bass because it's slow and falls rapidly to the deep water where the fish are.

Bankhead Reservoir's best fishing spots

1 to 3. Excellent spring pocket. Mouth is excellent in early spring with grub or Getzit. Up in pockets for shallow-water during spawn.

4. Mouth of Yellow Creek. Good spring and fall staging area.

5. Deep water bend in Yellow Creek. Rocks hold lots of crawfish. Good jig fishing area. Brushtops out in water.

6. Tan Troff Branch. Good boathouses and piers with brush. Jigs and grubs in spring.

7. Shoal Creek. Excellent point. Good year round.

8. Camp Creek. Good blowdowns. Shallow water in back. Some spring bass.

9. White Oak Creek. Left fork has grass and blowdowns. Good in spring.

10. Walker County Shoals Creek. Good bluffs in mouth. Grubs in mouth in winter.

11. Back of creek. Lots of grass, lily pads. Good spawning area.

12. Hurricane Creek. Tremendous number of piers and boat docks. Jig-and-pigs in brush year round. High banks block out wind on windy days.

13. Short Creek. Full of pine and hardwood blowdowns. Grass for 200 yards on right bank going in. Excellent spinnerbait and flippin' area. Both deep and shallow water.

14. Friley's Creek. Lots of flats. Right bank has lily pads, grass on weeds all the way to back. Good in spring, early summer and fall.

15. Mouth of Friley's Creek. Good year round.

16. Coal Bed Creek. Narrow creek with deep water with grass and blowdowns both sides. Good topwater fishing under overhanging bushes. Good fishing year round.

17. Good pocket. Deep water with blowdowns. Limited grass. Logjams in mouth. Good year round.

18. Islands. Often passed up. Good grass. Good fishing on all sides of islands.

19. Prescott Creek. Good spawning area. Left bank good pockets with blowdowns and grass.

20. Good bay. Warms good in early spring. Weeds, lily pads, blowdowns and boat docks. Sleeper hole.

21. Big bend in little river. Good island. Heavy cover and rocks in deep water. Good year round.

22. Pocket in bend of river. Good water depth. Good year-round fishing.

23. White Branch. Mouth has grass on both sides. Good spring fishing with jigs and spinnerbaits.

24. Back of White Branch. Good crankbait area in spring. Flat of lily pads in back. Back pond warms up early in spring.

25. Mouth of Bluff Creek. Good brush pile in mouth with weeds on right side. Excellent in dead of winter. Good worm or jig-and-pig.

26. Piers and boat docks in Bluff Creek. Good brush around them.

27 to 30. Excellent pocket. Spring spawning area. Shallow water with grass.

31. Mouth of Richardson Slough. Right bank has two good pockets just inside mouth. Good spring fishing in grass.

32. High bank in Richardson Slough. Deep water. Overhanging bushes. Good topwater fishing.

33. Large grass and lily pad patch on left bank of Lost Creek. Big fish area.

34. Pockets with grass below steam plant. Good area for big fish in early spring and in dead of winter.

35. Steam plant. Area just below discharge good year round with crankbait.

Bankhead Reservoir

Bankhead Dam to Little Shoal Creek

Bankhead Reservoir

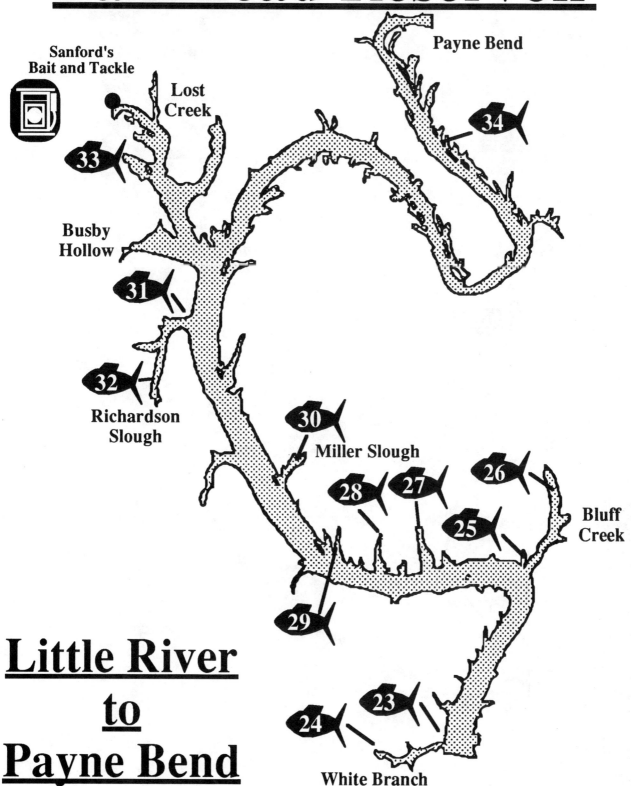

Sanford's
Bait and Tackle

Lost
Creek

Payne Bend

34

33

Busby
Hollow

31

32

Richardson
Slough

30

Miller Slough

28 27 26

25

Bluff
Creek

29

Little River
to
Payne Bend

24 23

White Branch

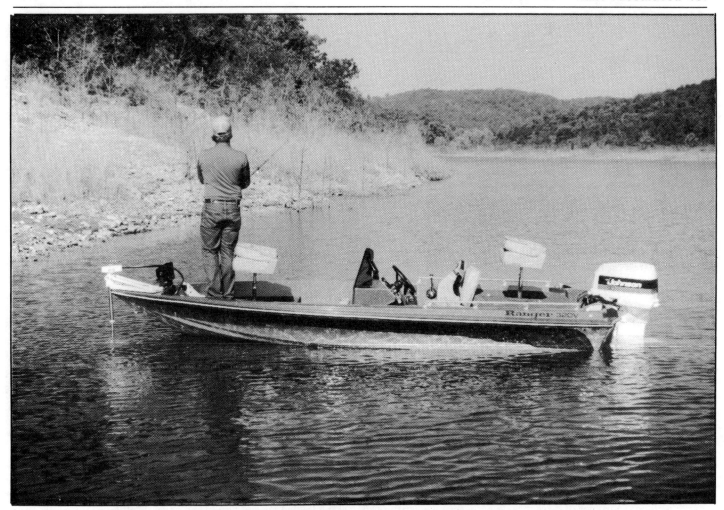

Lake Tuscaloosa

I f you were rating Alabama's lakes in terms of ease in catching bass, Lake Tuscaloosa would end up near the bottom with other deep, clear lakes such as Smith Lake and Inland Lake.

To make matters worse, Lake Tuscaloosa is almost void of structure; it lacks waterflow almost year-round and has a severely depleted shad population.

But never doubt the lake has bass in it. That was proven in June of 1989 when the Bass Anglers Sportsman Society (BASS) brought its federation national championship to the lake. Extremely good catches during the three-day tournament opened the eyes of a lot of anglers who had traditionally ignored the lake.

The problem with Lake Tuscaloosa is the fishermen rather than the fish. Fishing deep, clear, structureless water is something most anglers are not accustomed to and after a few unsuccessful trys, most give up and go elsewhere.

The result is a lake that receives little fishing pressure. That, coupled with deep, clear water computes into numbers of big fish. Those who have learned to properly fish the lake are more than glad

that most anglers think of it as a lake for waterskiing.

Spring bass fishing

SKELTON BEND TO BINION CREEK

Flat, wide, dingy water greets the angler fishing this end of Lake Tuscaloosa during the spring. Weed-filled creeks, stump-filled flats and islands dot the landscape. This area is as close as Lake Tuscaloosa anglers get to fishing a reservoir that resembles other reservoirs in the state.

Three creeks offer good spring fishing. Binion Creek offers relatively shallow, dingy water and is an excellent spring spawning area. It boasts a few weed-filled sloughs. Chartreuse/black spinnerbaits with a single gold willowleaf blade work well in the weed-filled sloughs, but medium-running, pearl-colored crankbaits and Carolina-rigged plastic lizards are needed for much of the rest of the creek.

Turkey Creek is a wide, shallow creek that offers weed beds on the

Lake Tuscaloosa Fact Sheet

Location, length, acreage

Lake Tuscaloosa is a 5,885-acre reservoir owned by the City of Tuscaloosa in Tuscaloosa County. It was formed by the backing up of North River. All of the timber was cut, piled up and burned before impoundment. The result is an ultra-clear reservoir void of structure. The reservoir stretches 27 nautical miles from Lake Tuscaloosa Dam to the small community of Samantha. The lake has 177 miles of shoreline and has a drainage area of 418 square miles. Both Tuscaloosa and Northport use the lake for their city water supply.

Lake Tuscaloosa Dam

Lake Tuscaloosa Dam is an earthern dam 1,280 feet in length. It has no generation facilities. It has a single concrete spillway.

Types of fish

Lake Tuscaloosa is stocked with Florida-strain largemouth bass, striped bass, hybrid bass, chain pickerel and walleye, and has a natural population of black bass, green sunfish, redear sunfish, bluegill, warmouth, longear sunfish, black and white crappie. Bullhead, channel and flathead catfish can be

Stocking history

Florida-strain largemouth	
1984-88	248,900
1989	58,900
1990	58,900
1993	6,124
1994	5,885

Striped bass	
1981	26,910
1984	33,600
1985	29,400

Hybrid bass	
1979	29,257
1980	1,013
1981	5,000
1982	60,100
1983	51,980
1984	30,000
1985	31,600

found, as can rough fish including carp, drum, spotted gar and longnose gar. Baitfish include threadfin shad, gizzard shad and skipjack herring, as well as numerous species of minnows and darters.

Impoundment

Construction began on Lake Tuscaloosa Dam in May 1967. Water first poured over the spillway in March 1970.

Configuration

North River was widened greatly by impoundment and fits the description of what most southern anglers consider a lake. It compares closely to Smith Lake in that hills and valleys were flooded by impoundment. The lake has an abundance of deep water. The lake's deepest point is 92 feet.

Major and secondary creeks

Besides North River, several creeks supply water to the lake. Binion Creek, Turkey Creek and Dry Creek are major water suppliers on the lake's upper end, while Carroll's Creek, Brush Creek and Clear Creek supply water to the lower end.

---

back side of Treasure Island, as well as weed beds in the back of the creek itself. Spinnerbaits and buzzbaits work well in the grass areas, as do plastic worms. Shallow-running crankbaits such as a Rapala work well on the fringes of these grass in early spring when the fish aren't yet buried in the grass.

Dry Creek, which can be found further north, is a shallow creek filled with grass beds throughout its length. The creek has excellent color in spring and offers excellent buzzbait fishing when the bass move shallow. This creek is home to a large largemouth bass population during the spring.

Once you go north of Dry Creek, you find nothing but the original run of North River, but the area can offer good spring fishing. This water is safe to navigate until you reach Skelton Bend. North of there, your boat motor's lower unit will discover rocks. The area above Skelton bend is littered with large boulders.

It's in this area you'll find is what is usually the lake's only moving, aerated water. Spinnerbaits, buzzbaits, Bang-O-Lures and floating worms are excellent spring baits here.

BINION CREEK TO CARROLL'S CREEK

The portion of the lake between Carroll's Creek and Alabama 43 bridge is much more spread out than portion of the lake below it. There's still plenty of 90-foot water in the main river channel, but this area offers plenty of flats and ledges around the banks, especially above Alabama 69.

Spring fishing is better than it is in the section of the lake below because of the shallow water and the fact this area will normally have some stain during the spring.

Deep diving crankbaits are good in February and early March as the bass begin staging out of the deep water and up the points and ledges. Plastic worms and jig-and-pigs can be effective.

During this time of the year, the bass will suspend in deep water along the ledges and points and occasionally race up on the flat to feed. Once the urge to spawn becomes strong, the fish will spend more and more time on the ledges.

Once the bass reach water 10 feet or less and stay there for long periods of time, spinnerbaits become the preferred bait. Many flats will be covered in dormant grass beds and this underwater cover offers excellent protection to baitfish and crawfish. A chartreuse spinnerbait with a willowleaf blade matched to the size of the bait and fished over the grass beds will produce the lake's best fishing of the year.

This section of the lake also boasts the lake's largest population of largemouth bass. This area has traditionally produced the lake's largest fish during spring months.

CARROLL'S CREEK TO LAKE TUSCALOOSA DAM

The lower end of Lake Tuscaloosa is the last place in the lake that takes on any color in the spring, that is if it does take on any color. It is not uncommon for this end of the lake to remain crystal clear year-round.

When the water surface temperature reaches 55 degrees, which is usually in late February or early March, the bass begin leaving their deep-water haunts and moving into shallow water in anticipation of the spawn. The spawn on this lake normally takes place from late March or early April through mid-May.

The bass begin their heavy feeding at this time, dining heavily on the distressed shad population, minnows, crawfish (their No. 1 food in this lake) and small sunfish.

Due to the lack of structure, the spring bass begin staging on the many points in the area. Keep in mind that bass in this lake are point-oriented year-round.

These bass are prone to backing off this time of the year at the slightest weather or sunlight change. They may be found on a shallow point one day, and suspended in schools 30 to 40 feet deep the next.

Spinnerbaits and buzzbaits aren't as effective on this end of the lake during spring months as you might expect. The bass want a slower topwater bait and the Bang-O-Lure fits perfectly. This lure thrown around shallow points and in shallow slough mouths this time of the year will usually produce fish.

On the days when the fish are backed off and suspended over deep water, trolling with Hellbenders and jigging with spoons is sometimes effective.

If your depth recorder shows schooling bass are staging 15 to 30 feet deep along the many stair-stepped ledges in early fall, a slow-moved worm or jig-and-pig can be effective.

When these bass actually go into the spawn, they do so in the extreme back of pockets and in creeks. Pockets with red clay or sand are best. Carroll Creek is one of the best creeks for spawning activity.

Hot weather
bass fishing

SKELTON BEND TO BINION CREEK

When the spawn is over and the water begins to heat rapidly, the days of finding fish with topwater baits end quickly. The bass leave the creeks and head for the cooler temperatures that can be found along the original North River channel.

Although the surface water may seem dead this time of the year, a slight water flow can often be detected in the original channel. Large spots and an occasional large striped bass can be caught by jigging spoons during the summer.

Night fishing is best during the summer as fish do sometimes move away from the channel toward shallow water. Deep-running crankbaits, spinnerbaits run along the bottom and jigging spoons are good baits for fish that you first mark with a recorder.

BINION CREEK TO CARROLL'S CREEK

Summer fishing is once again point-oriented, but anglers also have the advantage of being able to fish around boathouses and piers at night. These piers and boathouse boast excellent fishing because they offer a bit of structure in a structure-starved lake. Most boathouses and piers have Christmas trees and brushpiles around their perimeters.

If an angler is fishing during the day, he must plan to fish deep-diving crankbaits, worms or jigging spoons for fish suspended along the points and ledges. These fish can be anywhere from 20 to 50 feet deep.

The angler choosing to fish at night will find much better fishing, however. The bass will move into the areas around the boathouses and piers to feed on the baitfish and crawfish that find protection in the brushpiles. Worms, jigs-and-pigs and grubs are the top baits for night fishing.

From May to September 90 percent of the fishing takes place at night.

CARROLL'S CREEK
TO LAKE TUSCALOOSA DAM

Once the spawn is over, bass head back to the deep-water points and suspend themselves there until fall.

Deep-diving crankbaits are effective in May and June, but in July and August jigging spoons are needed because bass are commonly found 35 to 60 feet deep.

Night fishing is best during summer months. One, it is more bearable to the angler because he doesn't have to deal with the sun or mosquitoes. Two, the fish move to shallower water because they feed at night in summer months. Three, ultra-light line isn't needed because line is harder to see at night.

Spinnerbaits are excellent for night fishing. A black, double-bladed spinnerbait with a black pork frog works best. Position your boat in deep water and cast to the bank, and begin a retrieve just fast enough to make the blades spin. Using this method, the spinnerbait drops down along the bottom as it falls off.

A plastic worm can be fished in much the same way, but flureo-scent line and a black light are needed so the angler can keep tabs on his line.

Lake Tuscaloosa is an excellent lake for night boating since there is nothing in the open water for the boater to come in contact with.

Cool and cold weather
bass fishing

SKELTON BEND TO BINION CREEK

The cooling weather of September and October trigger bass to move toward shallow water to find baitfish and crawfish on which to gorge to store fat for the winter.

Crawfish or shad-colored, deep-running crankbaits, jig-and-pigs and worms can catch these fish after they are first located with a depth finder . The mouths of creeks and sloughs next to deep water tend to hold the fish better than other areas.

BINION CREEK TO CARROLL'S CREEK

Fall fishing is similar to fall fishing in the lower part of the lake, except this area occasionally gets some color due to heavy rains. When this water gets stained, fall fishing can be excellent by Lake Tuscaloosa standards.

When August passes and cooler temperatures begin to creep in, the bass will begin a gradual move to shallow water. Worms, deep-diving crankbaits and jig-and-pigs work well.

The wider expanses of water between the Alabama 69 and Alabama 43 bridges offer the best fall fishing. Boathouses, the mouths of sloughs and weedbeds next to deep water are typically the most productive areas.

When cold weather arrives, the fish move out on the ledges next to the natural river run and become hard to find. It's possible to find large schools of bass in 50 or 60 feet of water in December or January. A depth finder is needed to locate the fish.

Once they are located, jigging spoons or jig-and-pigs will sometimes take fish.

The strikes at that depth are gentle, so anglers must pay close attention.

CARROLL'S CREEK
TO LAKE TUSCALOOSA DAM

When fall arrives, bass abandon the super-deep water and move into shallower water, usually 15 feet or less. This shallow water holds a good supply of oxygen, which also attracts baitfish and crawfish.

Primary areas for fall bass include the areas around rock walls and in the rocky portions of creek mouths.

The spotted bass is the major bass species in the lake and spotted bass like rock bluffs.

The 4-inch plastic worm in transluscent colors such as watermelon, apple, pumpkin seed or salt and pepper, fished with 6-pound test line, makes a perfect fall combination.

Lake Tuscaloosa's best fishing spots

1. Weed-filled, shallow pocket next to Hagler Road Bridge. Excellent spawning area for largemouth and spots. Good spring fishing with topwater. Last slough deep enough to fish in as you head north.

2. Mouth of weed-filled slough. Excellent fishing in early spring and October and November. Worms or spinnerbaits.

3. Weed-filled slough. Treetops and brush on left bank. Good spring spawning for bass. Only slough large enough to fish in until you reach Dry Creek.

4. Mouth of slough. Excellent fishing in early spring and early fall.

5. Dry Creek. A solid weed bed.

6. Weed beds next to deep water.

7. Trash and brush piles in entrance to Dry Creek.

8. Weed beds is shallow water.

9. Island. Trash and weeds surround island.

10. Shallow pocket above Bull Slough Bridge. Man-made trash piles. Good fishing in spring and fall. Excellent spawning area.

11. Bull Slough Bridge. Man-made brush piles adjacent to main river channel. Main river channel cuts directly against west bank under bridge.

12. Sharp bend in original river channel. Excellent fishing in early fall.

13. Weed beds around front of Treasure Island.

14. Weed beds in back of Turkey Creek. Good spring spinnerbait fishing. Excellent spawning area.

15. Good sharp points and deep sloughs. Fishing good on points with worm in summer. Back of pockets filled with weeds. Good spring fishing.

16. Area between island and bank. Fish like a creek mouth. Area comes off banks shallow and fall directly into river channel.

17. Stump-filled shallow area on backside of island. Adjacent to deep water. Good spring fishing.

18. Underwater road bed. End of original road is used for boat ramp. Old bridge that crossed the river there was exploded and collapsed into water. Concrete and steel rubble still remains. Good night summer fishing with worm.

19. Alabama 43 Bridge. Riprap under bridge along both banks. Good fishing year round.

20. Good slough. Riprap from bridge area curves up into slough for good distance. Good weed beds and brush piles. Good in early spring and early fall.

21. Bridge. Good spring and fall fishing around pilings. Creek above bridge is shallow.

22. Underwater islands in upper end of Binion Creek. Dangerous area to navigate, but good spring fishing can be found between islands and cuts. Weed beds and brush piles around islands.

23. Backside of island east of main river channel. Adjacent to deep water. Good fall fishing.

24. Boathouses. Treetops and trash in shallow water next to original river channel. Excellent summer fishing at night.

25. Sharp River bend. Underwater island well-marked with buoys. Good in summer.

26. The Narrows. Good stretch with boathouses and piers. Trash and brush around those structures. Good year round.

27. Weed-filled slough. Excellent spawning area.

28. Tierce Patton Farm Road bridge. Riprap along east banks under the bridge. Pilings also hold fish.

29. Deep bank with trash along west bank. Good at night in summer and late fall.

30. Boathouses. Good brush piles off end of structures in deep water. Good summer fishing.

31. Deep slough. Excellent fishing year round.

32. Lary Lake Road bridge. Bridge is narrow, but slough widens past bridge. Good weedbeds and trash in back of slough.

33. Points along south bank. Good fishing year round.

34. Boathouses next to main channel. Lots of trash around structures.

35. Good weedbed-filled slough.

36. Excellent stretch of lake. Deepwater, trash, boathouses. Good year round.

37. Underwater road bed.

38. Horseshoe-shaped underwater dam. Located 100 yards off of north bank. Five to 10 yards wide. Located in 15 feet of water, but deep water nearby. Excellent summer fishing. Locate dam with depth finder and mark with buoys. Back off and fish with deep-running crankbaits or worms.

39. Beacon point. Weed-filled sloughs on both sides of point. Boathouses and islands, also. Excellent spring spawning areas. One of best fishing areas in the lake.

40. Excellents sloughs filled with boathouses and weeds. Adjacent to deep water.

41. Steep rock walls with trash and brush at base. Excellent

summer fishing at night. Adjacent to deep water.

42. Alabama 69 bridge. Riprap on both banks. Pilings hold fish year round.

43. Tierce's Slough. Long, deep, weedbed-filled slough. No boathouses. Good spot-holding area.

44. Boathouses and piers with brush.

45. Weedbed-filled sloughs. Also good points outside.

46. Good point. Early spring fishing. No trash or weeds, but good ledge.

47. Good, long-sloping point. Excellent summer fishing.

48. Good points for summer fishing.

49. Hamner Creek. Weedbeds and trash. Good points in mouth of creek. Good year round fishing.

50. Island. Good fishing around island in early spring.

51. Mayor's Point. Boathouses with brush. Excellent fishing in hot weather.

52. Carroll's Creek Island. Weedbeds on back side. Good spring fishing

53. Back of Carroll's Creek. Weedbeds and boathouses. Good spring spawning area.

54. Excellent point for year round fishing.

55. Underwater island. Located in 8 feet of water, but adjacent to 110 feet of water. Top of island filled with brush tops. Good year round.

56. Brush Creek. Lots of weed-filled pockets. Deep points.

57. Weed-filled pocket.

58. Weed-filled pocket.

59. Good point.

Lake Tuscaloosa

Skelton Bend to Binion Creek

Hagler Road Bridge

Binion Creek

Dry Creek

Treasure Island

Turkey Creek

1
2
3
4
5
6
7
8
9
10
11
12
13
14
15
16
17
18
19
20
21
22

43

Binion Creek to Carroll's Creek

Hamner Creek

Tierce Creek

Colson Marina

Lake
Tuscaloosa

Bob's Marina

Lake Tuscaloosa

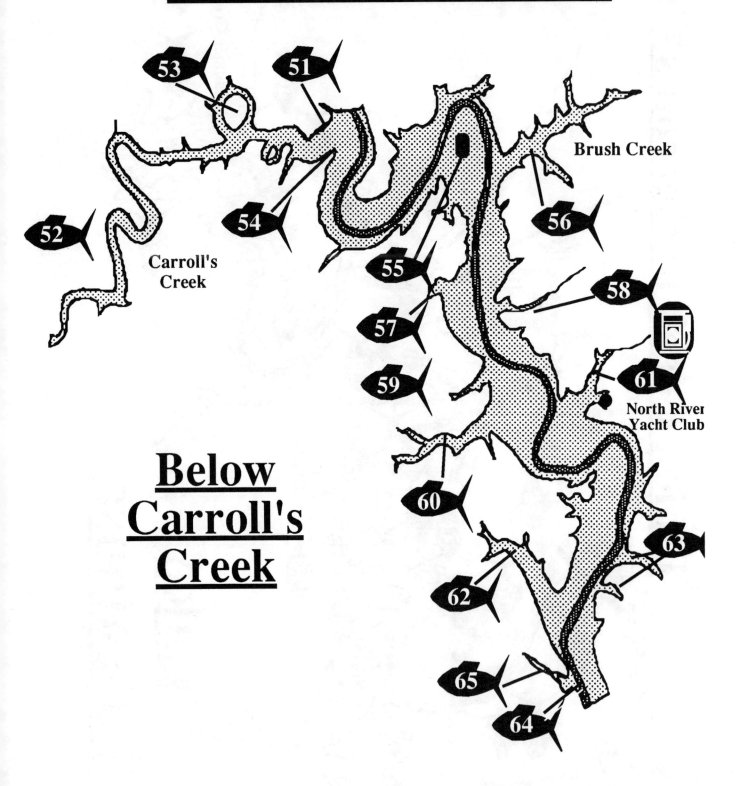

Brush Creek

Carroll's
Creek

North River
Yacht Club

Below
Carroll's
Creek

Lake West Point

Lake West Point lacks the vast structure that its downstream neighbor Lake Eufaula enjoys, but anglers who frequent the Chattahoochee River reservoir find the easy-to-locate roadbeds, rock piles and underwater bridges and trestles more to their liking.

The 16-inch size limit imposed on the lake years ago has resulted in an excellent bass fishery. According to the state's Bass Anglers Information Team annual report, Lake West Point annually ranks near the top of state lakes in the production of bass 5 pounds or larger.

It should be noted that only a small portion of the lake is in Alabama, and a non-resident Georgia fishing license is needed by Alabama anglers to fish most of the lake. An Alabama fishing license is honored only on the small portion of the lake west of the Rock Mill Road (Highway 109) Bridge.

So when you've got the licenses straight, this becomes a lake to enjoy.

Spring bass fishing

CHATTAHOOCHEE RIVER ABOVE HIGHLAND MARINA

The presence of excellent springtime fishing in nearby Yellowjacket Creek and further downstream in Wehadkee Creek makes bass fishing almost a wasted effort in this portion of Lake West Point.

The only exception to that rule is in early spring when the bass haven't gotten into the creeks and sloughs to spawn and heavy rains causes the release of large amounts of water upstream. The swift current resulting from the released water forces the bass to escape in the mouths of the numerous creeks, sloughs and pockets throughout

the upper end, with this being more pronounced the further you go upstream.

These creeks, pockets and sloughs will get muddy immediately after the heavy rains and fish will be impossible to catch, but several days of swift water will suck the muddy water out.

The shad and other baitfish will be forced into the pockets to escape the current, and the bass will follow. Brightly colored crankbaits (chartreuse or orange) work nicely in the mouths of these pockets when the water is dingy, but the color should be toned down all the way to white as the water clears.

Spinnerbaits with a pork chunk work nicely in the small pockets and logjams in the main river itself during this period.

YELLOWJACKET CREEK

For the angler who loves fishing visible structure in spring, Yellowjacket Creek is just what the doctor ordered.

The back end of the creek is full of grass and explosive topwater action is common there. There are numerous bridge pilings and acres of standing timber. Less visible, but easy to locate rock piles and deep points are also abundant.

Bass determined to spawn will start working their way up this creek sometimes as early as February. They don't have to travel far to find shallow pockets and sloughs in which to spawn, but many make a run as far back in the creek as they can go.

The area between the U.S. 27 bridge and Young Mill Road bridge is full of standing timber and is a spinnerbait fisherman's heaven. A 3/8-ounce spinnerbait with a chartreuse and black skirt and a nickel willow-leaf blade work in this shallow standing timber has won many tournaments.

The same pattern will also work in the standing timber in the north

Lake West Point Fact Sheet

Location, length, acreage

Lake West Point is a Army Corps of Engineers reservoir on the Chattahoochee River in East Central Alabama and West Central Georgia. Only a small portion of the lake's western boundary lies in Alabama, but Alabama fishermen routinely fish the entire lake. An Alabama fishing license is only good west of the Georgia 109 bridge.

The 25,900-acre reservoir stretches 147 nautical miles from West Point Dam in Troup County, Ga. to Buford Dam in Gwinnet County, Ga. The area above Franklin is run-of-the-river and not figured into the reservoir acreage. The reservoir drains 3,440 square miles and has 525 miles of shoreline. Full pool is 646.3 feet.

Lake West Point Dam

Lake West Point is impounded by an 896-foot-long concrete dam and spillway. The length of the dam, including earthern banks, is 7,250 feet. The dam has six spillway gates 50 feet by 41 feet each. The dam has 3 hydraulic turbines and 3 generators capable of producing 193 million Kilowatts of electricity annually.

Configuration

The Chattahoochee River overflowed its banks greatly when impounded by Lake West Point Dam. The ledges caused by this flooding are evident as far north

Stocking history

Hybrids

1984 87,800

Because the majority of Lake West Point is in Georgia, the Georgia Game and Fish Department does the majority of the lake's stocking.

as the Franklin community in the lake's upper reaches. The lake also has numerous creeks widened greatly by the impoundment.

Major and secondary creeks

Lake West Point is influenced by several large incoming creeks. Yellowjacket Creek in the lake's middle section is a major water supplier. It is fed by Beech Creek, Shoal Creek, Jackson Creek and numerous small, unnamed streams. Whitewater Creek and Thompson Creek are small water suppliers on the lake's west side above the Pyne Road Bridge. Wehadkee Creek is major water supplier on the west side and is fed by Caney Creek. Stroud Creek is a major creek and is fed by Finley Creek. Veasey Creek is a major creek and is fed by Gay Creek.

Impoundment

Construction began on West Point Dam in June 1966 and impoundment began in October 1974.

Types of fish

The lake features popular species such as largemouth bass, white bass, hybrid bass, and black crappie, channel catfish, blue catfish, longear sunfish, redbreast sunfish, dollar sunfish, redear sunfish and bluegill. A few spotted bass and white crappie may show up from time to time.

---

bank of Beech Creek, in the back of Beech Creek and in any of the grass beds throughout the creek. Buzzbaits and floating worms also work in the grass beds.

Flippin' in the grass beds and standing timber is also a good pattern in the early spring.

HIGHLAND MARINA
TO LAKE WEST POINT DAM

Unlike many Alabama reservoirs, the lower end of Lake West Point boasts enough deep water outside of the original river channel that bass don't find it necessary to suspend themselves in the channel itself to find water warm enough to tolerate.

It's not unusual to locate water 40 to 45-feet deep as much as 200 yards from the channel on the lake's lower half.

This means some adjustment to the normal patterns that many anglers use in early spring.

Anglers fishing the late-winter/early-spring pattern on most Alabama reservoirs traditionally fish the ledges next to the original river channel. The fish suspended in the channel in winter begin to make frequent trips to these ledges as the water warms and their appetites improves.

Should a fish leave the original channel on this end of Lake West Point, however, it is likely to still find itself in as much as 65 feet of water.

It's best to consider anything between the banks in this area the main river channel and pretend you don't know the original channel exists.

A multitude of long-running ridges, humps, road beds, old home foundations and even an old peach orchard can be found in water deep enough to satisfy bass during the cold winter months. It is these areas - not the main river channel - that the bass will begin leaving in the early spring.

A tremendous amount of easy-to-locate roadbeds (see map) lead directly from the main channel all the way up to the banks.

The route that automobiles once took to get to the river before the lake was impounded is now a natural roadway for bass (and other species) to migrate from deep water to shallow water during the spring.

In the late-winter/early-spring period, the better bass anglers first check the timber- and brush-lined humps, ridges and long-running islands with deep-running crankbaits and jig-and-pigs. The water is often dingy during this time, so a chartreuse or bright orange deep running crankbait like a Mann's 30-Plus or a Bagley's DB3 makes a good weapon. If you go the jig-and-pig route, try a black with brown pork frog or a chartreuse pork frog trailer.

Should these areas prove to be unsuccessful, and they probably will once the weather gets tolerable enough to fish, it is then you start fishing the bass's natural routes to more shallow water.

Rainbow Creek, Wehadkee Creek, Indian Creek, Maple Creek and many of the large shallow pockets and shallow sloughs have road beds leading directly from deep water right into their mouths. You don't have to be a rocket scientist to understand the significance of that.

An angler can use his depthfinder to locate these east-and-west running roadbeds and drop marker buoys along their length. He can then fish from deep to shallow water and back on these road beds to find the depth the bass are on any given day.

Deep-running crankbaits, spinnerbaits, jig-and-pigs and worms can be successful. A 3/8-ounce chartreuse or yellow-skirted spinnerbait with nickel blades will work better in dingy water, but don't hesitate to switch to a white bait with gold blades if the water is clear.

It should be noted that roadbeds aren't the only location to find moving spring bass, however. The lake's lower half is full of wide, long, sloping points that serve the same function as the roadbeds.

They can be fished with the same baits and with the same patterns as the road beds.

Buck bushes are something of a novelty particular to Lake West Point, but don't ignore their presence when spring is in full force and the bass have worked themselves up to shallow water. These bushes are normally out of the water, but good spring rains will put one and two feet of water around them.

Bass love the bushes as a means of structure. Buck bushes can be found on the river and up in the creeks and they can offer tremendous topwater action with buzzbaits. On the main river, the bushes are often the last stopping point before the bass move into the creeks with spawning on their minds.

WEHADKEE, STROUD AND VEASEY CREEKS

Easy-to-locate structure is a feature that make many bass anglers fish this area and this area only.

The back of Wehadkee Creek is full of standing timber and much of it is visible even in highwater conditions. There is standing timber in some pockets and sloughs off of Wehadkee Creek, including Caney Creek. There also are a few islands scattered throughout the length of Wehadkee.

Other fish-holding structure includes fallen timber, piers, roadbeds and underwater bridges. There are a limited amount of weed beds.

Bass begin moving into this area looking for spawning spots in early spring. The fish will move great distances, with many moving to the standing timber in the rear of Wehadkee Creek.

The standard springtime baits can be used to take these fish. A 3/8-ounce white sinnerbait with nickel blades is the best bet since the water is usually clear.

A spinnerbait fished around the timber and stumps can produce quality fish.

Floating worms, buzzbaits, Bang-O-Lures, Rapalas, plastic worms and a host of other baits can also be successful.

Before the fish get into the spawn good and after they come off, crankbaits fished on the points and around bridge pilings can produce fish.

Key areas to look for are include the Dewberry Access area in Wehadkee Creek (bridge pilings, an island, an underwater bridge, roadbeds and sloughs and pockets are in close proximity), the back of Wehadkee Creek (visible standing timber) and the Caney Creek area (an island, standing timber and a roadbed are close by).

An angler can find success in just about any area, however, if he applies what he knows about springtime bass fishing.

Hot weather bass fishing

CHATTAHOOCHEE RIVER ABOVE HIGHLAND MARINA

This end of Lake West Point is virtually run of the river with only a few flats and no real widening of the river. Almost all of the creeks and sloughs in this end are too shallow to fish during the months when water levels are low.

There is relatively good fishing in this section of the river during the summer months, with the odds greatly increasing whenever there is some water flow. The mouths of the creeks and the ledges adjacent to flats is the best bet for summer fishing, with a Prissy shad, a plastic worm or lizard rigged Carolina style or a medium-running crankbait the best bet to take the fish.

The mouths of sloughs and creeks found in the bend of the river hold the most bass. Bass will school on these bends during summer months.

Fishing at daybreak or at night is the best opportunity to catch these fish when the water is off.

YELLOWJACKET CREEK

Yellowjacket Creek is similar to most large creeks on Alabama reservoirs in that it will hold some bass year round. The relatively deep water found in the main channel of Yellowjacket Creek (45 feet deep a half mile into the creek), as well as relatively deep flats, tend to hold bass better than other such creeks however.

Boat houses, piers and docks can be found along the creek and some are in enough deep water to interest summer bass. The bass not only find shade there, but many docks have brushtops and Christmas trees around them which also attract baitfish. An electric red worm skipped under the piers will catch some of these fish.

Around bridge pilings in deep water, a spoon will also take some fish.

It is rare that you'll find the lake's better fishermen fishing this creek or any creek on the lake in summer, however. The lake's larger bass are enjoying the cool comfort of the deep, oxygenated water in the main river area.

HIGHLAND MARINA TO DAM

Even as late as the end of June and early July, you'll find a few post-spawn bass hanging around the mouths of all of the major creeks in Lake West Point's lower end.

These natural funnels for baitfish are in unusually deep water (55 feet in Maple, Bird and Wehadkee creeks, 45 feet in Wilson, Alligator and Rainbow creeks). These extreme water depths in the creek mouths allow the fish to tolerate a creek mouth this time of the year.

Shallow-running crankbaits fished on the secondary points in and around the mouths of these creeks can sometimes produce tremendous numbers of bass. Spinnerbaits can also be highly successful.

Don't doubt stories that some anglers catch good fish in these creeks year round. Deep-water piers and bridge pilings can produce bass during the hottest days of the summer and the coldest day of the winter, but these will usually be smaller fish than you'll find outside of the creeks.

Once hot weather arrives, most of the bass have begun their trek back out into the river. The road beds that the bass followed into these creeks are their highways back into deeper water.

Worms fished on top of and beside these roadbeds in water between 6 and 15 feet will catch good bass early in the summer. The roadbeds also offer excellent night fishing in late May and early June. Spinnerbaits slow rolled down the length of the roadbeds can be deadly.

Once the searing heat of late July and August arrives, the bass disappear from the roadbeds. They scatter to the deep, structure-covered mounds that parallel the main river channel and to the long, deep sloping points. Very few of these hot-weather bass will be found suspended in the original river channel.

WEHADKEE, STROUD AND VEASEY CREEKS

Whether you fish this area during the summer depends on whether you're playing or seriously trying to catch fish.

Relatively deep water (up to 35 feet) can be found in Wehadkee Creek, Veasey Creek and Stroud Creek and this water will hold some hot-weather fish. Smaller bass will find refuge under the deep-water piers and docks during the hottest part of the day, then slip into deeper water early and late. Other smaller bass will find refuge around the bridge pilings under numerous bridges.

A good rule of thumb is that you will not find the quality bass in these creeks during the hot summer months, however. The better fish will have exited the creeks and taken up residence on the deep humps, islands and ledges.

Cool and cold weather bass fishing

CHATTAHOOCHEE RIVER
ABOVE HIGHLAND MARINA

Although this upper end isn't the best spot to find fall bass, whenever there's enough rainfall to allow a boat into the sloughs that have timber or stumps, flippin' can produce some fish.

Wolf Creek and New River Creek both are filled with timber relatively close to their mouths and these areas hold bass in the fall. A black jig-and-pig with a brown frog pork chunk, 20-pound line and a flippin' stick is all that is needed.

HIGHLAND MARINA TO DAM

Once the state gets a break from the unmercifully hot weather of August, the gradual cooling of the water in the lower end of Lake West Point sends bass to more shallow water. The anticipation of a long winter will send these fish into a feeding frenzy to fatten up. The fishing can be terrific.

These bass will slowly move from their deep-water haunts via the same routes they used to find shallow water in the spring: the many roadbeds and long, sloping points.

These bass won't seek out the same shallow-water spots, however, and actually the water they'll eventually settle into isn't shallow by spring standards.

These fall bass may make and occasional foray into 2 to 5 feet of water, (they've been known to even move into grass on the rare occasions the water is up that high), but finding fish at that depth isn't something an angler can count on.

These fall bass will settle onto the ridges in water 10 to 15 feet deep and hang close to rocks, stumps and fallen timber that offer both structure and an ample supply of food.

The ledges can be located with the use of a depthfinder and a good topographic map. The map produced by Atlantic Mapping Company is an excellent map of the lake and these ledges can be located easily.

The maps are available at most tackle shops in the area, or by writing Atlantic Mapping Co., P.O. Box 7391, Marietta, Ga., 30065 or by calling (404) 426-5768.

An angler should locate the ledges on the map, then pinpoint them with his depthfinder. The ledges should be traveled slowly until fish are marked. Marker buoys help pinpoint the ledges holding fish.

Several lures can take the fish. Crankbaits, worms, jig-and-pigs or Prissy Shads can be successful.

The bass' venture into more shallow water is short-lived, however. Once the water temperature begins to drop into the mid-50's and lower, the bass move to the deep-water humps, islands and off the end of some of the points that have dropoffs.

Slow-moving lipped or lipless crankbaits can take these fish, but a jig-and-pig or spoon is your best bet. Locate the areas that have standing timber and you'll find cold-weather fish.

YELLOWJACKET CREEK

If you ask a tournament fisherman if bass can be caught in this area during the cool and cold-weather months, his answer will likely be a strong "no." The 16-inch fish he needs to weigh in during a tournament is a tough creature to locate here this time of the year.

Fall fish will make a move in this direction, however, and can often be found in the mouth of the creek as far up as Cameron Mill Road bridge. The deep water found here along with access to shallow water ledges makes this a natural spot for actively-feeding fish to corner some shad.

WEHADKEE, STROUD AND VEASEY CREEKS

Fall and winter fishing here is much the same situation as summer fishing there. It's possible you'll catch some bass, but these bass are generally going to be yearlings under 2 pounds. The larger fish are hanging in the deep water out on the main river.

The only exception to this is in the fall when the bass move into the mouth of Wehadkee Creek. These fall bass – and these are often quality bass – gather along the secondary points inside the creek mouth and are prime candidates for crankbaits, worms and jig-and-pigs.

The road bed (see map) running across the mouth of the creek starts in 15 feet of water on the north bank and runs southward as deep as 50 feet and back up to 5 feet of water on the south bank. You're likely to find fish at some depth somewhere on this roadbed during this time.

This roadbed holds quality fish in fall and early spring, and some fish are taken off of it year round. Plan to use a jig-and-pig or spoon here during the fall and early winter.

Other types of fishing

HYBRID FISHING

In a lake where a largemouth bass must be 16 inches long before taking it home to the frying pan, the annual introduction of 20 hybrid bass per acre in West Point Lake is good news for meat fishermen.

But never doubt that those who fish for sport haven't been well pleased. Less than 10 years ago, only one angler in 10 who used a guide requested to fish for hybrid bass, but many guides on the lake have witnessed a reversal.

The evolution of West Point Lake into the top hybrid lake in the Southeast and a lake where 7-pounders are common is undoubtedly behind that change.

The hard-fighting cross between the female saltwater stripe bass and the male white bass have a dual pattern in the spring months. A number of hybrids feel the urge to spawn, even though it's impossible for them to do so. These fish make a false spawning run upriver and end up at the head of the lake near Franklin. Anglers generally leave the fish alone.

Beginning approximately April 1, the remainder of those spring hybrids begin suspending themselves over the standing timber above West Point Dam. These fish will be in 30 to 35 feet of water, but once a school of baitfish enters the area, the hybrids will rush to 12 to 15 feet of water to feed. These feeding fish must be marked with a depthfinder and by pinpointing them by lining up spots on the bank.

Bucktail jigs, Rat-L-Traps, Little Georges or a Mann's Mann-O-Lure will take the feeding fish. The angler should throw well past the school and retrieve the lure back to the boat with a hopping motion.

Once summer arrives, the hybrids move from standing timber and position themselves over underwater islands, sandbars and roadbeds in 15 to 25 feet of water.

The fish will lie dormant and refuse to take a bait until current is moving. The moving of water through West Point Dam triggers the fish into a feeding spell and bucktail jigs, jigging spoons, deep-diving crankbaits and live shad can catch them.

Fall and early winter is a transistion period for the hybrids and fishing is generally poor, but a sudden drop in barometric pressure will send the schooling fish hitting topwater all across the lake's lower third.

Crazy Shad, Bang-O-Lures and other topwater jerk baits will catch these fish, while a Little George or jigging spoon kept in the boat on another rod can catch fish when they submerge.

Lake West Point's best fishing spots

1. Excellent fall fishing ledge. Deep drop into standing timber. Worms or jig-and-pig.

2. Small underwater island in main river channel. Good spot for schooling bass and hybrids in summer. Lots of brush on top.

3. Excellent flat in bend of river. Lots of standing timber.

4. Mouth of Fish Creek. Points on both corners.

5. Excellent point for bass in late spring, summer or fall when water is moving.

6. Whitley Road Bridge pilings. Fifteen feet of water. Good riprap. Crappie at night.

7. Excellent point for bass.

8. Underwater road bed leading to rubble of collapsed underwater bridge. Bridge rubble directly in main channel.

9. Good Rat-L-Trap fishing in mouth of creek.

10. Highway 219 (Mooty Road) bridge pilings. Good rip-rap on both sides.

11. Underwater road bed .

12. Good shallow hole. Location of farm pond before lake was impounded.

13. Underwater road bed.

14. Two underwater islands in 25 feet of water located in sharp bend of river. Good brush on top. Excellent in summer for bass with worm.

15. Standing timber-filled slough. Excellent for spinnerbaits much of the year, topwater in late spring. Crappie fishing in summer.

16. Good creek. Standing timber throughout. Good spring spawning area. Topwater, spinnerbaits and worms for bass. Also find crappie here.

17. Underwater road bed.

18. Underwater road bed.

19. Underwater islands 35 feet deep in main channel. Covered with brush.

20. Underwater road beds.

21. Underwater road beds.

22. Mouth of creek. Good holding areas for bass in spring when floodgates are going. Fish escape here.

23. Standing timber area.

24. Good crankbait area in creek along south bank.

25. Good pocket for spawning bass. Topwater or spinnerbaits.

26. Where creek forks in back, excellent spinnerbait area. Lots of standing timber.

27. Small underwater island in main river channel in 25 feet of water. Excellent for schooling bass when current is being pulled.

28. Excellent pocket with lots of good points.

29. Underwater road bed.

30. Underwater hump. Main channel runs around both sides. Excellent for schooling summer bass when water is on or off.

31. Underwater road bed.

32. Good pocket with flats. Crankbaits or spinnerbaits.

33. Long, underwater island. Island splits main channel. Lots of brush on top. In 30 feet of water. Excellent is summer with deep-diving crankbaits or in dead of winter with jig-and-pigs.

34. Underwater island. Brush piles on top.

35. Underwater island with standing timber on top. Adjacent to main river channel. Excellent spot for spooning in summer.

36. Location of small lake before West Point was impounded.

37. Small depression. Location of small farm pond before lake was impounded. Good topwater area in spring.

38. Underwater road bed.

39. Bridge pilings in Yellow Jacket Creek. Lots of tournament-releasd fish gather here. Good year-round.

40. Good coves with grass.

41. Grass beds at fork of creek.

42. Mill Road Bridge pilings. Good rip-rap. Good crappie spot at night.

43. Small bridge. Same as above.

44. Underwater road bed.

45. Underwater bridge.

46. Underwater bridge.

47. Mooty Bridge Road bridge pilings. Tournament fish also gather here.

48. Standing timber area.

49. Bridge pilings in Beech Creek. Good spring fishing for crappie.

50. Underwater island with standing timber surrounding it in 5 feet of water. Excellent topwater in late spring.

51. Stumps on west bank.

52. Mill Road Bridge pilings. Located over location of small pond before lake was impounded. Good rip-rap. Good spring fishing for crappie and bass.

53. Underwater bridge.

54. Underwater road bed.

55. Good fishing around bridge pilings year-round.

56. Lots of standing timber. Excellent spinnerbait fishing in spring. Also good crappie fishing in spring on west bank.

57. Good spawning area for bass and crappie in back of Yellow Jacket Creek.

58. Good spawning area for bass and crappie in back of the creek.

59. Site of large lake before lake was impounded. Excellent spring spawning area for bass and crappie.

60. Good spawning area in Half Moon Creek. Standing timber and grass. Good depression left by old farm pond before lake was impounded.

61. Whitaker Road Bridge. Good spring fishing around pilings. Deep water adjacent to shallow water. Good crappie fishing at night in late spring, early summer under the bridge.

62. Underwater road bed.

63. Underwater trees. Site of an old orchard before lake was impounded.

64 through 68. Underwater road bed.

69. Old houses flooded by lake's impoundment, houses are collapsed, but rubble and foundations remain. Good worming area.

70. Small, underwater island. Top of island in 35 feet of water. Good summer worming area.

71. Large underwater island. Top of island in 35 feet of water. Some brush. Crappie on top in summer. Good worming for bass.

72. Underwater road bed.

73. Location of farm pond before lake was impounded. Good spring spawning area for bass and crappie.

74. Underwater road bed.

75. Underwater road bed. Rubble from collapsed bridge in main creek channel 25 feet deep. Good summer crappie fishing.

76. Underwater road bed.

77. Location of farm pond before lake was impounded. Good spring spawning area for bass and crappie.

78. Standing timber in 15 feet of water. Good spring spawning area. Spinnerbaits for bass; minnows for crappie.

79. Antioch Road Bridge pilings. Holds pre-spawn and post-spawn crappie and bass.

80. Small underwater hump. Good location for stripers in summer.

81. Excellent pocket. Adjacent to main river channel. Fish run up on ledge in summer to feed.

82. Foundations of homes covered by impoundment.

83. Underwater railroad trestle. Across shallow water over main channel and back into shallow water. Old railroad bridge across main channel. Sometimes holds stripe in summer. Some bass year round.

84. Underwater road beds.

85. Long underwater island. Check for schooling stripers and hybrids in summer and winter.

86. Underwater road bed.

87. Standing timber area. Good spring spawning area for crappie and bass. Spinnerbaits and buzzbaits for bass, minnows and jigs for crappie.

88. Standing timber area. Good spring spawning area for crappie and bass. Spinnerbaits and buzzbaits for bass, minnows and jigs for crappie.

89. Excellent spring spawning area. Location of large lake before West Point was impounded. Holds both spawning bass and crappie.

90. Underwater road bed. Good spring pre-spawn and post-spawn holding area for crappie and bass.

91. Underwater road bed. Good spring pre-spawn and post-spawning holding area for crappie and bass.

92. Foundations of two old homes. Both in shallow water. Good spinnerbait and buzzbait area.

93. Underwater road bed. Runs from 10 feet deep to 45 feet deep. Can find several species up and down road year round.

94. Old home foundations. Some 10 feet deep, some 45 feet deep.

95. Highway 109 bridge. Good rip-rap. Year-round fishing for all species.

96. Underwater road bed.

97. Small underwater island in 45 feet of water. Top of island in 35 feet with some brush. Located close to main channel. Good hybrid and striper area.

98. Long, winding underwater road bed. Some brush on top.

99. Wilson Creek. Excellent year-round fishing. Good buck bushes.

100. Back of Wilson Creek. Good spring spawning area. Brush and standing timber.

101. Underwater road bed.

102. Underwater road bed.

103. Underwater islands in 45 feet of water. Top of islands 40 feet. Stripe and hybrids.

104. Shallow underwater road bed.

105. Pronounced small hump in 25 feet of water.

106. Rainbow Creek. Standing timber in mouth.

107. Stumpy area on east bank. Good buzzbait and spinnerbait area.

108. Underwater road bed.

109. Underwater road bed.

110. Good spring and fall area for bass and crappie. Small farm pond previous to impoundment.

111. Underwater road bed.

112. Underwater island that splits main channel. Good striper and hybrid area.

113. Underwater road bed.

114. Underwater road bed.

115. Underwater road bed.

116. Underwater islands in 65 feet of water. Shows good signs of hot summer stripers, but tough to catch.

117. Old home foundations.

118. Underwater road bed.

119. Underwater road bed in Veasey Creek

120. State Line Road bridge pilings in Veasey Creek.

121. Back of Veasey Creek. Good spring spawning area.

122. Good spring spawning area for bass and crappie. Location of old farm pond.

123. Underwater road bed.

124. Underwater road bed.

125. Good pockets in Veasey Creek

126. Old building foundations.

127. Underwater road bed.

128. Underwater road bed in Stroud Creek.

129. Underwater road bed with collapsed bridge in channel of creek.

130. Bridge pilings in Stroud creek. Good spring bass and crappie.

131. Back of Stroud Creek. Good spawning area.

132. Line Road bridge pilings. Good crappie area in spring.

133. Good bass point in Wehadkee Creek.

134. Underwater road bed.

135. Small depression that holds fish on sudden spring weather change. Site of old farm pond. Difficult to find. 15 yards due east of intersection of road bed and creek channel.

136. Small depression in 15 feet of water. Holds spring bass and crappie. Site of small farm pond before lake impoundment.

137. Excellent points in Wehadkee Creek.

138. Underwater road bed.

139. Underwater bridge.

140. Underwater road bed.

141. Underwater road bed.

142. Underwater road bed.

143. Spur 109 bridge pilings in Wehadkee Creek

144. Good bass and crappie spawning area.

145. Railroad trestle. Good spring fishing around pilings for bass and crappie.

146. Standing timber in back of pocket. Good spring spawning area for bass and crappie. Spinnerbaits and worms for bass.

147. Underwater railroad bed.

148. Underwater road bed.

149. Standing timber area. Good spring bedding area.

150. Underwater road bed.

151. Collapsed underwater bridge.

152. Large standing timber area. Good spring bedding area for bass. Topwater, worms and spinnerbaits.

153. McCosh Mill Road Bridge pilings. Good in spring for crappie.

154. Good fishing around bridge pilings in spring.

155. Underwater road bed.

156. Underwater bridge.

157. Alligator Creek. Good spring area in back. Fishing good in mouth of creek almost all year.

158. Underwater road bed.

159. Numerous old home foundations in 25 feet of water.

160. Underwater road bed.

161. Underwater hump that splits main river channel flow. Good area for summer stripers.

162. Old home foundations in 15 feet of water. Holds small bass in fall.

163. Underwater road bed.

164. Underwater road bed.

165. Underwater road bed.

166. Long, underwater island in 55 feet of water. Good summer area for stripers using downriggers.

167. Underwater island that splits main river channel. Deep. Holds summer and winter stripers.

168. Underwater road bed.

169. Deep hole in 15 feet of water. Hole is 25 deep in deepest part.

170. Underwater road bed.

171. Numerous old home foundations in 25 feet of water. Excellent worming area for bass in summer.

172. Underwater road bed.

173. Deep hole in 35 feet of water. Site of old pond. Good worming area in August.

174. Underwater road bed.

175. Old home foundations.

176. Underwater road bed.

177. Site of old orchard in 65 feet of water. Adjacent to main river channel. Good summer and winter stripe area with downriggers.

178. Underwater road bed.

179. Old home foundations in 15 feet of water.

180. Good depression in shallow water. Good topwater area for bass and schooling hybrids.

181. Old home foundations in 5 feet of water. Topwater for bass.

182. Old home foundations.

183. Depression in 35 feet of water. Old farm pond.

184. Underwater road bed.

185. Old home foundations right of edge of road bed in 15 feet of water. Good worming area.

186. Large, shallow depression. Good area for hybrids and bass to chase shad. Watch for shad popping topwater.

187. Underwater road bed.

188. Glass Bridge Road Bridge. Good spring area for crappie and bass around pilings.

189. Good depression that holds fish on sudden spring weather change. Holds crappie and bass.

Lake West Point

Above Yellowjacket Creek

Fish Creek

Lake West Point

Yellowjacket Creek

Whitewater Creek

Turkey Creek

Highland Marina
to
Highway 109

Lake West Point

Yellowjacket Creek

Lake West Point

Wehadkee, Stroud & Veasey Creeks

Lake Eufaula

No Alabama lake is more well known across the world than Lake Eufaula. During its heyday in the late 60's and early 70's, it was truly one of the finest bass lakes on this continent. Today, it is annually among the top two or three lakes in Alabama, and more often than not, No. 1. Alabama will never again see a lake with the tremendous offerings that Eufaula offered when it was first impounded.

The fish-rich Chattahoochee River was impounded in 1963, flooding thousands of acres of fertile farm land, much of it already loaded up with fertilizer and animal wastes. Sewage from Atlanta and other large cities from points north may have been pollution in those areas, but by the time it traveled down the Chattahoochee River to Lake Eufaula, it was fertilizer in its purest form.

The large amount of "fertilizer" in the lake virtually made it the world's largest private pond. The nutrients resulted in a near-perfect food chain.

Couple all of these positive aspects with the fact that numerous farm ponds and private lakes already full of large bass were flooded and their fish released into waters already filled with big fish and you

had a situation like Alabamians, or other Americans for that matter, will never enjoy again.

Lake Eufaula will never again see fishing like it had in its glory days, but it still offers Alabama fishing at its best.

Spring bass fishing
ABOVE SOAPSTONE CREEK

When the first warm days of spring come to Lake Eufaula, a young man's fancy indeed turns to love - love of big bass.

It takes only a few warm days of spring weather to kick shallow water in this end of the lake up in the 55-degree range, and this sends the bass from their deep-water winter haunts into water much more accessible to fishermen.

The areas near the mouths of Cowikee Creek's North, Middle and South Forks are full of shallow bars lined with stumps, as well as ditches filled with brush and other structure. The Chattahoochee River boasts similar areas, as well as a good number of points.

When these areas are adjacent to deep water, bass use the deep

Lake Eufaula Fact Sheet

Location, length, acreage

Walter F. George Reservoir, better known to fishermen as Lake Eufaula, straddles the Alabama-Georgia line on the Chattahoochee River. The 45,181-acre reservoir, sandwiched between Columbus, Ga., to the north and George W. Andrews Reservoir the south, draws fishing pressure not only from Alabama, Georgia and Florida anglers, but from across the nation as well.

The popular fishing lake begins at Eagle-Phenix Dam just below Columbus and stretches 87 nautical miles to the Walter F. George Dam. Florence Marina sits almost directly at the halfway point, although the marina sits at the upper end of what most consider to be the fishing lake. The lake boasts 640 miles of shoreline. A total of 7,507 square miles drain into the lake. Full pool is 190.0 feet.

Walter F. George Dam

Walter F. George Lock and Dam is 13,585 feet wide and 114 feet tall at maximum height.

The dam has four hydraulic turbines, each capable of passing 6,000 cubic feet of water per second. The dam also has four alternating current generators capable of annually producing 436 million kilowatt hours of electricity. The Army Corps of Engineers owns the dam and sells power to Alabama Power Co. and Georgia Power Co.

Each of the dam's 14 42-foot-by-29-foot spillway gates can pass 10,000 cubic feet of water per second in flood conditions.

Lake Configuration

Lake Eufaula's upper-end is run-of-the-river from Eagle-Phenix Dam to the River Bend Park area, a distance of approximately 24 miles. The river widens greatly there for about three miles, but narrows again and is more or less run-of-the-river for 18 more miles, until it reaches the Florence Marina area. Below that point, the river widens to form what most consider to be Lake Eufaula.

The lake widens dramatically and sloughs, pockets, flats and incoming creeks dot the landscape all the way to Walter F. George Dam.

Stocking history*

Florida-strain largemouth	
1986	13,800

Hybrids	
1975	49,000
1976	69,075
1977	99,938
1979	59,790
1980	32,307
1982	105,000
1983	120,630
1984	108,200
1986	99,700

* Does not include stockings by Georgia Game and Fish

Major and secondary creeks

Besides the Chattahoochee River, Lake Eufaula is fed by numerous major and secondary creeks. Cowikee Creek is the major supplier of water in the lake's upper end, while Soapstone Creek, Bustahatchee Creek, Rood Creek, Little Barbour Creek, Grass Creek and Turner Creek are smaller inlets.

The lake's middle section boasts major water suppliers in Chewalla Creek, Barbour Creek, Cheneyhatchee Creek and White Oak Creek, while Tobannee Creek is a smaller inlet.

The lake's lower section is fed by Pataula Creek - its biggest water supplier - and lesser creeks in Drag Nasty Creek, Thomas Mill Creek, Sandy Creek and Hardridge Creek.

Impoundment

Construction began on Walter F. George Dam in May, 1956, and the dam was placed into service in May, 1963.

Types of fish

The lake features popular species such as largemouth bass, white bass, hybrid bass, and black crappie, channel catfish, blue catfish, longear sunfish, redbreast sunfish, dollar sunfish, redear sunfish and bluegill. A few spotted bass and white crappie may show up from time to time. The lake also has species of gar and carp.

Gizzard shad, threadfin shad and several species of minnows are primary baitfish.

---

water as a spring staging area. The bass will hang in 12 to 15 feet of water, but will occasionally move up into the shallow water around structure to ambush shad. The cold fronts that roll through this time of the year always send the bass back deep, but only temporarily.

At this time of year, medium-running crankbaits such as a Bagley's Killer B2 or DB3 fished slowly across the structure will produce bass. Fishing the crankbaits slowly is the key. These fish are still in water that makes them sluggish and a fast bait is impossible for them to catch.

When the water warms to 60-degrees, the bass will move closer to shallow water to feed and in anticipation of moving into their shallow spawning areas. Keep in mind that structure still is critical. Areas without stump rows, brush-filled ditches or grass will not have fish.

Spinnerbaits become the weapon of choice at this point. A chartreuse or chartreuse/white spinnerbait with a No. 4 or No. 5 Colorado blade does well. Fish a 1/2-ounce spinnerbait early because bass will still be holding on the outside of structure and you'll need a heavier lure that will drop quickly when the water suddenly deepens. When the fish move up into shallow water, throw a lighter 3/8-ounce or 1/4-ounce spinnerbait that can be worked in the grass.

Another key lure during this period is the buzz bait. Any noisy lure such as a Lunker Lure fished in or around weeds often will produce violent strikes. This offers some of the most exciting fishing that can be found on the lake.

When water temperature reaches 65 degrees, fish will disappear from these areas and head into the creeks and sloughs to spawn.

The good part about fishing this area of the lake during the spring, besides the number of good fish it produces, is that whether or not water is being pulled is not important. This means fishing has the potential to be good most hours seven days a week.

SOAPSTONE CREEK TO WHITE OAK CREEK

Early springtime will find bass in this section of the lake beginning to move from the main river channel and scattering to the ledges, points, creek mouths and the ditches that run from the main channel into the flats of the main lake.

These long ditches are one of the secrets of the lake's best springtime bass anglers. They are prime bass fishing areas because they act as interstates for fish moving from deep water to the grass. The best way to locate these long ditches is to first buy one of the several detailed topographic maps of Lake Eufaula. The Lake Eufaula map published by Atlantic Mapping, Inc., is excellent. It is the map most commonly found in marinas and bait shops.

Locate these long ditches with your depthfinder by idling across the flats. After a ditch is detected, drop a marker buoy. Criss-cross the area until you pinpoint the direction of the ditch. Mark its length with buoys.

Worms, spinnerbaits, buzzbaits, jig-and-pigs and medium running crankbaits fished in these ditches will produce bass.

After the water temperature reaches 58 to 60 degrees and bass have traveled the length of the ditch and reached the grass, spinnerbaits, buzzbaits, worms and Pogo Minnows work well.

The large creeks in the lake's middle section act much like bass highways just as the ditches do. White Oak Creek, Tobannee Creek, Cheneyhatchee Creek and Barbour Creek are excellent spawning areas. White Oak Creek offers the best grass beds.

WHITE OAK CREEK
TO LAKE EUFAULA DAM

If just catching bass, not trophy bass, is what takes the kinks out of your line, there's no better place to fish than on Lake Eufaula's lower end during the spring.

Unlike the area of the lake above White Oak Creek, the painstaking art of locating ditches and river channels isn't necessary. Bass gather on the visible, rocky points and this makes fishing relatively simple for even the most basic of bass fishermen.

This area has few creeks, so when spawning time arrives, most bass ease their way off the points and simply work their way into the nearest slough.

The Alabama side of the lake from White Oak Creek to the Hardridge Access Area boasts numerous points and sloughs. Crankbaits are good in early spring when bass are staging on the rocky points, and worms and 1/2-ounce spinnerbaits work well when the bass move up the points into more shallow water. Buzzbaits also will catch these fish, but usually only early and late.

The bad part about fishing this part of the lake during the spring is that it's wide, and even the slightest wind deals havoc with efforts to fish. During March, this area can sometimes get down-right choppy.

Hot weather
bass fishing

ABOVE SOAPSTONE CREEK

It's common for anglers on this end of the lake to to report catching smaller bass in the grass and shallow water until early- or mid-May. These are fish that are no longer spawning and have returned to shallows because of preferable water temperatures and access to shad. Other bass that have spawned by this time will have moved out to the points.

It's at this time that two patterns will work. Spinnerbaits will take fish in the shallows, while crankbaits are needed for bass on the points.

After the end of May, easy-to-get-to fish become a thing of the past. The largemouth bass retreat to the river and creek channels to escape increasingly warmer water temperatures. These bass bunch up in schools, frequently suspended along ledges in 12 to 18 feet of water. Bass like these areas because they not only provide cooler,

oxygenated water, but because they also offer easy access to the stump-ridden ledges that hold shad.

Plastic worms and crankbaits thrown into shallow water and reeled off the ledge is the key to catching bass. Bass don't suspend themselves all along these ledges, however. The secret is finding something irregular along the channels, such as a sharp bend or a large concentration of brush or stumps. The sharp river bend (see map) directly across from Rood Creek, the sharp bend exactly one mile above Rood Creek and the sharp bend 1 1/2 miles up from Rood Creek are key areas.

Unlike in spring, pulling water is critical to good fishing during hot weather. Moving water sends the shad scurrying and sparks the bass into a feeding frenzy.

On the Cowikee Creek side, the entire crooked stretch of the creek channel across from Lakepoint Marina State Park is good.

For those unfamiliar with the lake, they should locate the ledges with a depthfinder and then drop marker buoys. This will ensure that you fish the areas you need to fish.

SOAPSTONE CREEK
TO WHITE OAK CREEK

By early June, the spawn is over and the fish have moved out of the creeks and flats and are searching for cooler water. The bass will gather in deep water near the mouths of White Oak Creek, Barbour Creek, Chenyhatchee Creek and Chewalla Creek, near the mouths of ditches that dump into the main channel and along the ledges of the main river channel wherever there's a bend with structure on it.

Some of the better areas with such bends are directly out from Old Town Park, directly out from the mouth of Chewalla Creek, 1.3 miles above the mouth of Barbour Creek, directly out from the mouth of Barbour Creek and the area above White Oak Creek.

Crankbaits or worms thrown into shallow water, pulled through the structure and allowed to drop into the main channel, will draw strikes from these fish. It is imperative that water be pulled for this pattern to be successful.

A few summer bass can be found in the creeks because of their deep water, but they can rarely be found farther up than the first bridges an angler will come to. These areas should be fished just as you would the main river.

WHITE OAK CREEK
TO LAKE EUFAULA DAM

Point fishing is the name of the game on the Alabama side of the lake during the summer. The mouths of most of the creeks and sloughs on this side sit within a few feet of the main river channel and when post-spawn bass exit, they are forced to head directly to the deep water. These bass will align themselves in the deep water adjacent to points, and they'll briefly brave the warmer water to dash to the points and feed on shad.

These points should be fished as you would the ledges upriver - with worms or crankbaits. Most of these bass, which school in large numbers as they suspend in the channel, lay dormant until power is generated. After the water is turned on, the bass rush to the backside of the points to chase shad that gather there to get out of the current.

On the Georgia side of the lake, it's different. The area from Pataula Creek to Sandy Creek is full of flats that you normally would avoid in summer, but a large number of fish-holding humps can be found in these flats. Once again, use a good topographic map to locate the humps, then use your depthfinder to pinpoint them. Worms and crankbaits on these humps can be deadly when water is being pulled.

Cool and cold weather bass fishing

Above Soapstone Creek

The first signs of cooler weather in late September and early October once again release the bass from their deep-water haunts and send them in search of shallow water.

Much as in early spring, the bass in early fall will stage themselves in 12 to 20 feet of water and occasionally move up into structure-filled shallows to chase shad. Cowikee Creek is an excellent area for activity as the many stumps seem to hold winter shad. Medium-running crankbaits are excellent for catching these bass.

As the water temperature continues to drop, the bass will feed more to store fat for the winter. They'll also move into shallower water. Dingy water warms better than clear water, as does water over pea gravel. Look for these areas. The area between Gamage Bridge Road to the U.S. 431 bridge is excellent. On the Chattahoochee River side, check out Little Barbour Creek and Rood Creek. Both have gravel flats.

Soapstone Creek To White Oak Creek

The cooling temperatures of October will move the bass out of the main channel and head them into the creeks, much as in the pre-spawn period. These fish won't actually get in the grass, but they will seek shallow water and position themselves on long points.

The mouths of Barbour Creek and Cheneyhatchee Creek are the main areas for this pattern. The mouths of these two creeks feature ditches that criss-cross the area, as well as a lot of sand.

The flats between Barbour Creek and Cheneyhatchee Creeks also are excellent. Several ditches link these two areas.

White Oak Creek To Lake Eufaula Dam

The lower end of Lake Eufaula isn't a good place to bass fish during the colder months. Anglers can enjoy brief success during the fall as a large number of bass pile up on the humps between Pataula Creek and Sandy Creek on the Georgia side, but when cold, cold weather arrives, the bass seem to disappear.

This is the time of year when the bass fisherman needs to crank the big motor and run north.

Other Types of Fishing

Crappie

Lake Eufaula's long history of excellent bass fishing has overshadowed the fact the lake is an excellent crappie hatchery.

There is nothing quite as impressive as entering one of the creeks off the main lake during February and suddenly seeing tremendous schools of crappie on your depthfinder. These schools can be so large that many anglers have passed them off as schools of baitfish.

These crappie make their spring spawning run up the creeks, and there is no better method of catching them than trolling jigs through the schools. Several rods out trolling chartreuse jigs at the 14-foot level almost guarantees success. Chewalla Creek and Cowikee Creek are excellent. Most of your better spring crappie fishing is in the lake's upper end.

Another method that works well is using a heavy lead to bump bottom along the stump-laden ledges next to the deep creek channels.

Other spring crappie can be found in treetops near the bank. A small spoon jigged in these treetops works exceptionally well.

For some reason, after the weather turns hot, the area of the lake from Cowikee Creek to White Oak Creek heats up for crappie fishing.

The secret to catching crappie this time of year is locating the structure directly adjacent to the river channel. Any time you find structure, you'll find crappie. These fish will be anywhere from 12 to 25 feet this time of the year.

Winter fishing for crappie is identical to fishing for them during the summer. They can be found at the same depths in the same structure on the ledges adjacent to the deepwater. Many will argue the point, but a spoon will put more crappie in the boat than will jigs or live minnows.

Hybrid Bass

Lake Eufaula has been stocked with literally hundreds of thousands of hybrid bass by both Georgia and Alabama fishery officials in recent years. Lake Eufaula offers tremendous fishing for this species.

The fish isn't capable of spawning, but it will make spawning runs into the middle fork of Cowikee Creek in mid-March. These fish run up this creek as far as possible in their attempts to spawn.

The fish will situate themselves in incredibly shallow and narrow water, so the smaller the boat you use, the better. The shallow portions of these creeks will sometimes have a 20-foot depression in them and the hybrids will gather there. Live shad can be used as bait, but Hopkins Spoons and Pogo Minnows probably work better.

Spring hybrid also can be found in some smaller creeks such as Wylaunee Creek and Rood Creek, but neither area can compare with Cowikee Creek's middle fork.

During hot weather, hybrids will move to 18 to 25 foot depths and hang around bends in the main river channel. These fish will occasionally, usually at daybreak and late evening, scoot into the shallow flats to feed on shad. These shad often will give away their location by seagulls which dive into the schooling baitfish to pick up cripples. If the hybrids are hitting on topwater, throw a topwater bait such as a Boy-Howdee. If they are feeding under the baitfish, throw a spoon or chrome Rat-L-Trap or similar bait. Allow the spoon or Rat-L-Trap to sink to the bottom and bounce it back to the boat.

The area between Cowikee Creek to the old railroad trestle below White Oak Creek is the best location to find these schooling hybrids.

The flats across from Old Creek Town Park is the best area of all.

When fall arrives, many of the bigger hybrids move up to the shallower water in the narrow area between the U.S. 82 causeway and the railroad trestle. Chicken livers fished from the bank produce a number of fish, but boaters find the best success with Rat-L-Traps and spoons.

Lake Eufaula's best fishing spots

1. Flats directly across from Florence Marina. Big bend in river. Lots of visible structure and incoming ditches into main river channel. Good year around for bass and crappie.

2. Sheer rock bank drops directly into river channel. Logjams. Flat water on both ends.

3. Rood Creek. Bass bed in back in April. Also spring crappie. Grass flats and stump rows throughout creek.

4. Location of ponds before river was impounded. Deep cut where dam was broken. Shallow flats. Underwater standing trees. Big bass in summer. Good spawning area in spring.

5. Wylaunee Creek. Dangerous area, but good crappie fishing in standing timber. Points produce good bass. Standing timber throughout middle of creek.

6. Underwater roadbed.

7. U.S. 431 bridge to intersection of Cowikee Creek and Chattahoochee River. Good year around area. Lots of flats with grass. Creek bends. 40-foot river channel. Bass and crappie year around.

8. Excellent fishing from South Fork to U.S. 431 Bridge. Best producing area on lake. Adjacent to Lakepoint Resort where most tournament bass are released.

9. South Fork Cowikee Creek. Good from Gamage Road Bridge to mouth of Middle Fork. Deep water. Stump rows. Lots of visible structure.

10. Middle Fork Cowikee Creek. Good area for spring bass and crappie. Visible tree tops. Good all seasons except summer.

11. Underwater roadbed.

12. Underwater roadbed.

13. Underwater roadbed.

14. Underwater roadbed.

15. The clothesline. River hits rocks out from Old Creek Town Park and heads directly for Georgia bank. Excellent bass, crappie and hybrid fishing. Nearby flats are excellent spawning area. 65 feet of water jumps to 10 feet.

16. Chewalla Creek. Top early spring crappie area. Trolling for crappie in early February produces slabs. Also good area for big spring bass.

17. Highway 82 causeway. Excellent crappie fishing around pilings. Same for nearby railroad trestle. Good both day and night. Riprap along causeway good for bass and hybrids. Most big hybrids come from this area. Also produces some trophy bass.

18. Underwater brush pile. Thirty yards southeast of buoy 93.8. Line up buoy 93.8 with tallest pine across railroad on northwest horizon. 15 feet deep.

19. Underwater hump. Directly below trestle. Leave Alabama side and line up with second piling. Go straight south. 65 feet of

water rises to 12 feet. Excellent for bass and crappie.

20. Underwater brush pile. 100 yards north of buoy 92.4 on old river channel. 15 feet deep.

21. Underwater road beds.

22. Underwater road beds.

23. Barbour Creek. Excellent spring crappie area to bridge. Good bass area. Sandy points. Crooked creek.

24. U.S. 431 Bridge pilings. Excellent crappie fishing day and night.

25. Corp crappie plot. Marked with buoy.

26. Underwater road bed exiting Cheneyhatchee Creek.

27. Bridge pilings in Cheneyhatchee Creek. Excellent crappie fishing at night.

28. Corp crappie plot. Marked with buoy.

29. Underwater brush pile. Directly across from first slough south of Cool Branch Park. Line southeast corner post of boathouse in slough with tall white-colored tree. Also, line up black buoy with water tower on west side of lake. 20 feet deep.

30. Corp crappie plot. Marked with buoy.

31. Underwater road bed.

32. Underwater road bed.

33. Underwater brush pile. Located 50 feet southeast of buoy 89.1 on old river bed. Line up three buoys to the north for correct alignment. 20 feet deep.

34. Big underwater brush pile. Go to first cove above White Oak Creek. Trees are east of the cove on old river channel (Alexander's Bend). Trees are on top of mound in 10 feet of water.

35. Underwater brush pile. Straight out of south point of Gator Hole slough. Line up south point with tallest pine in back side of slough. 15 feet deep.

36. Underwater brush pile. Northeast of the south point of Parmer Branch. 15 deep adjacent to drop-off.

37. Underwater brush pile. 150 feet northwest of buoy 87.8 on edge of old river channel.

38. Corp crappie plot. Marked with buoy.

39. White Oak Creek. Bridge pilings offer good crappie fishing. Riprap offers good bass fishing.

40. Underwater road bed.

41. Underwater road beds.

42. Underwater road bed across mouth of Drag Nasty Creek.

43. Underwater brush pile. Proceed west out of Drag Nasty Creek, along the south edge of the creek channel until the southwest corner post of the metal boathouse lines up with the large pine tree on the next point south. 15 feet deep.

44. Underwater road bed.

45. Corp crappie plot. Marked with buoy.

46. Underwater brush pile. South of first small island that is above the mouth of Pataula Creek. 13 feet deep.

47. Corp crappie plot. Marked with buoy.

48. Pataula Creek. Shallow. Excellent springtime spawning area for bass and crappie. Good fishing to bridge. Stumps and grass beds.

49. Old Clay County (Ga.) 39 highway roadbed crossing mouth of Pataula Creek. Excellent for big bass in spring.

50. Brushpile on top of old Clay County (Ga.) highway 39 roadbed, approximately 400 feet south of old Clay County (Ga.) 39 bridge.

51. Brushpile on top of old Clay County (Ga.) highway 39 bridge. Approximately 500 feet south of bridge.

52. Gopher Ridge island. Shallow water night fishing with buzzbaits.

53. Underwater road bed.

54. Underwater brush pile. Line up south point of Thomas Mill Creek with next point up creek. Proceed due east across old river channel. Brush located on Georgia side on top of huge mound in 23 feet of water.

55. Underwater cedar tree pile, 100 feet southeast of north point of Otho Branch. 16 feet deep.

56. Underwater brush pile 100 feet northeast of south point on Otho Branch. 16 feet deep.

57. Underwater road bed.

58. Underwater brush pile on Alabama side of main river channel, on second point above No. 60.

59. Underwater road bed.

60. Underwater brush pile. Immediately north of the rocky point at the north end of Holiday Shores subdivision. 15 feet deep.

61. Pockets off main river channel. Excellent bass fishing in back of sloughs in spring, excellent bass fishing in mouth where it falls into main river channel in summer.

62. Underwater road bed.

63. Sandy Creek. Flats, weedbeds. Good for bass and crappie in spring.

64. Corp crappie plot. Marked with buoy.

65. Underwater road bed.

66. Underwater road beds.

67. Underwater brush pile 50 feet northwest of big rocks at the point of the cabled off swimming area at Sandy Creek Park. 12 feet deep.

68. Hardridge Creek. Good bass fishing in mouth only.

69. Underwater road beds.

70. Underwater brush pile immediately south of the north point of Hardridge Creek. On edge of drop off. 16 feet deep.

71. Underwater brush pile. Go east of Pine Tree Point in Hardride Creek until you reach drop off. Trees are located on edge of dropoff. 16 feet of water.

72. Underwater cedar tree pile. East of the south point of Hardridge Creek. Follow 15 feet water until it drops off. Trees are at dropoff in 15 feet of water.

73. Underwater brush pile on point south of Hardridge Creek mouth. 15 feet deep.

74. Corp crappie plot. Marked with buoy.

75. Underwater tree pile 40 feet north of the south point of the first cove north of the dam on the Alabama side. 12 feet deep.

76. Underwater brush pile 20 feet north of the dam on the Alabama side adjacent to the first "No Parking" sign from the west point of the dike road. 14 feet deep.

77. Underwater brush pile 40 feet northwest of riprap at south point going into east bank area boat ramp. 13 feet deep.

78. Riprap around dam. Good on both sides of the channel and along dam for hybrids and stripes. One of the first areas big fish move into during the spring.

79. Underwater brush pile northwest of second point moving north from the dam on the Georgia side. 13 feet deep.

80. Underwater brush pile 50 feet west of first point north of the dam on the Georgia side. 13 feet deep.

81. Underwater brush pile 20 feet north of the dam at the first "No Parking" sign on the Georgia side. 10-14 feet deep.

Florence Marina

Grass Creek

Turner Creek

Little Barbour Creek

Omaha Road

Rood Creek

Wylaunee Creek

Bustahatchee Creek

Soapstone Creek

Lake Eufaula

Chattahoochee River to Soapstone Creek

Cowikee
Creek
North
Fork

10

Cowikee Creek
Middle Fork

Cowikee
Creek
South
Fork

9

Gamage Bridge
Road

Lake
Eufaula
Cowikee Creek

431

Lakepoint
Resort

7

8

11

Soapstone Creek

431

KOA Campground

Old Town
Creek Park
Chewalla
Marina

Chewalla
Creek

Barbour
Creek

82

Tobannee Creek

Central
railroad

Chencyhatchee
Creek

Lake Eufaula

Soapstone Creek
to
White Oak Creek

431

White Oak
Creek

Midlake Bait & Tackle

Sandy Creek

White
Oak
Creek

Drag Nasty
Creek

Pataula Shores

Pataula
Creek

41

42

43

44

47

48

46

45

97

95

50

49

51

52

53

57

39

Fort Gaines
Highway

Sandy Branch

Thomas
Mill
Creek

54

55

56

58

59

62

63

Sandy Creek

60

61

64

67

65

66

69

97

71

70

77

78

79

80

68

72

73

74

81

Lake
Eufaula

Hardridge
Creek

75

76

White Oak Creek
to
Walter F. George Dam

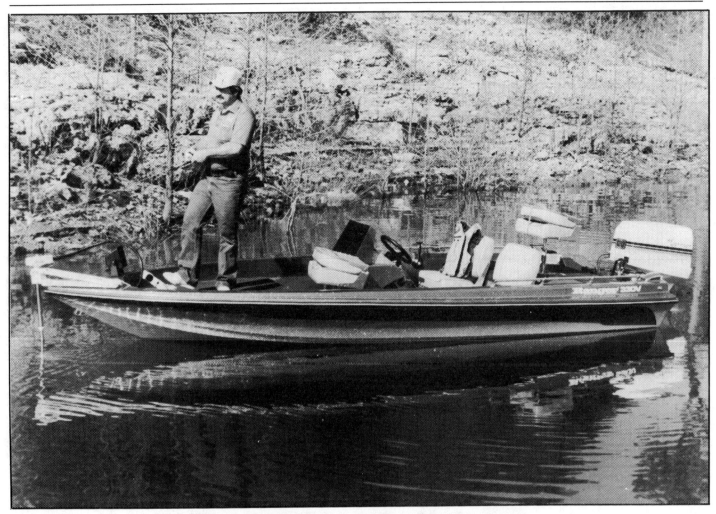

Lake Harris

Take a fish-rich river which receives agricultural run-off. Isolate it from metropolitan areas. Leave much of the surrounding structure intact. Impound the river. Stock it with more than 135,000 Florida-strain largemouth. Leave it's already-thriving crappie population intact.

That's the recipe for a tremendous bass and crappie fishing lake.

Lake Harris is the newest reservoir in Alabama, completed in 1983. With land costs, labor costs and enviromental concerns being what they are, many experts predict this will be the last reservoir built in the state.

Lake Harris has many of the same ingredients which made Lake Eufaula one of the nation's best bass lakes when it was impounded. Fortunately for the lake, it doesn't get the publicity or the pressure Lake Eufaula once received.

The lake lacks a nearby chamber of commerce to boast of the lake's potential, or local fishermen who like to talk. The Sports Center, a small tackle shop in Lineville, has photos of 16-pound and 14-pound Lake Harris largemouths on its wall. The fishermen who caught the fish asked that the news and photos of the catches not be released to newspapers. The lake has given up several 12- and 13-pounders, too.

Spring bass fishing

TALLAPOOSA RIVER

The steep rocky bluffs on the lake's lower end, the standing timber and the roadbeds and creek channels on the outside fringes of the standing timber, are the winter homes of many bass. It's from these areas that the bass will begin moving when spring arrives.

So few anglers are accustomed to fishing new, deep, clear-water reservoirs that many anglers have trouble fishing pre-spawn bass on this lake. During construction of Harris Lake, much of the standing timber was left intact. Many anglers new to this lake tap their depthfinders in disbelief as they find themselves in 100 feet of water and can still see timber sticking out of the water.

Many fish suspend themselves 30 feet deep in these trees during the winter, while others may be 40 feet deep on the roadbeds on the

Lake Harris Fact Sheet

Location, length and acreage

This Tallapoosa River reservoir is primarily in Randolph County, with a small portion of the upper end in Cleburne County and a small part of Fox Creek across the Clay County line.

The 10,660-acre reservoir begins at R.L. Harris Dam approximately 30 miles southeast of Anniston and stretches more than 27 nautical miles to the head of the lake, which is approximately three miles above the Randolph County 88 bridge (Lee's Bridge.)

The lake drains 1,453 square miles.

Impoundment

Construction began on R.L. Harris Dam Nov. 1, 1974, and it was placed into service April 20, 1983.

R.L. Harris Dam

R.L. Harris Dam is 1,142 feet wide and has six 40-foot-by-40-foot spillway gates. It has two hydraulic turbines and two alternating current generators.

Configuration

The upper end of Lake Harris is river like with only narrow ledges as far south as the power line that runs between the communities of Swag and Liberty, but there the the lake takes on a shape anglers love. The lake widens greatly and has literally

Stocking history

Florida-strain largemouth

1986	1,500
1987	10,138
1988	21,300

Hybrid bass

1983	160,750
1985	53,551
1989	19,000

thousands of sloughs and points. Both shallow water and deep water points and sloughs can be found throughout the lake's lower portion.

Major and secondary creeks

Besides the Tallapoosa River, Harris Lake is fed by numerous creeks and streams. The Little Tallapoosa River, which enters the reservoir 10 miles above the dam, is the major water supplier.

The Little Tallapoosa River is fed by Panther Branch, Wolf Creek, Bear Creek, Henson Branch, Mud Creek, Wedowee Creek, Pineywood Creek, Andanley Branch and Allen Branch.

Fox Creek, Triplett Creek, Miles Branch, Lane Branch and Ginhouse Branch are water suppliers on the lake's lower end below the Little Tallapoosa River intersection.

Above that intersection, Mad Indian Creek, Fuller Creek, Mill Branch, Sandy Creek, Hunter Branch, Gobbler Creek, Lost Creek, Little Ketchepedrakee Creek and Ketchepedakee Creek supply water to the reservoir.

Types of fish

Lake Harris features popular species such as largemouth bass, spotted bass, white bass, hybrid bass, saltwater stripe, white and black crappie, channel catfish.

Also present are flathead catfish, blue catfish, longear sunfish, redear sunfish and bluegill. The lake also has several species of gar, drum and carp.

As for baitfish, gizzard shad, threadfin shad and minnows are present.

---

lower end. It takes many anglers a tackle box full of jig-and-pigs or spoons and lots of practice before they master the feel of fishing that deep.

Fortunately, the warming water that comes with spring flushes the bass out of these deep haunts. They begin the staging process by moving to the points that have brush and timber. Slow baits such as a jig-and-pig or a big-bladed spinnerbait are needed in February when the fish are still sluggish and have yet to start their pre-spawn feeding frenzy.

A 1/2-ounce or 3/4-ounce brown or black jig with a weed guard should be used when fishing a jig-and-pig, and it should be tipped with a No. 5 brown or black pork frog. Many anglers opt for a full ounce jig - if they can find it - because of the water depth. For those wanting to use a spinnerbait, a chartreuse/black 1/2-ounce or 3/4-ounce spinnerbait is needed. It should be outfitted with a large nickel blade. The larger blade forces the angler to fish the bait slowly.

The angler has a tough pattern to fish here. He should position his boat in deep water and cast into 15 feet of water, then fish the bait slowly allowing it to fall deeper and deeper. Many anglers fish the bait too quickly, not allowing to fall back to the bottom on each retrieve.

These bass eventually will move into more shallow water where fishing smaller-bladed spinnerbaits and worms are more feasible.

When the water temperature hits the 65-degree range, the bass will slide off the points and begin to look for spawning areas in the back of the warmer pockets filled with brush and timber.

Both topwater baits and spinnerbaits are strong at this time. A 5/

16-ounce white or chartreuse/orange spinnerbait with a single-spin No. 5 Colorado nickel blade outfitted with a curly-tail grub trailer works well in these spawning areas. Almost any topwater bait, including buzzbaits and cigar-shaped baits, work well around the standing timber.

The lower end of the lake below the Alabama 48 bridge offers the best spring fishing, but the river as far as Ketchepedrakee Creek isn't bad.

Keep in mind that many of the pockets, because of the sunlight they receive and the shallow water in them, are much warmer than others in the spring. A water surface temperature gauge is a must.

There are several areas to concentrate during the spring. The three creeks entering Hunter's Bottoms (all are usually referred to by locals as Hunter Creek) is a key spawning area, as it Fox Creek. Triplett Creek is another good area. Mad Indian Creek is one of the best areas in the upper lake.

THE LITTLE TALLAPOOSA

The baits and patterns that work well on the Tallapoosa River also work well on the Little Tallapoosa. The main difference in fishing this part of the lake in spring is that it lacks the multitude of standing timber found on the big river. Anglers in this area must spring fish in areas much like those that hold spring bass in other Alabama lakes.

There are several key areas on the little river side. Wedowee Creek lacks standing timber, but is full of boat docks, piers, pockets and a brush-covered creek channel with many tight bends.

Allen Branch is a small creek with a good running branch in the back. It also has boat docks with brush around them.

The series of pockets (No. 42 on the map) are also good for spring fishing.

Hot weather bass fishing

THE TALLAPOOSA RIVER

Following the spawn, the bass will spend a brief amount of recovery time in the mouth of pockets and on the outside fringes of the standing timber in the pockets. They'll rest for a day or two, then feed heavily before going to deep water.

Spinnerbaits, topwater baits and especially lipless crankbaits such as Rat-L-Traps are effective at this time.

Once the water temperature in the pockets and sloughs gets unbearable, the bass slide off into the deep water and take up residence in the standing timber, usually suspending themselves 30-feet deep or so. Fishing for these fish is relatively tough.

A plastic worm or plastic lizard flipped against the timber should be allowed to fall to the depth of the fish showing on the depthfinder. The plastic bait should then be bounced around to attract the fish and entice them to strike.

A pattern that works well is doodlin', the strange technique developed for use in the deep, clear lakes in California. This pattern uses light line - 6-pound test or less - and a 3/16 bullet weight and a 4-inch plastic worm. The fish are first spotted on the depthfinder, then the worm is counted down to the correct depth. Once on target, the tip of the rod is shaken violently causing the worm to jump around erratically. It is a deadly pattern for these suspended fish.

The real drawback to the pattern is that the fish are on timber, and 6-pound test line is not conducive to cranking them out of it. The increase in the number of hookups with bass make the pattern worth using, however.

Some of the summer bass on this river will move up to the water surface at night, and during the early-morning or late-evening hours. Topwater baits fished around the visible tree tops can be good at this time.

A few other fish will hold on the few timber-covered points in 15 or 20 feet of water. Worms or spoons are good on these fish, but they are almost always smaller fish.

Key areas for this type of fishing on the lower end is the deep timber in Hunter Creek and Fox Creek. On the upper end, the standing timber on the right bank as you enter Mad Indian Creek is good.

THE LITTLE TALLAPOOSA

The summer patterns that work on the Tallapoosa River also work on the Little Tallapoosa River. Standing timber is evident on the left bank for approximately 2 3/4 miles as you enter the creek and the bass will suspend in that timber during summer months.

Wedowee Creek offers poor fishing during the daylight hours because it receives so much recreational boat traffic. It does offer good fishing around the many points and boat houses at night, however.

Cool and cold weather fishing

THE TALLAPOOSA RIVER AND THE LITTLE TALLAPOOSA RIVER

If you're looking for exciting fall fishing, you can do no better than Lake Harris. The bass school heavily on the lake during this time and it's not uncommon for better anglers to catch and release as many as 75 bass per day.

The bass begin chasing shad in the open water and are easy prey. A multitude of baits are good at this time, including Pop-R's, Rat-L-Traps, Little Georges and spoons.

A pair of binoculars are beneficial. An angler can pull his boat into the middle of the lake and use the field glasses to scan the water for schooling activity. This is recognized by the ripple on the water surface punctuated by bass hitting shad.

When the angler spots this, he should run the boat to within 100 yards of the fish, then use the trolling motor to ease up on them.

The angler should keep at least two rods rigged. One should have a topwater bait and the other a Rat-L-Trap, Little George or spoon.

When the fish are hitting topwater, the topwater bait should be cast well past the school and worked through it. When the topwater activity stops, a sinking bait should be cast well past the area and worked through it.

Surprising to most, much of this activity takes place right in the middle of the river. It's not unusual to catch these schooling fish 300 yards from the bank. This type fishing is best in the morning and evening, but on overcast days may go on all day long.

When the bass aren't schooling, they can be found in the same locations you found them following the spawn. The road beds in 15 to 20 feet on the lower end are good for worm fishing, while the outer fringes of the standing timber in the pockets is conducive to spinnerbait and topwater fishing.

This schooling activity and shallow water fishing decreases as winter arrives. The bass head back into the deep timber and suspend. Spoons, jig-and-pigs and worms should be used then.

Other types of fishing

CRAPPIE FISHING

Springtime crappie fishing on this lake brings back memories of the good old days. The multitude of standing timber through this lake provides the habitat crappie need to thrive.

Brushy pockets on the lower end hold the most easily accessible crappie in spring. These fish spawn in the timber in less than 18 inches of water. A live minnow fished on a No. 2 thin wire gold hook on 6-pound test line under a float is hard to beat. A 14-foot telescoping fiberglass pole allows an angler to gingerly swin the bait into place, but spinning tackle or spincast tackle will suffice.

The most deadly pattern during the pre-spawn and post spawn periods is spider fishing, however. A boat may be outfitted with as many rods as possible, each tipped with 6-pound test line and a jig. With the rods pointing out the side and the back of the boat, the trolling motor is used to troll the jigs through the water.

A 3/16-ounce jig with a white head and black body is excellent for this type of fishing.

Hunter Creek, Fox Creek and Mad Indian Creek are key spots for this type of fishing, as are the flats next to the standing timber on the left bank of the Little Tallapoosa River.

The angler working the trolling motor must watch his depthfinder carefully, speeding up to raise the jigs when humps and structure is sighted or slowing when the water deepens.

This type of fishing requires two anglers. One controls the bait while the other reels in fish. When a fish is on, the boat operator never slows. Allowing the boat to slow or stop will tangle the jigs in structure.

During the hot-weather months, the crappie move deeper, suspending themselves in the timber or in the deeper creek channels. Spider fishing works at this time, but most anglers fish a tight line.

Hunter Creek is one of the better creeks at this time.

Fox Creek isn't that good. Triplett Creek and Mad Indian creek are also good.

The bridge pilings on any bridge on the lake will hold crappie at night during summer. Live minnows should be fished under a lantern in this pattern.

Lake Harris' best fishing spots

1. Good long, sloping point above the dam. Excellent spring spot for bass and hybrids.

2. Excellent timber pocket. Good in spring and summer.

3. Underwater road bed. Leads out from timber. Shallow part of road good in spring, deeper part good in summer.

4. Steep rock wall falls directly in river channel. Lot of spotted bass. Summer fishing.

5. Standing timber pockets. Good in spring and summer.

6. Ginhouse Branch of Hunter Creek. Good creek channel and brush; no standing timber. Good year round for bass and crappie.

7. Lane Branch of Hunter Creek. Right bank full of standing timber to the back. Good year round for bass and crappie.

8. Miles Branch of Hunter Creek. Good year round for bass and crappie.

9. Excellent point in Miles Branch.

10. Steep rocky wall in Hunter Creek. Excellent for bass in summer.

11. Good fishing in back of pocket. No standing timber, buts lots of brush.

12. Steep rock walls. Good in summer.

13. One Tree Island. Riverside of island is deep; backside shallow. Bass work their way around island different times of the year.

14. Back of pocket. No standing timber, but lots of brush. Good spring fishing.

15. Rock Crusher area. Big boulders. Summer night fishing for bass.

16. Underwater road bed. Original path that rocks were carried from crusher to dam.

17. Collapsed underwater bridge. Good bass fishing in August. Forty feet deep.

18. Road bed leading to bridge. Goes from shallow water to deep and back shallow. Good bass fishing.

19. Brushy pocket. Good spring fishing.

20. Fox Creek. Good year round for bass and crappie.

21. Standing timber in tight bends of Fox Creek. Good year round.

22. Underwater hump. Good year round.

23. River ledge. Good summer fishing.

24. Timber pockets. Good in spring.

25. Standing-timber-filled pockets. Good spring and fall.

26. Good summer schooling area in bends.

27. Standing timber in back of pocket. Good spring and summer.

28. Right bank of Triplett Creek. Good standing timber. Left bank steep, rocky bank.

29. Alabama 48 bridge. Good crappie fishing at night in summer.

30. Timber-filled pocket. Timber on both banks.

31. Standing timber on right bank of Mad Indian Creek. Good year round.

32. Sharp bend in creek channel of Mad Indian Creek. Good summer and winter area for crappie.

33. Back of Mad Indian Creek. Well-defined creek channel. Steep rocky bank on left that falls into channel. Good summer, fall and winter.

34. Standing timber on pockets on left bank. Good spring and fall.

35. Foster bridge pilings. Good crappie fishing at night in late spring, summer and fall.

36. Ketchepedrakee Creek. Good fishing in the mouth year round.

37. Stump rows. Good in summer for spotted bass.

38. Excellent river bend in Little Tallapoosa. Good shallow point. Good in spring.

39. Allen Branch. No standing timber, but good boat docks with brush. Good year round fishing. Spring bass and crappie in brushpiles, summer bass on points and creek channel.

40. Excellent timber point sloping into river channel. Good year round.

41. Timber-covered island. Good spring fishing.

42. Standing timber pockets. Good spring fishing. 43. Underwater hump next to deep river channel. Also road bed on top. Excellent summer fishing for bass.

44. Wedowee Creek. Excellent points, creek bends and boat houses and piers with brush. Good year round except during the day in summer. Much recreational boat traffic. Good at night in summer.

45. Good bass and crappie fishing in back of Wedowee Creek. Good brush around bridge pilings in creek. Good creek channel.

46. U.S. 431 bridge. Good bass fishing around riprap and pilings; good crappie fishing under the bridge at night.

47. Good stump rows in river channel bend. Crankbaits or worms year round.

48. Old U.S. 431 bridge. Same as 46.

Lake Harris

Ketchepedrakee Creek

Lee Bridge

36

Little Ketchepedrakee Creek

Foster Bridge

35

Gobbler Creek

Fuller Creek

Above Mad Indian Creek

Mad Indian Creek

34

33

32

31

Lake Martin

L ake Martin has been a lake Alabama fishermen have enjoyed for generations. Its bountiful supply of large-mouth, spotted bass, crappie and catfish have since 1926 filled the creels of grandfathers, their children and their grandchildren.

The lake has seen some major changes in its days. It became the first Alabama lake to be stocked with striped bass in 1965 and in 1976 became one of the first non-county lakes to be stocked with hybrids.

The stocking of both types of those fish have given the lake two exciting new fisheries.

Another change that affected the lake was the construction of Harris Dam in 1983. This dam blocked the lake's natural water flow and prohibited the flow of many nutrients that fertilized the water through the years.

As a result, Lake Matin has gotten clearer and clearer and fishing has become tougher.

Anglers appear to be adjusting well and, despite a down cycle in the late 1980's, fishing for a variety of species is still excellent.

Spring bass fishing

ABOVE PINEYWOODS MARINA

The area of Lake Martin above U.S. 280 bridge may or may not be a good location to fish in spring. It all depends on the water level.

When the water level is at winter pool, spring fishing can be extremely difficult on the lake's upper end. This area contains a large amount of structure, but the pockets with structure may have only five or six inches of water during the early spring period some years.

During the springs when there are some good rains, these pockets can offer good fishing, especially when the water is rising.

Charteuse/white and chartreuse/black 1/2-ounce spinnerbaits outfitted with a No. 11 pork frog trailer (black or chartreuse) and a big willowleaf blade should be the first lure used in this area early in the spring.

Britt Creek, Sturdivant Creek and Coley Creek are the three creeks to concentrate on. The other creeks and sloughs above these areas often don't have enough water to hold fish. These three creeks don't

Lake Martin Fact Sheet

Location, length and acreage

Lake Martin is one of four Alabama Power Company reservoirs on the Tallapoosa River. It is bordered to the north by Lake Harris and to the south by Yates Lake. The 39,000-acre reservoir begins at Martin Dam in Elmore and Tallapoosa Counties and stretches to Harris Dam, approximately 30 miles southeast of Anniston. The head of the lake is considered to be Irwin Shoals, 28 nautical miles above the dam. Since the installation of Harris Dam, boat traffic is unable to go further upstream than Irwin Shoals. The lake has 700 miles of shoreline and drains approximately 3,000 square miles.

Impoundment

Construction began on Lake Martin Dam July 24, 1923. It was made operational Dec. 31, 1926.

Lake Martin Dam

Lake Martin Dam is 2,000 feet wide and sits 168 feet high at its highest point. It was constructed with 431,000 cubic yards of concrete and cost $17 million to complete. The dam has 20 30-foot-by-16-foot spillway gates capable of passing 3 million gallons of water each under flooding conditions. The powerhouse is outfitted with four hydraulic turbines and four alternating current generators capable of producing 336 million kilowatt hours of electricity each annually.

Configuration

Lake Martin, formed by the backing up of the Tallapoosa

River, offers wide water throughout its length.

Nowhere along that length does the water stay in the original river channel.

Major and secondary creeks

Besides the Tallapoosa River, Lake Martin is fed by numerous creeks. Kowaliga Creek is the largest, being nearly as large as the remainder of the lake.

Kowaliga Creek offers Lake Martin little water, however, as it enters the lake less than 1{ miles above the dam. Kowaliga Creek is fed by Oakachoy Creek, Pike Creek, Chapman's Creek and Little Kowaliga Creek.

Hillabee Creek is the first creek offering water below Irwin Shoals.

Coley Creek, Britt Creek and Sturdivant Creek join Hillabee Creek above the U.S. 280 bridge.

Elkahatchee Creek, Dennis Creek, Wind Creek, Madwin Creek and Manoy Creek are creeks above Young's Island, while Sandy Creek, Perue Creek and Blue Creek are on the lake's lower end.

Types of fish

Lake Martin features popular species such as largemouth bass, spotted bass, white bass, hybrid bass, saltwater stripe, white and black crappie, channel catfish, flathead catfish, blue catfish, longear sunfish, redear sunfish and bluegill.

The lake also has several species of gar, drum and carp.

As for baitfish, gizzard shad, threadfin shad and several species of minnows are present.

Stocking history

Florida-strain largemouth

1983-88	175,718
1990	38,299
1992	40,000
1993	40,000
1994	40,000

Striped bass

1965-78	135,556
1979	51,000
1980	143,750
1981	230,300
1982	100,800
1984	17,990
1985	100,000
1987	8,000
1988	16,900
1989	17,544
1990	78,000
1991	120,012
1992	119,672
1993	120,220
1994	120,014

Hybrid bass

1976	31,000
1982	104,883
1983	100,460
1984	100,000
1985	99,800
1986	99,138
1987	39,100
1988	39,200

have any weeds, but do have blowdown timbers, man-made and natural brush piles and rocks. If you catch these areas at the right time, you'll find tremendous fishing. Catch them at the wrong time and you'll waste a day of fishing.

PINEYWOODS MARINA TO LAKE MARTIN DAM

Lake Martin is a clear lake. You may find some stain early in the year, but rarely anytime else. They key to finding the big bass in this clear water during the spring is locating the right shallow rocky points. These points, almost always on the north bank, hold the heat and radiate it into the nearby water. The large largemouth bass will concentrate in these areas.

Find one of these rocky points with man-made brush piles on it and you will almost be guaranteed good fishing.

Being a good bass fisherman on this lake, or any lake for that matter, takes some effort. It's not unusual to come to this area of the lake in early January when it's too cold to be outside and find some of this lake's better bass fishermen out riding and looking, dressed like mummies. This lake's low water level during this time of the year exposes the man-made brush piles. The angler who comes to this lake in January with a notebook and pencil and nothing else is the angler who will have success here in the spring.

Another key location for spring bass in this lake for late February

and early March is the red clay points that have a few scattered fist-sized white rocks on them. No one has ever been able to successfully explain (or at least they don't want to explain) why the points with these rocks hold fish like they do. One guess, and it sounds farfetched, it that at one time an angler somewhat unfamiliar with the lake filled his boat with these rocks and whenever he caught fish on one of the points, he threw these rocks on them to mark them. If that's the case, the man was fishing from a battleship because there are a lot of these points and an awful lot of these rocks.

Nevertheless, the bass use these points for staging areas this time of the year.

Piers can offer some good fishing in the spring, but most of these piers are too far out of the water this time of the year to offer any help. The brush around the piers, if deep enough, can hold some fish, however.

There are several good area to concentrate on below Pineywoods Marina. Wind Creek, despite the fishing pressure and the amount of boat traffic, is one. Madwin Creek and Manoy Creek are also good spring fishing areas. The area behind Woods' Island, if you can catch it right, is also good.

Sandy Creek is a large creek that if you're willing to learn it, can hold your fishing attention all day in the spring. Its real drawback is the fact it's usually one of the first creeks to muddy in the spring and it will sometimes get too muddy to fish. It also holds the stain longer than most creeks on the lake. Its points, brush piles and piers hold numbers of fish, however.

All four of these creeks offer excellent bass fishing in the spring, but the key to being successful is fishing them enough to learn where the man-made brush piles are. This is where you'll find your quality fish.

A variety of baits will take fish in this part of the lake. A white spinnerbait is probably the most deadly, but only after the water temperature is over the 55-degree mark. Small, shad-colored crankbaits, Carolina-rigged lizards, jig-and-pigs, buzzbaits, topwater twitch baits and worms will all take fish here. Worms will take fish on this lake year round.

KOWALIGA CREEK

Kowaliga Creek is basically a lake in its own. The massive creek is nearly as large as the remainder of the lake. It contains both deep and shallow water, but it has one major drawback. It normally stays extremely clear year round. Fishing there can be doggone tough.

There is usually a 10-day span in the spring (usually right before Memorial Day) when this area offers tremendous fishing - a jubilee if you will. The water rises significantly during this 10-day period and covers the brush under piers. The largemouth quickly move into this brush and a jig-and-pig flipped into the structure often produces numbers of big fish. Spinnerbaits are often effective at the same time for spotted bass on the fringes of the structure.

Several areas of this creek can offer good spring fishing. The best area is the back of Little Kowaliga Creek, past Real Island. A large number of the pockets have man-made brush piles and fallen timber. Also, look for piers with rod holders and lights. These piers usually have brush around them. Buzzbaits, spinnerbaits and Rapalas all produce fish in these areas.

Always keep in mind that light line is an absolute must all times of the year.

Hot weather bass fishing

ABOVE PINEYWOODS MARINA

The lake's upper end offers little good summer fishing, even at night. It's possible to catch a few ledge fish in the mouth of Hillabee Creek, around the rocks near the back of the island downstream of Hillabee Creek, and around rocky points, but you're better off fishing below Pineywoods Marina.

PINEYWOODS MARINA TO LAKE MARTIN DAM

Combine deep, clear water, high surface temperatures, crazed water skiers and an unrelenting sun and you have a recipe for bass fishing at its worst in Alabama. Lake Martin unfortunately has all four ingredients. Bass are extremely spooky and stressed in this lake during the summer and it's no mystery why.

During the day in the summer, an angler with a depthfinder will often locate small schools of bass off the deep rocky points on the main river channel, but locating these fish and putting them in the boat are two different things. These fish are not only deep, they are also non-aggressive and spooky.

Anglers have attempted to entice the fish to strike for decades with a limited amount of success. Worms and crankbaits have been the main weapons.

Lake Martins' bass anglers have improved their success ratio recently, however, by taking a cue from California bass fishermen, for whom fishing deep, clear warm reservoirs is a way of life. The pattern they use is known as "doodlin."

Doodlin' requires a light spinning outfit, 6- or 8-pound test line, a 4-inch worm, a 3/16-ounce weight and an orange glass bead. The bead is placed above the weight where it will bump it and make noise. The worm should be rigged with an exposed hook rather than being rigged Texas-style.

Once small schools of bass are located on deep points, the boat should be positioned directly on top of the fish. The plastic worm should be counted down to the exact depth of the fish and the rod tip shook up and down quickly. This causes the worm to bounce erratically right in the face of the fish and it drives them crazy. Most believe the fish strike out of anger rather than wanting to feed, because a worm dropped the same way and not shook most often won't evoke a strike.

This pattern will produce good numbers of summer fish.

All the water skiers and bright sun in the world aren't going to keep bass from eating, however. That's why when the sun goes down on Lake Martin in the summer, it's time to get out the fishing rods to do some serious fishing in the lake's deeper creeks.

A tremendous number of piers on this lake have brush around them and a large number have lights. These lighted piers with brush attract baitfish and the bass are rarely far behind.

Worms, small crankbaits and an occasional topwater bait are the lures to use. The boat should be positioned as far as possible away from the piers in the dark water. Long casts are the key.

Many of the better anglers also fish deep in the creeks during the summer at night and catch good fish doing so. Worms and crankbaits fished on deep points with brush will produce these fish.

Another pattern - a strictly-for-fun pattern - is fishing a flyrod around pier lights at night. A white fly with wide white wings mimicks the small moths that fly around these lights. The small bass wait until these moths hit the water and then hit them hard. Plan to use a long, 4-pound leader, however.

KOWALIGA CREEK

Skiers, big boats and the crystal clear water makes Kowaliga Creek a difficult place to fish between Memorial Day and Labor Day. The best advice is to fish elsewhere on the lake at this time, but a an angler with a little patience can catch some fish there.

A doodlin' worm fished 25 deep on the deep rocky points and the ledges with sharp drop-offs is the best bet to catch bass during the day, but plan on fighting the waves from the boat traffic all day, especially on weekends.

Night fishing is best. Spinnerbaits, small crankbaits, Sassy Shads and an occasional topwater bait will take fish around lighted piers in the area from the sailboat club to Needle's Eye.

Cool and cold weather bass fishing

ABOVE PINEYWOODS MARINA

The narrow water above Pineywoods Marina can offer some good fall and winter fishing if the area has some water depth. Hillabee Creek is full of structure including downed trees, big rocks and brush. Spinnerbaits, topwater, small crankbaits and worms will catch both fall and winter fish around this structure.

PINEYWOODS MARINA TO LAKE MARTIN DAM

Three baits tell the story of fishing this area of the lake during the cool and cold months. Bring a few white spinnerbaits, a few topwater baits such as a Crazy Shad or some type of chugger and a Carolina-rigged lizard and leave the rest of your tackle box at home.

Any of those baits can produce fish this time of the year. A Crazy Shad fished around shallow rocky points, brush piles and piers offers the most exciting fishing during the fall, but spinnerbaits are more effective if you can find water with a little stain.

Madwin Creek, Manoy Creek, Sandy Creek and Wind Creek are key creeks for topwater this time of the year, but can also be productive for spinnerbaits if they have a little water color due to heavy rains. Elkahatchee offers the best spinnerbait fishing. Elkahatchee Creek has some funky-colored water at times, depending on what color dye a local manufacturer in the area is using at the moment.

All of the above creeks, except Elkahatchee, can offer some good late fall fishing with Carolina-rigged lizards fished on deeper, rocky points.

Another pattern that works in this area during the cold-weather months is pitchin'. Pitchin' with a jig-and-pig is basically the flippin' pattern with longer casts. The clear water makes flippin' tough. Look for man-made brush piles on deep points to pitch in.

Many anglers believe this is the state's best lake for December and January fishing.

KOWALIGA CREEK

If you fish for sheer enjoyment and would rather feel a tug on your line rather than struggling for hours in an attempt to catch the big one, Kowaliga is an excellent place to fish during the fall.

Christmas-tree colored Nip-I-Didees fished before the sun gets over the trees is the top producer. Points and islands next to the main creek channel begin producing topwater bass (mostly spots) as early as mid-September. These fish will gather in these areas for several weeks before moving up on the flats and in the back of sloughs and creeks.

The area behind Pine Point Marina (formerly Veasey's) is a prime area during this time. Pitchford Hollow, Chapman Creek above Needle's Eye and the open water above The Narrows are prime locations for fall fishing. All three of these areas will have a limited amount of stain during this time and shad gather there.

Once the sun gets over the trees, it's strictly worm fishing time. These areas are full of crawfish at this time and bass feed heavily on them. The crawfish will be brown and their pincers will have a lime color. Due to that, a motor oil worm with a chartreuse firetail has withstood the test of time in this area.

The dead of winter means jig-and-pig time. The fish caught on that bait will usually be larger than any fish you catch in this area any other time of the year. Deep points with brush tend to hold these bass during January and February.

Other types of fishing

HYBRID AND STRIPE FISHING

Lake Martin received its first stocking of striped bass in 1965 and pretty much held the title of stripe capital of Alabama until Smith Lake began to challenge that crown in the late 1980's. Smith Lake, although it is now producing numbers of fish in the 20-pound-plus range, isn't ready to challenge Lake Martin in size of fish, however. Lake Martin has produced hundreds of 30-pound fish, several 40-pound fish and at least one 51-pounder.

Saltwater stripes, hybrid bass and white bass all start the year off in the early spring by making a spawning run (stripes and hybrids can't spawn, but do try) into the area above U.S. 280 bridge and, over on Kowaliga Creek, into the area above the narrows.

These fish can be caught by several methods. The most exciting, but least productive, method is fishing a Redfin or Woodchopper lure on topwater. A 20-pound fish hitting a topwater bait is unlike anything most anglers have ever seen. These topwater baits should be fished early on long sloping points and in narrow pockets.

The most productive method, but probably the most boring, is fishing a live shad on a free line. Twenty-pound test line outfitted with nothing but a hook shuld be used with a live shad hooked through the nostrils. With the boat floating in the mouth of pockets or creeks, the shad should be given plenty of line and be allowed to roam free. It's not uncommon to fish three or four hours without even a strike, then catch a 30-pounder using this method.

Another spring pattern, especially early in the morning when the stripes and hybrids are shallow, is to use a small balloon as a float with a live shad. This allows the shad to run into shallow water without the boat scaring the fish off.

After Memorial Day, the stripes and hybrids will move back into the area around Pineywoods Marina, Bay Pines and Young's Island. The fish will hold on points and in the main river channel until approximately the first of June. Tightlining live shad at the depth the fish are is the only viable way to catch these fish.

The first of June will see these fish move further down river, gathering below the sailboat club, Blue Creek and Kowaliga Creek. These fish will normally stay in these areas on into the fall. Once again, tightlining live shad is the best method of catching these fish. The better stripe and hybrid anglers locate these fish with their depthfinders before daylight and fish them until approximately 8 a.m. After the sun gets high in the sky, the fish disappear into the depths and are almost impossible to locate.

(For more details on stripe fishing, see the Smith Lake section).

Lake Martin's best fishing spots

1. Big boulders in main river channel. Good fishing in spring. 5-10 feet deep.

2. Island. Good in spring when water is up. Topwater.

3. Mouth of Hillabee Creek. Good when water is up in spring.

4. Island in mouth of Hillabee Creek. Stumps on downstream side of the island. Good spring fishing with topwater.

5. Excellent point when water is up. Good spring and winter.

6. Underwater point leading to main channel. Good behind point when water is moving.

7. Excellent point adjacent to island. Good funnel area in spring.

8. Underwater island. Good for schooling bass and hybrids in spring, summer and fall.

9. Railroad trestle. Good night fishing for crappie under bridge with lights.

10. Underwater road bed.

11. Good point. Old building foundation out from point.

13. Lower point in Sturdivant Creek. Excellent fishing year round.

12. Underwater railroad bed in Sturdivant Creek. Good spring and summer. Locate by finding where railroad ties run into sandy bank on left side of creek.

14. Piers filled with brush in Sturdivant Creek. Excellent year round fishing.

15. Excellent point for hybrid fishing early in the year.

16. Excellent slough below U.S. 280 bridge. Many piers there surrounded by Christmas trees and other brush. Good in spring and fall.

17. Pockets north of Pineywoods Marina. Downed trees, brush around piers, rocky secondary points. Good year round.

19. Elkahatchee Creek. Good spring and fall with topwater baits, spinnerbaits. Good color.

18. Dennis Creek. Lot of red clay points and man-made brush piles.

20. Underwater road bed.

21. Underwater road bed.

22. The Narrows. West bank very deep. Great winter fishing with hair jig or grub. Some good fishing in February.

23. Underwater road bed.

24. Excellent slough full of piers with brushpiles.

25. Underwater road bed.

26. Madwin Creek. Full of rocky points, gravel flats and brush-filled piers. Good year round.

27. Manoy Creek. Spring and fall. Deep creek, but full of points.

28. Logjams and blowdown timber. Willow-leaf spinnerbaits in spring and fall.

29. Underwater road bed.

30. Underwater road bed.

32. Wind Creek. Good spring fishing for crappie in back slough.

33. Gas pumps island at Wind Creek State Park. Long point. Fish released from tournaments gather there.

31. Excellent spring fishing in back of Wind Creek. Good shallows with some weeds. Small crankbaits and spinnerbaits in very back.

34. Young's Island. Southwest point is long, deep, rocky. Holds bass on and off year round.

35. Woods' Island area. Lots of good sloughs with blowdown brush. Roadbed runs from bank to Woods' Island to Young's Island on south points.

36. Underwater island. Key area. Top of island is 8 feet deep at winter pool and covered with brush. Good spotted bass area year round. Also, some stripe school there.

37. New Hope Church area. Sloughs behind church full of man-made brush piles. Excellent spring fishing. Gravel bottoms good for spawning bass.

38. Underwater road bed.

39. Island with stumps on west bank.

40. Underwater road bed.

41. Underwater island with stumps on west bank.

42. Underwater islands with stumps on west bank.

43. Underwater road bed.

44. Underwater road bed.

45. Big Sandy Creek. Everything you need for all day fishing in spring and fall. Blowdowns, brush, rocky points.

46. Slough at mouth of Sandy Creek. Long, gravel-covered points and brushpiles. Excellent spring fishing. Brushpiles good in fall.

47. Wicker Slough. Excellent spring fishing. Gravel bottom with blowdown timber. Gravel points have stumps. First long slough on right is full of bass during pre-spawn.

48. Blowdown timber in back of slough. Good spring fishing.

49. Stumps on southwest side of island. Good spring fishing.

50. Underwater boulders on northwest side of small island. Good year round fishing.

51. Underwater road bed from bank through middle of channel and back up other side. Key area. Good year round.

52. Stumpy bank on east side of slough. Good spring fishing.

53. Underwater road bed completely across Blue Creek. Good year round.

54. Underwater road bed.

55. Underwater road bed.

56. Underwater road bed.

57. Stump-filled sloughs. Excellent spring fishing with buzzbaits and spinnerbaits.

58. Underwater road bed.

59. Underwater road bed.

60. Underwater driveway. Home foundations on both sides. Good spring fishing.

61. Underwater road bed.

62. Underwater road bed. Runs parallel to old creek channel. Good spring fishing area.

63. Underwater road bed. Adjacent to old creek channel. Good spring fishing.

64. Underwater road bed across Cooper Creek. Both deep and shallow water. Good year round.

65. Underwater driveway.

66. Underwater road bed across mouth of Blue Creek.

67. Mouth of Kowaliga Creek at Dixie Sailing Club. Tremendous schooling area for hybrids in summer before 8 a.m.

68. Underwater road bed.

69. Underwater road bed. Surrounded by old home foundations.

70. Underwater road bed.

71. Underwater road bed.

72. Underwater road bed in slough.

73. 63 bridge pilings. Good crappie fishing area at night with lights.

74. Underwater islands. Good spring fishing.

75. Good ledges next to shallow island. Good year round.

76. Excellent fishing point in spring.

77. Stump-filled slough. Good spawning area. Buzzbaits and spinnerbaits.

78. Good pockets for spring bass fishing.

79. Island in shallow water next to deep water. Good spring and fall area.

80. Mouth of pocket with good ledges. Good year round.

81. Excellent point for spring fishing. Out from Real Island Marina.

82. Excellent spring fishing point.

83. Shallow water island. Good spring fishing area.

84. Good spawning pockets.

85. Underwater rock point. Good early in fall and spring. Some good year-round fishing.

86. Underwater humps covered with brush piles. Marked fish attractor.

87. Man-made brush piles on banks and under piers in slough.

88. Big rocks off of point out from Castaway Marina. Marked with danger sign. Good spotted bass fishing.

89. Good rocky point with brush.

90. Underwater rock piles. Marked with danger sign. Nearby pockets have stumps on points. Some brush in back of pockets.

91. Excellent point. Deep rock piles.

92. Long gravel-covered underwater ledge.

93. Steep ledge out from rock wall. Good year-round fishing.

94. Good trash-filled pocket.

95. Excellent point. Rocky with quick drop.

96. Point with rocks. Out from house with sliding board.

97. Islands next to deep water. Good spring and fall fishing area before sunup with buzzbaits and Nip-I-Didees.

98. Back of Jack's Hollow. Lots of man-made brush piles.

99. Good stump-covered point. Out from big house. Good fishing in sloughs on both sides. Good fishing around islands in spring and fall. Good ledge fishing in area, too.

100. Good point with underwater rock pile.

101. Underwater rock pile. Good year-round fishing. Visible when water is down 8-10 feet.

102. Slough in back of Kowaliga Marina. Filled with rocky points and brush. Big iron pipe on left bank with automobiles sunk beside it. Lot of trash sunk around autos.

103. Big slough. Blowdown timber and rocks. Piers on right side have brush.

104. Block wall on point. Falls into deep water. Good topwater area in spring and fall.

105. Long point. Good spotted bass year round.

106. Excellent point above islands. Holds fish year round.

107. Good pockets. Filled with trash. Good spring and fall.

108. First point on left in Needle's Eye holds lots of fish. Back of pocket also good.

109. Excellent point right before the Narrows.

110. Pleasure Island. Pockets behind island contain pea gravel. Good spawning area for bass.

111. Back of Porter Branch. Ski course area. Entire pocket good. Full of brush.

112. Excllent series of points and slough. Many brush piles.

113. Good points and pockets. Brush usually visible.

114. Big rocky point. Good year round.

115. Good pockets. Lots of small points. Full of brush.

116. Back of Little Kowaliga Creek. Good flats. Good spawning area with brush.

Lake Martin

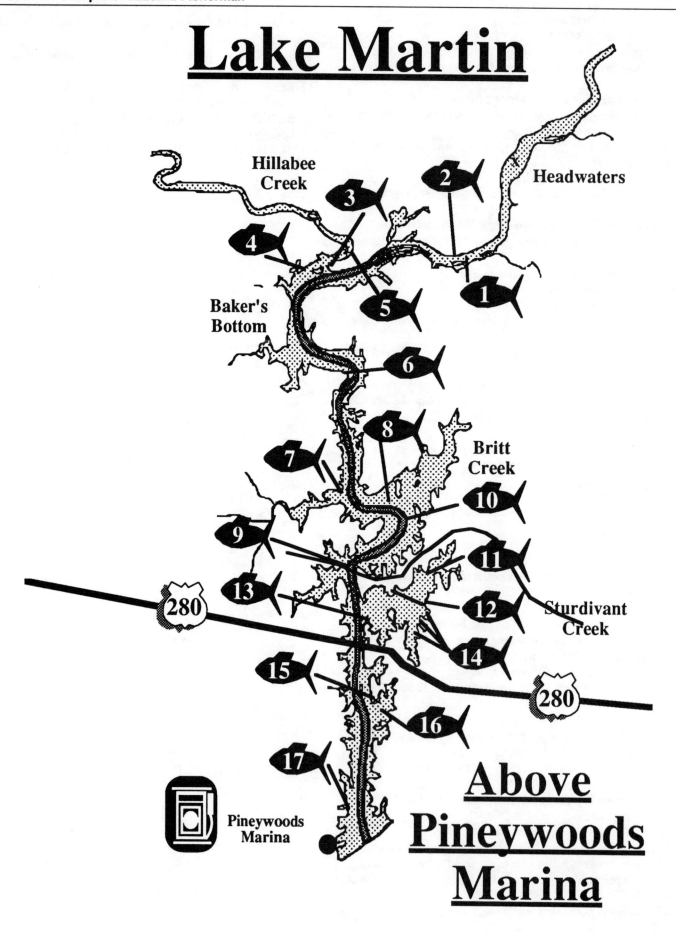

Headwaters

Hillabee Creek

Baker's Bottom

Britt Creek

Sturdivant Creek

280

280

Pineywoods Marina

Above Pineywoods Marina

Lake Martin

Elkahatchee Creek

Bay Pine Marina

Madwind Creek Marina

Manoy Creek

Sandy Creek

Wind Creek State Park

Wind Creek

Wicker Slough

Pleasure Point Marina

Pineywoods Marina to Pleasure Point Marina

Lake Martin

Pleasure Point Marina to Lake Martin Dam

Kowaliga Creek

Perue Creek

Blue Creek

Bama Park

Chuck's Marina

Stillwaters Resort

49 50 51 52 53 54 55 56 57 58 59 60 61 62 63 64 65 66 67

Lake Martin

Kowaliga Creek

Jones Bluff Reservoir

J ones Bluff Reservoir is living proof that a reservoir that flows through a major metropolitan area can still offer excellent fishing. Bass, crappie, bream, catfish and hybrid are plentiful in this lake. The lake flows along the northern edge of Montgomery's downtown.

This reservoir has long been known to area fishermen and according to statistics released by the state, is one of Alabama's most-fished bodies of water. The lake took on national significance in 1981 and 1982 when BASSMASTER Classics were held there. Fitzgerald, Ga.'s Stanley Mitchell won the 1981 Classic with 15 fish weighing 35.2 pounds and Paul Elias, of Laurel, Miss., won the 1982 Classic with 15 fish weighing 32.8 pounds.

Spring bass fishing

PARKER'S ISLAND TO THE EASTERN BYPASS

The section of the Alabama River that winds its way through Montgomery is little more than straight river banks. Because of a lack of creeks for the water to back up in, it's prone to flooding conditions during the spring and is often extremely muddy. For those reasons, the upper end isn't normally the place to plan a spring fishing outing.

During those years when spring flooding isn't a problem, a few fish can be caught in the upriver area, however. The area around Parker's Island and the Dead River area is full of sand bars, pea gravel bars and logjams. A one-half-ounce chartreuse/white spinnerbait with gold blade and a No. 11 chartreuse pork frog trailer is the best bait in this area.

Anywhere the river bends is worth a look in the spring. The outside of the bend will have deep water, but the inside bend will be shallow bars, many times with trash and logjams. The same spinnerbait should be fished in these bends.

Never pass up the mouth of Coosada Creek. This small creek offers one of the few areas where largemouth can escape the swift current and fish gather in the mouth, muddy water or not. Several days without rain is usually needed to suck the mud out of the creek during spring floods, but don't hesitate to go up in the creek and fish the line where the muddy water and clear water meet. Fish are

Jones Bluff Reservoir

Location, length, acreage

Jones Bluff Reservoir, officially known as Lake Robert F. Henry, is a long and winding Alabama River reservoir in Lowndes, Autauga, Montgomery and Elmore counties.

The reservoir begins at Robert F. Henry Lock and Dam in Lowndes and Autauga counties approximately 15 miles east of Selma and stretches 80.5 nautical miles to Walter F. Bouldin Dam. Jones Bluff Reservoir has 373 miles of shoreline and drains 16,300 square miles.

Impoundment

Robert F. Henry Lock and Dam became operational January 22, 1972.

Robert F. Henry Lock and Dam

Robert F. Henry Dam is 646 feet wide and 75 feet high. The powerhouse encloses four 17,000 kilowatt turbine/generator units.

Configuration

Jones Bluff Reservoir is virtually run-of-the-river above U.S. 31 with only a sprinkling of creeks and flats. Below that point, the river comes out of the original channel a good bit more thus creating ledges and pockets.

Major and secondary creeks

The Coosa River and Tallapoosa River merge to form the Alabama River at the head of Jones Bluff Reservoir and the lake gathers most of its water from the two rivers.

The reservoir's upper end lacks large creeks, with Galbraith Mill Creek, Coosada Creek and Pine Creek being small creeks which enter above U.S. 31.

Below U.S. 31, Autauga Creek, Catoma Creek, Pintlala Creek, Noland Creek, Log Cabin Creek, Bear Creek, Tensaw Creek, Swift Creek (fed by Yellow Water Creek) Cypress Creek, House Creek (fed by Spratt Branch) Brown Branch, Beaver Creek and Prairie Creek supply water to the lake.

Types of fish

Jones Bluff Reservoir features popular species such as largemouth bass, a small population of spotted bass, white bass, hybrid bass, saltwater stripe, white and black crappie, channel catfish, flathead catfish, blue catfish, bullhead catfish, longear sunfish, redear sunfish, green sunfish, warmouth, and bluegill. The lake also has several species of gar, drum and common carp. As for baitfish, gizzard shad, threadfin shad and several species of minnows are present.

---

sometimes gathered there in numbers.

If you enjoy fishing escape areas in the spring, give the backside of the islands a try, too.

Further downstream, the Jackson Lake area is worth a look. This oxbow lake is full of cypress trees and holds spring bass. The gravel pits (No. 9 on the map) is a good spawning area, but high water is needed to get into the area and high water usually means muddy water. If you can find a happy medium, give the pits a try.

Don't mistake the listing of several areas in this upper section as an endoresement for fishing the area during the spring, hoever. Rarely will you ever find the lake's better fishermen in this area during spring tournament time.

EASTERN BYPASS TO TALLAWASSEE CREEK

Once you pass downstream of the Eastern Bypass bridge, you will discover two things you will like - wider water and water with less stain.

Unlike the upper end of the lake, this area has many wide creeks which will back up and lessen water levels during heavy spring rains. The water still will be high at times, but it's less muddy and fishing isn't affected nearly as much.

Cooter's Pond, Catoma Creek, Pintlala Creek, Noland Creek and Tallawassee Creek help to alleviate the spring flooding problem.

The key to fishing this area in the early spring is determining exactly where the fish are. These fish will be leaving the deep water of the main channel and staging themselves up the ledges on their way to the creeks.

Deep-running crankbaits and Texas-rigged lizards are key baits at this time. Let the water clarity determine the bait color. Heavily stained water will call for a lime or chartreuse crankbait or a dark worm with a chartreuse or orange tail. Less stained water will require more subtle colors, such as a shad-colored crankbait or a pumpkin-seed-colored 7-inch Zoom lizard.

All of the upstream and downstream points leading into the creek mouths are surrounded by 2- to 4-foot sycamore stumps, and the dirt has washed away from the tremendous root systems of these stumps. It is excellent structure to hold staging fish. Bring lots of baits when you come, however. These roots keep a lot of crankbaits.

Once the water hits the 62- to 65-degree range, bass will have spawning on their mind and will move into the creeks using the channels and ditches as their roadways. These fish will stack up in bends of the original creek channel and hold until the water temperature allows them to move to the ledges. Fishing can be confusing during this time because the fish will flip-flop from the channel to the ledges depending on the weather. Worms and Sassy Shads are good baits when the fish are holding in the channel, but buzzbaits and 3/8-ounce Strike King spinnerbaits with big willowleaf blades are best when the fish move to the ledges.

One of the better secrets of the lake's spring tournament fishermen is using a blue/chartreuse, straight blue or straight red spinnerbait. These spinnerbaits tend to catch sluggish fish that are tired of seeing white or chartreuse baits thrown at them day-in and day-out.

Go with a gold blade in light stain conditions and a copper blade or a painted orange or charteuse blade when the water is heavily stained. Use a No. 11 pork frog trailer, a twin-tail frog or a 3-inch chartreuse grub to dress up the baits.

One of the strangest things about this lake is that the pre-spawn and post-spawn bass on the ledges in the spring often roam open water, rather than sticking close to structure. It's not unusual to throw a spinnerbait or buzzbait onto a muddy ledge void of structure and catch fish. Why are they there? Who knows?

There are several creeks to concentrate on during the spring. Cooter's Pond has lots of shallow water conducive to spring bass fishing. Catoma Creek is an excellent spring fishing area. It has the structure, flats and bends that concentrate fish and make locating them easier. Several junkyards were covered when the lake was impounded. There are also a lot of stumpy points in shallow water.

Noland Creek is a deepwater creek, but it has some flats and shallow points that hold spring fish. Pintlala Creek is narrow, but it has a lot of hard bends, blowdown timber and stumps in shallow water that make excellent spawning areas.

Tallawassee Creek is one of the better creeks for spring fishing. The Corps of Engineers left several stands of timber in the creek bends to attract fish. Some of it has rotted and fallen, leaving stumps at the water level. This was also one of the original stocking areas for the lake and many anglers believe a large number of those fish have stayed in the area.

TALLAWASSEE CREEK
TO ROBERT F. HENRY LOCK AND DAM

Anglers will notice several distinct changes in the lake once they go downstream of Tallawassee Creek. For starters, the water clears noticeably. The water is also wider and has more grass.

The patterns used in fishing this area in the spring is virtually the same as the stretch of lake above it. You may want to go to a lighter spinnerbait and switch to a silver blade, but pattern-wise, very few changes are in order.

Crankbaits and worms should be fished in the mouth of the creeks early, and spinnerbaits and buzzbaits are needed when the fish move up into the creeks.

If there is a pattern change on this lake, it's paying more attention to the grass. The grass that can be found in 5 feet of water will hold fish and the fish will be there before, during and after the spawn. This grass provides all the basic necessities including food, cover and oxygenated water.

Artificial crawfish and jig-and-pig flipped into this grass can produce some trophy fish this time of year.

There are numerous areas to concentrate on in this end of the lake in the spring. Newport Landing Slough is full of standing timber in the back and is an excellent spawning area. Tensaw Creek has both deep and shallow water and is full of good points that hold bass pre- and post-spawn.

Swift Creek shouldn't be overlooked. There is much farming in the area and animal wastes and fertilizer wash in and keep it stained. It is one of the earliest creeks on the lake to warm and the first place on the lake you can catch a fish with a spinnerbait each year. This creek is virtually a private pond.

Cypress Creek has many humps and ledges, as well as grass the first few hundred yards inside its mouth. The west bank is deep and the right bank somewhat shallower. The back end is full of cypress trees, hence its name. This creek can be rated good for spring fishing.

House Creek is the camp out spot on the lake. Tent-pitchers and private campers frequent the area. House Creek is narrow and over-fished. Pass it up.

The Three Fingers area, officially known as Cooper Howard Creek, is an excellent spring spawning area. The east fork stains good from farming and warms much earlier than the middle two forks, which are usually clear. Weeds, standing timber and points can be found on all three fingers and fishing can be excellent, especially on the west fork in March.

Brown Branch is a narrow creek surrounded by extremely high bluffs. Its water is much too deep for spring fishing.

Beaver Creek is a wide creek that is good in early spring. Its mouth is full of trash, floating debris, logjams and blowdown timber. There is some grass up in the creek. This creek has a lot of shallow water and is buzzbait territory.

Prairie Creek, the first creek above Jones Bluff Dam, is an excellent spring fishing area. It has a well-defined creek channel and lots of structure.

Hot weather
bass fishing

PARKER'S ISLAND TO EASTERN BYPASS

If there's a good time to fish this end of Jones Bluff Reservoir, it's during the hot months of summer. Unlike most lakes in Alabama, this lake gets a good amount of water flow during hot weather and this water movement triggers the bass into feeding.

Water will move in this area nearly every weekday during the summer and the lack of creeks makes the water flow more forceful here than any other area on the lake.

The outside bends of the main river channel are the areas to concentrate on during this time. Lots of baitfish gather in these bends when water is being pulled. Rat-L-Traps, spoons, Little Georges and plastic worms will take the bass gathered in these bends.

The Big Curve area has deep banks with blowdown timber and day-in and day-out is the top producing bend on the river's upper end.

If water isn't being pulled, don't waste your time in this end of the lake during summer.

EASTERN BYPASS TO TALLAWASSEE CREEK

Before Jones Bluff Reservoir was impounded, chainsaws took down all the timber that would eventually be underwater. This left ledges full of standing stumps.

Anywhere along these stump-filled dropoffs is a threat to hold schooling summer bass, but they gather best in the river bends because that's where the bait gathers. These bends also have more blowdown timber because the moving water erodes these banks more quickly.

It's not unusual to find smaller bass up in this blowdown timber from dark to 7 a.m. during summer. Worms and topwater baits will normally take these fish.

The bigger fish will stay off in the deep water, however, electing to suspend themselves along the ledge. They will make occasional runs onto the ledge to feed. The best method to locate these fish is to watch for shad. Shad will ripple the water and actually jump or get knocked out of the water while the bass are feeding on them.

The angler can use several baits at this time. A worm is probably the best bait, but a Sassy Shad fished on light line is close behind. Some opt for small, medium-running crankbaits, but the number of baits lost doesn't justify their use.

During the night or during the wee hours of the morning, don't hesitate to throw a topwater lure such as a Bagley's Bang-O-Lure where the ledge meets the deep water.

Once again, moving water is the key in this area. With the water off, it's possible to fish your heart out at daylight and not get a bite, then when the sun gets high, have the water start moving and load the boat. Having the water move is often like flipping a light switch or ringing a dinner bell.

If you're a creek fishermen, several creeks in this area have water deep enough to support summer bass. Catoma Creek and Pintlala Creek have such water.

Pintlala Creek is a creek you should especially keep an eye on. This narrow creek has shade trees on both banks and the amount of shade these trees provide results in a creek with a lower water temperature than the creeks around it.

Pintlala Creek also has a lot of blowdown timber and brush which hold fish on the banks during the summer.

Tallawassee Creek
To Robert F. Henry Lock and Dam

Because of the amount of water flow this lake gets during the summer months, the water flow into the creeks - especially the gaps - is well-pronounced. The bass like gathering in these areas.

One of the top baits during the summer is 1/4-ounce hair (bucktail) jigs. White/yellow or white/chartreuse colors seem to work best. These baits apparently match the size of the shad hatch well because they are dynamite this time of the year and not much use the rest of the year.

The bucktail jigs should be cast into the creek mouths when the water is moving and hopped back to the boat. The hair jig rarely produces big fish, but it produces numbers of fish.

Worms and Little Georges also will work in the creek mouths, and on the ledges as fished in the lake's middle section.

The flats and creek mouths above the dam are some of the best areas for this type of fishing.

Cool and cold weather bass fishing

Parker's Island to Eastern bypass

Once again, moving water is the key to good fishing on Jones Bluff Reservoir in the fall. Falls rains and the pulling down of Lake Martin to winter pool means there will be water movement almost every day during September, October and November.

There's a lot of visible topwater activity with bass busting shad on top in the outer bends, behind islands and in the mouths of creeks - the traditional escape areas for shad.

The smart angler keeps two loaded rods in the boat. A small Tiny Torpedo or Crazy Shad should be on one rod, while a Rat-L-Trap or Fish World Pogo Shad should be on the other.

Use the topwater baits when the bass are knocking shad out of the water, being careful to position the boat as far away as possible and still cast well past the schooling activity.

When the school of bass suddenly go under, switch to the Rat-L-Trap or Pogo Shad and and throw past the school and rip the lure back to the boat.

One of the tricks of the better anglers is that when a school suddenly goes under, they rush to the scene to get a look at wounded shad that may be left on top. This allows them to see the size of the baitfish and match their lures to that size. That matching is of utmost importance.

The bass will often be shallow when the water isn't running in this area - early in the morning, late in the evening or on overcast days.

A spinnerbait, Jitterbug, Jumpin' Minnow or Rapala can work.

Key areas to concentrate on are the ditch across Parker's Island, the backside of Mud Island, the Big Curve area, the Jackson Lake area, the mouth of Coosada Creek, and the primary points on flats and the mouths of the strip mine areas.

Eastern bypass to Tallawassee Creek

Fall fishing in this area is exciting because it offers so much opportunity for topwater fishing. If you purchase no other bait this time of the year, make sure your tackle box has a Christmas-tree colored Nip-I-Didee. This tried and true lure is strong on this area of the lake in the fall.

As mentioned before, stumps can be found throughout the flats in this area and are especially concentrated on the main points. A Nip-I-Didee fished on the points early on cool mornings often produces 30 to 40 bass a day when you catch it right.

Other baits that are productive include buzzbaits and worms.

When water is being pulled, and it's often, fishing can be good all day long.

A good number of fish migrate up into the creeks during this time, too. Cooter's Pond, a hotbed for recreational boating and skiing, can offer good fishing in the back where the grass and lily pads are.

This is an excellent flippin' and buzzbait area.

Both Catoma and Pintlala creeks are excellent fall fishing areas to concentrate on, too. Both creeks have good concentrations of shad.

Tallawassee Creek
To Robert F. Henry Dam

The cool and cold weather patterns change very little when you enter the lake's lower end. Just as in the middle section, you'll find some fish in the mouth of creeks, some in the creek channels and others up on the ledges of both the main river and the creeks.

Deep-diving crankbaits fished along the underwater bends in the creek channels is one of the best ways to take quality fish and is a little more effective on this end than in the middle or upper section.

Tensaw is a good fall creek, but it is small and receives a lot of pressure. Cypress Creek is another area to key on, but it is often filled with crappie fishermen. The Three Fingers area is a good fall fishing area, with the western finger usually holding the better fish.

Brown Branch is one of the lake's few creeks that enter in a bend, and as a result, current forces large numbers of shad into it. Although it's a deep creek, it offers excellent fall fishing.

Beaver Creek probably offers the most schooling activity, but only on the years when the shad are in there. Some years you won't find a shad in the creek. This creek is full of logs and stumps.

Prairie Creek offers erratic fall fishing. Stay away in the fall.

Jones Bluff Reservoir's best fishing spots

1. The ditch. Ditch connects the Alabama River to the Tallapoosa River through Parker's Island. Excellent spring fishing area. Tight mouths, but opens up to 25 acres of excellent fishing.

2. Intersection of Alabama and Tallapoosa Rivers. Excellent sandbar for summer and fall fishing.

3. Flats meet river channel. Good summer schooling area.

4. Mud Island. Good area in spring.

5. The "Big Curve" area. Good summer area. Baitfish load up in curve's upper end.

6. Island. Downstream point good when current is moving.

7. Flats adjacent to main river channel. Good in spring.

8. Jackson Lake. Oxbow lake. Natural lake with cypress trees. Good in spring.

9. Good escape area when current is moving. Bass school on this point.

10. Gravel pits. Good in spring when water level allows.

11. Location where Montgomery dumps its sewage. Known as the "Shad Hole." Good year round fishing in area.

12. Gravel pits. Good spring fishing.

13. Brick pilings. Good bass fishing when current is off.

14. County line bend. Excellent summer fishing as baitfish gather in bend.

15. Tyler Goodwin Bridge debris. Underwater debris. Good summer fishing with worm.

16. Bridge pilings and riprap on both sides. Good summer fishing area.

17. City storm sewers entrance. Spring rains bring warm water off of pavement. Key spring area during rains.

18. Pocket. Good escape area.

19. Bridge pilings and riprap.

20. Flats. Excellent crappie fishing in spring.

21. Good flats. Same as No. 20.

22. Island. Falls directly into main river channel on west side. Shallow water on east side. Good fishing on both upriver and downriver points.

23. Good spring fishing in what was a private lake before water was impounded.

24. Mouth of ditch. Good year round.

25. Good bend in river. Good summer fishing.

26. Small ditch going to Cooter's Pond. Good fishing in mouth in spring.

27. Entrance to Cooter's Pond. Good ledge fishing in spring and fall.

28. Good spring spawning area around island.

29. Good spring fishing around island.

30. Standing timber patch. Good spring fishing.

31. Lily pads in back of Cooter's Pond. Good spring and fall.

32. Bridge pilings. Good spring fishing in the narrows.

33. Crescent Lake. Can get an aluminum boat in area. Good spring fishing.

34. Mouth of Pine Creek. Excellent fishing in mouth during summer.

35. Good points in mouth of Pine Creek.

36. Bridge pilings. Pilings on both sides in shallow water good for spring crappie.

37. Bridge pilings under railroad trestle. Good crappie fishing.

38. Excellent cuts.

39. Good sandbar points.

40. Autauga Creek. Lot of moving water in creek. Good summer-time area.

41. Good sandbar points. Good in spring, summer and fall.

42. Mouth of Catoma Creek. Excellent year-round.

43. Grass filled cuts.

44. Excellent bank. Blow down timber.

45. Islands. Good spring fishing around island with spinnerbaits and topwater in spring.

46. Antioch Creek. Mouth offers good year-round fishing.

47. Backside of island. Good area when current is moving.

48. Standing timber.

49. Mouth of Noland Creek. Good year-round.

50. Noland Creek. Good spring and fall.

51. 'Possum Bright Bar. Underwater island. Good summer area.

52. Sheer dropoffs. Good summer fishing on ledges.

53. Mouth of Pintlala Creek. Good year-round.

54. Bridge pilings. Good spring area for bass. Good in summer for crappie at night.

55. Railroad trestle. Good spring area for bass and crappie.

56. Mouth of cuts full of standing timber. Excellent spring crappie area.

57. Tallawassee Creek. Good in spring and fall for bass and crappie.

58. Downstream point of Tallawassee Creek. Excellent year-round fishing.

59. Standing timber filled slough.

60. Mouth of Log Cabin Creek. Good spring staging area.

61. Mouth of Rocky Branch. Points good in early spring and summer.

62. Standing timber-filled slough.

63. Bear Creek. Mouth of creek is good fall area.

64. Tensaw Creek. Good spring and fall.

65. Pockets. Good spring and fall.

66. Flats. Good spring fishing.

67. Mouth of Swift Creek. Good year-round.

68. Creek channel. Well-defined. Good year-round.

69. Dutch Island. Stumps on upper end. Good spring and fall.

70. Grass filled flats.

71. Cut-off. Excellent when water is moving.

72. Stump-filled slough.

73. Mouth of Cypress Creek. Good spring, fall and summer.

74. Cypress Creek. Lots of grass. Cypress trees in back.

75. House Creek. Good fall creek. Lots of shad.

76. Grass flats.

77. Mouth of cut. Good year-round for bass.

78. Three-fingers area eastern finger. Good color from farm runoff.

79. Middle fork. Deep water.

80. West fork. 5-6 foot of water.

81. Brown Branch. Deep water. Excellent in spring.

82. Mouth of Beaver Creek. Good when current is moving on points.

83. Beaver Creek. Cypress trees in back.

84. Cut-off. Good spring fishing.

85. Big flat. Some spring fishing with topwater.

86. Excellent summer and fall schooling area for bass around island.

87. Ivy Creek. Now dredged out. Boat ramp in back. Good spring fishing.

88. Pier-filled slough. Brush around piers.

89. Long, sloping underwater point. Good year-round.

90. Slough. Primary downriver point good year-round. Some grass in slough.

91. Grass filled slough.

92. Island in mouth of Prairie Creek. Good water with grass behind island.

93. Mouth of Prairie Creek. Downriver point good except in winter.

94. Excellent point.

95. Good year-round fishing around islands. Adjacent to channel.

96. Grass filled sloughs. Mouth silted in, but good fishing in back.

97. Rip-rap above dam. Excellent spring fishing. Good rest of year.

98. Good pockets in spring.

Jones Bluff Reservoir

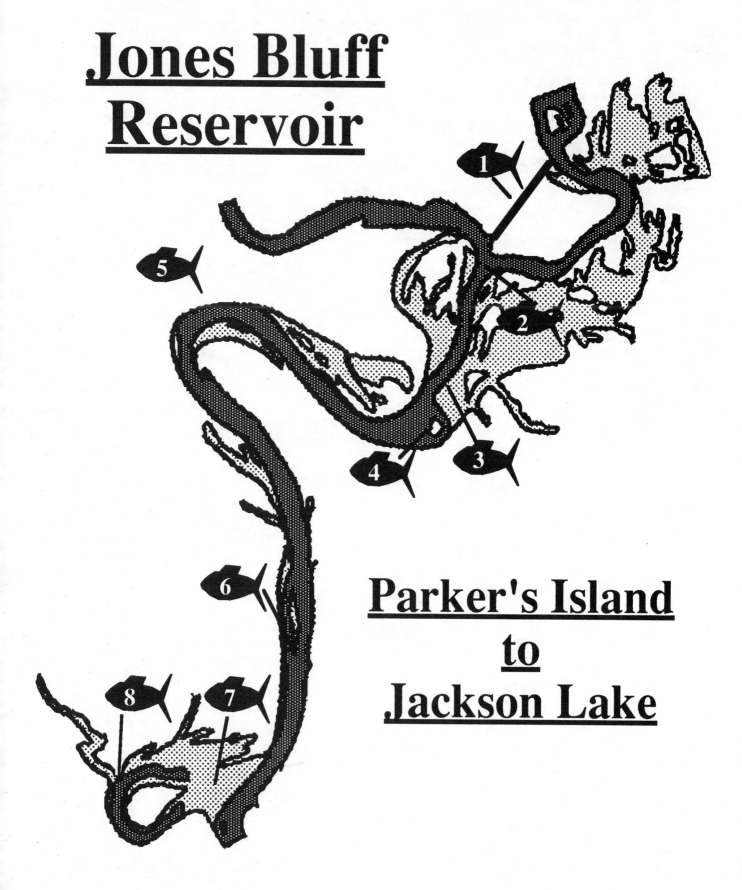

Parker's Island to Jackson Lake

Jones Bluff Reservoir

Jackson Lake
to
Eastern Bypass

Eastern Bypass to U.S. 31 Bridge

Jones Bluff Reservoir

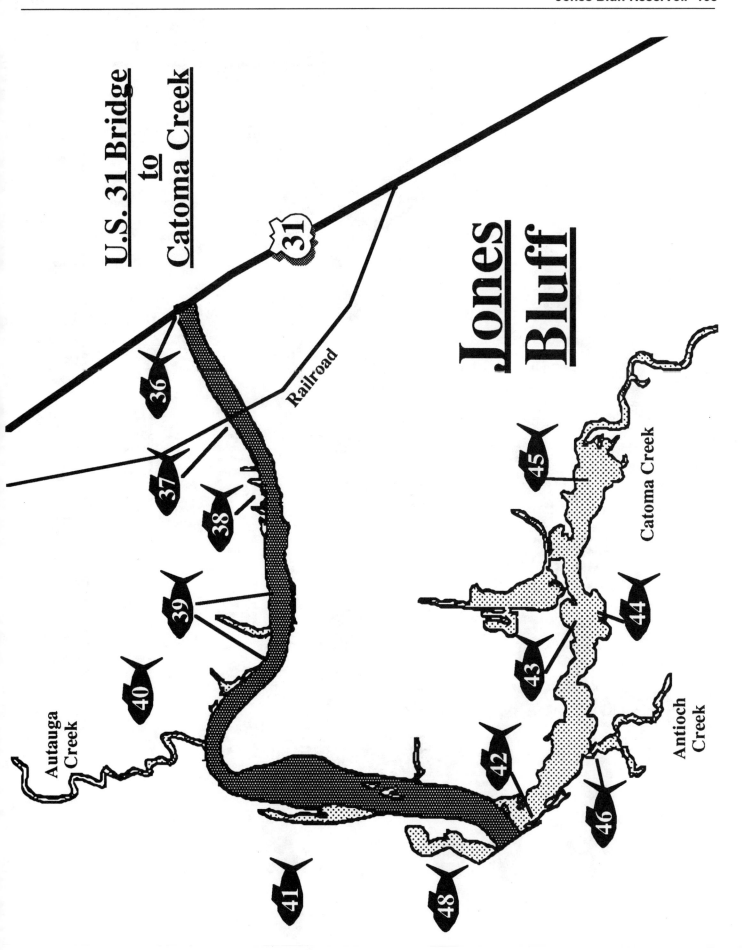

U.S. 31 Bridge
to
Catoma Creek

31

Railroad

Jones
Bluff

Catoma Creek

Antioch
Creek

Autauga
Creek

36

37

38

39

40

41

42

43

44

45

46

48

Jones Bluff Reservoir

Catoma Creek
to
Swift Creek

Swift Creek

Tallawassee Creek

Log Cabin Creek

Noland Creek

Jake's

Pintlala Creek

Jones Bluff Reservoir

Dutch Island

Dutch Bend

Cypress Creek

House Creek

Brown Branch

70

69

72

71

73

74

78

79

76

75

81

80

77

Jones Bluff Reservoir

Ivy Creek

83

82

Beaver Creek

85

84

87

86

89

88

Henderson's Landing

90

91

92

95

93

Prairie Creek

96

98

94

97

Robert F. Henry Lock and Dam

Beaver Creek to Dam

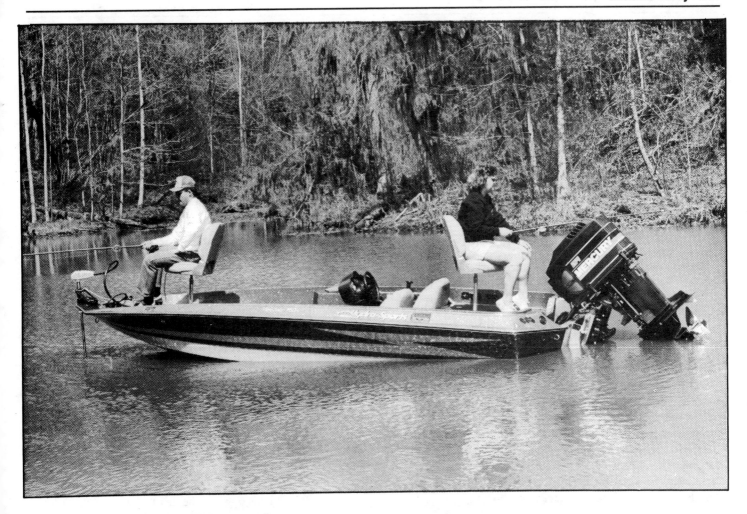

Miller's Ferry

The impoundment of the Alabama River to form Miller's Ferry Reservoir flooded thousands of acres of timber to create a remote lake perfect for bass and crappie. According to data compiled by the state from the annual Bass Anglers Information Team (BAIT) surveys, Miller's Ferry is always near the top of the list of the state's finest bass lakes. Creel surveys also show it is normally one of the state's top crappie producers.

You'll find something rare on this lake, too. From Gee's Bend to Canton Bend, a distance of approximately 9 miles, the river flows north. That's something seen on only one other lake (Pickwick) in Alabama.

Spring bass fishing

MILLER'S FERRY LOCK AND DAM
TO GEE'S BEND

Probably nowhere else in Alabama is a water surface temperature gauge as valuable as on Miller's Ferry Reservoir in the spring. The lake's combination of spring-fed and non-spring-fed creeks and sloughs, as well as its long, thin sloughs and pockets protected by shade trees, results in widely varying water temperatures throughout the lake early in the year. It's not unusual to find two sloughs side-by-side, one being 5 degrees warmer than the other.

There are two other key factors in fishing this lake and they apply year round - water clarity and water movement.

This is a stain lake. Almost never will you find clear water. Even in the dead of winter, rarely will you see water with three-foot visibility.

This lake is sandwiched between two hydro-electric plants and current is common. During the spring, you'll often find water being pulled or pushed 24 hours per day. An angler can call 682-4896 to find load schedules. Keep tabs on the water schedules. Every trip to the lake should be preceded by a call to that number. Water movement during the spring, especially when the water level is dropping rapidly, hurts fishing.

The quality bass in this lake spend the winter deep in the main river channel, but 55-degree water temperature will snap them out of thedoldrums and start them toward their spring activity. They'll

Miller's Ferry Fact Sheet

Location, length and acreage

William "Bill" Dannelly Reservoir, better known to fishermen as Miller's Ferry, is an U.S. Army Corps of Engineers reservoir on the Alabama River. The 17,200-acre impoundment is in southwest Alabama in Wilcox and Dallas counties. The lake begins at Miller's Ferry Lock and Dam 10 miles northwest of Camden and stretches 103 miles to Robert E. (Bob) Woodruff Lock and Dam, which backs up Jones Bluff Reservoir.^

The lake drains 20,700 square miles.

Impoundment

Construction was complete on Miller's Ferry Lock and Dam in November 1969. Power production didn't begin until April 1970.

Miller's Ferry Dam

Miller's Ferry Dam consists of a long earthern dike and a

Stocking history

Florida-strain largemouth

1981-90	156,388
1991	34,575
1992	42,804
1993	34,520
194	70,611

Hybrids

1983-88	396,400
1989	68,900
1990	51,600
1991	52,200
1992	51,076
1993	182,040
1994	55,060

Striped bass

1973-84	639,608
1986	31,900
1988	16,900
1989	17,544
1990	29,200
1991	34,584
1992	33,971
1993	34,487
1994	3,400

994-foot concrete spillway. There are three hydraulic turbines and three alternating current generators.

Major and secondary creeks

Miller's Ferry is blessed with several large incoming creeks. Shell Creek and Mill Creek are water suppliers on the lake's lower end. Foster Creek, Pine Barren Creek, Chilatchee Creek, Bogue Chitto Creek, Rum Creek, Whiteoak Creek, Big Cedar Creek and Big Swamp Creek are water suppliers on the upper end.

Types of fish

Miller's Ferry features popular species such as largemouth bass, a small population of spotted bass, white bass, hybrid bass, saltwater stripe, white and black crappie, channel catfish, flathead catfish, blue catfish, bullhead catfish, longear sunfish, redear sunfish, green sunfish, warmouth, and bluegill.

The lake also has several species of gar, drum and common carp. As for baitfish, gizzard shad, threadfin shad and several species of minnows are present.

---

begin staging out of deep water by moving up the ledges and points. Their food needs increase with this movement.

Jig-and-pigs and Carolina-rigged plastic worms and lizards, and to a lesser degree deep-diving crankbaits, are key baits during this time of year. This is the time for fishing patiently, and both jig-and-pigs and lizards can be fished deep and slow. Many of the better anglers report success by throwing a Carolina-rigged lizard on the deep points showing fish on the depthfinder and literally allowing it to sit there 5 minutes or more, the only movement being the lizard moving slightly in the current.

For fish suspended on the ledges, a deep-diving crankbait with extreme action, such as a Bagley's Smoo, should be used. The strong action of this bait causes the lure to move slowly just as the fish like it.

Once the water temperature jumps to the 62 to 64 degree range, the bass will be on their pre-spawn feeding binge and periodically will be up on the ledges and in the creeks and sloughs chasing shad.

Shell Creek, Mill Creek, Alligator Slough, Houseboat Slough and any of the structure-filled sloughs and flats next to the main river channel will hold these pre-spawn bass.

The increased water temperature will have increased the metabolism of the fish and they will be much quicker. A white or chartreuse/white 1/4-ounce spinnerbait with gold blades and a pork-frog trailer or a topwater buzzbait should be the angler's top choices.

Both baits can be fished around the blowdown timber, standing timber, stumps and brushpiles found throughout this end of the Miller's Ferry.

The spinnerbait and buzzbait works more effectively early in the spawning period when the fish are feeding heavy, but a 7-inch

Carolina-rigged spring lizard - either red-shad or pumpkinseed are the top colors - may be needed when the fish are beginning to feel the stress of the spawn and are holding closer to timber.

This lake has a short spawning period for reasons no one can seem to explain.

It boils down to the fact that most of the fish here spawn all at once rather than at staggered intervals as they do many other places.

The fish on Miller's Ferry come off the bed looking for action and heavy feeding is the norm the first two weeks following the spawn. These fish can be found in the same areas you found them in the pre-spawn period, but keep in mind the water temperature will now be 70 degrees or warmer compared to the 64 to 68 degree range when they were here earlier.

Increase the speed of the bait accordingly. Smaller blades on spinnerbaits will speed up that bait.

Lipless crankbaits such as the Rat-L-Trap can be effective, as are buzzbaits and other topwater lures. And of course, worms will take fish, too.

GEE'S BEND TO BOGUE CHITTO CREEK

The only difference in fishing this area in the spring is the name of the creeks. Buzzard Roost is a shallow, timber filled slough perfect for spring spawning. Pine Barren Creek is a timber-filled creek that offers excellent spawning grounds throughout much of its length. Foster Creek has a lot of deep water, but does have some shallow ledges that will hold spawning fish. The Gold Mine is a shallow water slough that will hold an occasional spawning fish. Chilatchee Creek is a wide creek that has a deep, well-defined creek channel with plenty of flats and islands and is perfect for spring spawning. Bogue Chitto Creek is similar to Chilatchee Creek, but has more structure.

Hot weather
bass fishing

MILLER'S FERRY LOCK AND DAM
TO GEE'S BEND

During years of normal rainfall, this lake will have at least some current moving some time during the day. If possible, aim for those times when there is moving water.

It's possible to find some bass in shallow water year round on this end of the lake, but as on other lakes in the state, these are almost always small fish. These shallow water fish can offer excitement for those who want to feel a tug on the line. Buzzbaits and other topwater will catch some fish early in the morning and late in the evening, especially on the shady banks in Mill Creek and Shell Creek. Plastic worms fished in or near the ledges on the creek channel will produce some fish up in the day. Rarely will these fish be larger than two or three pounds, however.

If you want big fish during the summer months, you have to work for them. The quality fish have more stringent temperature and oxygen requirements and the larger fish will be in deeper water, namely on deep humps and points on the main river channel or in the mouth of creeks.

The deep points in the mouth of Shell Creek, Mill Creek, the humps and brushpiles out from the mouth of Rex's Hole Slough, the underwater sandbar in Canton Bend (No. 28 on the map) and the deep points in the original creek channels in the mouth of Cotton-house Slough, Alligator Slough and River Bluff Slough are prime locations to search out with the fish finder.

What the depthfinder shows you should determine how you fish for these fish. A few scattered fish should be approached with a deep-diving crankbait, jig-and-pig, a Texas-rigged worm or Do-Nothing worm. Deep, schooling fish should be attacked with a jigging spoon or Little George.

A day of riding on the river with the depthfinder won't be wasted, especially if the current is off and fishing would be poor. Locate fish and come back to them when the current is moving and they are feeding.

GEE'S BEND TO BOGUE CHITTO CREEK

Once again, the fishing pattern doesn't change when you move up into this area. It's possible to catch fish year round in some of the creeks with deep channels such as Pine Barren Creek, Bogue Chitto Creek and Chilatchee Creek, but don't expect big fish. The fishing for bass in the main river channel is so difficult for so many anglers that most are willing to settle for small fish, however.

This portion of the lake does have several easy-to-locate sharp river bends and creek mouths that hold fish. Because of the large amount of timber in this lake and the current, sharp bends in the river are normally full of logjams and this is prime habitat for summer bass. Gee's Bend, the bend directly across from Camden State Park, the bend one mile above Foster Creek and the bend before you reach Bogue Chitto Creek are prime areas for this type of fishing. A jigging spoon works wonderfully in this area, but plan to use a heavy spoon

like a Mann's Mann-O-Lure or a big Krocidile because they hang up easily in the timber. The weight of the lures are often enough to pull the hook out of wood. Another excellent bait is a jig-and-pig. Some anglers try to use worms, but it's hard to detect a strike on a worm at these depths.

When you locate one of the logjams, throw a marker buoy and anchor. You must be directly on top of one of these spots to be effective.

Also, don't hesitate to fish the mouths and secondary points of Chilatchee Creek, Pine Barren Creek and Bogue Chitto Creek with deep-diving crankbaits.

Cool and cold weather bass fishing

MILLER'S FERRY LOCK AND DAM
TO GEE'S BEND

The cooling temperatures of October will see a lot of fish movement in this end of Miller's Ferry Reservoir.

The bass will leave the deep water they inhabited during the summer and seek out thermal refuges such as Mill Creek, Shell Creek and Marina Slough. Not only will the water be cooler, they'll also be full of shad.

The bass this time of the year won't be steadfast on any structure, but rather will be mobile. Large schools of bass will follow large schools of shad up and down the length of the creeks.

Any shad imitation bait such as Rat-L-Trap, Sassy Shad or spoon will catch these fish. The easiest method of locating these fish is simply watching for shad trying to jump out of the water and bass hitting them on the surface.

It's a good idea to have at least one topwater bait tied on a rod during this period, too. A Jumping Minnow, Bang-O-Lure, Crazy Shad, Boy Howdee or Devil's Horse cast into the school while they are on top can result in some explosive topwater action. When the school submerges, go back to the previously mentioned baits.

During the dead of winter, the bass return to the same areas you found them in the summer, possibly a little deeper. It becomes finesse fishing time again then. A jig-and-pig is a bait you can't beat during this time.

GEE'S BEND TO BOGUE CHITTO CREEK

In October, the bass head back to shallow water and there's plenty of it on this portion of the lake. Concentrate on Buzzard Roost and Pine Barren Creek, for its there that shad migrate. The same can be said for Chilatchee Creek, Foster Creek, Lidell's Slough and Bogue Chitto Creek.

Other types of fishing

CRAPPIE FISHING

The thousands of acres of wide, structure-filled water on Miller's Ferry Reservoir makes for a tremendous crappie fishery. Locals here jest if that Weiss Lake is the crappie capital of the world, this must be the crappie fishing capital of the universe.

Many of the wide creeks not only have underwater stumps,

standing timber, blowdown timber and brush piles, they are also blessed with deep creek channels next to shallow flats. You will notice that any lake in Alabama that has that combination - and that includes well-known crappie hotspots Weiss Lake, Lake Eufaula, Aliceville Lake, Gainesville Lake, Demopolis Lake and others - offers tremendous crappie fishing.

As you may expect, this structure-filled shallow water means excellent crappie fishing in the spring. Arguably, it's the best spring crappie fishing in the state.

When the water temperature reaches the 65-degree mark, the crappie begin to ease out of the deep water that held them during the winter and begin to seek out the flats next to their eventual spawning beds. These spawning beds will have a water depth of 1 to 3 feet (18 inches is preferred) and some form of structure.

On this lake, water that fits that description is almost everywhere you look, so the smart angler has several factors he uses in determining where to find the prime spawning water.

First, he looks for spawning flats near deep water. Not only does this allow the crappie access to the flats during the staging process, it also tends to allow the area to stay somewhat clearer during the muddy water conditions this lake often encounters during spring spawn time.

Second, he looks for banks that receive long periods of sunlight and areas that aren't next to large shady trees.

Third, he looks for underwater structure that isn't blatantly obvious. These areas receive extreme fishing pressure and cause fish to be spooky during what is a stressful period for them.

During the pre-spawn period, crappie will move up on the flats when the water temperature hits 65 degrees, but will usually not go to the 18-inch water until the temperature hits the 68-degree mark. A good rule-of-thumb is that the 65-degree water will make them think spawn, but it takes 68-degree water to make them act it out.

During the pre-spawn period, one of the best patterns is to use 4- or 6-pound test line on a spincast or spinning reel outfitted with a 1/32-ounce lead head chartreuse jig and a popping cork. This rig allows the angler to cover vast amount of water during the period the crappie are roaming and feeding heavily right before the spawn. These fish will be in open water and not holding tight to structure.

The popping cork not only allows the jig to be set at different depths, it also allows some noise to be made to attract attention. The angler should cast the rig parallel to the bank away from structure and pop the jig back to the boat.

If you think you're in an area that is holding fish, don't hesitate to experiment with varying depths and jig colors.

Once the fish move in tight on structure, leave the spinning and spincast tackle at home and finesse-fish with a cane pole or fiberglass pole, the longer the better. Outfit this rig with 4- or 6-pound test, a small foam cigar float and either a jig or live minnow.

This rig allows the angler to swing the bait exactly to a spot with a gentle splash. It also eliminates many of the inaccurate casts that result in tangles, and eventually scared fish.

The jig or minnow should be placed as tight to the structure as possible. The better fish will usually be buried in the thickest roots, limbs and brush.

Miller's Ferry's widest water - Pine Barren Creek, Mill Creek, Shell Creek, Gee's Bend and other such areas - are the most popular spring fishing areas and for good reason, but the smaller sloughs that sit next to the main river channel also hold their share of crappie in the spring.

There's no question why crappie fishing is more popular then than any other time of the year - they are easier to get to. Once you begin pursuit of crappie the rest of the year, plan for a little work.

Deep-water summer fishing takes a little effort, effort many anglers aren't willing to do. Following the spawn, many of the better crappie slide out of the flats into the deep river and creek channels. These summer crappie will hold on deep points, ledges and humps - the same areas you will find summer bass.

Many anglers argue these crappie are distinguishable from bass on the fish finder, however. The crappie travel in tight schools and will often appear as a large school of baitfish. A school of 20 or 25 crappie can be in an area no larger than the size of a bathtub.

A spincast or spinning reel outfitted with 4- or 6-pound line should be used for these fish with either a jig or live minnow as bait.

Since you will be fishing deeper than you did in the spring, go with a heavier jig than you did in the spring if you plan to jig fish. A different color of jig likely will be needed, too. A dark green, white or smoke grub may be needed if the water is clear, while a chartreuse/white or chartreuse/black may be needed if the water is dingy. Do a little experimenting.

If you plan to use a live minnow, use a split shot 18 inches above the bait. This will keep the minnow down, but will also give it some room to move around.

In either case, fish with a tight line rather than a float. Locate the crappie with a depthfinder, or fish in areas you know hold fish, and drift the bait over them.

Fall crappie fishing varies every year on this lake. During the fall of many years, there will be a two or three week period where they will move shallow and can be caught near where you caught them in the spring. Other years, they never make this shallow run. During those times, you will find them where you found them in summer.

The dead of winter - January and February - is prime time for deep crappie fishing. Structure in 20 feet of water next to the river bank holds the fish. When water is being pulled, these fish fed heavily. Because of the water flow, a heavier 1/4-ounce jig is needed to put the bait where you want it.

Buzzard Roost and the mouth of Mill Creek and Shell Creek are prime areas for this type of fishing.

Miller's Ferry best fishing spots

1. Beaver Dam in Marina Slough. Good spring fishing.
2. Beaver Dam. Good spring fishing.
3. Standing timber. Good spring area with buzzbaits and spinnerbaits. Good early spring with jig-and-pig.
4. Boat docks. Good all year. Lots of brush.
5. Underwater road bed.
6. Marker buoy. Good crappie fishing at night.
7. Standing timber.
8. Slave ditch. Narrow channel dug by slaves to irrigate adjacent fields. Good path for bass to move back-and-forth from shallow water to deep water. Good spring and fall.
9. Slave ditch.
10. Shell Creek. Good year round fishing.
11. Man-made fish reef. Good year-round for a variety of species.
12. Snags. Good year round.
13. Good trash-filled slough. Good spring fishing area.
14. Slave ditch.
15. Slave ditch.
16. Slave ditch.
17. Underwater hump in Mill Creek. Good summer, fall and winter.
18. Underwater hump in Mill Creek. Good summer, fall and winter.
19. Standing timber. Good year round.
20. Mill Creek. Good year round.
21. Underwater stumps.
22. Underwater brushpiles.
23. Underwater road bed.
24. Underwater brushpiles.
25. Rex's Hole Slough. Good spring fishing in back. Good spawning area.
26. Standing timber area. Good year round.
27. Location of farm pond before lake was impounded. Good summer schooling area.
28. Underwater sandbar. Good summer schooling area.
29. Cuts. Good spring fishing area for bass and crappie.
30. Slave ditch.
31. Slave ditch.
32. Slave ditch.
33. Slave ditch.
34. Stumps next to island. Excellent spring buzzbait area. Spinnerbaits and worms early summer.
35. Stumps next to island. Deeper than No. 34. Jig-and-pig all year. Topwater in spring.
36. Underwater road bed.
37. Slave ditch.
38. Slave ditch.
39. Slave ditch.
40. Alligator Slough. Full of standing timber. Good fishing year round with jig-and-pig. Deep slough.
41. Slave ditch.
42. Man-made fish attractor.

43. Location of two farm ponds before lake was impounded. Adjacent to creek channel. Good worm fishing area in summer.
44. Swimming area. Good fishing on point year round.
45. Legion Hut Slough. Some good spring spring fishing around brush piles.
46. Log Barge Slough. Good crappie fishing all spring.
47. Bamboo Slough. Good bass and crappie fishing in spring.
48. Ellis Landing area. Well-defined creek channel. Good crappie fishing in spring.
49. Underwater road bed.
50. Cypress trees. Good in spring for crappie around trees. Bass fishing good all year.
51. Underwater road bed.
52. Slave ditch.
53. Mouth of Gee's Bend. Good year round fishing. Deep channel in mouth. Good spring fishing in shallows.
54. Man-made fish attractor in Houseboat Slough.
55. Man-made fish attractor in River Bluff area.
56. Standing timber and stumps. Good year round fishing.
57. Slave ditch.
58. Stump flats around slave ditch.
59. Gold Mine or gravel pit area. Good year round.
60. Liddell's Slough. Good bass and crappie year round.
61. Standing timber in Liddell's Slough. Good year round.
62. Location of farm pond before lake was impounded. Good worm area in summer.
63. Standing timber throughout Buzzard Roost area. Good year round.
64. Good bass fishing around island in Foster Creek during spring.
65. Foster Creek. Good year round.
66. Man-made fish attractor in mouth Pine Barren Creek.
67. Standing timber throughout Pine Barren Creek.
68. Man-made fish attractor.
69. Man-made fish attractor. Tires and brush. Big pile.
70. Chilahatchee Creek. Good year-round fishing for bass and crappie.
71. Location of pond before lake was impounded. Excellent spring fishing area.
72. Man-made fish attractor in mouth of slough.
73. Man-made fish attractor in mouth of Bogue Chitto Creek.
74. Island adjacent to creek channel. Good year round fishing. 75. Underwater stumps. Good in spring and summer.
76. Standing timber.
77. Creek bend. Good spring fishing.
78. Location of pond before lake was impounded. Good spring topwater area.

Miller's Ferry

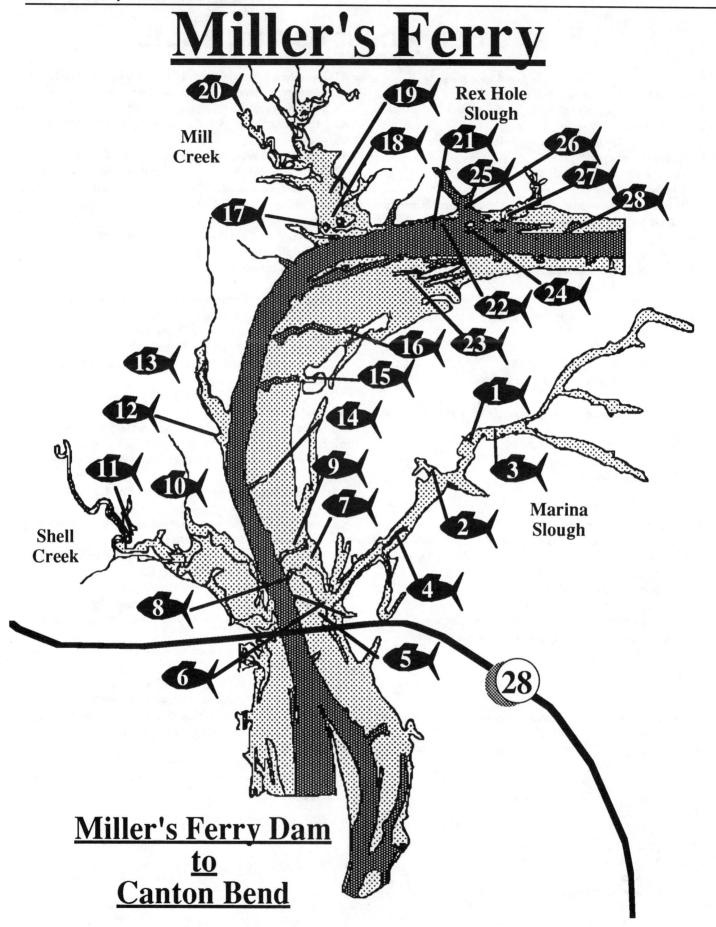

Mill Creek

Rex Hole Slough

Shell Creek

Marina Slough

Miller's Ferry Dam to Canton Bend

Miller's Ferry

Canton Bend
to
Houseboat
Slough

Alligator Slough

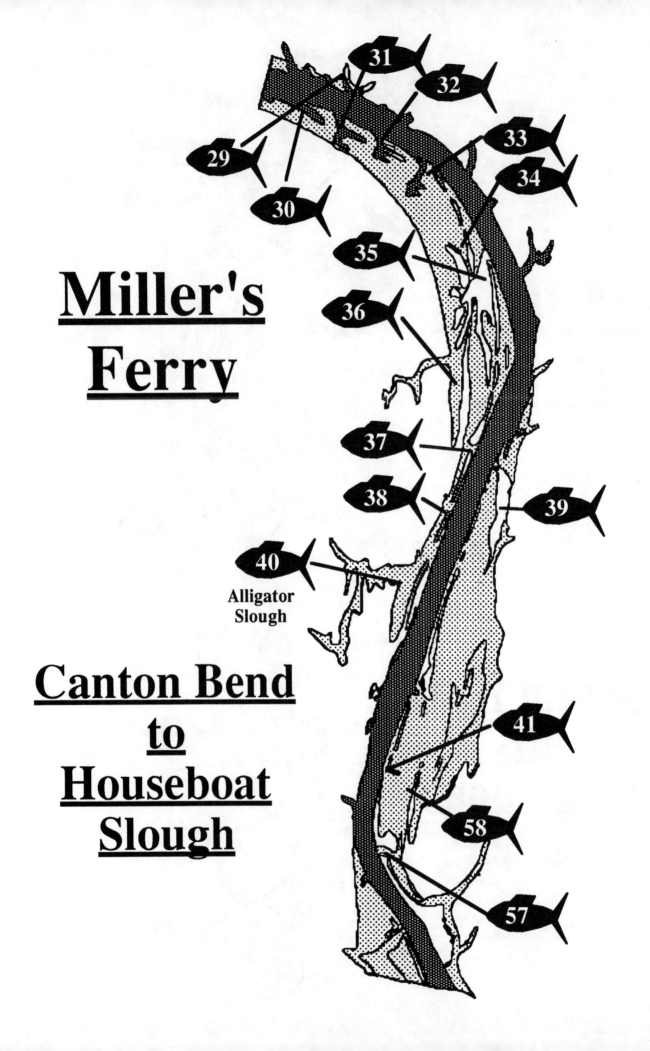

Miller's Ferry

Canton Bend
to
Houseboat
Slough

Alligator
Slough

Miller's Ferry

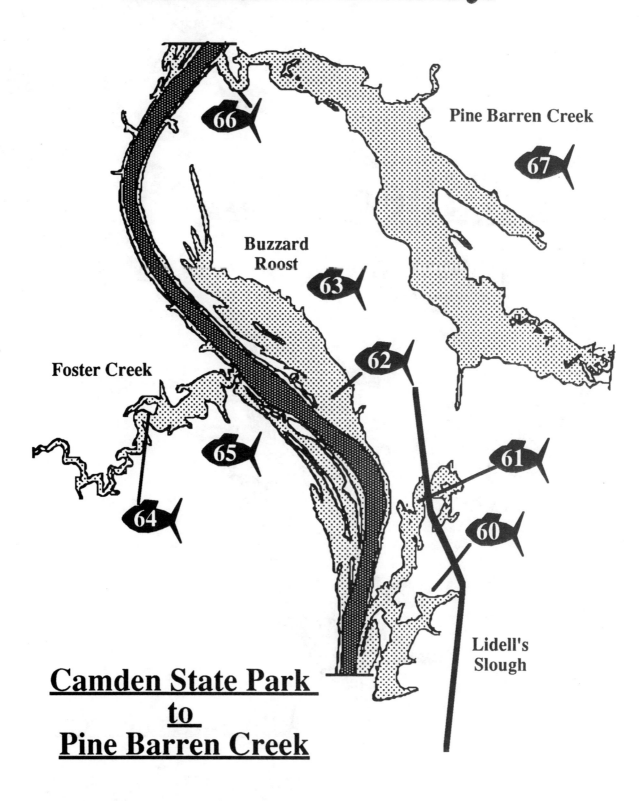

Pine Barren Creek

Buzzard
Roost

Foster Creek

Lidell's
Slough

Camden State Park
to
Pine Barren Creek

Bogue Chitto Creek

Miller's Ferry

Chilatchee Creek

Pine Barren Creek
to
Bogue Chitto Creek

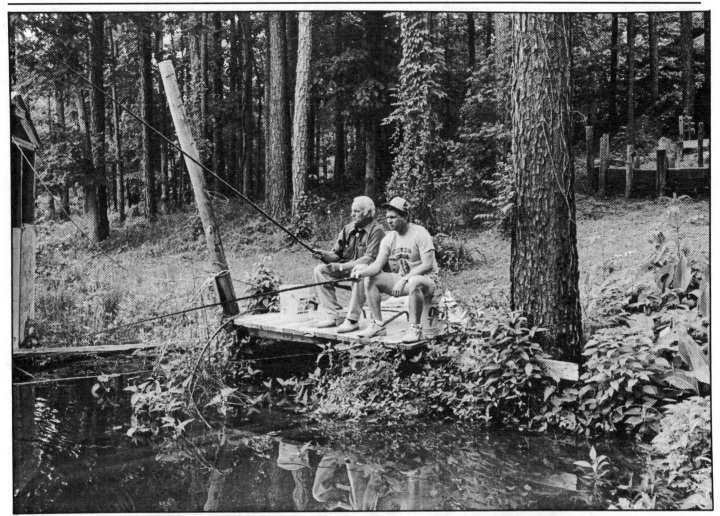

Aliceville Lake

liceville Lake, impounded in 1979 as part of the Tennessee-Tombigbee Waterway project, is a structure-
fisherman's dream. Grass, standing timber, cypress trees
and well-defined creek and river channels make for the type fishing
even the most basic of fishermen find easy.

The straightening of the main channel by the dredging of Hairston
Bend Cut-Off, Coal Fire Creek Cut-Off and Pickensville Cut-Off
resulted in flooded lowlands left in their pristine state. The original
river run in these areas is void of big boat traffic which damages the
banks and surrounding standing timber and grass beds.

The stocking of 100,000 Florida-strain bass into the lake in 1980
has resulted in terrific fishing with the lake just now hitting its peak.
Two bass larger than 14 pounds were caught from the lake in 1989
and 10-pound-and-better bass, most of them caught on topwater,
have been common.

The lake suffered a major setback in the summer of 1989 when a
decision was made to spray the milfoil and hydrilla with chemicals
in an attempt to eradicate them. This decision by the U.S. Army
Corps of Engineers has hurt fishing on the lake.

Spring bass fishing

TOM BEVILL LOCK AND DAM
TO LINDSEY CREEK

Once winter begins to loosen its hold in early February, the bass
on the lower end of Lake Aliceville start thinking spawn.

Most bass begin a staging pattern that sees them stair-step up out
of deep water, never hesitating to dive back deep with the slightest
change in weather conditions.

These bass move up on points and begin a feeding ritual that
prepares them for the difficult spawning time which lies ahead.
Long, sloping points leading directly from deep water to grass-
covered flats act like an interstate and offer a route that not only has
the structure the bass desire, but food as well. Both shad and bream
use these points as their route to shallow water.

During this transition period, several baits will produce fish. Keep
in mind that the cold-blooded bass are still sluggish from a long

Aliceville Lake Fact Sheet

Construction

Construction began on Tom Bevill Lock and Dam in March of 1974 and the lake was opened to navigation in December of 1979.

Tom Bevill Lock and Dam

Like all locks and dams on the Tenn-Tom Waterway, Tom Bevill Lock and Dam lacks power generation facilities. The $45 million facility has a gated and fixed six-crest spillway over the dam and a 110-foot high, 600 foot wide lock.

Configuration

From Columbus Lock and Dam to mile marker 320, Aliceville Lake is strictly river run. From mile marker 320 to Tom Bevill Lock and Dam, the lake broadens widely. Lowland flooding as a result of impoundment made for excellent fishing. At five locations on Aliceville Lake, cut-offs were dredged to straighten the channel and to shorten the distance barges must travel. The creation of Hairston Bend Cut-Off, Coalfire Creek Cut-Off and Pickensville Cutoff in the lake's lower end (the end available to Alabama fishermen) left the original river run undisturbed and resulted in a structure-filled haven for fishermen.

Stocking history

Florida-strain largemouth

1981	20,000
1985	20,000
1986	43,700
1987	16,400

Major and secondary creeks

Besides the Tombigbee River, Aliceville Lake is fed by numerous incoming creeks. Mile Creek, Green Creek and Mustard Creek are on the lake's upper end and out of the fishing area open to Alabama fisherman.

In the area open to Alabama anglers, Arkansas Creek, Lindsey Creek, Nash Creek, Kincaide Creek, McCower's Creek, Cedar Creek, James Creek and Coal Fire Creek are major water suppliers.

Types of fish

Aliceville Lake features popular species such as largemouth bass, a small number of spotted bass, white bass, hybrid bass, a few saltwater stripe, white and black crappie, channel catfish, flathead catfish, blue catfish, bullhead catfish, longear sunfish, redear sunfish, green sunfish, warmouth, and bluegill.

The lake also has several species of gar, drum and common carp and grass carp.

As for baitfish, gizzard shad, threadfin shad and several species of minnows are present.

---

winter and water temperatures still on the cold side. The baitfish they are after are suffering from the same conditions and are slow themselves. When choosing a bait, remember that in early spring, the bait must be fished slowly. As the water temperature warms, allow the speed of the bait to increase.

During this early spring period, relatively heavy, slow baits like jig-and-pigs, three-fourths-ounce spinnerbaits, large, deep-diving crankbaits or Carolina-rigged worms or lizards work best. Weight is needed because many fish are still deep and you want a bait that falls quickly into deep water.

As an early spring bait, jig-and-pigs are hard to beat in this area. If the water is heavily stained, and it usually is this time of the year, a 1/2-ounce or three-fourths-ounce brown jig with brown/orange skirt and a brown pork frog trailer works wonderfully. If spinnerbaits are to your liking, a three-fourths-ounce white/chartreuse with a chartreuse pork from trailer and nickel willow leaf blade work well. This color can be seen well in dingy water, the weight will drop it quickly and the big willow leaf blade will force you to fish it slowly.

Early in the spring, search for long, sloping points leading to grass-covered flats that are receiving a lot of sunlight. These flats will often have a surface temperature as much as three degrees warmer than other areas and fish will concentrate in the slightly deeper water next to these flats.

Keep in mind that this time of year, any small body of water even one degree warmer than adjacent water will often hold fish.

Once the water warms to the point that bass can stay in the shallow water comfortably, spinnerbaits, Rat-L-Traps, shallow-running crankbaits, jig-and-pigs and worms will take fish near the grass. Rat-L-Traps are the easiest bait to fish and produce the most fish, but jig-and-pigs tend to take the larger fish.

Once the water temperature hits the right mark, usually around 65

degrees, these fish move into the weeds to spawn. At that point, spinnerbaits, buzzbaits and plastic worms and lizards become the deadly baits. Once these fish are in the weeds, it possible you'll find no better bass fishing anywhere else in Alabama.

Noisy buzzbaits make for the most exciting fishing, but a floating lizard fished patiently will take the bigger fish.

The Big Bee Valley Landing area, Lindsey Creek, Pumpkin Creek, Little Coal Fire Creek and Big Coal Fire Creek, and the sawdust pile that connects Little Coal Fire and Big Coal Fire are key bass fishing areas in the spring.

There are also generous stands of timber in this area of the lake and you can find spring bass in these areas. Standing timber also tends to warm the water quicker than vacant water. Most of the standing timber in this end of the lake is in seven feet of water, however, and normally only big bass spawn in the timber. That sounds good, but the patches of standing timber are so thick that it may take all day to fish a quarter-mile-long stand of it. Fishing this standing timber in the spring normally isn't worth the hassle when fishing the weeds can be so productive.

It should be stressed that navigating this area of Aliceville Lake is treacherous. Shallow water and stumps are everywhere. Many rookie anglers have left early with their lower units separated from the rest of the outboard motor. Proceed with extreme caution.

LINDSEY CREEK
TO HAIRSTON BEND CUT-OFF

Once the angler moves into this section of the lake, he's faced with a much different fishing situation than he finds on Aliceville Lake's lower end.

Acres of standing timber, rather than weeds, are predominant and these trees hold the majority of spawning bass. Except for Arkansas

Creek, much of the weeds found in this area are unproductive for spring fishing because they are found in water much deeper than the super-productive weeds on the lake's lower end.

There's little argument what the most productive spring bait is in this area. Because of the vast acreage of standing timber, spinnerbaits, with their ability to cover a lot of water quickly, are a must. A 1/4-ounce mixed-color spinnerbait such as a chartreuse/black, chartreuse/blue or yellow/black tipped with a black pork frog are perfect. The spinnerbait should be tipped with two No. 4 willow leaf blades.

You'll find yourself in a Catch 22 situation here when it comes to line selection. Lighter lines result in more strikes, but heavier lines make for better odds of getting a fish out of heavy timber. The best choice is a medium-sized line such as 14-pound-test and a prayer that the water will have a good amount of tint to conceal the line.

Plastic lizards and jig-and-pigs are two more key baits anglers use with great success here. Their only drawbacks is inability to cover water quickly. This areas biggest spring fish are usually caught flipping jig-and-pigs, but due to the amount of standing timber, it would literally be possible to go a 1/4-mile and flip 500 trees in that distance. If you're looking for that fish of a lifetime, and have time and patience to flip, that is the pattern and this is the place you need to be.

This area is so full of standing timber that holds fish that narrowing down a few good fishing locations is difficult. The standing timber near the mouth of Hairston Bend and the mouth of Arkansas Creek are good places to start, however.

Summer bass fishing

TOM BEVILL LOCK AND DAM TO LINDSEY CREEK

Once the spawn is over, the bass direct their attention to their basic needs of cover, oxygenated water and food.

Unlike in most Alabama reservoirs, the big bass on this lake don't head directly to the original channel to suspend themslves on the ledges for the summer. Aliceville Lake's big bass head for the weeds to bury themselves underneath the foilage.

A small percentage of fish will make their way to the main channel, but these are almost always smaller, yearling bass.

The heat reflecting ability of the thick weeds is incredible. Water temperature underneath them sometimes is as much as 8 degrees cooler than surrounding water in July and August. The weeds also put off oxygen, and play home to baitfish.

Some of this grass appears so thick that it would be possible to walk on it during the summer, and fishing these weeds isn't an easy chore. Buzzbaits and floating worms are about the only lures that offer success, but when they are successful, it is a sight to behold. An 8-pound bass exploding through the grass to take a bait is a moment to remember. These large bass sometimes leave a hole in the grass the size of a No. 2 washtub.

Although most good bass fishermen stress light line in summer, fishing light line in this grass during the summer is an an exercise in futility. You must go with 14-pound-test or stronger to have any chance of pulling these bass out of these weeds.

It should be noted that one buzzbait outproduces all others on this lake. The Boogerman Racket Buzz has several characteristics which make it successful. First, it is a buzzbait designed for weeds. It's body is surfboard-shaped which gets it on plane quickly and allows it to pass through weeds easily. Second, it propeller is designed to bump the body as it spins, thus making a noise. Third, its body is made of tin and lead, rather than just lead. This allows the buzzbait to make a tink, tink, tink sound rather than a clack, clack, clack sound.

The lake's better bass anglers swear by the bait, but they make one slight adjustment to it. They straighten the shaft, remove the propeller, put a bead on the shaft, put the propeller back and re-bind the shaft. The bead keeps weeds from choking the propeller and stopping its ability to spin.

This bait is produced in Illinois and is rarely found in Alabama. It's use is almost exclusive to Aliceville Lake and can usually only be found at Pickensville Marine and other tackle stores on the lake.

Deciding which grass to fish is as difficult as fishing it. You'll find acres and acres of unproductive grass, but will then find a small patch full of fish. The reason isn't known, but the lake's better anglers have discovered one tendency. Bass seem to hold wherever two different types of weeds or grass merge together. Milfoil, hydrilla, coontail and several other grasses can be found on the lake.

LINDSEY CREEK TO HAIRSTON BEND CUT-OFF

Summer fishing in Alabama is normally a less-than-thrilling experience. Deep fish, as well as weather that forces robins to pick up worms with potholders, combine to make many anglers stay at home and watch Bill Dance re-runs on television.

This area of Aliceville Lake is a rare exception. Being able to fish deep-water weeds and visible standing timber does something to the angler's inner-mind. Most anglers agree that being able to fish visible structure that the mind believes holds a fish is much better rather than fishing an underwater hump.

This area of the lake is overwhelmed with standing timber and has enough grass to keep most anglers happy. It also provides for the type of fishing most anglers enjoy most - worm and topwater.

The construction of Hairston Bend cutoff during the building of the Tenn-Tom Waterway resulted in Hairston Bend becoming a fisherman's dream. Due to the bypass of Hairston Bend, no longer does traffic from big boats disturb the area and its standing timber and other structure is left unharmed.

This area, as well as Arkansas Creek, are summertime fishing delights.

For the topwater fisherman, the standing timber offers the chance for a strike behind every tree. Buzzbaits, Pop-R's, Bang-O-Lures, Crazy Shad, twitch baits and other topwater lures offer terrific fishing in the early-morning hours, after sunset and all day on overcast days.

Plastic worms or lizards are the best weapons during daylight hours. Fished around the deep standing timber in the mouths of Hairston Bend or Arkansas Creek, or in the bends of the original river channel in Hairston Bend, these baits produce the majority of the summertime bass.

Cool and cold
weather bass fishing

Tom Bevill Lock and Dam
to Lindsey Creek

A lot of anglers don't enjoy fall fishing on Aliceville Lake. Locating fall bass is most often a difficult chore. But when bass are located, they'll often be schooling and it's not unusual to catch large numbers of big fish.

Many anglers wrongly believe that the weeds that offered such good fishing in the spring and summer will offer the same type fishing in the fall. They won't. The reason these fish leave these weedy areas in fall is simple. The weeds begin to die during the fall and the decaying process robs the weed-area of oxygen.

More often than not, in early fall, the fish end up in shallow-water flats (3 to 7 feet of water) adjacent to deep water, but not necessarily near the weed beds they inhabited during the summer.

Small, sinking crankbaits such as Rat-L-Traps are the lures to use this time of year. But instead of quickly retrieving that lure across the shallow water, it is best to hop it across the bottom as if jigging a spoon in shallow water. Cast the lure and allow it to settle to the bottom, then rip it off the bottom a few feet before allowing it to settle again. When the lure is falling, pay close attention because it is at this time when the fish strike.

Big Coal Fire Creek is an excellent fall fishing area. An island-like flat sits adjacent to the main river channel there. This flat sits three feet under the water and falls off into six feet of water on all sides. Pumpkin Creek is another excellent fall fishing area.

These fish will stay in these flats and creeks until January.

When extremely cold weather comes in January and February, you have to pick your days to fish. When the temperatures have been in the 20's and 30's for a week or more and suddenly you have a 42-degree day with another such day forecast for the following day, go fishing.

Aliceville Lake warms quickly and a quick warming will send winter bass moving in search of food. Jig-and-pigs, worms and slow-moving crankbaits will be needed as fish head for areas adjacent to the weedbeds.

Lindsey Creek
to Hairston Bend Cutoff

Having a temperature gauge on your boat is the key to fishing this area during the cool and cold weather months. During early fall, the influx of any cool water from incoming creeks can trigger bass into their fall feeding frenzy. The mouths of McCower's Creek and Cedar Creek where they dump into Hairston Bend are areas to watch for early fall feeding activity. Also keep an eye on the mouth of Arkansas Creek where it dumps into the flooded flats.

The fall bass are coming out of their deep-water summer pattern from the main river channel which runs through Hairston Bend, Coal Fire Creek and the Pickensville Cut-Off area. The deep water in these areas is adjacent to structure-filled flats and the bass will come right out of the deep water to feed in these flats when the water cools.

The key to finding these fish is a temperature gauge. A stretch of cooler water, which may be caused by an incoming creek, underground spring or just being in the shade, will hold numbers of fish. One of the best baits this time of the year is a shad-colored, medium-running crankbait, but be forewarned that it is a difficult bait to fish in these waters. Hangups are common, so bring a plug-knocker and a handful of crankbaits.

Once the water cools to the point that the bass are too sluggish to chase crankbaits, a jig-and-pig becomes the bait to use. This bait is much more weedless than a multi-hook crankbait and hangups are less likely. A 1/2-ounce black/brown jig with a black pork frog trailer works best as the pork frog gives the bait added buoyancy and further prevents hangups.

Casting into standing timber is difficult, and casts longer than 20 feet are tough and not advised. Any fish further than 20 feet out in the timber is an unlikely candidate for the net.

Other types of fishing

Crappie

The massive amount of standing timber and weeds present in Aliceville lake make it an excellent lake for crappie fishing.

Many of the lake's better crappie fishermen believe crappie fishing here is the best kept secret in Alabama.

Crappie fishing is best during the spring when the fish move into the shallow water to spawn. These fish can be found in two locations during this time.

The better fish leave the original river channels in the Coal-Fire Creek Cut-Off area and the Pickensville Cut-Off area and move into the weed beds adjacent to the deep channels.

Naturally, the better fish are the toughest to get at during this time. Better fishermen use a long, telescoping fiberglass pole such as a B'M Crappie Pole outfitted with 12-pound test line and a curly-tail chartreuse jig with a white lead head. This setup can be used to gingerly reach over and drop the jig right into the holes in the weeds. This produces the true slabs.

An easier, but less productive method is to line up parallel to the weed beds and, using a spinning or spincast reel, cast a jig hanging 18 inches below a cork as far as possible and as close to the weeds as possible. This rig shold then be "popped" all the way back to the boat. This popping draws attention and the jig right on the weedline is often too much for the fish to resist.

These fish can also be fished in the traditional method, and that's with a minnow and cork fished near the weedline. This method is good right before and right after the spawn when the fish are holding just outside of the weeds in 5 or 6 feet of water.

Although the cut-off areas offer the best fishing, any timber- or weed-filled slough or pocket adjacent to the main river is likely to hold fish during this time. The same patterns will work there.

Following the spawn, the crappie will hold on the flats in about 5 to 10 feet of water until June. Stumps and blowdown timber will concentrate these fish. Live minnows fished under a cork is the best bait.

Once the hot part of the summer arrives, the crappie in Aliceville Lake head for deep water. The fish that head to main river channel are often difficult to locate, so the better fishermen head to the cut-off areas. Crappie gather here in the original river channel and stay until winter. The cut-off areas are by-passed by the big boat traffic, thus the crappie find an undisturbed summer.

One of the better patterns used by the lake's best crappie fishermen at this time is trolling. A multi-rod setup with jigs set at varying depths will produce tremendous numbers of fish. Experimenting with jig colors and jig depths may be needed to fine tune this pattern.

Another summer pattern that works well is bottom-bumping with live minnows. The crappie change their pattern very little during the fall. Most of the better fish stay deep in the channels, only occasionally making a run to the ledges to feed. Trolling or bottom-bumping works best, but a live minnow fished under a cork over a ledge with structure on the lip will produce some good fish.

Winter crappie fishing is tough on Aliceville Lake. The fish get deep in the channels and are seemingly lifeless. A pattern that works to stir up these fish is first locating the fish with a fish finder, then jigging a spoon such as a Mann's Mann-O-Lure right in there faces. This will usually provoke the fish into striking.

Aliceville Lake's best fishing spots

1. Island in Hairston Bend. Excellent shallow water fishing in spring.
2. Standing timber in Hairston Bend. Excellent fishing year round.
3. Excellent point in Hairston Bend. Standing timber adjacent to deep water channel. Good fishing in shallow timber in spring and fall, good fishing in channel summer and winter.
4. Upper end mouth of Hairston Bend. Excellent fishing for schooling summer bass.
5. Cedar Creek. Good standing timber. Good all year except hot summer and coldest part of winter.
6. Lower end mouth of Hairston Bend. Excellent fishing for schooling summer bass.
7. Mouth of Arkansas Creek. Difficult to locate. Island surrounded by standing timber just inside mouth. Weed beds in upper crook. Excellent spring fishing in mouth and along creek. Prime fishing area in mouth in the fall.
8. Island located in flats west of main river channel. Surrounded by weed beds. Excellent in spring. Good in summer.
9. Location of private lake before lake was impounded. Excellent shallow water spring fishing.
10. Excellent stand of standing timber in shallow water adjacent to main river channel. Good year round fishing.
11. Back of flats. Good grass beds. Good spring fishing with buzzbaits.
12. Island in shallow flats. Good spring fishing around island with topwater.
13. Standing timber patch.
14. Standing timber patch.
15. Underwater island adjacent to main river channel. Good year round fishing.
16. Island splits main river channel. Excellent summer schooling area for small bass all around island.
17. Standing timber in mouth of Kincaide Creek. Excellent spring spawning area for bass and crappie. Excellent jig-and-pig or topwater area for spring bass.
18. Standing timber patch. Good spring spawning area for bass and crappie.
19. Standing timber in back of Kincaide Creek.
20. Islands in Kincaide Creek.
21. Mouth of James Creek. Excellent area for schooling summer bass.
22. Island in James Creek. Good spring fishing.
23. Island in James Creek. Good spring fishing.
24. Standing timber in James Creek. Good year round fishing for bass and crappie.
25. Standing timber in back of James Creek. Excellent spring fishing for bass and crappie. Surprisingly good bass fishing area in fall.
26. Good ledge fishing area in summer.
28. Underwater island adjacent to main river channel. Good summer fishing for bass with deep-running crankbaits or Rat-L-Trap. Good fall and winter fishing with jig-and-pigs.
27. Visible island adjacent to main river channel. Good year round fishing.
29. Underwater island in mouth of small, unnamed creek. Adjacent to main channel. Excellent area year round. Jig-and-pigs late winter, early spring. Good summer schooling area for bass.
30. Standing timber in small creek. Excellent buzzbait area. Excellent spring and fall area for crappie.
31. Mouth of Lindsey Creek. Excellent summer and fall. Excellent buzzbait area in standing timber in spring.
32. Standing timber in back of slough in Pumpkin Creek area.
33. Standing timber in back of slough.
34. Standing timber in back of slough.
35. Man-made underwater brush pile.
36. Man-made underwater brush pile.
37. Man-made underwater brush pile.
38. Man-made underwater brush pile.
39. Standing timber in back of Pumpkin Creek.
40. Long row of man-made brush piles.
41. Mouth of Pumpkin Creek. Full of underwater islands. Good year round fishing.
42. Underwater island at fork of main river channel and Coal Fire Creek Cut-Off. Good summer and fall schooling area for bass.
43. Islands adjacent to original river channel. Good spring and summer fishing for bass.
44. Islands off of point. Good spring spawning area.
45. Man-made underwater brush pile.
46. Massive man-made underwater fish attractor.
47. Man-made underwater brush pile.
48. Large slough full of standing timber.
49. Standing timber-filled slough.

50. Standing timber patch.
51. Boat lane cut in standing timber patch.
52. Island. Excellent spring spawning around island.
53. Man-made brush pile.
54. Standing timber in back of slough.
55. Large, man-made brush pile.
56. Island. Good topwater area.
57. Massive man-made brush pile.
58. Man-made brush pile.
59. Standing timber.
60. Standing timber.
61. Large man-made cedar tree pile.
62. Standing timber.
63. Standing timber.
64. Island. Good spring and fall fishing area.
65. Small man-made brush pile.
66. Man-made brush pile between two stands of standing timber.
67. Man-made brush pile.
68. Man-made brush pile.
69. Large underwater cedar tree pile.
70. Standing timber adjacent to main river channel. Excellent year round fishing.
71. Standing timber adjacent to main river channel. Good year round fishing.
72. Fork where original river channel and Coal-Fire Creek Cut-Off meet. Excellent summer schooling area. Good year round fishing.
73. Standing timber in back of slough. Excellent spring spawning area for bass and crappie.
74. Point where original river channel and Coal Fire Cut-Off meet. Good year round fishing.
75. Man-made cedar tree pile.
76. Man-made brush pile.
77. Man-made brush pile.
78. Island. Good spring fishing.
79. Island. Good spring fishing.
80. Man-made brush pile on point.
81. Man-made brush pile.
82. Point of original river channel and Coal Fire Creek Cut-Off. Good summer schooling area.
83. Large islands above dam. Good spring spawning area for bass and crappie.
84. Good year round point.
85. Island adjacent to main river channel. Good year round fishing.

Aliceville Lake

Mile Marker 322

Arkansas Creek

Cedar Creek

Mile Marker 322
to
Kincaide Creek

Aliceville Lake

Crawford Lake

Coal Fire Creek

Pumpkin Creek

Crawford Lake to Dam

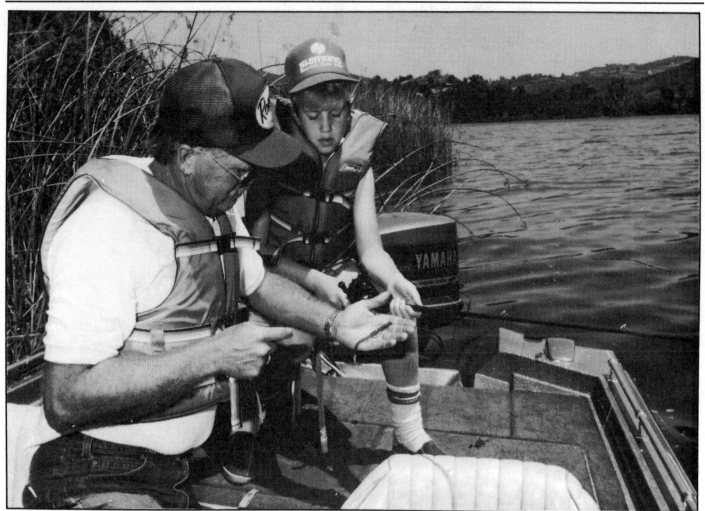

Gainesville Lake

Take a major river located away from a major metropolitan area, impound it, fill it full of standing timber and grass, straighten out its curves with cut-off areas, stock it with more than 60,000 Florida-strain largemouth and what do you have? A situation like you'll probably never see again in Alabama.

It's been said the creation of lakes Gainesville (1978), Aliceville (1980) and Harris (1983) forever ended the creation of new, major lakes in Alabama. Enviromental concerns, construction costs and the lack of feasible locations for impoundments will probably end the building of major lakes in this state.

Gainesville Lake is one of the newest lakes in the state and it was just coming into its own in 1989. Terrific crappie fishing, coupled with reports of a 16-pound and 14-pound bass caught in the lake by one angler in one day in January 1989, brought nationwide publicity to the lake. The lake that was a secret for many for years, is no secret anymore.

Another factor that will help the lake continue its progress was the decision in 1989 to let the grass grow. While the U.S. Army Corps of Engineers decided to spray Aliceville's weeds, Gainesville's weeds were left intact.

Spring bass fishing

TOM BEVILL LOCK AND DAM TO ALICEVILLE BRIDGE

The upper end of Gainesville Lake is strictly run of the river from Tom Bevill Lock and Dam to Aliceville Bridge, and as a result spring bass fishing is limited. But take note that "limited" doesn't necessarily mean poor.

Whenever you have a situation where the upper end of a lake is river run and the number of incoming creeks is few, the creeks are forced to concentrate bass during the spring spawn. The result is terrific fishing in areas easy to pinpoint.

One doesn't have to be a fisheries biologist to see that the Big Creek Cut-Off area (see map) has wonderful spring possibilities. By being the only incoming creek within a 4-mile stretch below the dam, bass seeking shallow water to spawn or shelter from the strong, muddy current caused by spring rains have no choice but to go there.

Gainesville Lake Fact Sheet

Location, length, acreage

Gainesville Lake is one of three Army Corps of Engineers reservoirs in Alabama on the Tennessee-Tombigbee Waterway. Only two of those reservoirs – Gainesville Lake and Demopolis Lake – are entirely in Alabama. The 6,400-acre reservoir begins at Gainesville Lock and Dam and stretches 40.7 nautical miles to Tom Bevill Lock and Dam. Mile marker 286 sits at the lake's halfway point.

Construction

Construction began on Gainesville Lock and Dam in November of 1972. The lake was opened to navigation in October of 1978.

Gainesville Lock and Dam

Gainesville Lock and Dam, in Sumter County above Gainesville, Ala., has a 225-foot-long fixed crest spillway. It also has a 110 foot by 600 foot gaited lock with a 36-foot lift capable of handling barge traffic.

Configuration

Gainesville Lake is virtually a river-run impoundment. The long, snaking Tombigbee River slightly overflows its original banks creating narrow ledges throughout its length. Good fishing areas

Stocking history

Florida-strain largemouth	
1978-90	92,900
1991	12,818
1992	12,827
1993	20,020
1994	12,800

Hybrids	
1982-88	152,910
1989	12,500
1990	13,000
1991	12,800
1992	12,800
1993	12,873
1994	51,959

Striped bass	
1978	36,000

were created when, during construction of the Tennessee-Tombigbee Waterway, eight cut-off areas were dredged to straighten the path for barges and other large vessels. Thanks to the cut-offs, the original river channels that were bypassed created excellent, undisturbed fishing habitat. The lake also has several large incoming creeks, a major incoming river (the Sipsey) and numerous large sloughs.

Major and secondary creeks

Besides the Tombigbee River, Gainesville Lake is fed by numerous creeks and two rivers. Big Creek, Owl Creek, Beaver Creek, Bogue Chitto Creek and Lubbub Creek are water suppliers on the upper end of the lake. The Sipsey River is a major water supplier that enters the lake above mile marker 281. Phanachie Creek and Wilkes Creek feed the lower end, as does Noxubee River.

Types of fish

Gainesville Lake features popular species such as largemouth bass, a small population of spotted bass, white bass, hybrid bass, a limited number of saltwater stripe, white and black crappie, channel catfish, flathead catfish, blue catfish, bullhead catfish, longear sunfish, redear sunfish, green sunfish, warmouth, and bluegill. The lake also has several species of gar, drum and common carp and grass carp. As for baitfish, gizzard shad, threadfin shad and several species of minnows are present.

There are similar situations downriver at Owl Creek Cut-Off area, Beaver Creek, Cedar Creek, Curry Creek, Bogue Chitto Creek and the many small standing timber-filled pockets. Keep in mind the further upriver you go, the stronger the current becomes during times of spring flooding and the stronger the current, the more important these incoming creeks become as a place for fish to escape.

The tailrace below Tom Bevill Lock and Dam (mile marker 306) produces bass year round, but access is difficult and most anglers choose to ignore the area. There's a launch at Ringo Bluff (mile marker 303), but getting there is an experience. The two-mile-long dirt road that leads to the launch is more than many anglers want to put their boats and vehicles through.

There's another landing, a good one, at Cochrane (slightly above mile marker 294), but the tailrace is a 12-mile boat ride from that point. Most anglers simply choose to head downstream to wider expanses of water. The result is a year-round fishery that receives little pressure.

Under normal early spring water flow conditions, pearl-colored Sassy Shads, chrome Rat-L-Traps and white grubs fished on the walls of the lock, in the eddy pool to the left of the dam and in the eddies behind logjams on both banks will produce both spotted and largemouth bass.

During the years of heavy spring rains, fishing in this area gets even better. The swift current forces bass to seek shelter to avoid being washed away. The diversion canal on the west bank, the logjams and eddy pools on both banks and the Big Creek Cut-Off area downstream on the east bank are the bass' only real options of

escape.

The diversion canal's walls and mouth are good for only a short period of time once the swift current begins. Rat-L-Traps fished in these areas will take fish that are feeding heavily in anticipation of having difficulty in finding baitfish for awhile. The diversion canal will quickly become as muddy as the surrounding water, however, and fishing will become difficult.

The procedure in the Big Creek Cut-Off area is different. This area will quickly muddy at the first sign of spring rains, but within a few days, the swift current will suck the muddy water out. Remaining is a clear-water refuge full of concentrated fish.

It is in this same Big Creek Cut-Off area, and in the other creeks and sloughs downstream, that these bass will eventually spawn. Standing timber and grass beds are common in the flats of these creeks and the typical spring baits - buzzbaits, spinnerbaits, twitch-baits and floating worms and lizards - take the fish.

ALICEVILLE BRIDGE TO BIG SLOUGH

Once the angler ventures below Aliceville Bridge, he'll find a lake so much unlike the upriver portion he may find it difficult to believe he's on the same body of water.

No fewer than three cut-offs have been dredged between Aliceville Bridge and Big Slough to straighten the winding river. The result is three slough-like areas full of standing timber, fallen timber, grass beds and a deep-river channel adjacent to ledges. It's simply Alabama spring bass fishing at its best.

The key location in this area is unquestionably the Dead River, Lubbub Creek Cut-Off area. This is the area that the 16-pound and

14-pound bass caught by Wayne Wiggins reportedly came from on Jan. 19, 1989. This double loop (see map) was once the original river channel, but dredging the cut-off during construction of the Tenn-Tom waterway left the area untraveled by big boat traffic.

This area features a well-defined river channel (in the west loop) and a well-defined creek channel through the Dead River area (in the east loop). The river channel loop is strictly run of the river and doesn't offer good fishing except at the four intersections, but the creek channel loop is a different matter.

The creek channel meanders its way through both standing and fallen timber and past the mouth of Lubbub Creek. Most of the standing timber has broken off at water level, or slightly above, and has fallen into the flats next to the banks and the channel. It's here that the angler will find some of the best bass spring spinnerbait fishing that exists in this state.

A 1/2-ounce white spinnerbait with some type of trailer – a white pork frog, a white split-tail eel, a white grub or a white worm – should be used. This area of the lake usually has good water color in spring, so tandem nickel willowleaf blades should be used to draw attention.

The only other pattern that should be considered is flippin'. A black/brown jig-and-pig used with 20-pound or larger line should be used for bigger bass in the standing timber in water 4 feet or deeper. The standing timber is in water from 1 to 11 feet deep.

The fish will be concentrated in water warmer than surrounding areas, so locating the fish can be somewhat difficult. The smart angler covers a lot of water quickly with the spinnerbait to locate fish, then switches to a flippin' pattern to cover that area thoroughly after the spinnerbait produces a fish.

Other good areas in which you can use similar patterns include the standing timber-filled slough known as Buzzard's Roost (a lot of late-spring tournaments are won there), the standing-timber filled pocket in the back of Cochrane Cut-Off, the standing timber-filled slough adjacent Catfish Bend, the standing timber-filled Pump House Slough (also has grass), and the loop known as Lard Lake. Lard Lake has both standing timber and grass.

Although spinnerbaits and jig-and-pigs are the key baits in these areas, buzzbaits can be productive, but to a lesser degree.

BIG SLOUGH TO
GAINESVILLE LOCK AND DAM

Once the angler moves downriver of Lard Lake, he finds a river that doesn't widen greatly the rest of the way to the dam.

Despite this area's lack of wide water, it does have incoming creeks and an incoming river (the Sipsey), as well as numerous grass-filled and timber-filled sloughs. While the area from Aliceville Bridge to Big Slough is best known as the lake's spring fishing area, spring fisherman will have no problem finding fish here as well.

Two areas stick out for spring fishing in this portion of the lake - the Sipsey River and Bend Lake.

Sipsey River is a long, navigable river which offers miles of good fishing. It's full of standing timber, a few islands, hundreds of good points and a well-defined channel adjacent to flats. This river has the structure and water depth to hold fish year round.

The Sipsey River's only real problem is that it's too obvious a spot. There's easy access and as a result, it's fished hard. The lake's better bass fishermen, especially at tournament time, stay out of the area.

That doesn't mean fish can't be caught there. The concentration of spotted bass can make for a fun day of fishing. The Sipsey is well known as a spinnerbait area in spring and fish found there like a falling spinnerbait rather than one pulled at a constant speed. An occasional pause to let the lure fall produces more fish for a reason that hasn't been explained.

Bend Lake isn't really a lake, but a slough fed by a small creek in the farthest reaches of the slough. This slough doesn't appear to anything special on the map, and many anglers pass it up for better-looking water. But the long, narrow slough is filled with timber from front to back and holds a lot of spring fish.

A Rat-L-Trap fished in the first few hundred yards of the mouth of Bend Lake is an excellent pre-spawn and post-spawn pattern, while spinnerbaits fished in the shallows around the standing timber is best during the spawn.

Several other areas are worth trying. If the angler likes grass and standing timber, Big Slough has just what the doctor ordered. The site of a large lake before Gainesville Lake was impounded, Big Slough is now connected to the main river and is an excellent spring spawning area. Spinnerbaits, jerk baits and buzzbaits are key baits in fishing this area.

Goat Slough has some standing timber in its left fork and offers excellent fishing in the spring and fall.

There is some standing timber in the first slough you come to while going south in Cook's Bend, as well as in the last slough you encounter before getting back out in the main river channel.

Phanachie Creek, which leads into Warsaw Bend, has some good standing timber above the bridge and will give up fish in the 3- to 5-pound range on buzzbaits spring, summer and fall. Bass spawn by the thousands in the creek, but where they spawn is protected by shallow water and anglers can't get there. The spawning flats, which lie out of the 10 to 12-foot channel are sometimes only a foot deep and boats can't hack it. When the spawn is on, fish elsewhere.

Turkey Paw Branch directly above the dam also has standing timber, as well as some grass scattered throughout. Turkey Paw is difficult to navigate. Angler should stay on the right bank halfway back into the creek, then move to the left bank. Turkey Paw is outstanding for topwater fishing spring and fall.

Topwater baits such as Lunker Lures and jerk baits work below Bend Lake better than they do in the areas above it.

Hot weather
bass fishing

TOM BEVILL LOCK AND DAM
TO ALICEVILLE BRIDGE

If you were to design an area non-conducive to summer bass fishing, it would probably look a lot like the upper end of Gainesville Lake.

This area, as said before, is strictly river run. Bass are unquestionably in this main channel during the hot summer months, but the lack of ledges and the small number of points doesn't give the angler structure to develop a summer pattern.

Save your gas and fish elsewhere during the summer.

ALICEVILLE BRIDGE TO BIG SLOUGH

The creek channels through the cutoff areas have water deep and cool enough that bass can comfortably reside there during the difficult months of summer. This is good news for fishermen because this keeps the bass out of the main river channel where they are much more difficult to locate and catch.

The water is usually cool enough that a good bit of topwater action takes place during the early-morning and late-afternoon hours. The deep channels next to ledges filled with standing timber make it easy for bass to chase shad and corner them. These ledges make excellent summer fishing.

The angler needs to keep two rods outfitted with different baits during these months. A rod with a jerk bait such as a Pop-R or Bang-O-Lure needs to be on hand when the bass are chasing shad on the ledges, and a rod with a plastic worm or lizard needs to be in reach when the bass are playing hit-and-run with the shad.

The angler needs to fish the worm or lizard on top of the ledges where they fall off into the channels, concentrating on areas with fallen timber, stumps and other irregularities. The mouth of Lubbub Creek and the fingers off the channel in Dead River are key areas.

Whenever the angler spots bass hitting shad on top of the ledges, he should quickly switch to the topwater bait. When the topwater ceases, he should quickly go back to the worm and throw on top of the ledge where the activity took place, slowly bring that worm back and letting it fall off the ledge. The bass will usually be suspended there two or three feet deeper than the ledge awaiting the shad to return to deep water. Be ready when the worm falls. The bass will often explode on the worm and a quick hookset is needed.

The Cochrane Cut-Off area, Catfish Bend and the mouths of Lard Lake and Pump House Slough are other areas where this pattern will work.

BIG SLOUGH TO GAINESVILLE LOCK AND DAM

The hot months of summer scatter fish widely in this area. The largemouths head to the points and dropoffs in the main river channel, while the spots move to the timber that has fallen into the main river.

Fishing for these spots can offer some exciting fishing. A large deep-diving crankbait fished on the fringes and between the limbs of the fallen trees takes the best fish. Spinnerbaits, worms and lizards can be fished in tighter, but they take fewer fish.

Deep-diving crankbaits can be used on points for largemouth, but this fishing is hit-and-miss. It's possible to come back from a long, hot day day of fishing with nothing to show but a sore arm from cranking a reel.

It's possible to catch a few summer fish in the creeks, but a good fish is rare. Phanachie Creek has a channel deep enough for summer bass, as does Warsaw Bend and Cook's Bend.

The message is this – you might catch some "great" fish in this area.

Then again, you may not.

Cool and cold weather bass fishing

TOM BEVILL LOCK AND DAM TO ALICEVILLE BRIDGE

During the fall and winter, bass fishing is a mixed bag here. The angler who finds fishing so good here in the fall often finds it dismal just a few months later.

Because the area lacks ledges and points, fall bass that are gouging themselves for the winter are forced to corner shad the only way they know how. That is by forcing them to the surface and to the banks.

The result is some spectacular topwater action in this area.

The angler needs three things to be successful during the fall. First, he needs a rod rigged with any kind of jerk bait such as a Pop-R, Devil Horse, Bang-O-Lure or Crazy Shad. It should be outfitted with 10 or 12-pound test line. This will be used to take bass schooling on topwater.

The second thing he needs is a rod rigged with a lipless crankbait. A chrome/black backed Rat-L-Trap or Pogo Shad, or a pearl Little George with a blue or black back, will work nicely. This rod should be outfitted with 8-pound test line. It will be used to take schooling bass that have been hitting topwater and have temporarily returned to below the surface.

The larger fish are often taken by this method. The larger bass often let yearling bass attack the school of shad and while they wait for the cripples that begin to fall.

The third thing the angler needs is a pair of binoculars. This will allow him to scan the water surface up to a half mile away for signs of schools feeding on topwater.

Once a school is sighted (the tailrace and the mouths of creeks are prime areas), the angler should make a dash in that direction, stopping at least 100 yards away. The trolling motor should be used to approach the schooling fish quietly. The angler should make the farthest cast possible.

Don't hesitate to throw a jerk bait in the middle of the schooling fish. Once the school submerges, pick up the other rod and throw the lipless crankbait well past the area where the fish went down and pull the bait through the area with an irregular jigging motion. The bass will often take the bait when it's falling.

Many anglers would rather catch one bass on topwater than 10 by any other method and if that's the case, this is the area and the time of the year. This exciting method of fishing is known locally as "jump fishing."

Surprisingly, this area is Dullsville when the water temperature drops into the 40's. The lack of structure doesn't concentrate the fish in any one area and they are almost impossible to locate. The other sections of the lake offer much better winter fishing.

ALICEVILLE BRIDGE TO BIG SLOUGH

It may be hard to believe, but the bass that bunched up so tight in this area during the spring and summer will be in even tighter schools during the fall months. That makes these fish difficult to locate, but once they are found, it's not unusual to load the boat with nice bass.

For the angler who loves to fish a Rat-L-Trap, this is it. The wobbling, noisy bait drives schooling fish crazy.

The angler should locate schools of bass or schools of baitfish (if the baitfish are there, the bass are nearby) with his depthfinder. The mouth of Lubbub Creek, the points of the cut-off areas, the mouth of Lost Slough, the mouth of the small creek in the back of Lost Slough and the mouths of Lard Lake and Pump House Slough are prime areas to find schooling fall bass.

Once the fish are located, the angler should back off the area as far as possible and cast the Rat-L-Trap well past the area. The retrieve should be just fast enough to keep the lure on a plane just over the schooling fish. An occasional pause that lets the lure fall slightly is often all that is needed to trigger the schooling fish into a feeding frenzy.

Once the water surface temperature dips below 50 degrees, bass fishing here gets difficult. The bass settle into the deep creek channels and on the points of the Cut-off areas and get sluggish. The winter angler needs to switch to slow-crawl fishing then. A jig-and-pig or a 4-inch worm fished slowly is the best shot at a good fish.

The only exception to this is on those rare occasions when several unseasonably warm days string together. This will kick the temperature in shallow water up to the 48-degree range and send baitfish scurrying to the area. Bass will follow. A worm or medium-running crankbait fished slowly in this shallow (4 to 8 feet) water will produce fish then.

Other types of fishing

CRAPPIE

The crappie fisherman who finds success on Aliceville Lake should have no problem finding similar success on Gainesville Lake. Gainesville Lake is remarkably similar to its upstream neighbor.

Just as Aliceville Lake, the massive amount of shallow structure next to deep water makes good crappie fishing year round. Crappie fishing is best during the spring when the fish move into the shallow water to spawn. The fish can be found in several locations during this time.

The majority of the better fish leave the original river channels in the Big Creek Cut-Off area, the Owl Creel Cut-Off area, the Dead River or Lubbub Creek Cut-Off area, the Cochrane Creek Cut-Off area, the Cook's Bend Cut-Off area and Warsaw Bend Cut-Off area to move into the weed beds, logjams and standing timber next to the deep channels.

Naturally, the better fish are the toughest to get at. Better fishermen use a long, telescoping fiberglass pole such as a B&M Crappie Pole outfitted with 12-pound test line and a curly-tail chartreuse jig with a white led head. This setup can be used to gingerly reach over and drop the jig right into the holes in the weeds. This produces slabs.

An easier, but less productive method is to line up parallel to the weed beds and, using a spinning or spincast reel, cast a jig hanging 18 inches below a cork as far as possible and as close to the weeds as possible. This rig shold then be "popped" all the way back to the boat. This popping draws attention and the jig right on the weedline is often too much for the fish to resist.

These fish can also be fished in the traditional method, and that's

with a minnow and cork fished near the weedline. This method is also good right before and right after the spawn when the fish are holding just outside of the weeds in 5 or 6 feet of water.

Although the cut-off areas offer the best fishing, any timber- or weed-filled slough or pocket next to the main river is likely to hold fish during this time. The same patterns will work there.

Following the spawn, the crappie will hold on the flats in about 5 to 10 feet of water until June. Stumps and blowdown timber will concentrate the fish. Live minnows fished under a cork is the best bait.

Once the hot part of the summer arrives, the crappie head for deep water. The fish that head to main river channel are often difficult to locate, so the better fishermen head to the cut-off areas. Crappie gather here in the original river channel and stay until winter. The cut-off areas are by-passed by the big boat traffic, thus the crappie find an undisturbed summer.

One of the patterns used by the lake's best crappie fishermen at this time is trolling. A multi-rod setup with jigs set at varying depths will produce numbers of fish. A little experimenting with jig colors and jig depths may be needed to fine tune the pattern.

Another summer pattern that works well is bottom-bumping with live minnows. The crappie change their pattern very little during the fall. Most of the better fish stay deep in the channels, only occasionally making a run to the ledges to feed. Trolling or bottom-bumping works best, but a live minnow fished under a cork over a ledge with structure on the lip will produce some good fish.

Winter crappie fishing is tough on Gainesville Lake. The fish get deep in the channels and seem lifeless. A pattern that works to stir up the fish is locating the fish with a fish finder then jigging a spoon such as a Mann's Mann-O-Lure right in their faces.

Gainesville Lake's best fishing spots

1. Aliceville Dam tailrace. Good spring, summer and fall for bass and crappie.

2. Mouth of Big Slough. Excellent during summer with Little Georges. Good in early spring with jig-and-pigs and worms.

3. Upper end of Big Creek Slough. Standing timber, grass beds.

4. Aliceville Bridge. Good around pilings in summer. Deep-diving crankbaits.

5. Pulpwood Canal. Holds summer fish.

6. Mouth of Dead River. Good worm area in summer.

7. Point in mouth of Dead River area. Good towater fishing in late spring, early summer.

8. Upper mouth of east loop entering Dead River. Excellent spring, summer and fall.

9. Lower mouth of east loop exiting Dead River. Excellent spring, summer and fall.

10. Fingers in Dead River. Full of standing timber. Excellent in spring.

11. Standing timber and ledges on inside bank of Dead River. Excellent spring, summer and fall.

12. Mouth of Lubbub Creek. Good summer fishing.

13. Lubbub Creek. Excellent spring, summer and fall. Spring and summer with spinnerbait on bends, fall with crankbait in bends. Also good creek for sauger and walleye in fall.

14. Buzzard Roost area. Full of standing timber. Excellent in spring with topwater. Good in fall with Rat-L-Trap.

15. Good springtime pocket full of standing timber.

16. Point of Cochrane Cut-Off. Good for schooling fish in summer.

17. Good standing timber. Good fall fishing area.

18. Standing timber filled slough. Good in spring.

19. Point in Catfish Bend. Good all summer and fall.

20. Mouth of Lost Lake. Good in summer and fall.

21. Lost Lake. Standing timber. Good topwater summer and fall. Tough area to get into, but it's possible.

22. Mouth of Lard Lake. Good in summer and fall.

23. Good standing timber and weeds in Lard Lake. Push pole territory. Good spring fishing with topwater. This area has given up several 12-pound largemouth.

24. Pump House Slough. Standing timber and weeds. Good in summer with buzzbaits.

25. Mouth of Big Slough. Good good island inside mouth. Good fishing year round first 100 yards.

26. Back of Big Slough. Area around culvert is excellent after a good rain. Water running in from culvert oxygenates water.

27. Mouth of Sipsey River. Good spring, summer and fall. Little Georges and Rat-L-Traps.

28. Moon Lake. Standing timber. Good in spring with spinnerbaits, summer with buzzbaits.

29. Sipsey River. Miles of standing timber. Weeds just starting. Good in spring when not muddy. Good in summer and fall.

30. Mouth of Goat Slough. Good fishing spring, summer and fall.

31. Left fork in Goat Slough. Full of standing timber. Excellent spring, summer and fall.

32. Right fork of Goat Slough. Good spring fishing with lizard.

33. Back of Cook's Bend. Good year-round fishing.

34. Timber-filled slough. Good spring fishing with spinnerbait, good summer fishing with buzzbait and worm.

35. Bend Lake. All standing timber. Good year round. Bass spawn on little points just inside mouth in spring.

36. Standing timber filled slough. Good year-round fishing.

37. Wilkes Creek. Standing timber in back. Weeds throughout. Good year-round.

38. Mouth of unnamed slough. Good in summer for schooling bass.

39. Back of slough. Grass and standing timber. Good year round.

40. Timber-filled slough. Good crankbait area in fall.

41. Mouth of Turkey Paw Branch. Lefthand bank is standing timber. Excellent with spinnerbait and jig-and-pig spring.

42. Back of Turkey Paw. Points of fingers offer good year-round fishing.

Tom Bevill Lock and Dam

Big Slough

Below Tom Bevill Lock and Dam

Gainesville Lake

Gainesville Lake

Tailrace to Aliceville bridge

Bogue Chitto Creek

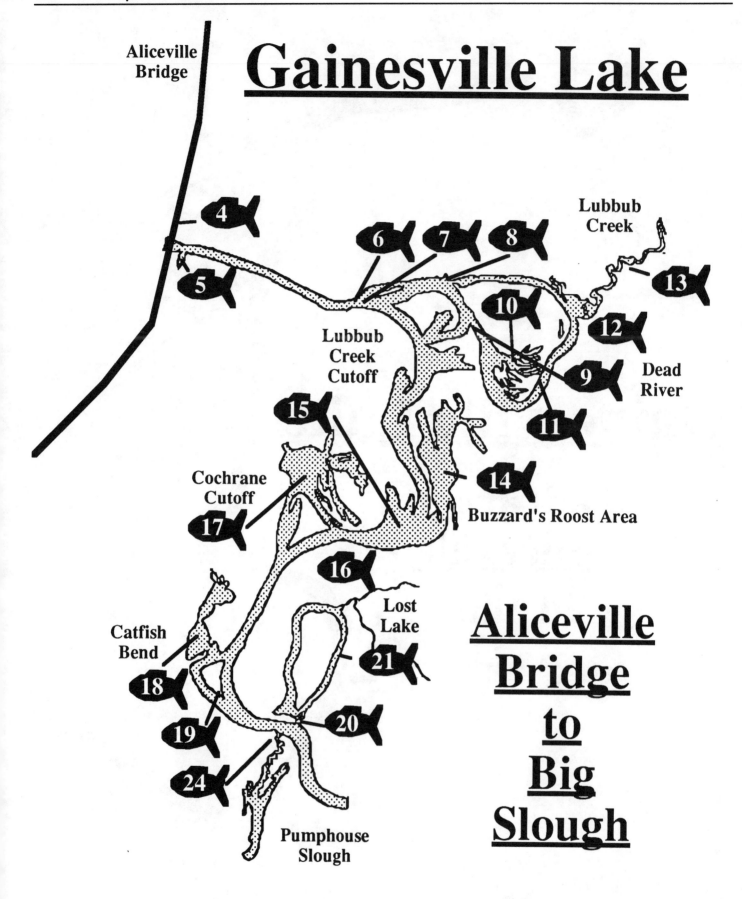

Aliceville Bridge

Gainesville Lake

Lubbub Creek

Lubbub Creek Cutoff

Dead River

Cochrane Cutoff

Buzzard's Roost Area

Catfish Bend

Lost Lake

Aliceville Bridge to Big Slough

Pumphouse Slough

Sipsey River

Moon Lake

Big
Slough

Gainesville
Lake

Goat Slough

Cook's
Bend

Big Slough
to
Bend Lake

Gainesville Lake

Fenache
Creek

Wilkes
Creek

Bend Lake
to
Mile Marker 271

Gainesville Lake

Mile Marker 271 to Dam

Turkey Paw Branch

Demopolis Lake

y no stretch of the imagination is Demopolis Lake a lake, at least by the standards of appearance set by many other Alabama lakes. The damming of the lake did little to change the original river channels. There isn't a wide spot anywhere on the main rivers that would give the appearance of most lakes in Alabama.

Demopolis Lake is unsual in another way. While most lakes are the result of the damming of a river, Demopolis Lake was formed by backing up two rivers - the Tombigbee and Black Warrior. It is possible for angler - in a a space of just a few feet - to fish different rivers with different water colors.

Although Demopolis Lake is unusual by most standards, many an angler would swap his best rod and reel for his home lake to have the structure Demopolis Lake has.

Standing timber and cypress stumps can be found tucked away in a large number of sloughs, swamps and creeks. Grass - seemingly hundreds of miles of grass - can be found everywhere.

The grass and shallow standing timber and cypress stumps means shallow-water fish easily accessible to most anglers.

Spring bass fishing

TOMBIGBEE RIVER ABOVE
THE BLACK WARRIOR RIVER INTERSECTION

Anytime a lake is blessed with shallow standing timber, shallow cypress trees and massive grass beds, it's a foregone conclusion that tremendous springtime fishing awaits bass anglers. The Tombigbee River section is a perfect model of water that offers spectacular springtime fishing.

The Tombigbee River section is full of both medium-depth and shallow-water sloughs, all filled with enticing springtime structure.

Bass in this section of Lake Demopolis have very few winter options. The main river has the only deep water to offer comfort for big bass during the harshest part of winter, and it's out of this main river and into the sloughs the bass move when the first warm weather approaches.

The shallow and medium depth sloughs, usually laden with good

Demopolis Lake Fact Sheet

Location, length, acreage

Demopolis Lake is an Army Corps of Engineers lake formed by the backing up of two rivers - the Tombigbee and Black Warrior, both of which are waterways navigable by barge traffic. Lake Demopolis is part of the Tennessee-Tombigbee Waterway system and a vital link in the chain of navigable waterways that tie middle America to the Gulf Coast.

Demopolis Lake stretches 68 nautical miles from Gainesville Lock and Dam to Demopolis Lock and Dam on the Tombigbee River, then 53 miles from Demopolis Lock and Dam to Warrior Lock and Dam on the Black Warrior. The lake has 10,000 acres of water surface and 500 miles of shoreline.

Impoundment

Construction on Demopolis Lock and Dam began in 1949 and was completed in 1954.

Demopolis Lock and Dam

Presently, Demopolis Lock and Dam has no power generation facilities. An application has been filed for a powerhouse by the Alabama Electric Cooperative, Inc. The lock and dam has a 1,485-foot open-crest spillway and with a navigation lock on the east bank.

Configuration

Demopolis Lake is virtually "Y" shaped, with the Upper Tombigbee River on the west side and the Black Warrior River to the east. The lake lacks the configuration of many Alabama lakes because it is

Stocking history

Florida-strain largemouth
1983-90	136,750
1991	20,534
1992	20,240
1993	20,020
1994	20,000

Striped bass
1984	50,000
1985	20,300
1986	20,000

Hybrids
1982-87	511,830
1988	21,300
1989	20,000
1990	20,400
1991	25,347
1992	20,000
1993	111,475
1994	100,941

virtually river run throughout its length. Incoming creeks, flooded swamps and large sloughs form the widest points on the lake. Nowhere on the lake does the main river widen to any degree.

Major and secondary creeks

Besides the grass, standing timber and other desirable structure in Demopolis Lake, there are a number of creeks, sloughs and swamps scattered throughout the length of both rivers. On the Tombigbee River, McConnico Creek and Birdine are water suppliers in the Rattlesnake Bend area, while Taylor Lake Slough, Logjam Slough, Spidle Lake Slough, Belmont Landing Slough, Culpepper Slough, Foscue Creek and Lock and Dam Slough supply water to the rest of the river below.

On the Black Warrior River side, Runaway Branch, Kelly's Slough, French Creek, Backbone Creek, Yellow Creek and and Big Prairie Creek are major water suppliers.

A small number of creeks which add small amounts of water or water during heavy rains dot both rivers.

Types of fish

Demopolis Lake features popular species such as largemouth bass, a small number of spotted bass, white bass, hybrid bass, a limited number of saltwater stripe, white and black crappie, channel catfish, flathead catfish, blue catfish, bullhead catfish, longear sunfish, redear sunfish, green sunfish, warmouth and bluegill.

The lake also has several species of gar, drum and common carp and grass carp. As for baitfish, gizzard shad, threadfin shad and several species of minnows are present.

stain due to heavy spring rains, warm much quicker than the main river. The dingy water absorbs heat rather than reflecting it as clear water does, and the warm water sends the grass on a growing binge which in turn oxygenates the water.

This warm, structure-filled, oxygenated water, combined with the baitfish that are attracted to it, computes into excellent pre-spawn, spawn and post-spawn water for bass.

These bass first move into the mouths of the sloughs and creeks and alternate between there and the main river as the weather does its usual early spring flip-flops.

Several days of sunshine will warm the mouth to the point the fish will find it comfortable enough to remain there, while the periodic cold snaps or cold nights will send them back to the deep water of the main river channel.

Crankbaits are the first effective baits. The points and secondary points inside the sloughs hold the fish, and medium running crankbaits will shake them loose. Shad-colored crankbaits such as Mann's 20-Plus, Bagley's DB3 and other similarly colored baits work well on the rare occasions the water is clear this time of year, while chartreuse and other brightly colored baits work well when the river has its normal spring stain. Belmont Landing Slough, Spidle Lake, Logjam Slough, Taylor Lake Slough, Birdine Creek, Birdine Slough and McConnico Creek are shallow-water refuges in which you'll find early spring bass.

When warm days finally begin to be followed by warm nights on

a regular basis, the bass will move into these areas and stay until post-spawn. The bass will hold temporarily on points, deepwater timber and in the grass and will feed heavily in anticipation of the spawn.

Lunker Lures, Nip-I-Didees, Spin-I-Didees, Bang-O-Lures, Jitterbugs, twitch baits or some other form of topwater bait will take these fish in exciting style, but die-hard spinnerbait or flippin' fishermen can also be successful with their favorite lures.

A chartreuse/white spinnerbait tipped with a chartreuse pork frog flipped into the back of the grass and brought through at a slow roll will provide vicious attacks. Odds are that any of the fish taken by any method this time of the year will be quality fish.

Every slough or creek between the Tombigbee River-Black Warrior River intersection and the upper end of Rattlesnake Bend cutoff is filled with grass, standing timber, stumps or cypress trees, and most have a combination of two or more types of structure.

It's these good hiding places bass seek out to build their beds. Most of the grass beds in these sloughs will be in 3 to 5 feet of water.

Once these bass have buried themselves in this grass and are serious about the spawn, flippin' becomes the best way to take the larger fish. A 1/2-ounce or 3/4-ounce jig with a pork frog chunk will punch its way through the grass and get down where the fish are. Anglers should concentrate on any grass patch where there's a small opening (this lets sun in and warms the water) or wherever two types of grass meet.

The number of days of flipping for those big fish are few, however. The big females lay their eggs and vacate the premises in short order. The males are left behind to guard the eggs. The males are always smaller fish.

Once the spawn is over, Demopolis Lake goes through a brief period that is unquestionably its best fishing time of the year. For two, three or four weeks, depending on the weather, the bass, reeling from the hardship of the spawn, begin to revitalize themselves by going into a feeding frenzy.

Both the males and females are hungry and the realtively cool water allows them to stay in the shallow structure to feed. Topwater action can be tremendous. Lunker Lures, Jitterbugs, Nip-I-Didees, Hula Poppers, Pop-R's, Bang-O-Lures, floating worms and lizards - just about anything that floats, will produce fish.

TOMBIGBEE RIVER-BLACK WARRIOR RIVER
INTERSECTION TO YELLOW CREEK

The patterns that lead to successful spring fishing on the Tombigee River on Demopolis Lake work just as well on the Black Warrior River fork. The only real difference between the two rivers during the spring is that following heavy rains, the Black Warrior normally will have somewhat less stain and will clear more quickly.

Medium or deep-running crankbaits or lizards rigged Carolina-style are effective when the fish first move out of the main river channel to the mouths of sloughs and swamps. The angler should use a 7-inch or larger lizard such as Zoom makes because the larger the lizard, the better it floats. A 7-inch pumpkin Zoom worked slowly in the mouth and secondary points can be deadly those first few days that the bass move shallow.

Once the bass begin their transition from the mouth to the shallow water back in the creeks, sloughs and swamps, spinnerbaits work wonderfully. You're going to find stained water most of the time, so use a chartreuse or chartreuse/white spinnerbait tipped with a chartreuse pork frog and a nickel willow leaf blade.

It should be noted that some creeks are clearer than others this time of year for one of two reasons. Either the slough or creek is deep, or it has a good creek running through it and pumping muddy water out of it. Pay close attention to that and the water temperature. The creeks that have moving water have good oxygen content and, thus, more active fish, but only in middle or late spring. Moving water is more difficult to heat and the creek with good moving water, in early spring, may be actually pumping cooler water on top of warm water. It's such little tricks that experts use to make the difference between good and great fishing.

Once in shallow water, topwater baits such as buzzbaits, floating lizards (once again, use the largest lizards you can find so they will float a hook) and twitch baits are the key. When hard on spawn and in the weeds, buzzbaits will work, but 3/4-ounce jig-and-pigs are sometimes needed to punch through the heavy greenery to get where the fish are.

A good buzzbait trick is to straighten the bend that holds the blade on and remove the blade. Put a small silver or orange plastic bead (both can be found at larger tackle stores) onto the arm and return the blade. Re-bend the arm to hold the blade in place. This bead will keep most of the weeds from tangling the spinning blade and will result in more time the lure stays in the water.

Just as on the Tombigbee fork, most spring fishing in the Black Warrior fork takes place in the creeks and sloughs. Having a good knowledge of the areas and the type structure they contain is important.

Dobbs Swamp is a shallow, multi-fingered swamp that lives and dies with spring floods and summer drought. It has a narrow opening, but opens to a wide expanse of water. The swamp is full of grass beds and fallen trees. In late spring and summer, the grass beds become so thick passage into the swamp will be blocked.

The shallow water is an excellent spawning area. Buzzbaits and other weed-proof topwater baits, as well as floating plastic lizards, work well during spring.

Runaway Branch is a moderately deep slough that has grass beds, scattered standing timber and much blow-down timber. Camphouses can be found on both sides of the branch and many have piers and docks laced with underwater brush piles. Worms, Sassy Shads and spinnerbaits work well in that brush during spring. There also is a landing accessible from U.S. 43.

Kelly's Slough is the closest slough to the old U.S. 43 bridge. The slough is void of points, and is fairly shallow. Camphouses and piers can be found in the slough and many areas surrounding piers are loaded with brush. Grass is predominant throughout its length and cypress trees can be found in the back. It's a natural location for the bass spawn. Buzzbaits, worms, spinnerbaits and topwater twitch baits work well.

The Citadel Cement Slough has a small opening laced with old bridge pilings, but it opens into a fairly decent-sized fishing hole. It has both deep and shallow water. Grass is found throughout the slough, as are steep lime rock banks. It offers only average spring fishing.

French Creek is one of the three largest creeks on Demopolis Lake. It is the deepest creek in the lake and the last creek on the lake to get muddy during spring rains. This wide creek offers islands, a multitude of points, rock banks, a well-defined creek channel and a small amount of grass. For the average angler, its spring fishing is only fair, but top anglers do quite well there in the spring. The multiple offerings of other creeks with grass and standing timber and the resulting shallow spring fish make other creeks a better bet for the average angler, however.

Powerline Slough is a slough that offers deep water in the front and shallow water in the back. It is full of grass throughout its length and has its share of standing timber in the back. It also has three major points. The shallow water in the rear offers excellent bass and crappie spawning. This slough is better known as a crappie producer, but nice bass can occasionally be found during the spring. The spring bass baits mentioned for other creeks and sloughs work well.

Backbone Creek is a long, narrow creek with moderately deep water. There is a launch site. It has a good stand of cypress trees in the back which offer a safe spawning area to bass in the spring. Spinnerbaits and topwater are best.

Yellow Creek appears on the map as a long, navigable creek, but anglers find difficulty in fishing more than 1/2 mile back. By being in a major river bend, the mouth of this creek has silted in and passage can be difficult. For the angler who finds water deep enough to get through, the shallow-water creek offers good points and grass beds. This is primarily a spring fishing area because passage is limited other times of the year.

Yellow Creek to Candy Landing

Big Prairie Creek is the largest water inlet on the Black Warrior side of Demopolis Lake and offers excellent fishing year round. It is possible to go as far as four miles back in Big Prairie and still find 17 feet of water. Yet, there is plenty of shallow water throughout to make for excellent spring fishing. There are plenty of grass-ladened shallow water ledges that fall directly into deep water and these are excellent areas to find spring bass.

In early spring, the bass will inhabit the deep water points and use these points as a highway to travel back and forth for brief feeding runs in shallow water. With your boat positioned in deep water, shad-colored deep-running crankbaits cast into shallow water and reeled down the deep point produce nice catches. Large (3/4 or 1-ounce) spinnerbaits with big blades also work well here. The heavy spinnerbait falls quickly down the steep points and the larger blades force the angler to fish the bait slowly at the speed these sluggish fish need.

The water normally isn't heavily stained here, so use spinnerbait colors such as white or shad and blade colors such as copper or gold that work well in clearer water.

Other baits that work well here in the early spring are jig-and-pigs, plastic worms and Carolina-rigged lizards.

Once the water warms to 65 degrees, the bass are thinking spawn and shallow water. Buzzbaits, spinnerbaits and other topwater baits mentioned elsewhere for fishing grass can be used.

These are not the best patterns for taking spring bass, however. If you've ever considered jiggerpole fishing, there are few places better than Big Prairie Creek for you to witness it at its best. (Jiggerpoling also works wonderfully on other grass-filled sloughs on this lake in the spring).

For those who haven't heard of the ancient art of jiggerpoling (a method your grandaddy probably used if he fished), all that is needed is an 18- to 20-foot cane or fiberglass pole, a large broken-back minnow bait and six inches of 100-pound-test braided Dacron saltwater fishing line.

The lure should be tied to the pole with the 6 inches of Dacron. Using the trolling motor, simply run the bait inches away from the fringes of the grass, all the while shaking the pole so the tip of the pole barely slaps the water with a steady rhythm. This may seem unnatural at first, but it gives the appearance of a minnow chasing a small bug and the result is an offering that the bass, hiding in the grass awaiting an easy meal, can't turn down.

This method of fishing is thorough. It allows the angler to cover every inch of the grass instead of casting every 15 feet or so.

When a fish decides he wants the bait, the explosions are tremendous. The angler must then swing the fish around to the opposite side of the boat into deep water and pull the pole in hand-over-hand to retrieve the fish.

Big fish are common, and a 5-pound bass on 6 inches of line is a thrill unlike any other you'll find in fishing.

If you're looking for water that has less fishing pressure than Big Prairie, Bream Slough is a moderately deep slough filled with grass beds. It's mouth silts in often which makes it difficult to get into, but getting inside with a small aluminum boat can have its rewards. Bream Slough is better known as a spring bream producer, but it does hold some bass, especially around the lone stump that can be found there.

Baker's Slough is another such place. It has a tiny mouth, but it is filled with grass beds.

Hot weather bass fishing

Tombigbee River above the Black Warrior River intersection

The thick, matted grass beds that can be found in Lake Demopolis provide enough shade and oxygen to allow bass to stay shallow longer into the summer than in most other Alabama lakes, sometimes as late as midsummer. Oxygen-producing grass, shade from large trees on the bank and deep water combine to provide tolerable summer bass habitat.

Several areas off the main river in this portion of the lake contain water deep enough to hold summer bass. It's not unusual to find bass holding on points in Rattlesnake Bend, Twelve-Mile Bend, Taylor Lake Slough, Spidle Lake and McConnico Creek even when the surface temperature passes the 90 degree mark. The deep south bank in Spidle Lake is a solid summer place to go. Twelve-Mile Bend is virtually nothing but river run filled with enticing structure, and the dredging of the Twelve-Mile Bend Cut-Off to divert barge traffic during construction of the Tenn-Tom Waterway turned this into an excellent summer fishing area, and other times of the year as well.

Twelve-Mile Bend is virtually a 12-mile-long deep slough.

Other key holding areas during this time are the wide mouths of Taylor Lake Slough and Spidle Lake. The fish suspended in the main channel dash into the wide areas to feed, but are always just seconds away from deep water again.

Deep-running crankbaits, Rat-L-Traps, plastic worms and Carolina-rigged lizards are the key baits to fish these points with during the dog days of summer.

Both Taylor Lake Slough and Spidle Lake have gradual slopes leading out of their wide mouths into the main river channel and a Carolina-rigged lizard or a Do-Nothing Worm can be effective.

If you're willing to swat mosquitoes and fish at daybreak or dusk, don't forget to bring your topwater baits along, even if common sense tells you it's not really topwater season.

Spidle Lake, Taylor Lake Slough and McConnico Creek are areas where shad surface near the mouth in the early morning and late evening hours and are attacked by small, schooling bass. Twitch baits and other injured shad or minnow imitations will often result in a limit of bass in minutes. Don't expect the bass to be quality bass, however. They're usually just big enough to stink up a frying pan.

Barge and yacht traffic on the Tombigbee River is cursed by many fishermen, but the disturbances do result is some good summertime fishing. The waves from the vessels have washed the bank from under a large number of trees and these trees have fallen into the river. The trees offer excellent summer areas for flippin'.

Tombigbee River-Black Warrior River intersection to Yellow Creek

Once the spawn is over, the fish hold in the shallow grass beds until summer's heat arrives and they then seek deeper water with milder temperatures.

The mouth of Runaway Branch is a summer schooling area on this portion of the lake. Chrome/blue-back Rat-L-Traps and similarly colored medium-running crankbaits are excellent when fish are schooling hard in open water. When the fish are running up on the ledges to feed, 4-inch Slider worms or Sassy Shads cast from deep water onto the ledges work well.

Summer bass also school in the mouth of French Creek.

Lesser fish can be found in both creeks, especially in the creek channel in French Creek. Another good possibility is fishing the piers and docks in both creeks. The fish find shade under the structures during the hottest part of the day, and for night fishermen, feed under them in the brush at night.

YELLOW CREEK TO CANDY LANDING

Summer fishing is rarely tremendous on any lake in Alabama, but the wide expanses of deep water found in Big Prairie Creek make it an excellent summer location by summer standards. Bass here can sometimes find enough thick, matted grass in relatively deep, cool water that they can find refuge, at least in the early morning hours, in the late afternoon or at night.

These fish won't be aggressive, so a slow bait like a heavily weighted worm, or a jig-and-pig that can punch through the thick stuff is needed.

Other fish here hold on the points in the deep creek channel. Worms, Carolina-rigged lizards or jigging spoons will take these fish.

A large number of bass head to the main river channel during summer and the fallen trees and logjams offer cover they need. Flippin' a jig-and-pig at the base of trees that are in 20 feet or water can catch the fish. The water is fairly clear this time of the year, so a brown/black jig-and-pig tipped with a brown or black pork frog works well.

COOL AND COLD WEATHER BASS FISHING

TOMBIGBEE RIVER ABOVE THE BLACK WARRIOR RIVER INTERSECTION

Cooling water temperatures in late September send bass fleeing from the dull, stale, deep water of summer. Just as for humans, this must be an enjoyable time of the year for bass. They find temperatures much more bearable.

And it's the time of the year for the bass to harvest and store food for winter. The cooler water sends the baitfish into shallower water and the bass readily follow.

Unfortunately, the shallow grass that made fishing so good isn't quite as enticing in the fall. Instead of growing, the grass is dying and robbing the water of oxygen. Some bass can be found in the grass that is struggling to stay alive, but most fish are moving in close to the fringes of this grass and hanging on points.

Spinnerbaits, worms and, to a lesser degree, topwater baits and crankbaits, are effective. Sloughs with shallow water falling into deeper water close to the mouth will hold the fish and they'll be actively feeding in anticipation of winter.

Placing a boat in the mouth of Taylor Lake Slough and casting a Carolina-rigged lizard or worm into the mouth of the creek and into the main river channel is an excellent fall pattern. Great numbers of bass coming into the shallow water to feed use this route.

Once the water temperature plunges, full bellies and lower metabolisms slow the fishes' feeding habits. The shallow water that offered the best pH and water temperature flip-flops and offers the worst conditions for fish, so they move to deeper water to compensate. There, they become complacent and uninterested in eating.

The same areas that offered refuge from the unbearable summer offer the same refuge for winter bass. A slow bait such as a jig-and-pig, a Do-Nothing worm or a heavy spinnerbait slow-rolled across the bottom right in the fish's face is needed to get a response.

These baits should be worked on deep points and in the main river channel around any tye of deep structure such as brush piles or logjams.

TOMBIGBEE RIVER-BLACK WARRIOR RIVER INTERSECTION TO YELLOW CREEK

Fall fishing can be quite good in this section of the lake. The logjams and fallen trees along the main river channel hold active bass, as do the mouths of Runaway Branch, Kelly's Slough, Citadel Cement Slough, French Creek, Powerline Slough, Backbone Creek and Yellow Creek. Bass will school and feed heavily in the main river channel near sharp bends such as those found near Hines Landing, Klies Bend and at the mouths of Backbone Creek and Yellow Creek.

When the bass are schooling and chasing shad on the top of the water, Rat-L-Traps, medium-running crankbaits, spoons or Sassy Shad thrown into the middle of visible schools will result in catches of small to medium bass.

At times, bass will leave the main river channel to feed on the narrow ledges found throughout the length of the river. Locating stumps and brush on these ledges is the key to finding fish when they're not schooling on top.

Because of the moderately deep water, both Runaway Branch and French Creek hold fall bass. The boathouses and piers hold quantities of small bass until the water temperature drops below 60 degrees, as do the fringes of the grass in 4 feet or deeper water.

Once winter sets in, fishing gets tough. Jig-and-pigs hopped along the bottom of points in the creek channels in Runaway Creek and French Creek will result in a few fish. The best route to go, however, is flipping the deep, fallen timber in the main river.

YELLOW CREEK TO CANDY LANDING

Fall fishing is usually on-again, off-again in this section of Demopolis Lake. The best bet is to watch for schooling activity in the mouth and on the secondary points in Big Prairie Creek, but that isn't much to depend on. Those fish will normally be there, however, even if they can't be seen. Worms, Sassy Shads and Carolina-rigged lizards work well on the points, but keep a Rat-L-Trap or twitch bait tied on another rod to be ready for any visible schooling activity.

The mouth or secondary points of any opening off the main river channel is a threat to erupt with schooling bass.

After the water cools somewhat, the mouth and banks of Power-plant Slough will hold some bass. Rat-L-Traps and medium-running crankbaits will work there.

The coldest part of the winter means jig-and-pig fishing again, with timber on the main river and deep points in Big Prairie holding the better fish.

Other types of fishing

CRAPPIE FISHING

The multitude of grass and standing timber in the wide creeks in Demopolis Lake make it a natural for crappie.

Although this lake doesn't produce the numbers of 3-pound-plus crappie some waters in this end of the state like Miller's Ferry produce, it can more than compete numbers-wise. This lake is a tremendous crappie-producer year round.

If this lake has a crappie fishing secret, it's the tremendous numbers of big fish it produces in November, December and January in the Demopolis Lock and Dam tailrace. Large numbers of large crappie move into the tailrace area during these months and position themselves in the deep structure approximately 300 yards below the dam. An angler should use a depthfinder to locate this structure, then anchor right on top of it. The structure includes rocks, trees and some steel beams.

This is a pattern that works best when there's no current or little current. Using ultralight tackle and 6-pound test line, drop live minnows hooked through the lips into the structure. This often produces numbers of crappie in the 2-pound range. One angler caught more than 1,200 crappie from this area during the three months in 1989.

Fishing up in the lake isn't bad either. During the spring, numbers of crappie move into the grass in French Creek and Powerline Slough, as well as other similar areas. The fish will hold on stickups and stumps in 5 or 6 feet of water until the surface temperature reaches 68 to 70 degrees, then will go to the banks to spawn on the fringe of the grass. Rarely will these crappie get up in the grass as bass do.

While off the banks, trolling jigs is an excellent way to take numbers of fish. Once the crappie are on the banks, a long, fiberglass pole and minnows are the way to go. The pole allows you to drop the bait right in the crappies' faces when they're holding tight to the grass.

Following the spawn, the crappie return briefly to the areas they held in before the spawn, then head to the deep creek and river channels. A double-hook rig with minnows fished in French Creek, Taylor Lake and Powerline Slough is an excellent way to take these fish.

In September and October, the cooling water temperature sends the crappie shallow again. Tree tops, stumps and shallow humps in 4 to 6 feet of water will hold fish. Live minnows or jigs can be used.

Demopolis Lake's best fishing spots

1. Mouth of McConnico Creek. Excellent spring fishing, good other times of the year. Full of grass beds and standing timber in deep water.
2. Point in McConnico Creek. Excellent year-round fishing.
3. Underwater island in McConnico Creek. Excellent spring and summer fishing.
4. Small sloughs on north side of the bank. Sloughs are full of grass beds. Excellent spring fishing.
5. Birdine Slough. Shallow slough offers excellent spring fishing.
6. Birdine Creek. Small creel muddies easily, but good late-spring fishing in grass beds and on structure on the banks.
7. Small, grass-filled slough. Excellent spring fishing. Good summer fishing in the mouth.
8. Small, grass-filled slough. Excellent spring fishing. Good summer fishing in the mouth. This slough and No. 7 are remotely located, so they attract large numbers of fish coming out of the channel in spring and late summer.
9. Rattlesnake Bend Cut-Off south intersection. Excellent worm fishing in early morning hours in spring and summer.
10. Rattlesnake Bend Cut-Off north intersection. Same as above.
11. Taylor Lake. Stays clear in spring. Good mouth for worm fishing. Grass, islands, standing timber and points.
12. Logjam Slough. Cypress trees in the back corners of both forks. Deep slough holds bass year round. Several good points and some grass.
13. Unnamed slough. Excellent spring spawning area. Grass beds equate to terrific buzzbait fishing. Normally impossible to get into during summer.
14. Mouth of Spidle Lake. Good fishing most of the year. Shallow water and grass beds directly in mouth.
15. Back of Spidle Lake. Grass beds and excellent spring spawning area.
16. Deep, south bank of Spidle Lake. Stays shady in summer. Good structure.
17. Belmont Landing Slough. Full of cypress trees and grass beds. Excellent spring fishing.
18. Culpepper Slough. Good worm fishing in mouth during summer. Standing timber in back and grass beds on north and south banks. A few good points. Good spring fishing.
19. Demopolis Yacht Basin Slough. Wide area directly off river. Some grass beds. Boat slips are good for crankbait fishing year round.
20. Island in Yacht Basin. Good topwater fishing around grass in spring.
21. Webbs Bend. East side is lime rock banks good for crankbaiting in summer.
22. Whitfield Canal. Points, grass, boat ramps and deep water. Some good fishing year round. Excellent area for worm fishing.
23. Shallow water in back of Whitfield Canal. Grass beds. Good spring fishing.
24. Grain Elevator Slough. Same type of fishing as Whitfield Canal.
25. Lock and Dam Slough. North of lock and dam. Very shallow. Excellent spring spawning area. Lots of grass, but little standing

timber. Good buzzbait area.
26. Foscue Creek. Deep slough with good year-round fishing. Points, grass, shallow water and islands.
27. Dobb's Swamp. Shallow water with grass beds and standing timber. Topwater fishing. Excellent spawning area.
28. Runaway Branch. Excellent year-round fishing. Deep water. Standing timber, grass beds, boat docks, points and cypress trees. Clear slough most of the year.
29. Kelly's Slough. Long, straight slough. Grass beds and standing timber. Worms, spinnerbaits and buzzbaits spring and early summer.
30. Unnamed slough. Connects with Demopolis Yacht Basin Slough in high water conditions. Grass beds and standing timber. Good worm fishing in mouth.
31. Citadel Cement Slough. Good grass beds and both deep and shallow water. Good year-round fishing.
32. Mouth of French Creek. Good year-round fishing.
33. French Creek. Largest water inlet on Black Warrior side. Good grass beds, standing timber. Deep water throughout most of creek.
34. Island in French Creek. Good spring fishing.
35. Roadbed in mouth of French Creek.
36. Powerline Slough. Very narrow opening. Standing timber and cypress trees. Good points. Shallow grass and deep water. Good year-round fishing.
37. Backbone Creek. Narrow slough with cypress trees in back half, grass beds in back. Clear slough. Good year-round fishing.
38. Yellow Creek. Shallow except at mouth, but well-defined creek channel. Grass beds. Good spring fishing with buzzbaits.
39. North bank of Bream Slough. Good grass. Excellent spawning area.
40. South bank of Bream Slough. Deep water. Good year-round fishing.
41. Baker's Bottom. Good spring slough.
42. Greene County Steam Plant inlet. Good year-round fishing.
43. Pilings on west bank. Good late spring, summer and fall with jig-and-pigs.
44. Boulders on east side. Good year-round fishing with worms, spinnerbaits and crankbaits.
45. Excellent stripe fishing area in winter months. Warm water discharge area.
46. Johnson Branch. Very shallow slough filled with grass beds. Good spring spawning area.
47. Unnamed slough. Grass beds and good points. Good spring fishing with topwater baits.
48. Mouth of Big Prairie Creek. Good year-round fishing. Good schooling area in summer and fall.
49. Island in Big Prairie Creek. Shallow water adjacent to deep water. Good in this area year round.
50. Underwater island in Big Prairie Creek. Good year-round fishing.
51. Underwater island in Big Prairie Creek. Good year-round.
52. Main creek channel in back of prairie creek. Up to 17 feet deep. Holds bass year round.

Demopolis Lake

Rattlesnake Bend area
(Twelve-Mile Bend)

McConnico Creek

Birdine Slough

Birdine Creek

Rattlesnake Bend Cut-off

Taylor Lake Slough

Demopolis Lake

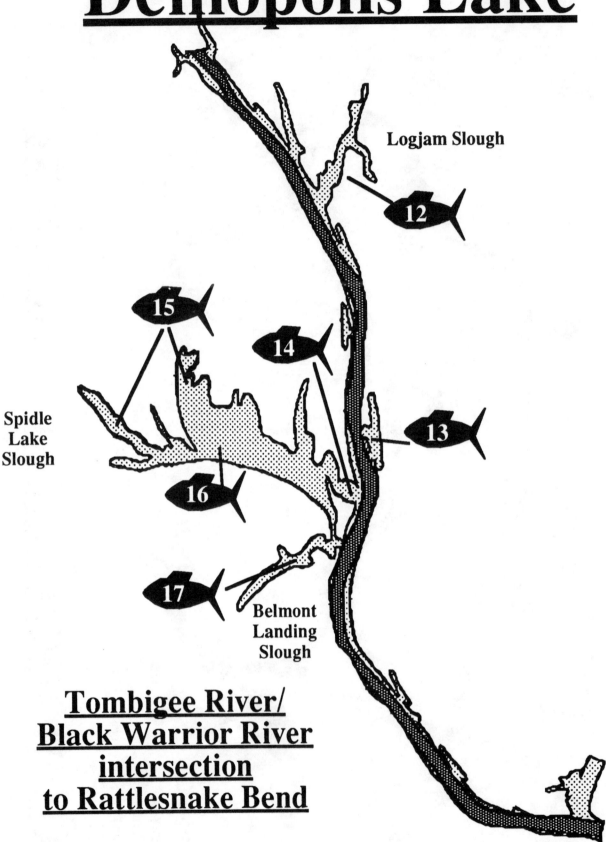

Logjam Slough

12

15

14

Spidle
Lake
Slough

13

16

17

Belmont
Landing
Slough

Tombigee River/
Black Warrior River
intersection
to Rattlesnake Bend

Demopolis Lake

Powerline Slough

36

Backbone
Creek

37

Kelly's
Marina

Kelly's
Slough

29

French
Creek

34

33

35

32

Citadel
Cement
Slough

31

Culpepper
Slough

30

20

Demopolis Yacht
Basin Slough

43

Runaway
Branch

28

18

19

21

Webb's
Bend

Whitfield
Canal

22

23

Dobb's
Swamp

27

Lock and Dam
Slough

24

25

Demopolis
Lock &
Dam

Foscue
Creek

26

Demopolis Lock & Dam
to
Yellow Creek

Demopolis Lock & Dam
to
Yellow Creek

Demopolis Lock & Dam

Demopolis Lake

Foscue Creek

Lock and Dam Slough

Demopolis Yacht Basin Slough

Webb's Bend

Whitfield Canal

43

Dobb's Swamp

Runaway Branch

Culpepper Slough

Kelly's Slough

Kelly's Marina

Citadel Cement Slough

French Creek

Backbone Creek

Powerline Slough

Mobile Delta

To the angler accustomed to fishing Alabama's reservoirs, the Mobile Delta can be a perplexing puzzle. Not only does the fisherman in the Mobile Delta have to worry about the myriad of factors that affect reservoir fishing - factors such as fronts, water color and water temperature - he must also worry such things as ebb tides, salinity, wind direction and salt lines.

The angler adept at fishing the Mobile Delta is a well-rounded fisherman capable of fishing anywhere.

The Delta is made up of several major rivers and numerous small creeks and shallow bays which offer widely and quickly changing fishing conditions.

For instance: The shallow bays offer excellent spring fishing, but the bays closest to the Mobile River muddy quickly and often become unfishable. It's also possible for spring fishing to be terrific, then suddenly have a north wind kick up and literally push the water out of the bay. To make matters worse, these same shallow bays and the creeks leading to them are often choked-off with weeds as the spring fishing gets good.

These same areas offer some good fall fishing, but by winter, many are too shallow to fish.

And then there's the perplexing problem of the fish themselves. During certain times of the year, an angler doesn't merely go bass fishing. A fish on the end of the line may be anything from a bass to a flounder. If you're looking for a variety of fish, this is your best bet in Alabama. Largemouth bass, striped bass, crappie, bream and several species of catfish are abundant here as they are in most Alabama waters, but a cast at the right time of the year in the Mobile Delta will also produce saltwater fish. Speckled trout, redfish, flounder, sheepshead, croaker, drum and jack crevalle are common at certain times.

Spring bass fishing

BELOW I-65

By the third week of February, water temperatures in the Mobile Delta usually have risen to the point that bass are thinking about the spawn. The bass leave the wide, deep waters of the main rivers where they spent the winter and head for the shallow bays. These shallow, weed-filled waters heat up the quicker than surrounding water and it here that the bass will lay their eggs and raise their young.

There are several key areas to concentrate on during the spring months. Chocolata Bay (also known as Chacalloochee Bay) is one of the first bays to hold spring fish and the bay that holds bass the longest. The area near the grass beds in the back offers excellent spring topwater fishing. Conway Creek, which is near Chocolata Bay, is a key area when a north wind is forcing the water out of the bay. Delvan Bay is a wide bay with a somewhat narrow mouth that offers good spring fishing. Grand Bay and Chukfee Bay are also key spring areas.

Little Bateau is a shallow water bay that is only a foot deep and it is rarely fished, but a flood tide causes fish to stack up in the mouth and it is worth a cast or two when those conditions are present.

Farther north, The Basin Negro, better known as Negro Lake, and Big Lizard Creek are also worth taking a look at. Mifflin Lake, which has its mouth below I-65 but extends well north of the interstate, is another key area.

Keep in mind that almost every raindrop that isn't soaked into the ground when it falls in this state ends up in the Mobile Delta. Much of the Tennessee River, the Tombigbee, the Warrior, the Black Warrior, the Coosa, the Tallapoosa and the Alabama River eventually flow into the Mobile Delta. Thus, spring rains all over the state have an effect on fishing here. Finding water not too muddy to fish is a key to good spring fishing.

It's not unsual to find a shallow bay full of muddy water in its mouth, but don't concede the fishing there without further investigative work. It is often possible to locate a distinct stain line separating muddy water from the clear somewhere in the bay. The northern half of these bays often clear up quickly after huge influxes of muddy water. The stain lines often offer tremendous fishing with most strikes coming by casting into the clear water and bringing it to the stain.

The shallow bays have a variety of grasses including Coontail and ribbon grass. All will concentrate fish.

Another key form of structure to concentrate on in the spring is the hundreds of duck blinds scattered throughout the Delta. When these duck blinds are located in shallow water, bass will almost always use them to spawn and they are hot both pre- and post spawn.

A wide array of lures will take spring bass from the Delta, none really much better than the other. A 1/4-ounce or 1/2-ounce spinnerbait, either white or chartreuse depending on the water clarity, is probably the most popular bait. It should be equipped with a single, small nickel blade and a pork frog trailer the same color as the skirt. The pork frog trailer is important because it keeps the spinnerbait buoyant and allows it to slip over the grass.

Topwater baits also are deadly. Buzzbaits with a bead placed in front of the propeller to discourage the gathering of grass is probably the most fun bait to use. It also covers a lot of ground quickly. Before the grass gets too thick, Nip-I-Didees, Bang-O-Lures and stick baits work well.

Another popular bait is the "Delta" worm. A "Delta" worm is nothing more than a purple worm with a white tail rigged without a weight so it will float through the grass. It is a deadly spring bait. The "Delta" worm's only drawback - if you consider it a drawback, is that it also produces a lot of flounder - this time of the year.

Bass larger than 5 pounds are rare in the Delta, so an angler can survive with 12-pound-or-less test line.

The Delta's largest bass are often caught in spring on live shiners fished around the duck blinds. Chocolata Bay usually gives up the Delta's largest spring bass.

On the occasions when a good, hard, north wind pushes the water and fish out of the bays in the spring, the deep creeks near the bays become the best locations to fish. The water will be churned up and spinnerbaits will be useless, but plastic worms rigged to fish on bottom will produce numbers of good fish. The small creeks near Chocolata Bay are especially deadly when the north wind pushes the water out. One of the key areas at this time is the small passes in the area. Bass stack up heavily in these passes at this time and its possible to catch numbers of good fish.

Spring Bass fishing

ABOVE I-65

Fishermen who bass fish in the Mobile Delta above Interstate 65 can witness a wide spectrum of circumstances during the spring. A south wind and a high tide results in high water that jumps the banks and fills the nearby woods. The very next day, the angler may find a north wind and a falling tide that pulls the water out as if someone had pulled the bathtub stopper. Fortunately, low tides and north winds are not common when the fishing gets its best.

On the occasions that the rivers and creeks jump their banks and flood the timber, bass will follow and take hold in the new-found structure. They will locate at the base of trees and stumps as far back as the water goes. They will stay there until the water recedes.

When an angler finds this situation, a spinnerbait fished in the thick stuff is difficult to beat. A 1/2-ounce or 3/8-ounce chartreuse/white spinnerbait with a single copper blade is best when the water has good stain. A white spinnerbait with white blades or a chartreuse bait with chartreuse blades is needed when the water muddies

The spinnerbait should be cast as far up in the trees as the water goes and slow-rolled through the stickups and trees, bumping every piece of structure possible.

There are several key areas which an angler can concentrate on during the spring months. Mifflin Lake is the best and all fishing should begin there. The I-65 bridge pilings in Mifflin offer excellent structure, especially pre- and post-spawn. Bottle Creek is another key spawning area, as is Tensaw Lake. All three locations offer Mobile Delta spring bass fishing at its best.

Summer Bass Fishing

BELOW I-65

Unfortunately for the spring angler, just about the time the shallow-water bays hits 65 degrees and it gets time for great fishing, the grass is often so thick it is impossible to fish the area.

The bass are on their post-spawn cycle by then and their instincts tell them to clear the area while they can still get out. These bass end up in the rivers.

This often happens by the end of May or the first of June. Mobile Delta bass are forced into a summer pattern earlier than the bass in many other areas in the state.

The rivers in the Delta lack blowdown timber and other similar structure which typically holds summer bass elsewhere in the state, but these rivers have their own brand of fish-concentrating structure, namely barge pilings and feeder creeks.

Barge pilings, which are large creosoted poles, are abundant on the rivers. They are usually found in 15 to 18 feet of water all up and down the rivers in the Delta, and all are a threat to hold bass. Chrome-colored Rat-L-Traps with blue or black backs, and crawfish-colored lipped crankbaits are the key baits in fishing these pilings.

All along these rivers you will find small feeder "creeks" which concentrate bass. These "creeks" may be only a foot wide in some places and are nothing more than a trickle of water, but they supply the river with a steady supply of seed shrimp, a tiny shrimp that is a major part of the diet of summer Delta bass. These feeder creeks are easily located by looking for a break in the heavy cane that lines the banks.

Seed shrimp are available at many bait shops in the Delta, or anglers may catch their own by using a fine mesh net to shake underneath tree roots on washed-out banks. Two or three of the small shrimp laced on a fine wire hook and fished under a small float and fished near the creek mouths will produce fish.

Quarter-size crab are another of the Delta bass' main foods during the summer months. Anything with crab coloring can evoke a strike.

A greenish/brown crankbait with a light-colored belly, or a motor oil worm with chartreuse tail, will catch bass.

Traditionally, the farther you go up in the Delta, the better the summer fishing. Both the Tensaw and Mobile Rivers offer good summer fishing near I-65. There's also some good fishing in Negro Lake, Mifflin Lake and any of the creeks or cuts that hold more than nine feet of water.

There's limited summer bass fishing near Interstate 10 and the bay, but what is there is excellent. A deep channel was cut through John's Bend years ago to allow barges to transport materials to build the interstate bridge and that deep water is excellent in June and July. Pay special attention to the hook in the bay and any grass that may be there.

Also, the mouth of the Blakely River where it dumps into the bay will concentrate bass in August when they gather to slaughter the shrimp.

ABOVE I-65

Summer fishing isn't great in the Mobile Delta, but nowhere else in Alabama is summer fishing great, either.

Tides are the key to the best fishing above I-65 in the summer. Bass gather on points when in-going or out-going tides are moving water, much like the do on reservoirs when water is being pulled.

Plastic worms become the Delta's top bait during the hot summer months.

A Pumpkin-colored Carolina-rigged worm fished around blowdowns and pilings on the rivers and lakes is tough to beat.

When an angler knows the location of deep-water underwater struture, flippin' can be deadly. A 1/4-ounce jig-and-pig with a piece of plastic worm tail is the best bait. Orange and black colors are strong in summer.

The many lakes in the area can offer good fishing in the daylight and sunset hours, but they close down completely when the sun clears the trees. Topwater baits and worms both work well.

Mifflin Lake and Tensaw Lake are key areas for this type of fishing.

The best summer fishing is definitely in the rivers, however. Visible, deep structure in the Middle River, Tensaw River and Mobile River should draw most of your attention. The north winds that occasionally hit the Delta during the summer shouldn't be a signal to not go fishing.

A north wind that pushes the water out the rivers and creeks force bass into the mouth of creeks and this is a good time to go fishing. The bass school heavily when this happens and this is one of your best chances to catch numbers of bass.

Cool and cold weather fishing

BELOW I-65

The Mobile Delta gets its least amount of rainfall in October and this enables the saltwater to make a surge into the rivers and creeks far up in the Delta. This is beneficial to the fisherman because this influx of saltwater normally kills the thick grass in the shallow bays. When rains do finally come, it is not unusual to see this dead grass floating away in large portions.

A bass angler must understand that the water in these creeks and bays literally separate with the saltwater moving to the bottom and the freshwater to the top. Bass have no difficulty living in this brackish water, despite its salt content.

The bass will gang up in the creeks near these shallow bays before they go back into a spring-like pattern. They stage in this deeper water much like they did in spring and in the same areas.

Shrimp - which bass love - make a run as far as the saltwater goes in the creeks and the largemouth follow and have no trouble finding a quality meal.

Bass will also gather in the rivers near the mouths of the feeder creeks at this time. These areas are as likely to produce redfish at this time.

Both white and chartreuse spinnerbaits and shallow-running lipped crankbaits in lighter colors are deadly during this time. Creek bends or stick ups will hold bass, as well as redfish, speckled trout and an occasional sheepshead.

Those who fish plastic worms in these areas often catch flounder, too.

Colder weather naturally sends bass back into deeper water and the deeper creeks that held bass in the post-spawn pattern in the spring will hold winter bass. Other key areas to concentrate on are the bridge pilings under I-10, U.S. 90 and I-65.

Jigging spoons, grubs and plastic worms will catch bass in these areas.

Many of the better bass anglers also live bait fish for bass during the winter months. Shrimp are productive when shrimp are present, but when the cold drives the shrimp out, most live bait anglers switch to shiners.

Many of the better anglers ride the river on low tide situations and take notes of structure that is showing and then fish those areas when the water is back up.

These areas are particularly productive during winter months and can be beneficial year yound.

ABOVE I-65

Water levels are usually low during the cool and cold-weather months, so deep banks with cover on both the lakes and rivers hold fall and winter bass. Sloping banks, even if they have cover, rarely hold fish during this time.

The better fall and winter fishing is below I-65.

Saltwater fishing

SUMMER
ABOVE I-65

The shortage of rainfall that this area traditionally sees during summer months allows heavy incoming tides to push saltwater up into the Delta. The lack of rainfall means there is no freshwater to push the saltwater back out. The brackish water eventually creeps well up into the Delta.

Redfish are usually the first saltwater fish to make the move into the Delta, followed by flounder, sheepshead and croaker. Bass anglers fishing white spinnerbaits are usually the first to discover the redfish have arrived.

Anglers wishing to catch redfish during the summer months

should concentrate on areas closest to the mouth of the bay since this water will have the most salt content.

Any of the small islands near the mouth of the bay is good with the north point usually holding the fish for some reason. Little Sand Island is probably the best of all these islands. Pinto Pass is another key area. Many a tourist visiting the USS Alabama has leaned over the rail and watched anglers load the boat with redfish and flounder in Pinto Pass. The submerged pilings east of Little Sand Island also offer good fishing. The piers all along the east bank of Mobile Bay offer good redfish, speckled trout and flounder during the summer.

One of first areas above I-65 to find saltwater fish in the summer months is the mouth of Grand Bay on the Spanish River. The point of Polecat Bay in the Spanish River is another excellent spot. Underwater stumps near the cypress trees across from the mouth of Bay Grass hold a lot of redfish during this time. The point of the Tensaw River where it meets Delvan Bay is another key area for redfish and flounder.

The pilings (called the "Old Battery") at the split of the Apalachee and Blakely River hold lots of sheepshead, croaker, and flounder. This "V"-shaped series of pilings once extended across both rivers to block boat traffic during the Civil War, many locals claim.

The upper point of the Apalachee and Tensaw rivers is full of sandbars and offers good fishing for redfish on live or dead shrimp.

Any sandy point is usually good because one side usually drops off into the river and the other leads to three to four feet of water. These sandy points are excellent on a falling tide.

For those wishing to strictly fish for flounder, the Blakely River where it passes under I-10 bridge is strong. The interstate bridge pilings 100 yards each way of the river hold lots, especially in June.

Natural baits are popular, with live or dead shrimp the best for redfish and live shrimp, bull minnows or shiners good for flounder.

The "fishfinder rig" is the best tackle setup. An 18-inch length of 20-pound mono should be topped with a swivel, followed by a barrel weight on the main line. This should be finished with a No. 6 treble hook. This rig allows a fish to pick up the bait and run with it while pulling the mono through the weight. The treble hook allows for a good hook set. If fishing strictly for flounder, opt for a 1/0 single hook rather than a treble hook.

COOL AND COLD WEATHER FISHING

There's no question that once the cool breezes of fall arrive, the saltwater fishing in the Mobile Delta heats up. The redfish and flounder will literally move as far up in the Delta as the shrimp and saltwater go. Catches of reds and flounder near the I-65 bridge are not uncommon. Speckled trout will not normally move that far.

The small island in Grandy Bay and the small island nearby in the Raft River holds both reds and flounder, as do the submerged pilings in the Mobile River. The dock pilings just above Grand Bay where the Spanish River and Mobile River meet is another key area. The angler who throws a Mann's pink and white Stingray grub can catch reds, flounder, bass and an occasional sheepshead.

When September arrives, the speckled trout will be at the head of the bay just south of the I-10 bridge. They will be staging in the cuts and channels feeding heavily on shrimp. The terns and seagulls will give the specks' location away as the dive for the shrimp injured by the attacking specks. Thise will usually last a month. Unfortunately, these easy-to-locate specks are usually small.

The middle of November usually signals the start of speckled trout season up in the Delta. This is when the quality specks move in. The mouth of Delvan Bay at the point point of the Tensaw River is usually one of the first spots where the specks gather in numbers. Any sandy point below Chuckfee Bay is a threat to hold specks then.

Cocahoe Grubs - chartreuse/black back, or smoke color - are normally the best bait for specks at this time, but unseasonably cold water will require white or pink Stingray Grubs. If the specks are finicky, a small curly tail grub like you would use for crappie fishing may entice them to bite. Either white or pink colors can be used.

A 1/4-ounce lead head is needed when the fish are off the bottom and a 3/8-ounce head is needed when the fish are on bottom. Most of the better anglers opt for 10-pound test line.

When the water is warm, a steady spinnerbait-like retrieve can be used. When the water gets colder, a jigging retrieve that allows the bait to hit bottom is needed.

Another pattern that works well is fishing a live shrimp under a popping cork. The sound of the float being popped in the water often draws the attention of fish.

Once again, terns and seagulls will give away the specks' location. One of the best-kept secrets of the better anglers is paying close attention to the large white pelicans that often accompany these birds. The pelicans aren't as quick and agile as terns and seagulls, so they'll actually swim along with the shrimp that the specks are feeding on rather than trying to fly and dive at the bait.

When the weather really turns cold, usually in mid-December or early January, rains have pushed much of the saltwater back out of the Delta. This forces the saltwater species back to the bay's head.

The Tensaw River, where it is 18 feet deep, and in the Apalachee where it's 17 feet deep just below U.S. 90, are key areas at this time. Grubs or live shrimp fished on the bottom will catch these fish.

Mobile Delta's best fishing spots

1. Lake Forest Yacht Club. D'Olive Bay good for speckled trout, flounder and redfish September through December.

2. I-10 bridge pilings. Blakely River. Flounder fishing in June, specks September, October and November.

3. I-10 bridge pilings in Ducker Bay. Bull minnows for flounder in May and June. Dead minnows for sheepshead.

4. John's Bend. Good spring bass fishing in shallow water, good summer fishing in deep cut in summer.

5. Devil's Ditch. Deep pass. Good for specks in fall, flounder on the points.

6. Seawall across from Mack's Bait and Tackle. Redfish in fall. Dead shrimp on bottom.

7. Pete's Island. Flounder and sheepshead on dropoffs and submerged pilings.

8. Underwater pilings south of Pinto Pass. Specks and reds.

9. Oyster shell reef. Fall fishing for specks, reds and flounder, good in summer when there is little rain.

10. Pinto Pass. Live or dead shrimp in summer for big specks,

good in winter on artificial baits.

11. The Cut. Redfish in small channel.

12. Point of Polecat Bay and Delvan Bay. Fall fishing for reds and specks.

13. Point of Tensaw and Delvan good in August-December for reds, specks and flounder.

14. Cypress trees and stumps. Fall and winter for redfish.

15. Delvan Bay. Good in spring for bass. In May, good for bream around duck blinds.

16. Bay Grass. Spring bass area.

17. Chocolata Bay. Good end of February for spawning bass.

18. Mouth of Conway Creek. Good when north wind pushes water out of Chocolata Bay.

19. Big Bateau. Lots of grass. Shallow. Fair in March and April for bass. Good April and May for bream around banks and duck blinds.

20. Deep water creeks around Little Bateau. Good bream fishing in spring.

21. The Old Battery. Specks, reds, flounder around pilings.

22. Sardine Pass, also known as Game Warden's Ditch. Conservation Department's headquarters here. Fair spring fishing.

23. Bay Minette Basin. Good spring bass fishing. Second best spit next to Chocolata.

24. Bay Minette Creek. Submerged timber. Lots of white perch.

25. Mouth of Mudhole Creek. Big sandbar on north side. Speckled trout and redfish in the fall.

26. Tensaw-Apalachee fork. Good sandbars. Specks. Very few reds. Live shrimp under popping corks in fall.

27. Crab Creek. Good worm fishing for bass around blowdowns in spring.

28. Raft River. North points of islands good in fall.

29. Grand Bay and Spanish River point. Specks and reds in fall.

30. Grand Bay. Bass fishing in spring before grass takes it over in May. Also good in fall.

31. Visible pilings where Spanish River and Mobile River meet.

32. Feeder creeks good in fall for bass. Shallow with lots of blowdowns.

33. Chuckfee Bay. March and April for bass. Good bream fishing around duck blinds.

34. Good feeder creeks for spring bass fishing.

35. Oak Bayou. Good fall bass fishing.

36. Gravine Island. Reds, specks and flounder fishing around sandbars.

37. Negro Lake. Good spring fishing for bass.

38. Ship Canal. Man-made cut. Good point for bass fishing.

39. Good bass fishing point.

40. Good stretch of bank on Tensaw River. Cypress stumps. Good in fall for bass, specks and reds.

41. Good bass fishing in mouth of cut.

42. Little Briar Creek. Full of weeds. Good spring bass fishing.

43. Big Briar Creek. Lots of weeds. Good spring fishing for bass.

44. North point of Twelve-Mile Island. Good fall fishing for reds.

45. Pilings under railroad trestle. Fair bass fishing year round. Some reds in fall.

46. Big Bayou Canot. Some logjams. Some bass.

47. Dead Lake. Good water depth. Bream and crappie.

48. Smith Bayou. Good weeds. Good spring fishing with buzzbaits.

49. Owl Creek. Same as 48.

50. Squirrel Bayou. Same as 48.

51. Duck Bayou. Same as 48.

52. Six Bits Creek. Same as 48.

53. Bat Creek. Same as 48.

54. Bayou Avalon. Some milfoil and hydrilla.

55. Big Lizard Creek. Reeds on bank with sharp dropoffs. Dropoffs hold bass year round.

56. Not shown on map.

57. Not shown on map.

58. Little Lizard. Some good bass fishing in late spring and late summer.

59. Dennis Lake. Good spring bass fishing.

60. Mifflin Lake. Good spring bass fishing.

61. Bottle Creek. Fair bass fishing around runoffs.

62. The "T". Powerline crosses just past interstate. Deep and shallow water. Some good bass fishing year round.

63. Briar Lake. Limited spring bass fishing.

64. Tensaw Lake. Fair spring fishing when water is high.

65. Island. North point good year-round.

66. Island. Clay point with lots of roots. Good year-round fishing.

67. Good stretch of river. Runoffs concentrate fish.

68. Watson Creek. A few spotted bass in mouth.

69. Douglas Lake. Fair bass fishing.

70. Chippewa Fingers good in high water in spring.

71. Good flippin' area. Lots of brush.

72. Grompau Branch. Good bass fishing in mouth when water is being pulled out.

73. Bayou Zeast. Fair in spring. No grass. Some cypress trees.

74. Dead Lake. Good year-round fishing for bass.

75. Good stretch in Stiggins Lake. Excellent in spring.

76. Bear Creek. Good summer area.

77. Sheppard Lake. Good spring fishing in back. Barges hold bass.

78. Cedar Creek. Fair spring fishing.

79. Lower Dead Run. Good year round.

80. Upper Dead Run. Same as 79.

81. Boatyard Lake. Fair year-round fishing.

82. Alabama River. Good cover. Many tournaments won here. Spots on sandbars.

83. Alabama River cut-off. Tombigbee side holds bass.

84. Bates Lake. Good spring fishing.

85. Jim Burr Lake. Good spring and fall.

86. Bilbo Creek. Fair spring and fall.

87. Hall's Lake. Fair spring fishing.

88. Fisher's Lake. Good spring fishing when water is up. Narrow opening, but opens wide.

89. Three Rivers Lake. Fair spring fishing.

Mobile River

90

Mobile Delta
Below the L&N Railroad

Mobile Delta
L&N Railroad
to
Douglas Lake

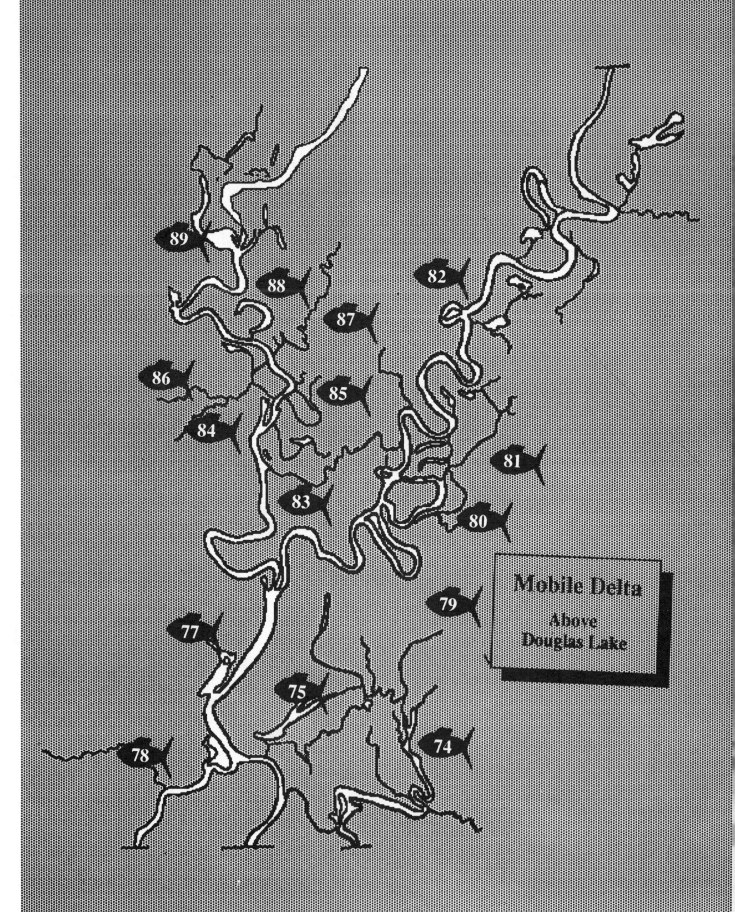

Mobile Delta
Above
Douglas Lake

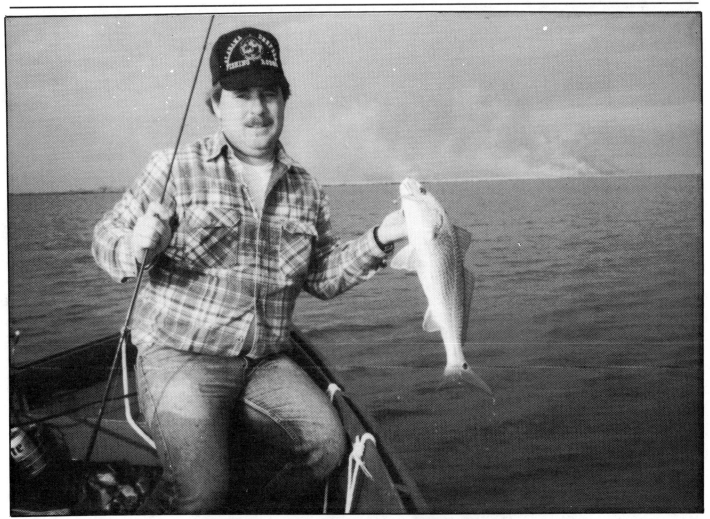

Mobile Bay

Despite its huge expanse of water, quality fishing on Mobile Bay is accomplished in only a tiny percentage of the area. The flat mud and sand bottom that is its predominant feature does not provide cover or harbor food for game fish.

NORTHERN END

There is a tremendous amount of one to three foot depth water in the northern end, punctuated by narrow winding channels that eventually drop to the 10 and 12 foot depth that is generally uniform for the length of the bay. Fishermen work bridge pilings, snags and brush for fresh water bream in spring and fall, and go for speckled trout in deeper holes in winter.

EASTERN SHORE

Dozens of piers jutting into the bay are worked for flounder in spring, summer and fall. Live minnows, live or dead shrimp or a Sting Ray Grub tipped with a bit of squid is cast around the piers and slowly retrieved, bumping the bait along the bottom. The flounder lay on the bottom waiting for an easy meal to happen by and when it does, pounce on the bait.

This same area can be worked successfully for Speckled Trout year around. They can be caught on live shrimp or minnow-shaped lures such as the blue and silver Rebel.

Each of the rivers flowing into the river can be worked for Flounder, Speckled Trout and Redfish, using the same type of lures.

The three species are the dominant gamefish of the lower bay and can be caught working channels, cuts, holes, piers, pipes, pilings and other structure - as sparse as it may be - for the length of the eastern shore, Bon Secour Bay and Fort Morgan peninsula.

CENTRAL BAY

The central bay is only lightly fished, and for good reason, there's not much there in the way of structure or quality fish.

The gas rigs are changing that somewhat. Found throughout the lower bay, these rigs are major vertical structures to provide cover and draw baitfish for the game species. Frequenting the rigs are Speckled Trout, Flounder, Redfish and some open gulf species.

Mobile Bay Fact Sheet

Location, size

Mobile Bay is an arm of the Gulf of Mexico, extending from the mouth of the Mobile River to its opening into the gulf between Dauphin Island and Mobile Point, a distance of approximately 35 miles. The bay ranges from eight to 18 miles wide, and is the dominant water body in extreme southwest Alabama.

Configuration

Mobile Bay is a bell-shaped body of water, with a dishpan type bottom severed in its central area by a 300- to 500-foot-wide ship channel. Except for the ship channel and a few deep holes, the flat bay bottom ranges from about 10 to rarely more than 20 feet in depth.

The bay begins as broad marshland on its western boundary, descending gently, with periodic oyster reefs near its lower end. The lower central body of the bay is interrupted by gas drilling operations, with rigs visible throughout the lower bay.

The eastern shore, particularly the northern two thirds, rises abruptly from the water's edge, forming high banks where developers have built fine homes and resorts. This portion of the bay is studded with piers jutting outward. The lower third of the eastern shore is dominated by the major sub bay, Bon Secour.

Except for the aforementioned oyster reefs, Mobile Bay's bottom is relatively free of structure except for buoys and drilling rigs. The ships that went down during the Civil War Battle of Mobile Bay now lay beneath the sand and mud bottom.

Because the bay lacks major structure, shrimpers frequently drag the bay both for food and bait shrimp.

Major and secondary creeks

Excluding the Mobile River Delta, which drains most of Alabama, some of Georgia and Mississippi, Mobile Bay is fed by a number of smaller rivers and streams.

In its northern reaches as the delta turns to bay, countless steams and sub bays dot the landscape. They include Grand Bay, Chacaloochee Bay, Delvan Bay, Ducker Bay, D'Olive Bay, Blakeley River, Apalachee River and Polecat Bay.

Southward from Mobile, which sits at the northwest corner of the bay, is Dog River and its tributaries Rabbit Creek, Alligator Bayou and Halle Mill Creek; Deer River, Fowl River and East Fowl River.

From north to south along the eastern shore are Fly Creek, Fish River and Weeks Bay, Magnolia River, Skunk Bayou, Bon Secour River and Oyster Bay.

Types of fish

In the upper reaches of Mobile Bay occasionally fresh water species such as largemouth bass and bream can be found from time to time. However, much more commonly, salt water species venture up into the brackish water, rather than vice versa.

Popular sport fishes found in bay waters include Black Drum, Bluefish, Blue Runner, Croaker, Flounder, Grouper, Jack Crevalle, Mullet, Pinfish, Redfish, Sharks, Sheepshead, Spanish Mackerel, Speckled Trout, White Trout and Whiting. Some of these fish are seasonal and can be found only part of each year.

A wide variety of baitfishes range in and out of the bay.

Again, live shrimp, artificial grubs, cut bait, white jigs and spoons will take these fish, with action being brisk at times.

Otherwise, the ship channel provides some action from Gafftopsail Catfish, Redfish and an occasional Black Drum. The Gafftopsail Catfish can be distinguished by an extraordinarily long dorsal fin. Unlike the common saltwater catfish, considered a pest and inedible, the Gafftopsail is considered good table fare. It can be caught on cut bait, squid or dead shrimp. A depthfinder is essential if you plan to catch Redfish in the channel.

WESTERN SHORE

From Dog River southward, the rivers and creeks flowing into Mobile Bay are prime locations for Redfish, Flounder, White Trout and Speckled Trout.

Also, work the piers and the sparse structure for Croakers, Flounder, Speckled Trout and occasional Redfish.

At the southern end of the bay - to either side of the Dauphin Island Bridge where Mississippi Sound joins the bay, work the bridge, the channel area and oyster reef area for Redfish, Speckled Trout, Black Drum, Jack Crevalle, Croakers and Sharks.

Near the eastern tip of Dauphin Island, try for Croaker, Sharks and Ground Mullet (Whiting).

HOW TO FIND 'EM

While catching fresh water species depends a great deal on presentation of the proper bait at the proper time, salt water fishing depends more on locating the fish.

Once they are found, any of several methods usually can be employed to put the fish in the boat.

Don't carry the point to extreme. Obviously flounder aren't likely to hit a mackerel rig trolled along the surface. But once located, the flounder probably can be taken on small spoons, jigs or grubs bounced slowly along the bottom, with live shrimp or even with cut bait.

The same goes for the other species mentioned. Check the fish dictionary for habitat and food preferences of each species.

Mobile Bay's best fishing spots

1. Upper bay flats and channels. Good bream in spring and fall. Fish holes for speckled trout in winter.

2. Eastern Shore piers. Countless piers jut into the bay from the northern end of the bay to Mullet Point where Bon Secour Bay begins, a distance of more than 10 miles. Fish piers and pilings from spring to January for speckled trout, summer trout and flounder.

3. Weeks Bay and Fish River. Fall and winter for Redfish, trout and flounder. Fish deep holes after cold snaps for speckled trout.

4. Magnolia River. Fall and winter for Redfish, trout and flounder.

5. Bon Secour Bay. Shallows extend for many yards from shore, then drop quickly to a depth of between 7 and 10 feet. Fish the dropoff for reds, flounder and trout. Work the shallows at night with a light and gig for flounder.

6. Oyster reef obstruction. Flounder, trout, drum, sometimes croaker. Depth rises from 8 to 6 feet.

7. Bon Secour River. Reds, flounder and trout. Work deep holes in fall and winter.

8. Flats behind Fort Morgan peninsula. Flounder follow this shoreline on their fall migration from the bay to the open gulf. Extremely good for flounder November through January.

9. Obstruction in bay. 12 feet. Trout, flounder, sometimes bluefish, blue runner, spanish and northern mackerel.

10. Intercoastal Waterway channel. Use fishfinder to locate reds, trout, croaker schools along channel. Work channel for flounder until early winter.

11. Drilling rigs. Trout, reds, bluefish, flounder, mackerel in spring and summer, drum, croaker. Circle rig and find side where baitfish are holding.

12. Ship channel. Bay drops abruptly from 10 to near 50 feet, and runs from mouth of bay to docks at Mobile on northwest corner of bay. Not a tremendous amount of fishing in channel, but it can be worked successfully for gafftopsail catfish, redfish and black drum.

13. Eastern tip of Dauphin Island. Channels and flats can be worked for ground mullet, sharks and croaker. Specked trout on both inside and outside of island tip.

14. Back of Dauphin Island. This large are of channels and flats encompasses the Intracoastal Waterway, Dauphin Island bridge and utility line structures, oyster beds, and a portion of Mississippi Sound. Try for reds, speckled trout, croaker, flounder, Jack Crevalle, drum and sharks. Use bottom finder to locate structure and fish. Use bottom alarm, if equipped, as depth can change abruptly.

15. Cedar Point Pier. Recently rebuilt fishing pier. Bait, some tackle, fishing information, snacks available. Parking. All bay species; same as 14.

16. Western shore has wide flats before dropping to between 7 and 10 feet. Try flats in warm weather at night for gigging flounder. Otherwise work area for croaker, flounder and speckled trout. Dropoff is primary area to check. A few reds are caught here, but it is not the bay's best area for reds.

17. Fowl River and East Fowl River. Croaker, flounder, trout and reds, particularly fall and into winter.

18. Dog River. Same as 17.

Perdido Bay

The jetties on the east and west sides of Perdido Bay's mouth are the primary fishing locations.

Skin divers and fishermen share the territory, particularly at high tide when gulf water rushing into the bay clears the water sufficiently for diver's to have some visibility. Fishermen with boats anchor off the jetties and cast toward them with artificial, cut or live bait. Those without boats stand on the rocks and cast outward. Those on the rocks have a much higher risk of losing fish and tackle in the sharp rocks.

Flounder lie in the sand just off the jetties, while Bluefish, Spanish Mackerel and Mullet cruise in schools just off the rocks. The Bluefish can be caught on 0- or 00-size spoons or blue and silver Rebel-style lures, fished with a rapid retrieve. Spanish are attracted to any of dozens of small lures - ranging from silver spoons 0 or 00 size to jigs and multi-hook rigs, almost all of which are manufactured specifically for Spanish Mackerel and are available at area tackle shops.

The Mullet are caught in cast nets, but occasionally can be caught on tiny dough balls. Few fishermen go for Mullet with a hook and line, however.

Live shrimp and bass-type, minnow shaped crankbaits are used to cast the jetties for Speckled Trout. The live shrimp also are deadly for Flounder, Grouper and Redfish. Grouper also are caught on live bait such as Pinfish or Mullet Minnows.

Dead shrimp or cut bait are effective for Redfish, Flounder, Sheepshead and Grouper.

Redfish and Flounder also can be caught on Sting Ray Grubs, which seem to be most attractive when tipped with a bit of cut bait or squid. They are cast, then slowly retrieved, allowing the grub to bounce bottom.

On the west side of the channel a concrete sea wall extends for several hundred yards. Many of the same species caught along the jetties can be found running along the wall. The same baits and fishing techniques can be used here as on the jetties.

Except at slack tide, current is swift in the channel. While smaller hooks probably will do best for general fishing, pyramid sinkers of

an ounce, sometimes more, work best to hold bait on bottom.

On the east side of the channel, perhaps a hundred yards north of the jetty, the sand is scalloped out forming a calmer, deeper pool. Bits of debris (food to fish) settle in the pool, and small baitfish, seeking refuge from the current, move in and out of the pool. It is an excellent spot to try for Flounder, using small Pinfish, Croaker or Mullet minnows that can be netted along the shore where you are fishing. This pool can be cast into from shore or by wading out toward it.

Turn left into Cotton Bayou just after you cross under the bridge and you will move across shallows, then will find a deep hole. This hole also is worth trying for Flounder, White and Speckled trout. Mullet can be netted in this area.

Trout are occasionally taken on live bait and by casting small minnow-like lures, spoons, jigs or Sting Ray Grubs in Cotton Bayou, particularly around piers and in deep holes. Use your depth finder.

Due north of the Alabama Point Bridge is Terry Cove, where many of the charter boats dock. Water in Terry Cove drops from flats along the shore to about 10 feet. Fish the dropoffs for White and Speckled trout.

The open water between Terry Cove and the tip of Ono Island sometimes hold Blue Fish. This can be an iffy proposition, but a quick scan with the fish finder or a quick troll with small spoons, jigs or minnow-shaped lures will reveal their presence.

The channel leading to Wolf and Perdido Bays is a winding one, pocked with holes and flanked by sand bars. In winter, the deep holes hold Speckled Trout that can be caught on live shrimp fished on bottom. In summer, the trout are scattered, often foraging along the channel edges for food. Work lures along these cuts.

Another narrow channel leads immediately eastward from the bridge to Old River. Redfish and trout can be caught in the mouth of Ole River, particularly where flats drop into deep water near pilings.

The Ono Island bridge is a good spot for Sheepshead and Speckled

Perdido Bay Fact Sheet

Location, size

Perdido Bay is the dividing line between Alabama and Florida, at Alabama's eastern boundary.

It is a multi-arm bay and is of amazingly large size, considering its small opening to the gulf at Alabama Point.

So small is the opening that after its discovery by the Spanish, they lost track of Perdido Bay for a time because when attempting to return to it, the seamen would overlook the small channel.

That small opening and the relatively high dunes around the mouth of the bay served well Jean Lafitte shortly after the turn of the 19th century when he and his band used the bay as a base of operations.

The bay runs northeastward for the better part of 20 miles, and to the northwest for perhaps 10 miles, counting all the twists and turns.

Configuration

From its mouth the bay appears to spread in every direction. To the west, Cotton Bayou parallels the gulf for the better part of two miles. Immediately eastward, Ole River separates Ono Island from Perdido Key. Just to the north a long, wide neck of water running east and west creates the north shore of 3 1/2-mile-long Ono Island and leads to the bay's two main lobes, Wolf Bay and Perdido Bay proper.

The geographic feature that keeps Perdido from being one huge open bay is a peninsula that runs east and west, a mile north of the bay's mouth.

The peninsula juts three miles eastward into the bay, making Wolf Bay a distinctly separate body of water.

The end of the peninsula is at Mill Point where the Intracoastal Waterway channel enters the bay.

The channel continues westward through a brief series of narrows and openings, with two major openings: Arnica Bay and Bay La Launch. This neck runs

westward for approximately two and a half miles to Sapling Point where Wolf Bay opens and runs north and south for approximately five miles before narrowing into a series of bayous.

Opposite the channel leading to Wolf Bay is the opening to the broad open waters of Perdido Bay proper, flanked to the northwest by Rose Point and to the southeast by Innerarity Point.

This area is severed by the Alabama-Florida line.

Major and secondary waters

The Perdido River, boundary between Alabama and Florida, is the primary tributary flowing into the bay, entering at the north end of Perdido Bay proper.

Otherwise, a number of small streams and bayous are only minor tributaries.

In the southernmost part of the bay, Cotton Bayou to the west and Old River to the east are not actually tributaries, but only sub-features of the bay itself.

Actual tributaries are found in Wolf and Perdido Bay proper. In Perdido, they include Bayou Garcon, Tarkiln Bayou, Soldier Creek, Palmetto Creek and Spring Branch.

In the approach to Wolf Bay and in Wolf Bay are Roberts Bayou, Stone Quarry Bayou, Ingram Bayou, Hammock Creek and Graham Bayou.

Types of fish

At the mouth of Perdido Bay, open gulf and bay species mingle around stone jetties that flank the mouth of the bay. Grouper, Sheepshead, Flounder, Redfish, Bluefish, Spanish Mackerel, Mullet, Speckled Trout, Croaker, Whiting, Sharks and Blue Runner can be found, although some only seasonally.

Once north of the Alabama Point bridge, the incidence of open gulf species diminishes rapidly. North of the bridge, the dominant species are White Trout, Speckled Trout, Redfish, Flounder, occasionally Blue Fish and Mullet.

Trout, while Mullet can be found running the river's shallower depths.

On the eastern end of Ono Island, work the cuts for Specked Trout. Just beyond the eastern end of the island, the Intercoastal Canal narrows and goes under the highway bridge that connects Perdido Key to Pensacola, Fla. Under the bridge is some hard rubble that holds trout, and is worth trying.

In Perdido Bay proper, Innerarity Point should be worked for trout and Flounder. Much of the bay's shoreline is marshy, with shallow flats extending outward for many yards. Watch the water and your depth finder carefully or you can find yourself grounded. The bottom drops off abruptly from one or two feet to 10 to 12 feet. White Trout, Flounder, Speckled Trout and Redfish should be sought along the dropoffs. While the entire shore can be worked, particular attention should be shown to the mouths of creeks, inlets and bayous.

On the northwest side of the bay, Red Bluff point and adjoining Soldier Creek should be worked. There are several piers jutting into the bay at Red Bluff and there are submerged pilings that tend to draw fish.

Soldier Creek as well as adjoining Palmetto Creek have channels of 8 to 10 feet that hold trout and Redfish. Take care navigating into the creeks since shallows abound.

From the opening at Rose Point that leads to Wolf Bay to Sapling Point where Wolf Bay opens, the mouths of Roberts Bayou and Ingram Bayou should be worked for Redfish and trout. Sapling Point also should be worked for specks.

In the upper end of Wolf Bay, Hammock Creek and Graham Bayou should be worked for Redfish, White and Speckled trout.

At mid-bay, Mulberry Point juts outward from the west. Work the dropoffs around the point for specks and Redfish.

Bay species such as trout, Redfish, Bluefish and Flounder are much better at certain times of the year than others.

For example, remember that specks are extremely sensitive to drops in temperature. Thus, after a cold snap, look for them ganged up in any little hole of deep water they can find. Sometimes a hole only two or three feet deeper than surrounding water will hold a huge concentration of fish. These fish may be sluggish, but live shrimp fished right in their midst will bring strikes.

Croaker and Whiting are almost year-around residents, however sometimes are hard to find in January and February, the coldest months.

Flounder also are found most frequently in spring, summer and fall. They tend to migrate into the open gulf in fall, and sometimes can be caught in great numbers during that migration, especially in the channel approaches to the mouth of the bay, which they all must pass through to get to the open gulf.

The spring, summer and early fall Redfish tend to be small, with the larger Redfish, called Bull Reds, moving in in mid-fall and remaining through Januay.

Sheepshead can be found around bridge abutments, piers or pilings - anywhere that crustaceans attach to structure. These fish feed on the crustaceans. They can be found year around.

While grouper can be found in the jetties year around, the often come in in numbers just before or after a major storm. They also seem to move into the shallower waters in cooler months.

The best Spanish Mackerel run is in mid-spring, when they sometimes literally swarm around the jetties, running the cuts. Some Spanish Mackerel hang around through the fall, but the numbers always seem fewer after the spring run.

White Trout are found most frequently in the spring through fall.

Perdido Bay's best fishing spots

1. Jetties flank each side of the mouth of Perdido Bay. These stone structure can be reached by land and by boat. Exact depth and channel configuration changes from time to time due to erosion, silting, channel dredging, storms, etc. Species include grouper, mullet, sheepshead, spanish mackerel, flounder, redfish, bluefish, croaker, whiting, Jack Crevalle, a few sand sharks and trout.

2. A concrete seawall runs for many yards along western side of channel into Perdido Bay. Many of same species as found on the jetties can be found here, although incidence of grouper is diminished. Current is swift, requiring significant weight to keep bait on bottom.

3. Unless altered by recent dredging, there is a significant dip in the bottom behind the jetty on the east side of the channel. Good flounder fishing in this hole in spring, summer and fall.

4. Entrance to Ole River has pilings adjacent to narrow channel. Check area in fall and winter for trout.

5. Ono Island Bridge. Fish around structure for sheepshead, trout, reds.

Also check Ole River channel for depth finder for same species, plus flounder and white trout.

6. A hole surrounded by flats just to the north and west of Perdido Pass Marina is frequently fished for trout, flounder and occasional reds. The shallower areas are worked by net for mullet.

7. Cotton Bayou. There is a free public boat ramp at the end of the bayou. The bayou can be worked for croaker, speckled and white trout, flounder and redfish.

8. Canals cut into subdivisions are worked for trout and croaker.

9. From Orange Beach Marine to Robinson Island, good area for white and speckled trout, ground mullet and croaker.

10. Bluefish roam cuts in area just inside mouth of bay, along with occasional blue runner and small mackerel in spring and summer.

11. Narrow and winding cuts and channel leading to main bay can be worked for speckled trout. Fish dropoffs from deep side, casting to shallow and working to depths in warm weather. Check deep holes in winter for trout ganged up.

12. Intercoastal canal. Check flats to either side for flounder and mullet, particularly in summer and fall. Work edges of channel in warmer months for trout, and deep holes for them in winter.

13. Bridge connecting Perdido Key to Innerarity Point has hard bottom around it. Particularly good in cool weather for trout.

14. Flats at Innerarity Point drop into channel of 20 feet. Check edges of channel for trout. In warm months use light and gig on flats to take flounder.

15. Tarkiln Bay and Bayou. Flounder, speckled and white trout.

16. Soldier Creek and Red Bluff and northward along shore. Work shallows in warm months for flounder at night. Fish dropoffs for speckled and white trout.

17. Perdido Beach area, Palmetto Creek and Spring Branch. Speckled and White Trout, Redfish.

18. Rose Point area. Fish point for flounder and trout.

19. Roberts Bayou. Redfish and Speckled Trout.

20. Ingram Bayou. Redfish and Speckled Trout.

21. Sapling Point where Wolf Bay opens to the north. Redfish and Speckled Trout.

22. Hammock Creek and other small streams opening into Wolf Bay near its northeastern end. Speckled Trout, White Trout and Redfish.

23. Northwestern end of Wolf Bay, including Graham Bayou. Redfish, White and Speckled Trout, particularly in cooler months.

24. Mulberry Point. Redfish and Speckled Trout.

25. Intracoastal Waterway. Use depth finder to find fish roaming edge of channel. Good, especially in cooler months, for reds, trout, flounder and (with net) mullet. This is a particularly good area for fresh water crappie fishermen in the fall since fish in the channel can be caught on live shrimp with the same bottom-fish-and-drift pattern used in Alabama

The waterway runs all the way to Mobile Bay and is spanned by the Alabama 50 bridge leading into Gulf Shores. Fishing is good along the length of the waterway. Particular attention should be given to fishing the several creeks flowing into the waterway, bridge structure, riprap and old tree structure remaining along the edge of the channel from when the waterway was cut.

26. Mill Point and Bear Point. Gig flounders in the shallows in warm months.

Perdido Bay

The Gulf of Mexico

The gulf itself is a monstrous circular pond, bounded by Mexico's Yucatan Peninsula, the east Mexican, Texas, Louisiana, Mississippi, Alabama and Florida coasts, with an outlet into the Atlantic through the Caribbean Sea.

The Alabama portion stands out in several ways:
• The Loop Current, part of the Gulf Stream circling through the gulf, edges closest to shore along the Alabama coast. Riding that current is a rich variety of fishes; tropical species from the south that cruise in in spring and out in fall, and bottom species that range in and out as water temperatures rise and fall.
• The gulf's major geologic feature - the DeSoto Canyon - nudges closest to shore nearest the Alabama coast, about 30 miles due south of the Alabama-Florida state line. There the bottom drops from a depth of just over 100 feet in stair-steps of craggy cliffs. They are overgrown with marine plants and animals, home for every step in the marine food chain. The canyon is a well from which dozens of kinds of fishes ebb and flow, depending on the seasons, temperatures and currents.

• Mobile and Perdido bays play vital roles. Ringing these bays are wetlands, breeding grounds and massive incubators of sea life; safe places for baby fishes to be born and spend their juvenile lives.
The inland rivers push nutrients - nature's fish food - from the north into the bays and out into the gulf.
Through a million years the gulf rose and fell from ice age to ice age. At times its shoreline was hundreds of miles north with its waters covering many of the Southeastern states. At other times great forests grew where fishes now swim. Underwater limestone rock rises from the bottom in thin ridges, signs of one-time luxurious shallow, warm-water coral reefs that now are covered only by small soft corals, sea fans and the few deep-water hard corals. These sparse patches of rock rise out of the sand mostly in east-west strips, paralleling the coast, and are home for remarkable concentrations of sea life.
• Sea turtles, mackerel, Cobia, Amberjack and Spadefish patrol waters over the reefs for easy meals from the schools of baitfish that swarm over the rock.
• Some reefs are pocked with holes - some say stumpholes from

The Gulf of Mexico

Location

Alabama meets the Gulf of Mexico for 53 miles of coastline. Additionally, Mobile and Perdido Bays provide the state with approximately 360 square miles of Gulf coastal water.

From the Mississippi state line to the mouth of Mobile Bay, the Alabama coast is protected from the open gulf by barrier islands, the largest being Dauphin Island, which forms the western tip of Mobile Bay's mouth.

Eastward from Mobile Point, the bay mouth's eastern tip, there are no barrier islands. However, since the Intracoastal Waterway was dug, the entire Alabama shore is technically an island since one must cross the intracoastal before getting to the coast.

Composition

The Alabama coastline is predominantly quartz-laden sand, brilliantly white, fine and soft. The sand has drifted into low dunes, held together by sea oats and scrub. Just inland the sand is puddled by lakes and overgrown by scrub, palmetto and coastal pines.

The soft blanket of sand stretches from the plant growthline for 70 or more yards before meeting the surf.

The descent is gentle and uniform, with only slight dips and cuts, making for ideal bathing beaches throughout the state's brief coastline.

The mild descent into gulf waters helps provide generally gentle currents and modest tides. As the bottom slowly descends, one or two sand bars break the slope. Once depths reach 70 feet, occasional rock outcroppings show up, and are enhanced by artificial reefs to attract gamefish.

Types of Fish

The northern gulf is a major fishery, with Mobile and Perdido Bays significant spawning grounds for many species of gamefish, crustaceans and baitfish.

The open gulf provides a year-round home for a number of gamefish species, and is a roaming ground for certain pelagic fishes that move in and out as the water temperature rises and falls season by season.

Gulf of Mexico fishes generally are divided by the environment where they are found: the surf, the reefs and wrecks or schooling in open water.

Surf gamefish include Bluefish, Blue Runner, Croaker, Flounder, Jack Crevalle, King Mackerel, Ladyfish, Mullet, Pompano, Redfish, Sharks, Spanish Mackerel and Whiting.

Reef and wreck gamefish include Amberjack, Barracuda, Bluefish, Bonito, Cobia, Grouper, Jack Crevalle, Porgy, Sharks, Red, Black and Vermilion Snapper, Spadefish, Triggerfish and some tunas.

Open water gamefish include Bluefish, Bonito, Boston Mackerel, Cobia, Dolphin, Jack Crevalle, King Mackerel, Blue Marlin, White Marlin, Sailfish, Sharks, Spanish Mackerel, Swordfish, Tuna and Wahoo.

Some species are found in more than one area. At times, open water fish may congregate around reefs and wrecks because structure draws baitfish and these open-water fish come in search of the baitfish. Others, such as the Cobia, run in nearshore open water in the spring, then settle around wrecks in summer.

Some species such as the tunas and mackerels tend to school, while others such as the marlins are solitary creatures.

The gulf also is home to literally hundreds of species of non-game fishes, baitfish and minnows.

---

prehistoric forests - and fractured into thousands of cracks and crevices. Lying in and shooling along the safety of these fissures are grouper, snapper, grunts, porgys and flounder. Circling the rock or hovering to the outer edge are the sharks and barracuda, ominous scavengers preying on the injured or careless, leaving the fittest to regenerate the life of the reef.

• Water temperature rises and falls with the seasons in greater extremes than any other location along the gulf rim. When summer water temperatures peak at 85 degrees or so, the mackerels, dolphin and billfish have surged northward into these waters and patrol the coast until winter cold fronts push them back toward their homes to the south.

• Bottom fishes move from the depths to the shallows, then back again as the water heats and cools.

• Great swarms of baitfish surge in and out of the bays with the heating and cooling of the water.

• As winter approaches this section of the gulf, it brings a succession of fast-moving weather fronts, packing strong winds that keep most sport-fishing boats in port through the cold months. It offers a brief respite to reef dwellers so heavily fished from spring through fall, allowing populations to rebuild as fish spawn or migrate into the structure.

In recent years, heavy fishing has taken some toll on gamefish populations. But the Alabama coast has fared better than some areas of nearby Florida where overfishing has greatly reduced fish populations.

Government regulators are likely to put additional limits on fishes and fishermen in coming years to safeguard the region's sea-life population. It may create tough times for commercial and charter fishermen; it certainly will force a discipline to take fewer fish, and perhaps a different style of fishing to ensure that future generations are able to experience the joys of a day upon the sea.

The Alabama Coast

Perhaps it is the idea that one is standing at the edge of the world that brings fishermen back again and again to venture into the gulf.

Perhaps it is the plentiful catches the area is known for, or the size of the fishes. Perhaps it is the great diversity of fishing and styles of fishing that are possible.

Whatever the reason, fishermen flock to this place by the thousands; unwind in its casual air, revel in its beauty, are awed by its mystery, respect its power and harvest its bounty.

THE SURF

The very thing that draws millions of visitors to the Alabama shore - the pristine white sand - is the same one that discourages many fishermen from trying their luck on the beach.

Because the surf lacks close-in reefs, rocks, vegetation or other obstructions that normally attract fish, many anglers view it as so many miles of desert when it comes to sea life.

A closer look reveals something vastly different. Actually, the surf is a treasure house of marine life.

Great schools of fish cruise near the beaches, and several types of game fish patrol the sandy bottom for bits of food washed up or crustaceans and shellfish that live in the shallows.

The key is knowing how to look for the fish. Many a surf angler has spent all day without so much as a nibble, while others fishing sometimes only yards away are filling their coolers.

If you plan to bottom fish in the surf, search for potholes and cuts in the sand bars. Water moves more rapidly in the cuts, and food particles accumulate in the potholes. The food and moving water attract fish.

These cuts and potholes are easy to detect, particularly on calm days, by the color of the water. The shallower the water, the lighter color it is. The deeper it is, the darker it gets. The shallowest water appears almost clear white; when it begins getting deeper it appear light green; in the cuts and potholes it appears blue to dark blue.

There are several other ways to find fish. Watch for birds circling and diving at the surface, or a dimpling of the surface. Those are indications of schooling fish. In extremely clear water on calm days you can actually spot schools of fish along the shore.

The schooling fish move in and out from the shoreline; some days they run in thick schools; other days they disappear completely. You just have to hunt them.

One thing about surf fishing: you probably will catch something, even if it is only a sea catfish or Pinfish.

Surf fishermen use tackle ranging from light spinning rigs - the same as they use back home for bream - to heavy surf rods. The only criteria is to select a rod capable of casting bait or a lure beyond the first sand bar (You don't even need to cast that far for Pompano or Whiting sometimes).

Just be prepared to have your line snapped once in a while with light tackle.

Bottom fishermen use smallish hooks on one- and two-hook rigs, held on the bottom by a pyramid or barrel sinker, usually about the size of those used or crappie fishing. Popular bottom baits are frozen squid and shrimp. A small bit of bait on a small hook will do fine. Some fishermen use cut bait, sand fleas, bits of shellfish or sand crabs.

Favorite artificial lures include jigs ranging from 1/4 to 3/4 ounce. Sting Ray Grubs and silver spoons in 00 or 0 size. A small three-hook mackerel rig is popular for casting natural baits such as cigar minnows.

During summer months, casting with lures or natural bait or bottom fishing all produce fish. In winter, surf fishing is limited mostly to bottom fishing.

A couple of handy gadgets that make surf fishing easier include a five-gallon bucket or medium-size cooler to keep your catch in and a three-foot length of stiff plastic pipe, of sufficient width for the butt of your rod to slide down into the pipe. You stick one end of the pipe in the sand and the butt of your rod in the other to keep it out of the sand when you don't want to hold it.

A caution: Wear clothes fit for wading and shoes you don't mind getting wet. And remember the sun. A person sunburns quickly with the rays reflecting off both the water and white sand.

PIERS

Some wag once said that piers were the poor man's boat into the gulf. Don't believe it. Pier fishing is something different - something all its own.

The structures jut into the gulf to beyond the breakers and provide a haven for fish and a place where fishermen can cast beyond the sand bars into waters holding Bluefish, Bonito, Flounder, Pompano, King and Spanish Mackerel, Cobia, Ladyfish, Whiting, Barracuda, Shark, Redfish, Black Drum, Boston Mackerel and Blue Runners.

Some fishermen come to the pier with light fresh-water tackle, fish for such smaller species as Flounder and Whiting and do just fine. For larger fish such as the King Mackerel and Bonito, heavier gear is needed. A light to medium surf rod is recommended - one that you can get some casting distance with.

Most all natural baits will draw action. For bottom fishing, either a one- or two-hook rig will do. Small to medium spoons, grubs and jigs in the 1/4 to 3/4 ounce size are most commonly used.

Some pier fishermen cast live or dead cigar minnows on an unweighted line for mackerel. They sometimes use a single hook through the minnow's mouth and out the eye socket, or a three-hook mackerel rig.

Piers can get crowded at times, particularly when fish are schooling. Remember to give the other fellow room at the rail and room to cast. If the fisherman next to you has a fish on, get your line out of the water. Otherwise there is a fine opportunity for a tangled line and a lost fish.

You are a good distance above the water on the pier. Large fish usually are gaffed to get them up and over the rail. Customarily the fisherman with the gaff shares it with others. Remember to put it back when you are finished using it. Pier fishermen know how tough it is to maneuver a fish from the water onto the pier, keeping it away from the huge crustacean-covered pilings that can separate a line so quickly, and then hoisting it onto the pier itself.

Keep your tackle box closed and away from the pier's edge. Don't leave sharp-finned fish for someone to step on. And keep tackle put away.

Pier fishing provides essentially the same action and the same species of fish as surf fishing.

JETTIES

To halt silting and erosion of channels, jetties of huge boulders and concrete have been built at the mouth of bays and in a few other areas along the Alabama coast.

Jetties are havens for an array of fish and other sea life. The cracks and crevices in the rocks draw shellfish, crustaceans, sea urchins, starfish and minnows - which draw bigger fish.

Fishermen either are addicted to the jetties or hate them. Some anglers fish jetties almost exclusively year around, and come home with heavy stringers of fish. Others swear they will never again fish jetties after leaving half their tackle tangled in the rocks. There is no question that you will use a quantity of tackle when fishing jetties. A fish will try to dive for the rocks when hooked; and if he gets to them, odds are he'll be able to drag your line across one and cut it.

Yet, such a variety of fish - and large numbers of them at certain times of year - make jetties favorite fishing spots. Not only will you find most surf species around jetties, oftentimes such reef fishes as Triggerfish and grouper and, on rare occasions, White and Red Snapper will move into the jetties, particularly during cooler months.

While many people use light fresh-water tackle for jetty fishing, others prefer light to medium surf tackle. Also, some anglers use slightly heavier than normal sinkers because of the strong tidal currents. A pyramid sinker is preferred over a barrel sinker since it will better stay put. A barrel sinker tends to roll in the current.

Open Gulf Fishing

BOTTOM FISHING

Much of the year, your chances of catching a variety of food fish are greatest bottom fishing. The bottom fish - such as snappers, Triggerfish, porgy and groupers - usually are willing biters, easily located (for those who know where to look) and caught with a minimum of expertise.

Almost every day of the year that the gulf is calm enough, charter and party (head) boats venture from Alabama ports into the gulf for bottom fish. In addition, some reefs and wrecks are close enough to shore that fishermen can reach them with their own boats and drift or anchor and bottom fish.

If you charter a boat or get on a party boat, your bait and fishing tackle is furnished. You use heavy tackle and natural bait - either cut bait, squid or, sometimes, live or dead whole baitfish.

The basic bottom-fishing technique is simple, but the fine points take practice to master. Bottom fishermen usually use a rig consisting of two hooks and a heavy sinker to hold the rig near the bottom.

Once the boat captain signals that it is time to fish, the fisherman simply lowers his line over the side of the boat until he feels the sinker hit bottom. Usually he will get a bite immediately. The tough part for the novice is being able to distinguish a bite - particularly a soft nibble - from the sinker bumping bottom. The second toughest part is setting the hook. It is tough because you are setting the hook from 100 or more feet away, and you are having to deal with that heavy weight in setting the hook. With a monofilament line you get a certain amount of stretch. And if you aren't careful, you will tend to momemtarily let your line go slack after trying to set the hook. This allows the fish a chance to get loose.

The crank up is a long one. Some boats offer electric reels for a modest fee. With those you have but to push a button to have your hook speeding to the surface.

If you lack your own boat, you have two choices: party boats, also known as head boats because they charge per head (fisherman), and charter boats.

Party boats are the least expensive way to spend a day on the open gulf. Depending on the boat and the day, these trips sometimes last a half day, sometimes a full day of 9 or 10 hours.

Most party boats are equipped with a galley where food and drinks can be purchased.

These generally are large boats, carrying 50 or more fishermen at a time, traveling to large reefs or wrecks, usually within 30 miles of shore.

The main advantages to party boat fishing is price and the fact that all bait and equipment is furnished to the fisherman. A full-day trip will cost in the $40 range, while half-day trips are in the $25 range.

Party boats are equipped with a variety of fish finders and navigation equipment and captains have no trouble locating fishing grounds.

Some argue that individual fishermen do not catch as many fish on party boats as they do on charter boats. That may or may not be the case, depending on the boat, the fisherman, and the day of the fishing

trip. If party boats sometimes do not deliver the same per-fisherman catch as charter boats, it may not be that one is fishing better territory than the other. Because of the size of his boat and the number of fishermen aboard, a party boat captain must stop over areas capable of holding large concentrations of fish. While these spots may be larger, they also may be more heavily fished than a tiny spot that a charter boat may offer to his group of a half dozen fishermen.

Secondly, the pure economics of 50 fishermen fishing a single hole dictates that while a party boat may get as many fish from one spot as a charter boat, the number of fish per fisherman may be less.

In addition, when 50 or more fishermen try to fish shoulder to shoulder there are going to be more tangled lines and more confusion. Party boats do have deck hands who help, but on party boats each deck hand often has more fishermen to watch out for than the average charter boat deck hand.

The final, and perhaps most significant, factor has to do with the skill of the fisherman. Every party boat takes out a large number of people each day who don't know anything about salt water fishing. And that factor alone keeps them from catching the numbers of fish they could catch if only they had taken some time to learn what to do.

A novice probably isn't going to have as much luck as an experienced fisherman. Most experienced fishermen always bring back heavy stringers from a day of party boat fishing. They aren't always huge fish, but there almost always are plenty of them. With some knowledge of salt water fishing techniques - even such things as how to properly bait the hooks, when to improvise and put a live bait on, how to detect a bite and how to set a hook - a party boat fisherman will bring more fish over the rail than he will know what to do with.

The other option is charter boat fishing. If you don't care for the larger boat or large number of fishermen, or want some personal and special attention from a captain and deck hand, charter boat fishing should be considered.

It costs more than party boat fishing, generally.

On the whole, these are smaller boats capable of carrying from 6 to 20 fishermen and are chartered by the hour or day, with the base rate figured on 6 to 10 fishermen, depending on the size of the boat. Additional anglers cost extra. Charter boat captains often will go fishing for the number of hours and on the hours that you specify.

With fewer fishermen, the captain and crew have more time to offer fishing tips, usually will move from one fishing spot to another whenever you want and usually will change from one style of fishing to another whenever you want.

Charter boats also furnish all bait and tackle. Lighter tackle often is available on charter boats - making it easier to detect bites and to do more kinds of fishing, to use lighter sinkers or even to use an unweighted line. Some charter boats offer live-bait fishing.

Some charter boats have galleys; some do not. Most allow you to bring your own lunch and beverages. Some require you to do so. Ask in advance.

A half day of charter boat fishing can cost $220 to $300, while a full-day trip can cost from $450 to $600, depending on the boat, number of fishing hours and type of fishing. Some boats offer overnight trips for an additional fee.

While charter captains often will fish for what the fishermen demand, the smart angler will ask the captain what's biting and take his advice.

Getting a Good Captain

Some captains catch more fish than others, just as in life some workers are more productive than others. Following are some tips on selecting a top-notch captain:

• Before booking your trip, talk to acquaintances who have fished Alabama gulf waters recently. Get the names of captains who have provided successful trips.

• If you arrive at the coast without having already booked your trip, visit the marinas. Notice the boats. While a neat, clean, well-kept boat won't catch fish by itself, it is an indicator of the care a captain gives.

• In addition to checking boat conditions, if you visit the marinas as boats are returning from a day of fishing you can see what they catch. Visit the same marina several times in a row if possible. While the good boats will consistently come in with catches, even the best ones have a bad day once in a while.

• Talk to the captain. If you don't care for his temperament, find another one. See if he seems genuinely interested in you catching fish and having a good time.

• Ask area residents, at motels and at fish houses, and with folks you see wandering around the docks about which captains do the best job.

Throughout much of the spring, summer and fall, the better boats are booked in advance, particularly on weekends. However, they are not so fully booked on weekdays. If you want a weekend trip, call in advance or you may not be able to find a boat.

Trolling

Party boats do not troll.

Charter boats offer two distinctively different types of trolling - inshore and offshore.

INSHORE

Inshore trolling means trolling not too far from the beach - usually within 15 miles of land and often within a mile.

When the mackerel are running, this type of fishing is often so fast and furious that a fisherman will want no more than a half-day trip.

Charter boats charge similarly for both bottom fishing and trolling.

Also, as with bottom fishing, boats chartered for trolling normally provide all tackle and bait.

Trolling can be much more a feast or famine proposition than bottom fishing. The migratory fish that are the bread and butter of the trolling fleets move in and out of the coastline; some years they are plentiful; other years scarce. One day a charter captain will fish hard for two or three fish, only to go out the next day and load the fish box.

Oversimplified, trolling is a matter of hooking a natural or artificial bait at the end of your line and towing it through the water, enticing a fish to strike what it thinks is its next meal.

The difference in lures generally is color and size, with smaller spoons and jigs for Spanish Mackerel, and larger dusters and natural baits more common for King Mackerel. Other trolling baits include natural and artificial squid, cigar minnows and large spoons.

Trolling boats congregate over reefs, wrecks, near cuts or channels and over any kind of obstruction or area that attracts baitfish. Often they will troll in a tight circle around buoys.

OFFSHORE

The warm Loop Current and the blue-black depths of the DeSoto Canyon are the cruising grounds for Sailfish, Wahoo, Tuna, Blue and White Marlin, big Dolphins and Swordfish.

These giants migrate into the waters during the spring, and roam the deep waters until the winter chill.

You troll for these big game fish. But it is different than inshore trolling.

An offshore trip often will take at least 12 hours, and possibly require spending a night on the open gulf. Because it requires more time to get to the deeper water, it costs more to troll offshore - generally $600 minimum for a group of six.

The search for big offshore fish involves hours of monotony, broken by moments of spine-tingling excitement. Even after reaching offshore fishing grounds, you may troll for hours before anything rises to so much as look at your bait.

Inshore, when a fish hits it normally instantly hooks itself. Offshore, a billfish sometimes will follow a bait for a long distance before striking; even then, it may touch the bait several times with its bill before actually taking it in its mouth. Sometimes a fisherman will fight a fish for a long time only to have it tear loose or break off.

One giant Blue Marlin is a prize catch. The success of an offshore trip is measured in the size of the fish you catch, not in numbers.

It is specialized fishing. Tackle is among the heaviest available. Lures are oversize. And the length of the trip requires some stamina.

Tidbits

SEASICKNESS

Anyone can get seasick. There are a number of remedies on the market these days. Don't wait until you are sick to take one. The smart angler checks with his druggist or physician ahead of time on the best seasickness remedy. Follow the instructions. Once you get out to sea, particularly on a party boat, there is no turning back until the captain has finished his day. To avoid seasickness, eat normally, avoid greasy foods and don't upset your normal routine. That includes not drinking alcoholic beverages heavily the night before you go out.

WHAT TO WEAR

Wear comfortable clothes. In winter you will need a jacket on most days. In summer, wear light clothes and a hat, and shoes that you don't mind getting wet. You will get bait and fish slime on your hands. Bring a towel to wipe them.

TIPPING

Charter boat deck hands normally are tipped 15 to 20 percent of the trip cost. That is, if they do a good job. A deck hand working hard can mean the difference in a successful trip and an unsuccessful one.

ON YOUR OWN

Do not challenge the open gulf in your bass boat, or any other vessel not properly equipped for such a large body of water. Piloting a small boat on the Gulf of Mexico can be an enjoyable experience. It also can be an exercise in pure terror and can end in disaster.

As seas go, the gulf is considered calm. Still, strong winter and spring winds can raise seas to more than 10 feet in a short time. Summer and fall seas are less fickle, generally calmer, and more predictable. Seas generally are flatter in those seasons.

Still, if you never have had experience on the open gulf, venture out cautiously - first into the bay, then a short foray into the open gulf. Build your confidence. Practice maneuvers until you are confident of the maximum seas that you and your boat are capable of handling safely.

Even before leaving port that first time, make sure your craft is rigged for open water. A ship-to-shore radio and compass are essentials. If you expect to catch any fish bottom fishing, a Loran receiver and depth finder also are musts. Spend some time learning to operate them; 10 miles out is no place to learn to program a Loran.

Many anglers say they would not venture out without a backup engine, while others frequent the gulf with only one; they say their will call for a tow if the engine breaks down.

The most efficient of life jackets are recommended.

An anchor designed to dig into soft bottom is suggested, along with rope approximately three times as long as the water depth you intend to fish in.

Basic salt-water tackle consists of a five- to six-foot boat rod and a level-wind reel. Rods of solid fiberglass, with the fiberglass extending through the butt handle, in five and six foot lengths are basic. New, strong, hollow rods of modern-day materials are available and are lighter than solid fiberglass. A good all-around reel is the 4/0 size. If you don't plan to venture out more than 15 miles or so, you can get by with smaller reels. If your fishing is to include heavy grouper and Amberjack, you may want to consider the slightly larger 6/0 size.

These reels should be equipped with 50 to 80 pound test line. Most fishermen now use monofilament, but braided line still is available and doesn't present the stretch problem of monofilament. There are more styles of hooks for salt water fishing than most fishermen even know of. Three items are important in hook selection: 1. Match the size of the hook with the kind of fish you are going for (remember that grouper and Amberjack have big mouths); 2. Salt water hooks need thick shanks to keep toothy species from biting them in half; 3. If you are undecided about which size hook to use, always pick the smaller of two choices.

TACKLE

Other important tackle peculiar to salt water are a gaff to hoist larger fish into the boat, a cutting board for cutting fish and squid into bait-size pieces and a marker buoy which can be purchased at tackle stores or made from an old plastic jug.

"A Big Pond"

The Alabama salt water angler with his own boat still is faced with a challenge. He can troll near shore or outward over the reefs. He can drift fish or bottom fish, use light tackle and play a fish all day long or use a heavy boat rod for big Amberjack or grouper.

But he still has to find the fish.

Mostly, the shore off the Alabama coast is a gently rolling to flat sand bottom outward for 20 or more miles. This gentle sea floor is occasionally interrupted by limestone outcroppings and artificial reefs - sunken ships, car bodies, concrete bridge rubble or just about anything else that fishermen could sink to attract fish.

The Gulf of Mexico is a big pond. Reefs, artificial or natural, are tough to find. Men who make their livings fishing the gulf fiercely protect the locations of the reefs that they personally build at much effort and expense.

There are many reefs built by the government for the pleasure boat fisherman, and the Loran numbers for those are available to the public. Many of the natural reefs are now well charted and their locations are becoming well known.

The locations of these fishing grounds are determined with a navigation tool known as a Loran. Oversimplified, the Gulf of Mexico is gridded by radio signals. An instrument known as a Loran receiver picks up two-set six-number signals.

Along the Alabama coast, one signal tells the captain generally how far south he is, while the other tells him how far east or west he is.

Once he locates an area where he spots a concentration of fish on his depth finder, he can forever return to that spot by logging the Loran numbers the receiver displayed while he was seeing fish on the fish finder.

How the map works

Following is a listing of Loran coordinates within reach of recreational boaters from Alabama ports.

Some of these locations are publicly built reefs designated for recreational fisermen. Some were contributed by area divers and fishermen and others are from reported shrimpers' hangs.

Some aren't exact, particularly the shrimpers' hangs. Sometimes they recorded the exact location of the hang. Sometimes they drifted off a bit before they made the notation.

Also, some artificial reefs made from metal objects such as car bodies rust away in time, and heavy seas move them around. Shifting sand sometimes covers reefs.

All to say, you might try some of these numbers and find nothing. If that is the case, run a pattern before giving up.

The maps were compiled by The Alabama Cooperative Extensive Service's Alabama Sea Grant Extension.

It was compiled with the best information available, and meticulously constructed.

Gulf Shores to Pensacola

No.	LORAN C	Structure
1	13326.3 47116.0	Casino Reef
2	13306.9 47102.8	Barge
3	13305.2 47103.0	Liberty Ship
4	13323.0 47013.0	Tenneco Rig
5	13326.3 47105.8 13323.0 47105.8	Airplane, tires, etc.
6.	13270.5 47108.0	Three Barges
7.	13277.5 47091.8	Bridge Rubble
8.	13263.9 47077.0	Russian Freighter
9.	13080.0 46995.0 13060.0 47000.0	Trysler Grounds
10.	13070.0 47020.0	Mobil Oil Platform
11.	13038.0 47046.0	Liberty Ship Wallace
12.	13059.2 47054.9	Lillian Bridge Rubble
13.	13069.2 47059.0	Liberty Ship Allen
14.	13046.7 47062.8	Lillian Bridge/ Kelley Pipes
15.	13417.5 47080.6	Boxcars
16.	13247.0 47081.7	Artificial Reef
17.	13247.5 47076.5	Artificial Reef
18.	13254.4 47062.4	Artificial Reef
19.	13248.0 47062.4	Artificial Reef
20.	13247.5 47068.1	Artificial Reef
21.	13250.2 47078.7	Boat
22.	13251.5 47064.2	Concrete Rubble
23.	13464.7 47040.9	Rock
24.	13511.4 47101.4	Liberty Ship
25.	13302.6 47098.2	Liberty Ship

Perdido Bridge Rubble put down in 1989

13044.4 47062.1	13050.4 47034.2
13045.6 46030.0	13053.2 47036.1
13045.6 47061.8	13055.5 47038.5
13047.5 47062.0	New Box Cars
13048.4 47032.0	12956.2 47002.2
	13038.4 47018.4

No.	LORAN C	Structure
26.	13278.1 47092.0 13244.3 47085.3	Hard bottom
27.	13227.6 47054.8	Hard bottom
28.	13233,7 47059.4	Hard bottom
29.	13191.2 47086.1	Amberjack hole
30.	13158.1 47060.8	Artificial reef
31.	13131.0 47079.0	Dutch banks/ Hard bottom
32.	13107.7 47061.8	Artificial reef
33.	13065.3 47060.3	Car or truck body
34.	13063.5 47087.1	Barge
35.	12979.5 47034.4	Barge or boat
36.	12956.3 47021.7	Boat

Fort Morgan Peninsula to Ala./Miss. Line

No.	LORAN C	Structure		No.	LORAN C	Structure
37.	12711.9 47027.4	Tulsa Wreck		56.	12848.0 47077.0	Shrimper's Hang
38.	12733.4 47018.6	Liberty Ship Anderson		57.	12882.7 47047.1	Barge
39.	12709.4 47013.6	Liberty Ship Edwards		58.	12900.9 47043.3	Boat
40.	12080.3 47027.0 12787.1 47025.9 12788.9 47050.6 12790.0 46858.8	Southeast Banks		59.	12911.0 47086.1	Shrimper's Hang
				60.	12954.7 47085.5	Shrimper's Hang
				61.	12959.8 47039.9	Shrimper's Hang
				62.	12629.2 47082.2	Shrimper's Hang
41.	12881.9 47045.5	Buffalo Barge I		63.	12638.2 47049.4	Shrimper's Hang
42.	12883.1 47045.8	Buffalo Barge II		64.	12652.2 47064.0	Shrimper's Hang
43.	12876.8 47044.3	Fort Morgan Pipes		65.	12652.5 47051.2	Shrimper's Hang
44.	12900.0 47045.0	Lipscomb Tug		66.	12655.0 47071.0	Wreck
45.	12957.8 47039.9	Tug		67.	12655.0 47071.0	Shrimper's Hang
46.	12948.1 47020.2	Liberty Ship Sparkman		68.	12655.0 47049.6	Shrimper's Hang
47.	12704.6 47028.7	Drydock		69.	12657.3 47063.5	Shrimper's Hang
48.	12650.0 47045.0 12655.4 47050.4	Southwest Banks		70.	12657.5 47052.9	Shrimper's Hang
				71.	12657.5 47084.7	Shrimper's Hang
49.	12806.7 47070.9	Shrimper's Hang		72.	12660.0 47042.0	Shrimper's Hang
50.	12808.0 47074.7	Shrimper's Hang		73.	12661.8 47077.4	Shrimper's Hang
51.	12813.0 47071.7 12813.4 47071.3	Shrimper's Hang		74.	12662.0 47064.5	Shrimper's Hang
				75.	12665.9 47081.8	Shrimper's Hang
52.	12816.0 47082.8	Shrimper's Hang		76.	12666.5 47068.2	Shrimper's Hang
53.	12820.0 47076.0 12820.0 47077.0	Wreck		77.	12667.8 47085.3	Shrimper's Hang
				78.	12668.7 47078.0	Shrimper's Hang
54.	12824.0 47071.8	Wreck		79.	12670.6 47049.8	Shrimper's Hang
55.	12833.1 47045.8	Shrimper's Hang		80.	12682.2 47081.9	Shrimper's Hang

Fort Morgan Peninsula to Ala./Miss. Line

No.	LORAN C	Structure	No.	LORAN C	Structure
81.	12684.0 47080.9	Shrimper's Hang	106.	12723.4 47036.3	Bridge Rubble
82.	12684.2 47067.9	Shrimper's Hang	107.	12724.6 47035.6	Bridge Rubble
83.	12684.2 47063.7	Shrimper's Hang	108.	12724.8 47035.1	Bridge Rubble
84.	12684.3 47069.9	Shrimper's Hang	109.	12726.7 47035.3	Bridge Rubble
85.	12685.3 47067.8	Wreck/Probably a boat	110.	12730.2 47035.3	Bridge Rubble
86.	12688.8 47043.8	Shrimper's Hang	111.	12735.3 47035.3	Bridge Rubble
87.	12688.8 47076.8	Shrimper's Hang	112.	12719.2 47034.5	Bridge Rubble
88.	12690.0 47060.0	Shrimper's Hang	113.	12720.5 47035.5	Bridge Rubble
89.	12697.9 47051.7	Bridge Rubble	114.	12709.7 47038.8	Bridge Rubble
90.	12698.0 47051.8	Bridge Rubble	115.	12717.0 47040.5	Bridge Rubble
91.	12708.7 47050.5	Bridge Rubble	116.	12704.9 47050.6	Shrimper's Hang
92.	12708.9 47050.6	Bridge Rubble	117.	12710.3 47027.2	Wreck
93.	12691.8 47049.9	Bridge Rubble	118.	12719.8 47077.1	Shrimper's Hang
94.	12703.7 47046.9	Bridge Rubble	119.	12721.3 47077.1	Shrimper's Hang
95.	12704.0 47046.9	Bridge Rubble	120.	12721.9 47054.9	Artificial reef
96.	12704.2 47046.9	Bridge Rubble	121.	12722.1 47069.4	Shrimper's Hang
97.	12704.4 47046.9	Bridge Rubble	122.	12722.1 47065.5	Shrimper's Hang
98.	12704.5 47046.9	Bridge Rubble	123.	12722.1 47067.5	Shrimper's Hang
99.	12713.5 47041.3	Bridge Rubble	124.	12722.9 47060.5	Shrimper's Hang
100.	12713.0 47041.4	Bridge Rubble	125.	12724.2 47062.9	Shrimper's Hang
101.	12726.2 47039.2	Bridge Rubble	126.	12724.5 47064.6	Shrimper's Hang
102.	12723.7 47036.4	Bridge Rubble	127.	12727.2 47070.0	Shrimper's Hang
103.	12720.3 47038.4	Bridge Rubble	128.	12731.4 47058.0	Shrimper's Hang
104.	12717.0 47036.5	Bridge Rubble	129.	12722.8 47076.7	Wreck
105.	12715.2 47035.7	Bridge Rubble	130.	12733.5 47060.4	Pipe

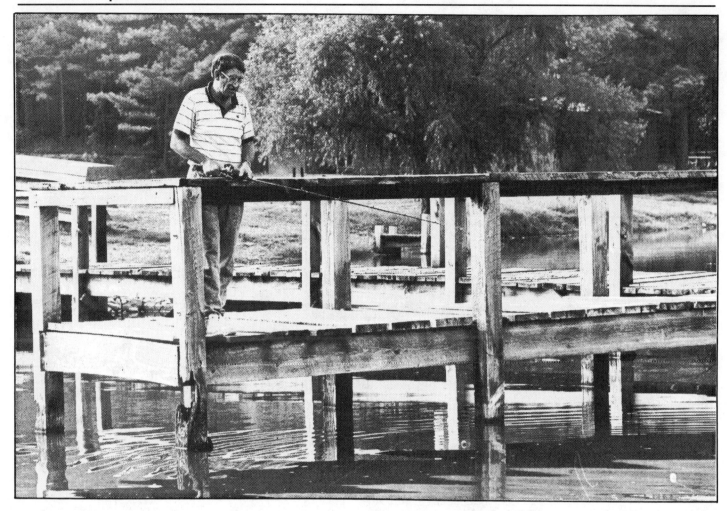

Alabama's State Lakes

Several sections of Alabama, including much of the southern third and much of midwestern portion, lack the large reservoirs that so many Alabama fishermen enjoy. But that doesn't mean Alabamians who live there don't have the opportunity to enjoy good fishing.

The Game and Fish Division of the Alabama Department of Conservation and Natural Resources manages 20 public fishing lakes concentrated in areas lacking sufficient natural waters to satisfy the fishing needs of the public. These lakes range from 13 acres to 184 acres.

These lakes are not just stop-gap measures to silence anglers who lack areas to fish, either. The lakes are well-maintained, including weekly fertilization. These lakes gave up a tremendous average of 113 pounds of fish per acre in a 1986-87 study.

Studies have shown these lakes are undoubtedly the angler's best opportunity to catch a fish five pounds or larger in Alabama. Washington County lake did even better than that in 1982 when it gave up a state record bass of 13 pounds.

That lake gave up 60 fish larger than 5 pounds in 1986-87, including two larger than 12 pounds and one 10-pounder.

All of these lakes are stocked with largemouth bass, bluegill and shellcracker and many now have crappie populations established. Some also have hybrid bass, channel catfish and rainbow trout.

Many of these lakes have most recently turned into a haven for those who like to fish for catfish. Those lakes which have channel catfish have been stocked 50 to 200 catfish to the acre depending on fish populations.

A feeding program for catfish has been started on every lake stocked with them in an effort to concentrate them for fishermen. An average of 10 to 20 pounds of catfish food per day is thrown on every lake from May through October. Sixteen of the lakes are equipped with automatic feeders which throw food to the catfish on two-hour intervals throughout the day.

The lakes are fertilized weekly during warm months to increase the production of fish and prevent the growth of obnoxious aquatic vegetation. In addition, each lake is checked for lime requirement every three years.

Each lake is sampled every spring by electrofishing to analyze fish

1. Barbour Co. Lake
2. Bibb Co. Lake
3. Chambers Co. Lake
4. Clay Co. Lake
5. Coffee Co. Lake
6. Crenshaw Co. Lake
7. Dale Co. Lake
8. Dallas Co. Lake
9. DeKalb Co. Lake
10. Escambia Co. Lake
11. Fayette Co. Lake
12. Geneva Co. Lake
13. Lamar Co Lake
14. Lee Co. Lake
15. Madison Co. Lake
16. Marion Co. Lake
17. Monroe Co. Lake
18. Pike Co. Lake
19. Walker Co. Lake
20. Washington Co. Lake

Alabama's state lakes

development. In addition, each lake is sampled with seine nets once a month from May to September to determine the success of the bass spawn and to determine fish balance in the lake.

The excellent maintenance and resulting good fishing is only one of the plusses these lakes offer, many anglers believe.

If you've ever fished one of Alabama's reservoirs, you've undoubtedly had your fishing interrupted at one time or another by water skiers, sailboaters, pleasure riders or swimmers.

These state lakes are strictly fishing lakes and other water activities are banned. Only five of the 20 lakes allow outboard motors to be used and then at trolling speed only.

Another management tool these lakes use is catch records. All fishermen are required to weigh every fish that is kept. These harvest records are computerized and the total harvests of all species on every lake is monitored. Harvests are regulated so no more than 30 pounds of bass per acre are removed each year.

For the convenience of anglers, each lake is provided with a concession building and an individual from the community is contracted to operate the concession.

The contractors are required to keep accurate records, weigh fish, fertilize the lakes, and keep the lake and grounds attractive. Everyone 12 years of age or older are is required to purchase a $1.50 ($2 at Pike County Lake) fishing permit for every trip to the lake and this is required along with a state fishing license. The concessionaires sell state fishing licenses.

Boat rentals are $2 per day and there is a $1 launch fee for those who bring there own boats. There is a $3 camping fee at the lakes which offer camping.

Paddles, cushions, life jackets, fishing supplies and food and drink are also available at concession stands.

The state lakes are:

1. **Barbour County Lake**. Location: 6 miles north of Clayton on Barbour Co. 49. Concessionnaire: L.R. Hurst. Mailing address: Rt. 1, Box 164-A, Midway, Ala. 36053. Phone No. 775-9595. Lake acres: 75. Land acres: 175. Fish species: Bass, bream, catfish, crappie and hybrids. Additional facilities: picnic areas, launching ramp, rental boats, camping available. Hours of operation: Sunrise to sundown six days a week. Closed Thursday.

2. **Bibb County Lake**. Location: 5 miles north of Centreville on Alabama 5. Concessionnaire: Billy Smith. Mailing address: Rt. 1, Box 539, West Blocton, Ala. 35184. Phone No: 938-2124. Lake acres: 100. Land acres: 520. Fish species: Bass, bream, catfish and crappie. Additional facilities: launching ramp, fishing pier, rental boats, self-contained campsites. Hours of operation: 5:30 a.m. to 8:30 p.m. six days a week. Closed Mondays.

3. **Chambers County Lake**. Location: five miles southeast of Lafayette on Chambers Co. 55. Concessionnaire: Thomas Royster. Mailing address: Rt. 3, Box 208, Lafayette, Ala. 36862. Phone No.: 864-8145. Lake acres: 183. Land acres: 453. Fish species: Bass, bream, catfish and crappie. Additional facilities: launching ramp, picnic tables, fishing pier, rental boats, barbecue pavillion. Hours of operation: 5 a.m. to 10 p.m. six days a week. Closed Thursday.

4. **Clay County Lakes**. Location: One mile west of Delta on Alabama 47. Concessionniare: Starr Knight. Phone No. 488-5359. Lake acres: 13, 23 and 38. Fish species: Bluegill, shellcracker,

Florida largemouth, channel catfish and hybrids. 343 land acres. Additional facilities: campsites, launching ramp, picnic table, fishing pier and rental boats. Hours of operation: Sunrise to sunset.

5. Coffee County Lake. Location: four miles northwest of Elba on Coffee County 54. Concessionnaire: Erma Kendrick. Mailing address: Rt. 2, Box 245, Elba, Ala. 36323. Phone No. 897-5501. Lake acres: 80. Land acres: 123. Fish species: Bass, bream, catfish, crappie and hybrids. Additional facilities: picnic tables, fishing pier, launching ramp, rental boats. Hours of operation: 6 a.m. to 6 p.m. six days a week. Closed on Monday.

6. **Crenshaw County Lake**. Location: five miles south of Luverne on on U.S. 331. Concessionnaire: Buddy Williams. Mailing address: P.O. Box 91, Luverne, Ala. 36049. Phone No. 335-3550. Lake acres: 53 acres. Land acres: 187. Fish species: Bass, bream, catfish, crappie and hybrids. Additional facilities: self-contained campsites, picnic tables, fishing pier, launching ramp and rental boats. Hours of operation: Sunrise to sundown six days a week. Closed Thursday.

7. **Dale County Lake**. Location: one mile north of Roy Parier Road (Dale County 36) in Ozark. Concessionnaire: Bobby Skipper. Mailing address: 707 Myrtle Drive, Ozark, Ala. 36360. Phone No. 774-9802. Lake acres: 92. Land acres: 263. Fish species: Bass, bream, catfish, crappie and hybrids. Additional facilities: Self-contained campsites, picnic tables, fishing pier, launching ramp, rental boats. Hours of operation: Sunrise to sundown six days a week. Closed Thursday.

8. **Dallas County Lake**. Location: 11 miles south of Selma on Alabama 41. Concessionnaire: Clay Evans. Mailing address: Rt. 1, Box 56, Sardis, Ala. 36775. Phone No. 872-0219. Lake acres: 100. Land acres: 207. Fish species: bass, bream, catfish, crappie and hybrids. Additional facilities: picnic tables and grills, fishing pier, launching ramp and rental boats. Hours of operation: Sunrise to sundown six days a week. Closed Tuesday.

9. **DeKalb County Lake**. Location: one mile north of Sylvania off of DeKalb County 47. Concessionnaire: Wiley Clifton. Rt. 1, Box 338, Sylvania, Ala. 35988. Phone No. 657-3000. Lake acres: 120. Land acres: 215. Fish species: Bass, bream, catfish, crappie and hybrids. Additional facilities: kiddie playground, picnic pavilion, barbecue grills, self-contained campsites with restrooms, launching ramp, rental boats. Hours of operation: Sunrise to sundown six days a week. Closed Thursday.

10. **Escambia County Lake**. (Leon Brooks Hines Lake). Location: 23 miles east of Brewton off of Escambia County 11. Concessionnaire: U.V. McDaniel. Mailing address: Rt. 5, Box 440, Brewton, Ala. 36426. Phone: N/A. Lake acres: 184. Fish species. Florida largemouth bass, bluegill, coppernose bluegill, shellcracker, channel catfish. Additional facilities. Picnic tables, launch ramp, fishing pier, rental boats. Hours of operation: Sunrise to sunset.

11. **Fayette County Lake**. Location: six miles southeast of Fayette on Fayette County 26. Concessionnaire: Linda Moore. Mailing address: Rt. 4, Box 217-C, Fayette, Ala. 35555. Phone No: (L) 932-4646, (H) 932-4586. Lake acres: 60. Land acres: 195. Fish species: Bass, bream, catfish and crappie. Additional facilities: picnic tables and grills, launching ramp, rental boats. Hours of operation: Sunrise to sundown seven days a week.

12. **Geneva County Lakes** (two lakes). Location: 10 miles south of Enterprise on Alabama 27, then right on Coffee County 65 for

seven miles. Turn right on Geneva County 64 for two miles, then right on Geneva County 63. Concessionnaire: Eleanor Tillman. Mailing address: Rt. 1, Box 197-A, Coffee Springs, Ala. 36318. Phone No: 684-6488. Lake acres: 32 and 33. Fish species: Bass, bream, catfish and crappie. Additional facilities: picnic tables and grills, launching ramp. Hours of operation: Sunrise to sundown, seven days a week.

13. **Lamar County Lake**. Location: eight miles west of Vernon on Alabama 18, then five miles north on Lamar County 21. Concessionnaire: Betty Pennington. Mailing address: Rt. 2, Box 178, Sulligent, Ala. 35586. Phone No.: 695-9002. Lake acres: 68. Land acres: 127. Fish species: Bass, bream, catfish and crappie. Additional facilities: fishing pier, launching ramp, rental boats, picnic tables and grills. Hours of operation: 5 a.m. to 10 p.m., seven days a week.

14. **Lee County Lake**. Location: six miles southeast of Opelika on Alabama 169, then one mile west on Alabama 29. Concessionnaire: Mrs. J.D. Mullins. Mailing address: Rt. 1, Box 403, Opelika, Ala. 36801. Phone No.: (L) 749-1275, (H) 776-9773. Lake acres: 130. Land acres: 272. Fish species: Bass, bream, catfish, crappie and hybrids. Additional facilities: picnic tables, launching ramp, rental boats. Hours of operation: Sunrise to sundown six days a week. Closed Thursday.

15. **Madison County Lake**. Location: seven miles east of Huntsville on U.S. 72, then left on Ryland Pike Road to Maysville. Concessionnaire: Mrs. R. Renfroe. Mailing address: 2501 County Lake Road, Gurley, Ala. 35748. Phone No.: (L) 776-3304, (H) 776-9773. Lake acres: 105. Land acres: 212. Fish species: Bass, bream, catfish, crappie, rainbow trout and hybrids. Additional facilities: launching ramp, fishing pier, rental boats, picnic tables and grills, self contained campsites. Hours of operation: Sunrise to sundown, seven days a week.

16. **Marion County Lake**. Location: six miles north of Guin on U.S. 43. Concessionnaire: Margel Guyton. Mailing address: Rt. 2, Box 75, Guin, Ala. 35563. Phone No.: 921-4747. Lake acres: 37. Land acres: 343. Fish species: bass, bream, catfish, crappie and carp. Additional facilities: rental boats, picnic tables and grills, launching ramp and fishing pier. Hours of operation: Sunrise to sundown, Sunday-Tuesday; sunrise to 10 p.m., Monday-Wednesday.

17. **Monroe County Lake**. Location: 12 miles north of Monroeville on Alabama 21 at Beatrice, then five miles west on Monroe County 50. Concessionnaire: Mrs. Melba. B. Fore. Mailing address: Rt. 1, Box 158, Beatrice, Ala. 36425. Phone No.: 789-2409. Lake acres: 94. Land acres: 151. Fish species: Bass, bream, catfish, crappie and hybrids. Additional facilities: rental boats, picnic tables, launching ramp, fishing pier. Hours of operation: Sunrise to sundown six days a week. Closed Thursday.

18. **Pike County Lake**. Location: Three miles south of Troy on Alabama 87, then right on Pike County 39. Concessionnaire: Joe B. Allen. Mailing address: Rt. 2, Box 38, Troy, Ala. 36081. Phone No.: 484-9161. Lake acres: 45. Land acres: 362. Fish species: Bass, bream, catfish, crappie and hybrids. Additional facilities: picnic tables, rental boats, launching ramp, fishing pier. Hours of operation: Sunrise to sunset six days a week. Closed Tuesday.

19. **Walker County Lake**. Location: three miles southeast of Jasper off old U.S. 78. Concessionnaire: Wayne B. Abbott. Rt. 5, Box 155, Jasper, Ala. 35501. Phone No.: (L) 221-1801. Lake acres: 163. Land acres: 299. Fish species: Bass, bream, catfish, crappie, hybrids. Additional facilities: Fishing pier, launching ramp, picnic tables, rental boats, self-contained campsites. Hours of operation: 5:45 a.m. to 7:30 p.m. six days a week. Closed Mondays.

20. **Washington County Lake**. Location: two miles west of Millry off Washington County 34. Concessionnaire: Mrs. Hulon Davis. Mailing address: P.O. Box 2, Millry, Ala. 36558. Phone No.: 846-2512. Lake acres: 84. Land acres: 161. Fish species: Bass, bream, catfish, and hybrids. Additional facilities: launching ramp, rental boats, picnic tables, grills, overnight camping. Hours of operation: Sunrise to sunset six days a week. Closed Mondays.

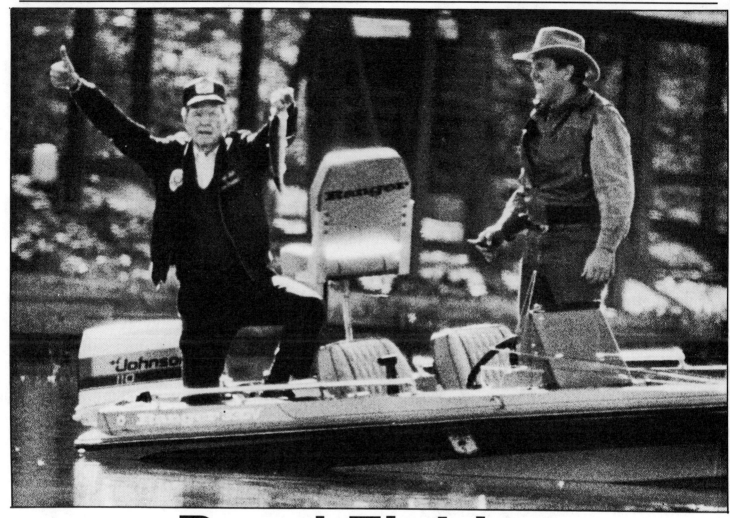

Pond Fishing

A n estimated 10,000 farm ponds and small lakes dot the Alabama landscape and a great number offer trophy fishing for those fortunate enough to have access to them. As a matter of fact, an incredibly large percentage of bass larger than 10 pounds and bream larger than one pound come from private waters. These farm ponds' and small lakes' better-than-average fishing is a result of two important factors.

First, fishing pressure is significantly less on farm ponds and private lakes than on public reservoirs. This lack of fishing pressure offers a calming effect to its inhabitants. Unlike public reservoirs where fish become "educated" by sometimes seeing five or six white spinnerbaits or 10 or 15 purple worms a day pass by their face, fish from these waters are less wary and strike more readily.

Secondly, the size of farms ponds and private lakes lend themselves to being better maintained than public reservoirs. Fertilization of the smaller bodies of water is common, whereas no public reservoirs receive fertilization.

Fertilization, it should be explained, accomplishes several things.

One, properly fertilized water blocks out sunlight and prevents unwanted vegetation, such as lily pads, from growing from the bottom and choking out a lake.

Two, fertilization provides a natural food chain for fish. Fertilized waters cause the growth of plankton which provides food for insects, as well as small minnows and other baitfish. These nutrient-ladened insects and small fish provide food for bream, which in turn provide food for bass and catfish.

The result is healthier, faster-growing fish than you'll find in reservoirs.

Even in farms ponds and private lakes not fertilized by man, they often receive the watershed from farms and gardens and as a result are fertilized much in the same way.

There's no better proof of what well-maintained bodies of water can produce than the two consecutive state record largemouth bass which came from private bodies of water no less than 57 days apart in 1987.

The first, a Florida-strain largemouth, was caught by Birmingham's

Lionel Bragan on Sept. 8 in a well-maintained pond in Cullman County. That fish weighed 15 pounds.

The second, caught by Birmingham's T.M. Burgin Nov. 3, came from a 22-acre private lake in Shelby County. That bass weighed 16 pounds, 8 ounces.

That lake, owned by Burgin, Norman Pless and Ollie McClung, is the picture of perfect management. It receives periodic fertilization, lime applications and 100 pounds of catfish food per day. The lake also gives up bream in the two-pound range and catfish over 25 pounds.

Incredibly, Burgin's bass wasn't a Florida-strain, state fisheries biologists determined. The state fisheries biologists believe it may be the largest non-Florida strain bass ever caught.

Fishing methods

One of the most exciting things about fishing farm ponds and private lakes is knowing that few are ever well-fished.

Unlike public waters where excellent fishermen chart every inch of every piece of structure with depth recorders, these smaller bodies of water are rarely ever attacked by anything stronger than a small jonboat and wooden paddle.

Fishing these farms ponds and small lakes is much like fishing reservoirs in that fish will relate to structure. Structure in these small bodies of water will range from fallen trees to ledges, humps, rocks, deep holes and standing drainpipes.

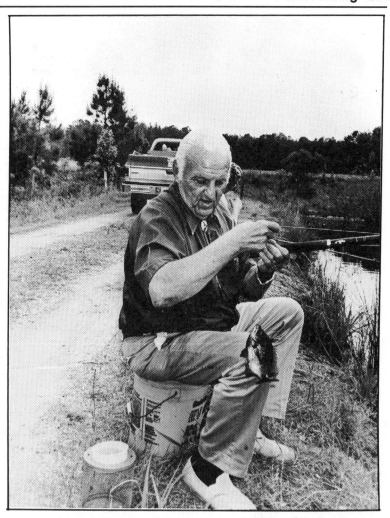

One of the most effective procedures in fishing these waters is, if possible, locating the owner or person who built the lake and has seen it without water in it. Then ask questions.

How deep is the deepest portion? Is that deep area around the dam or elsewhere? Were trees cut when the pond or lake was built? If so, do the stumps remain? How about creek channels cutting through? Any ditches or ledges? Was debris piled when the lake was built? If so, where? Does shallow water offer sand or pea gravel? Are there incoming creeks? How about underwater springs that may offer cooler or warmer water than the rest of the lake?

Having a few of those questions answered can immediately put the lake's underwater image in your head and give you an idea where fish are likely to hide.

If that isn't possible, a portable depthfinder will work wonders. Slowly travel the lake charting its depth. Using a pen and pencil, draw the lake's outline as you imagine it. Fill in depths on the map and record any irregularities such as ditches, humps and deep holes.

If you don't have access to a portable depthfinder, a string and lead weight works well, albeit slower. Mark the string off in five foot increments and drop it often as you tour the lake. Hopefully, you'll sometimes hang in stumps, brush and limbs and break off the string. The inconvenience that causes is well worth the knowledge gained.

This deliberate study of the lake may very well take up an entire fishing day, but it will result in better fishing. It is estimated that as much as 75 percent of the water in a lake is unproductive. Eliminating this water will mean you'll spend 75 percent more time fishing where the fish are going to be.

Bank fishing

Fishing from the bank of small lakes is an age-old fishing method that works well. But just as fishing from a boat, eliminating unproductive water is the key to successful fishing.

Bass fishing from the bank is sometimes more efficient than bream or catfishing because the bass angler is usually on the move and is more likely to stumble upon productive water.

Bream and catfish anglers are more likely to sit and wait in one spot for long periods of time before it dawns on them the area just isn't holding fish.

Locating structure from the bank isn't that difficult of a chore, however. A cheap pair of Polarized sunglasses will work wonders and many times when circling the lake on foot, the angler can see into the water and see fallen trees, stumps and other cover.

A small weight (no hooks) attached to the fishing rod's line makes for an excellent depthfinder. A cast and a glance at the line's angle will quickly tell you the waters depth. Throw often and look for ledges, humps and brush. A slow retrieve will help you feel for structure as the weight bounces along the bottom.

Freshwater Fish

Bass, largemouth - (black bass, trout, green trout, bigmouth bass). The largemouth bass is the most common bass found in Alabama waters. The stumpy largemouth is easily identifiable by its coloration, which begins as a white belly, switching to moss green and eventually to dark green as you go up the body to the dorsal fin. A dark horizontal line runs the length of the fish's body and separates the white underbody from its darker upper half. Other characteristics that separate the largemouth from its cousin, the spotted bass, is a jaw that extends past the eye, and a toothless tongue. The largemouth bass can be found in all reservoirs, rivers and streams in Alabama, as well as in private lakes and ponds. Two distinct strains of largemouth, the northern and Florida strain, are present in Alabama. The difference in these two species, however, is not obvious to the untrained eye. Scale counts and tissue samples are the only true methods of identification.

The state record for largemouth bass is 16 pounds, 8 ounces.

Bass, redeye - This bass is native only to central and northern Alabama and Georgia and southeastern Tennessee. In Alabama, it can be found in the Chattahoochee, Coosa and Warrior river systems. The redeye bass is similar to the spotted bass and smallmouth bass and they are likely its closest cousins. All have red eyes or a considerable amount of red in the eyes, scales on the base portion of the soft-rayed second dorsal fin and an upper jaw that doesn't extend past the eye. The fins are redder in color. The eyes will actually glow bright red when the fish feeds.

Bass, smallmouth - (smallie, brownie, bronzeback). The smallmouth bass has the almost identical shape and fin placement of its cousin, the spotted bass, but its coloration makes it impossible to confuse the two. The smallmouth has a dusky bronze color with distinct, dark vertical bars. It also lacks the dark horizontal bar that runs the length of the bodies on largemouth and spotted bass. The smallmouth has red eyes.

The range of the smallmouth is limited in Alabama. Almost all are confined to the Tennessee River and its drainage system. Some smallmouth have been stocked in Smith Lake, but catches are rare. Some smallmouth also have been stocked in Yates and Thurlow Reservoir.

Bass, spotted - (spot, Kentucky spot). The spotted bass is often confused with its cousin, the largemouth, but distinguishing between the two isn't difficult. The spotted bass has more of a torpedo shape than the stocky-looking largemouth. It also has several rows of spots below the horizontal dark line that runs the length of its body. These spots may be faint or distinct.

There are other identifying characteristics. Approximately 95 percent of all spotted bass have teeth on their tongue. These teeth appear as a raspy patch. A light blue/green coloring also can be found on the jaw of most spotted bass. The spotted bass' jaw does not extend past its eye.

Spotted bass can be found in all Alabama reservoirs but become less common south of Montgomery.

Bass, striped - (stripe, striper, saltwater stripe, rockfish, line-sides). The striped bass is a saltwater fish that has adapted to fresh water. This fish commonly swam from the Gulf of Mexico into Alabama waters early this century, but locks and dams have halted most of this migration. Striped bass are now stocked in most Alabama waters.

Having a slimmer body than the white bass or hybrid bass, the fish is easily identified by its silver appearance and its seven distinct, olive-gray stripes. These stripes are rarely broken, and the first stripe below the lateral line is complete to the tail.

The striped bass' tongue also has two tongue patches. Striped bass commonly grow to 20 pounds in Alabama. The state record is 55 pounds. The striped bass can be found statewide, but stocking has been discontinued in the Tennessee River.

1ST STRIPE BELOW LATER
DISTINCT AND COMPLETE

Bass, hybrid - (stripe, striper, hybrid bass, wiper). The hybrid bass in Alabama is a fish literally built in a laboratory. Biologists strip the eggs from the female striped bass and fertilize them with the milt of the male white bass. The resulting fry is technically a hybrid striped X white bass. The small fish are raised in laboratory jars, then holding ponds, before being stocked in Alabama waters.

This fish boasts several characteristics of both parents. It has the shorter, chunkier appearance of the white bass, as well as the white bass' frenzied feeding style. It has two tooth patches on its tongue, just as the striped bass, and the first stripe below the lateral line is distinct and complete to the tail. The remainder of its stripes are distinct and definitely broken, however.

Bass, white - (stripe, white laker). The white bass is much shorter and chunkier in appearance than the striped bass, and rarely do these

fish grow larger than three pounds. These fish are often confused with both striped bass and hybrid bass, but need not be.

It has the silver color and seven stripes just as the stripe and hybrid, but its stripes are faint, and the tongue has only a single tooth patch. The first stripe below the lateral line is not distinct, nor complete to the tail. The white bass can be found statewide.

Bass, yellow - (Barfish, brassy bass, stripe, streaker). The yellow bass can be found in the lower Coosa drinage area and in the Mobile Delta, as well as Inland Lake. It resembles its close relative, the white bass, but it's golden yellow sides and irregular stripes set it apart. It is smaller than most large bluegills, but has a more bass-like shape. The flesh is white, flaky and better tasting than the white bass.

Bowfin - (mudfish, mud pike, dogfish, griddle, grinnel, cypress trout). The bowfin is recognized easily by its flat head, long, stout body and its long dorsal fin. It also has a mouth full of sharp teeth. The males have a spot on their tail surrounded by an orange-yellow halo. Bowfin have lungs and can gulp air from the surface. The bowfin is considered poor as a food fish. The bowfin can be found statewide.

Buffalo - The buffalo is the largest member of the sucker family and is often confused with carp because its dorsal fin is similar. The buffalo can be distinguished from the carp in the fact it has no spines in any of the fins, only soft rays. The toothless mouth is large and wide and slants downward when closed. The smallmouth Buffalo can be found statewide, except in the Chattahoochee River drainage system. The bigmouth buffalo is found only in the Tennessee River. It is rarely eaten.

Carp - The carp is an imported fish, brought to the U.S. in 1877. The carp is actually a member of the minnow family and the largest member of that family. It is a close relative of the goldfish. All have deep bodies, small, retractable mouths, a forked tail, a single, long dorsal fin on the back and unusually large scales. Colors range from olive brown to gold. The carp has two soft barbels, or whiskers, on each side of the mouth. The carp is a delicacy in Europe, but rarely eaten in Alabama. It is found statewide.

Catfish, bullhead - There are several species of this catfish in Alabama. The black bullhead can be found statewide except for the Chattahoochee River. The brown bullhead and the yellow bullhead can be found statewide. The snail bullhead and the spotted bullhead can be found in the Chattahoochee River only. All are similarly shaped and their colors vary so greatly that colors can't distinguish them. All have double dorsal fins, barbels, large heads and lack scales.

Catfish, blue - The blue cat often is confused with the channel catfish, but its deeply forked tail sets it apart. The blue catfish also has a straight margin on its anal fin as compared to the rounded fin of the channel cat. The blue catfish is found in all Alabama waters except the Chattahoochee River.

Catfish, channel - (spotted cat). Adults of this species are silver-gray to almost black in their upper body, while juveniles may have scattered black spots. It may be distinguished from its close cousin, the bullhead, by its slender tail base and its widely forked tail fin. The channel cat is found statewide.

Catfish, flathead - (Appaloosa cat, yellow cat). This is the largest catfish found in North America, and 100-pounders have been recorded. Both the body and head are flattened, and the protruding lower jaw further distinguishes this fish from other members of the catfish family. This fish is normally a dirty brown color and peppered with black sashes.

This fish is found everywhere in Alabama but the Chattahoochee River system.

Catfish, white - (Albino cat) The white catfish is not white at all. The white cat is shaped like a bullhead, but has the coloration of the channel catfish.

Crappie, white - (papermouth, government perch, white perch). Many anglers believe there is only one species of crappie, with the white crappie being the female and the black crappie being the male. That is not the case.

The white crappie is a species that boasts a white/silver body with scattered dark spots that tend to form vertical bars on its body. The white crappie can tolerate much warmer water than the black crappie.

Any crappie larger than 3 pounds is considered a trophy. The state record for white crappie is 4 pounds, 8 ounces. The white crappie can be found statewide except in the Chattahoochee River.

Crappie, black - Other common names: papermouth, government perch. The body of the black crappie is basically silver in color and often boasts a purplish sheen. The body also is heavily peppered in black spots. The black crappie has 7 to 8 dorsal fin spines.

The state record for black crappie is 4 pounds, 4 ounces. The black crappie can be found statewide.

Drum, freshwater - The freshwater drum is easily distinguished by its two dorsal fins and its forked tail. It has a deep body, humped back and blunt nose. It's color is light, but has a light mist of hues ranging from pink to purple. It is considered a trash fish by most anglers in Alabama, although it is excellent when blackened, as is its saltwater relative, the redfish. The drum can be found statewide, except the Chattahoochee River drainage system.

Gar, alligator - This fish, which dates to prehistoric times, has a head much like an alligator, hence its name. It can be distinguished from other gars by its double row of teeth in the upper jaw, its broader

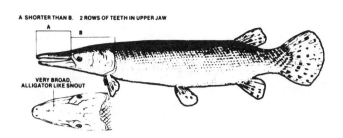

snout, and by the fact it can grow to 200 pounds. Other gars rarely exceed 50 pounds. It is found in many reservoirs and rivers.

Gar, longnose - The longnose gar is the most common gar found in Alabama. It has a longer, more slender body than other gars and has a long, narrow mouth full of teeth. It has large diamond-shaped scales that form a tough body of armor that often deflect arrows of bow fishermen. The fish isn't considered edible. Its green eggs are poisonous, causing severe illness in humans and death in small animals.

Gar, spotted - The spotted gar is easily identifiable by its spots, which cover its mouth, body and fins. It has a broad snouth and a mouth full of sharp teeth. It is often confused with the Florida gar, which is similar in appearance. It is possible to tell the difference by measuring from the eye to the rear of the gill plate. If it is more than 2/3 the length of the snout, it's a spotted gar, while less than 2/3 is a Florida gar. It can be found statewide.

Muskellunge - (Muskie, great pike) The muskellunge is a popular northern gamefish stocked in some Alabama waters. A long, slender fish, its dorsal fin is located well back on its body near the tail. The mouth is large and wide, and reaches well back to its eye. The mouth is full of teeth.

This fish has been stocked in the Tallapoosa River system.

dorsal fin vs. 19-20 in the walleye. The flesh is firm, white and delicious. This fish can be found in the Tennessee River drainage system.

Perch, yellow - (striped perch, lake perch, American perch) - This fish, rarely found in Alabama, resembles a bass, but is a true member of the perch family. Its most striking characteristic is its golden-yellow body with 6 to 8 dark bars which extend from the top of the back to the belly. It is also "sway-backed" in appearance. It can be found in the southern half of the state.

Sunfish, bluegill - (bream) The bluegill is found statewide in Alabama waters, including private lakes and ponds. A common forage for the largemouth bass, it is recognizable from other sunfish species by its solid black gill tab and the dark vertical bands that run the length of its body. Breeding males, which have a dark yellow or rust red breast, are well known for guarding the eggs in their beds during the spring spawn.

The bluegill is a noted hybridizer, often breeding with other members of the sunfish family to produce some unusual combinations.

Bluegill larger than 1-1/2 pounds are extremely rare, but the state record is 4 pounds, 12 ounces. That fish also is the world record. The bluegill is found statewide.

Pickerel, chain - The pickerel is often confused with the pikes and muskies because of its similar torpedo-like body shape, but it can be distinguished with its body markings. The sides are yellowish to greenish and overlaid with a chain-like pattern of black lines. This fish can be found statewide.

Sauger - The sauger is closely related to the walleye and the two are almost identical in appearance. The sauger has distinct dark spots on the dorsal fin. The sauger has 17 to 20 soft rays in the second

Sunfish, green - (green perch, sand bass) - The green sunfish has a larger mouth and thicker, deeper body than most fish in the sunfish family. The fish has an extended gill flap with is bordered in black around light red, pink or yellow. The body is usually brown to olive green with a bronze to emerald green sheen, paling to yellow-green on the lower sides and yellow or white on the belly. There are emerald or bluish spots on the head. The fish has excellent, white, flaky flesh. This fish is common statewide.

Sunfish, longear - (bream). Although this fish rarely grows larger than 1/4 pound, its coloration arguably makes it one of the most beautiful fish in Alabama waters.

Its white-bordered, jet-black gill tab, which gets considerably large in the adult male, is the fish's most distinctive characteristic. The fish's back and sides are blue/green and broken by dark vertical stripes. The body also is peppered with yellow and emerald spots. The belly and sides of the head of breeding males are often bright orange-red.

The state record for longear sunfish is open. Any longear sunfish larger than 0.4 pounds is eligible. The longear sunfish is found statewide.

Sunfish, redbreast - (bream). The redbreast sunfish's less-than-distinctive shape causes it often to be referred to only as a bream, but the fish can be identified easily by two distinct characteristics. Easily noticeable is the flaming, burnt-orange breast of the adult and the greatly elongated black strap-like gill tab, which gets longer with age.

The state record for redbreast sunfish is open. Any redbreast sunfish larger than 0.75 pounds may be entered. The redbreast sunfish is found only in the Coosa and Tallapoosa rivers and Lake Guntersville.

Sunfish, redear - (shellcracker, stumpknocker, bream). The redear sunfish is found statewide in Alabama, but rarely is it called by that name. The well-developed grinding teeth in its throat are used to crush snails, mollusks and other type shellfish, hence its more common Alabama name, shellcracker.

The redear sunfish is shaped much like its cousin, the bluegill, but several characteristics separate the two. The shellcracker is much lighter in color and lacks the light blue to dark blue gills. It also has a distinctive scarlet border on its gill tab, as compared to the solid black gill tab of the bluegill, and lacks the bluegill's vertical black bands.

The redear sunfish prefers clear, still water with abundant vegetation and finds its home around submerged logs and stumps.

The state record for redear sunfish is 4 pounds, 4 ounces.

Trout, rainbow - The rainbow trout isn't native to Alabama waters, but has been stocked in a few locations. Colorization of this fish varies greatly, but it is noted for its broad pink stripe alond the middle of the sides, interlaced with black spots. The fish is normally caught flyfishing, but can be caught on whole kernel corn and spinners. The flesh of this fish ranges from white to pink and is delicious. This fish has been stocked on a trial basis in Smith Lake, in the Smith Lake tailrace, at Tannehill State Park near Birmingham and Madison County Public Lake. Individuals have stocked the fish in several of the clear, cold streams near Springville in St. Clair Co.

Walleye - The walleye is another fish imported into the state and stocked in small numbers. It is the largest member of the perch family. It has large glassy, opaque eyes. The walleye, often confused with the sauger, differs from that fish by its dorsal fin has a prominent dark blotch. The lower edge of the tail is white-tipped. The flesh is white to pink and one of the best meats of freshwater fish. The walleye was stocked years ago and can be found in state's upper half and in the Conecuh River.

Warmouth - (Bream) The rust and orange-colored warmouth has a more robust shape than its daintier cousins in the sunfish family. Several rust-colored streaks radiating from the fish's red eyes across the gillcovers also help to identify the fish. Found statewide.

Saltwater Fish

Amberjack – An elongated (three and a half to four times longer than it is from top to bottom) fish easily identified by a dark slash mark that comes across the eye. They are greenish gray on the back and lighter on the belly. The fish averages from five to 30 pounds and is frequently caught by party and charter boat fishermen. Amberjack exceeding 100 pounds are occasionally taken from norther gulf waters. Inshore Amberjack are found over reefs and wrecks, seeming to prefer structure that offers a significant profile. The further offshore you fish, the larger the Amberjack seem to be. These fish cruise over the reefs, preying on smaller reef fishes. They are caught by fishing live bait (chofers, white snapper or other baitfish) or jigging with 3/4- to 2-ounce jigs. Once in a while one is caught on cut bait. Ten years ago, fishermen spurned Amberjack. However as other game species became scarce and restaurants popularized the firm, flavorful flesh, its popularity grew. Always one of the toughest fighters in the sea, in the past decade the Amberjack also has risen high in the rankings as a most sought after species. In fact, fishing pressure on Amberjack has led to stringent creel limits.

Barracuda – Feared only slightly less than sharks, these large, long, slender fish do have an impressive array of sharp teeth. However, their threat to man is greatly exaggerated. These fishes are silvery with black blotches up and down their sides. They are commonly four feet long, but have been known to range up to near 10 feet. These fish hang around reefs and wrecks, especially in the spring and summer months. They are not commonly sought after as game fish. Most often, in fact, fishermen notice they are around when a fish they have hooked comes aboard cut in half. They can be caught with live bait such as a hard tail or small bonito or with a tube lure fished at fair speed. Not many people eat Barracuda, despite its white flaky meat.

Beeliner (Vermillion Snapper/Mingo Snapper) – This smallish red-colored snapper goes by many names and is hauled from the gulf by fishermen in tremendous numbers. These fish average a pound or less, but in areas of light fishing pressure, particularly offshore, they are caught ranging to seven or eight pounds. These fish are common around reefs and wrecks year around. They are caught by bottom fishing with cut fish or squid on small hooks.

Black Drum – This heavy fish is distinguished by flesh-like chin whiskers. Younger ones are lighter with dark bars, becoming dark all over as they get older. While a record Black Drum will be more than four feet long and weigh mor than 150 pounds, they average less than 10 pounds. These fish are found in bays, particularly in deep holes, along ship channels and around oyster beds. The fish is usually caught coincidentially on cut bait by bottom fishermen. While the flesh is edible, the larger ones tend to be wormy. And, they have such tough hides many fishermen don't want to go to the trouble of cleaning them.

Bluefish – Shading from a blue-green back to silver sides, this longish fish commonly ranges from one to five pounds and one to two feet long. Larger ones as found along the Atlantic coast are not common in the northern gulf. They are found year-around, with several good runs coming in winter. This is a frenzy feeding fish, with cigar minnows the best natural bait and Rebel or Rapala lures the best artificials. A bucktail jig or bucktail spoon also is effective. Lures are cast, must as a bass fisherman would cast and retrieve a crank bait. These fish are found around jetties, near reefs and wrecks and schooling into bays. The fish have strong, sharp teeth which should be avoided when extracting a hook. While the Bluefish reputation as a fighting game fish is legend, its reputation as a food fish is lacking. The flesh is considered only average table-fare, soft and with a strongish taste. When fileting, take care to cut out the red streak running down each side. That improves the flavor dramatically.

Blue Runner (Hardtail) — This smallish shallow-water fish is greenish on the back and upper sides, shading to a yellowish-silver, and with translucent fins. It runs about a foot long on average, peaking at about 20 inches. They average about a pound, and almost never reach five pounds. The Blue Runner is found in greatest abundance from spring to mid summer. The fast, hard-hitting fish is important not so much for its food value, but because it is easily caught on small silver spoons or white jigs close to shore by surf fishermen, and because it makes such good live bait for larger game species. They are caught along the beaches, and particularly around jetties, cuts and channels. They also range into the bays. They can be caught with light spinning tackle. Food value is only fair, and usually prepared grilled. Be sure to cut out the dark lateral line when cleaning. Removal will improve taste of the flesh.

Bonito (Little Tunny) — This is a steely-blue and silver fish that looks to be a cross between a tuna and mackerel. It ranges from three to five pounds, fights like a fool when hooked and can be caught almost anywhere in the gulf - from piers to blue water. They are more rarely found in bays. They are found year around in the northern gulf, but the winter ones seem a bit smaller than those found in summer. While they are occasionally caught on cut bait by bottom fishermen, they are more frequently caught on live bait or on trolled mackerel rigs. For all its game fighting abilities, the fish is generally considered a dud when it comes to table fare. The meat is bloody and is used for shark bait as much as anything.

Boston Mackrel (Atlantic Mackerel/ Northern Mackerel) — This bluish, greyish, silvery mackerel is found in the northern gulf most commonly through the spring and early summer. It is caught in the bays and shallow gulf by trolling small spoons or jigs. The fish rarely weighs more than two pounds, with one pounders more common. Surf fishermen sometimes catch this small mackerel on light spinning tackle. These mackerel are edible with a taste similar to the other mackerels.

Cobia (Ling) — This large fish ranges in color from a dark yellow-brown to a dark bluish-slate color on top and shading to white on its belly. Often a loner, this fish averages 12 pounds or more. Fourty pounders are not uncommon, with a record fish going over 100 pounds. It is caught in the spring off the beach in the surf by casting feather jigs or pinfish to them. They also are caught the rest of the year over wrecks and artificial reefs with jigs and live bait. They are found both on the bottom and at mid water over wrecks. Small Cobia are caught in the bays in summer, but usually are under the keeper limit of 33 inches. These fish are excellent food fare.

Croaker — This fish can be identified by a mouth slung just underneath a rounded nose, dark vertical bars running from their backs down their sides and their small chin barbels. This pan-fish ranges upwards to four or five pounds, but is commonly found to weigh a pound or so. They are found all year long in the northern gulf in every location - offshore reefs, bays, channels, the surf. The fish is an important one because it can be easily caught from shore with light tackle by the casual angler. Once located, they are easily caught with small hooks on bits of cut squid, shrimp or fish. They are among the best tasting of the common bottom fish.

Dolphin – Don't get this excellent game and food fish mixed up with the mammal called by the same name. The fish looks like a rainbow of blues, greens and yellows, with the stripes running the length of its long, sleek body. The male differs from the female in that he has an extremely high forehead, giving him a squared-off look in the front. The Dolphin is among the fastest of all fishes, striking and fighting viciously. Size runs from small school Dolphin of two to five pounds to tackle-busters of more than 50 pounds. They are found both inshore and offshore, but rarely are caught from land or piers. Most are caught trolling with spoons, jigs or bait; however, bottom fishermen catch them on cut bait from time to time. Like Amberjack, Dolphin are easier to catch if the first one hooked remains in the water drawing others into a feeding rally. Dolphin are frequently found around floating objects and floating mats of grass or weeds. The fish is common in the northern gulf from spring through fall. Food value, excellent.

Flounder – This flatfish comes from a large family of fishes whose distinguishing characteristics are that they swim and lie on their sides, and often spend much of their time almost covered in the sand. A Flounder's top side is a mottled brown and it can change color to match that of its surrounding. Its other side (the one that sits on the sand) is white. This important game and food fish as a year-around inhabitant of the northern gulf, moving into shallow water, sometimes right up to the beach in warmer weather, and into deeper water off shore in cooler months. It averages a pound or two and can range to well over 15 pounds, although that is rare. It can be found in many types of water and terrain - depending on the season. They are caught in the gulf around reefs and wrecks, on sandy bottoms in bays, channels and the surf, and grass beds. Light casting or spinning tackle or light surf rigs can be used. Fish the bottom with live or dead shrimp or cut bait, live minnows or by casting a spoon or jig and retrieving it slowly along the bottom. Flounder also are gigged at night by shining a strong light into shallow water as you wade along or from a boat. If you move quietly and slowly, a Flounder will not move so long as the light is on it and can be easily gigged. Food value, excellent.

Grouper – There are 40 or more species of grouper, and several live in northern gulf waters - Jewfish, Gag (Black), Red, Kitty Mitchell, Yellowfin, to name a few. But more than 90 percent of those caught are the Red Grouper and Black Grouper. Groupers as a whole are large fish and prolific ones. From the giant Jewfish that can weigh more than 700 pounds to several sea basses that average less than a pound. The average red or black grouper ranges from five to 25 pounds. Most have the general shape of a fresh-water largemouth bass. These fish are found in bays, offshore and inshore, year around. Virtually all groupers are bottom feeders and will take cut bait on occasion, however live bait such as small white snappers or pinfish are much preferred. These fish live around reefs, wrecks, rocks and other underwater obstructions. These are excellent food fishes. Size and bag limits are under discussion by government authorities; check with local tackle shops for new legislation.

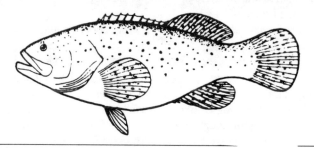

Jack Crevalle – It is a light olive-green color on the back, shading to gray, gold and yellow along the sides to the belly. It has a black spot on the gill cover and a deeply forked tail. It has a heftier body and blunter head than other members of the jack family. A savage striker and fighter, these are constantly moving fish. Due to their poor food quality, fishermen normally don't seek out Jack Crevalle. However, once a fisherman catches one he likely will catch more since they travel in schools. On light salt water tackle a 20 to 30 pound Jack Crevalle can fight for a half hour or more before being landed. They are fairly common in the gulf in spring and summer, moving into the bays in late summer and fall. They can be caught trolling just off the beaches, inshore and in channels along jetties. They also can be caught on cut bait. This fish ranges from three or four pounds to 40 pounds. Food value, poor.

King Mackerel – This may be the most important sport fish of the northern gulf. Anglers by the thousand troll inshore waters in the late spring, summer and fall for these sleek, silvery battlers, with whole fleets of charter boats dedicated to their capture. This pelagic, or migratory, fish makes its way up the Florida peninsula, arriving in northern gulf waters usually in April. Their arrival depends on the warming of inshore waters. The fish is black to navy blue on the back, shading to silver on the sides and white on the belly. Its tail is forked and its mouth has an array of pointed teeth. Migrating northward in the spring and then back southward in late September or October when the cool fall winds blow, the King Mackerel travel in schools, sometimes several miles off the shore, sometimes just outside the breakers. Some years they arrive in vast numbers; other years they are hard to find. Their size and where they swim seems to have little to do with each other. The pier fisherman casting with live minnows has a chance to catch a record-size king as does the charter boat trolling miles off shore. However, odds do greatly favor the charter boat because of its ability to move to the fish instead of waiting for the fish to come to it, as the pier fisherman must do. These fish average five to 10 pounds, and rarely range to more than 50 pounds. Light to medium surf or boat rods are needed. Fishermen cast for king with live bait, jigs or spoons from piers or from boats anchored or tied to buoys. More often, fishermen troll for kings around buoys and over reefs and wrecks. In the warmest months, schools of kings can be seen cutting through baitfish on the surface and are trolled for with dusters trailing cigar minnows. At other times they drop beneath the surface and the most effective trolled bait is natural or artificial squid. Trolling for king should be on the slow side. Due to fishing pressure, a limit of two fish per day has been imposed. Also there may be a closed season. Check with local authorities. Food value, good. The flesh is a bit soft and to the oily side, making it a bit stronger than some.

Ladyfish (Skipjack) – A long, slender fish, dark gray or greenish on the back, silver on the sides and white on the belly, the Ladyfish is most common in northern gulf waters in the spring and summer. The fish is common at a pound or two, but occasionally goes to five or six pounds and three feet in length. They are caught along the coastal sandbars, around cuts, jetties, and sometimes schooling in bays. This tough gamefish is no lady when it comes to vicious strikes and hard runs. Unfortunately, neither does she get respect as table fare. They sometimes are used as cut bait on fishing boats.

Marlin, Blue – These giants are blue on top, shading to white underneath. They average between 200 and 300 pounds, with the potential of reaching between 500 and 1,000 pounds. These billfish are found strictly offshore. While they never come inshore, they are found closest to land in the hottest part of summer. They can be found in northern gulf waters until the onset of winter. They are known for their speed, leaping ability and strong fight. Fishermen troll large jigs and natural bait at high speed in the ocean currents for

the Blue Marlin. While fishermen may spot several marlin in a day and even have three or four nose the bait, a single fish in a day is a success story. Blue Marlin is growing in popularity as a food fish, and is frequently grilled like fresh tuna.

Marlin, White – This marlin, much smaller than the Blue Marlin, is caught in the same area as his larger cousin. The White Marlin averages 50 to 60 pounds, and usually does not exceed 150 pounds. It is bluish-black on top, shading to white towards its belly. It has colored lines or hues of purple along its back. It is fished for in the same manner and areas as the Blue Marlin, and at the same times of year. Again, it is not caught in great numbers, but rather is sought for its fighting ability. While its food value is considered only fair, it is highly sought in certain parts of the orient.

Mullet – This round-nosed fish is silvery colored, and has faint stripes along each side. It averages around 2 pounds, and can be found ranging to near 10 pounds. It roams the surf and bays in both small groups and large schools, with schools growing quite large in the autumn. Fishermen often see large schools of them, but rarely do these fish take a hook. Mullet generally are vegetarians and moy are caught by netting. Than can be taken on small hooks baited with doughballs. They die quickly when out of water and do not freeze well.

Pinfish (Chofer) – Some call these bright blue and yellow striped fish sea bream. They are an important baitfish because they are one of the few salt-water fishes that can live long enough in captivity to be carried into the gulf as live bait. They also are important because there are lots of them almost year-around, close to shore in the surf, around piers, grass beds, throughout bays and even around near reefs. They can be reached by the casual fisherman and will take most any bit of cut bait and are tough fighters for their size. Kids love catching them. They grow to about a pound and a half, ranging in size and shape to that of the fresh-water bream. They are edible, but a strong iodine flavor makes them only fair eating.

Pompano – It is a roundish fish, silvery to yellow-gold in color, with a deep forked tail. It ranges upward to an average of just under two pounds. One over five pounds is considered trophy size. They are most commonly found in the northern gulf in the early spring and again in late September and October. The Pompany is caught in the surf on light tackle. Favorite baits are fiddler crabs, sand fleas and small jigs. Just cast the bait into the surf, then ever-so-slowly bump it along the bottom back to shore. Some say this is one of the finest tasting fish found in northern gulf waters.

Porgy (White Snapper, Key West Porgy) – There are actually several varieties of the white snapper as this fish is widely known, but they all are such close cousins few outside the marine biology community will appreciate the ifferences. Basically they are a whitish fish with pink or blue or green tinting, particularly around the head. One large species, known as the Key West Porgy, is mottled light brown over white. They can easily be identified by the strong small jaws and the molar-like teeth. The average one runs a pound or two, but they can range to 10 pounds or more. They can be found in bays, channels, around piers and pilings, on occasion. But mostly they are caught bottom fishing in the open gulf around wrecks and reefs. They are primarily bottom feeders, living on shellfish and crustaceans. Food value, good.

Redfish (Red Drum, Channel Bass) – This is perhaps the most famous and most sought after of the croaking fishes. It is a goldish, red fish, with a heavy body, underslung mouth and a dark spot at the tail, just before the tailfin begins. They are the largest and noisiest of the croakers. School reds range from three to eight pounds, while bull reds commonly run 15 to 20 pounds or more. They are found year-around in the northern gulf, with bull reds arriving in large numbers in the late fall. In recent years, season on Redfish in some areas has been closed because of the toll taken by heavy harvesting. When they can be caught, they are found in the gulf and in the bay, in deep holes and along channels. They are caught on live bait such as Pinfish or shrimp or on large spoons trolled slow and deep. Best fishing time is at slack tide. Medium to heavy surf or boat rods are necessary. Food value, good.

Sailfish – This is the smallest of the gulf billfish, and most commonly caught. Thanks to its huge dorsal fin - its sail - the Sailfish also is a unique gamefish. The Sailfish's fin and upper back are a deep blue. It has a green stripe along its side, and a greenish white underside. It commonly reaches 40 to 60 pounds and, unlike other billfish such as the marlin and Swordfish, the Sailfish ranges into inshore waters. It rarely is caught within a mile of shore, although juveniles have been caught in the bays. Mostly it is caught more than a mile off shore by trolling, usually with the same baits used for marlin or King Mackerel. Trolling tide and weed lines, much as one would for Dolphin, seems to produce good results. It roams the northern gulf from April through September. The pink flesh has excellent food value.

Sharks – The Hammerhead, Sandbar, Dusky, Bull, Nurse, Lemon, Tiger and Black Tip all are common in northern gulf waters. All have the distinctive dorsal and tail fins, and most have the distinctive pointed head - except for the easily identified hammerhead and the more flat, rounded head of the Nurse. The Hammerhead is a brownish shark, weighing to 600 pounds. The Bull, Sandbar and Dusky sharks also are grayish to brownish, with the Dusky and Bull ranging to 600 pounds, while the Sandbar ranges to

250 pounds. The Black Tip, Nurse and Lemon sharks are somewhat smaller, ranging up toward 300 pounds maximum. The largest shark common to the northern gulf is the Tiger, a grayish shark with light stripes, that will go over 1,000 pounds. They are year-around inhabitants, but summer months seem to bring them in larger numbers. Except for the Nurse Shark all have prominent teeth and can cause a nasty wound. All the sharks are found in the open gulf, with several such as the Black Tip and Sandbar also common in the bays. They can be caught trolling mackerel-type lures or by fishing cut bait (the stinkier the better) in mid water, preferably near structure such as a reef or wreck. These sharks are primarily nocturnal feeders, but can be caught day or night. Sharks are curious fish; if you anchor and fish for them with cut bait such as Bonito or Skate, make lots of noise and, if you are fishing at night, put out lots of light. Sharks will come around to see what's going on. Food value, excellent. However, if you intend to eat a Shark, gut and head it as soon as it is caught. The Shark stores urea in its liver. When caught the fish releases the urea into its body, tainting the meat. Dressing the fish immediately prevents the spread of the urea.

Sheepshead – This large member of the Porgy family is of typical panfish shape, and is distinguished by its dark vertical stripes on a lighter background. It has teeth like a sheep. The fish is common in the two to six pound range, and is frequently found in bays, channels and inshore. It is a favorite target for spearfishermen and for bridge, jetty, bay and pier fishermen. The fish is found nibbling on the crustaceans attached to pilings and rocks and is usually caught on shrimp. They are an excellent food fish, but difficult to clean due to heavy scales and big bones.

Snapper, Black and Red – These prized food fishes are of similar size and shape, however are easily distinguished from each other by the Red Snapper's bright red color and the Black Snapper's gray with just a hint of red tint. They are found in northern gulf waters year around, although heavy fishing has reduced their numbers. Since these fish multiply and grow fairly rapidly, proposed

size and bag limits should improve populations quickly. Ranging from keeper-size of just over a pound to trophy weight in excess of 40 pounds (the Black Snapper ranges to about 10 pounds), the Red Snapper averages two to 10 pounds. These snappers are commonly found in depths from 50 to more than 300 feet, hanging around reefs, wrecks or artificial reefs. While most are caught in the open gulf, more than one surprised angler has found them in the bays. They are notorious nibblers, and are caught bottom fishing on cut bait (squid or fish), dead minnows such as Cigar Minnows or live baitfish. These fish will work their way up the water column and larger ones are known to hang out at the edge of a wreck; thus, larger snapper are sometimes caught on an unweighted line with a live baitfish. These snappers are considered among the world's finest food fish.

Spadefish – This member of a tropical fish family is shaped similar to the Triggerfish and the Angel Fish. It is a silver fish with prominent vertical stripes. The bigger the fish gets, the lighter the stripes. The Spadefish averages just over a pound and can grow to more than five pounds. It is a schooling fish, lazily cruising back and forth over reefs and wrecks; sometimes moving near shore to be around jetties, piers or seawalls - anywhere it can find an abundance of jellyfish, a staple of Spadefish diet. They are easily located in warm months and can be caught on small hooks baited with bits of jellyfish. It is considered to have good food value.

Spanish Mackerel – This mackerel, next to his big brother King Mackerel, is one of the most important and most sought after fish along the northern gulf. Many feel that it tastes better than the King, and he certainly can be found in the area earlier in the year than the King. The Spanish is a long, slender fish of dark blue to silvery white from back to belly, and with gold spots along its sides. It has a mouth of serrated teeth and a deeply forked tail. This is a smallish mackerel, ranging from an average of about two pounds up to five pounds or maybe a little more. The heaviest run of Spanish along the northern gulf is in March and April, dying down as May wears on. There is another run in early August, usually of fish larger than those of the spring run. Stragglers can be caught throughout the warm-water months. These fish school about in the near shore gulf, into channels and the mouths of the bays, feeding on baitfish. They usually are caught by trolling small spoons or jigs or by casting from piers.

Speckled Trout (Spotted Weakfish) – This member of the drum family is shaped something like a freshwater trout, thus its name. It is darker on the back, changing to a silver color on the belly. It is spotted on the upper half of the body. Speckled Trout average from one to eight or nine pounds. They are found in channels, bays and brackish rivers emptying into salt water year around. However, cooler months are considered best for them because the fish frequently gang up in deep holes in bays and rivers when the weather turns cold. Otherwise they scatter across the wide bays, foraging for food. In winter months the best bait is live shrimp. In summer, however, bays are flush with smaller "trash" fish that will steal the shrimp before a trout ever has a chance at it. A live bait minnow, spoon or minnow-like plug that you would use for bass fishing are preferred lures. In summer concentrate fishing around grass flats where they roll into deeper water; fish from the deep-water side. They are considered good table fare, expecially when prepared fresh. The Speckled Trout is a soft-meat fish and does not freeze well.

Swordfish – This offshore gamefish is easily identified by the prominent sword-like bill, much broader than that of the marlins. The fish is purplish on the back and lighter on the belly. An eight-foot Swordfish is not unusual and it has been known to grow to 15 feet. It is a loner and lives in the deep waters of the offshore currents, but is sometimes seen basking near the surface or cutting through surface baitfish. It is caught by trolling natural bait, usually squid, mostly during the warmer months. It is a prized food fish.

Triggerfish – This rounded fish is easy to identify by its solid to mottled gray rough thick skin and by its three dorsal spines. One of these spines "unlocks" the others so they can be depressed and folded into a notch on the fish's back - thus, the trigger of the Triggerfish. It averages about a pound, and can range to more than 10 pounds. Triggerfish are found in bays, channels, wrecks and reefs inshore and offshore. They are extremely common on any inshore obstruction. They will take a bite out of anything that looks like meat, and are notorious bait stealers with their big squirrel-like teeth and tough lips (A note here: This can be a foul-tempered creature that won't hesitate to take a plug out of you if you are so careless as to get within biting proximity.) They are found year around, caught bottom fishing with cut bait, small hooks and light to medium tackle. For many years the Triggerfish was considered a trash fish, perhaps because its tough skin made it a little troublesome to clean. During the past decade, however, fishermen have come to prize the excellent firm, white meat.

Tuna – These fishes are shaped like torpedoes. They are swift, muscular, with pointed heads and forked tails. They vary in color but generally have a bluish, blackish to white cast, sometimes tipped with some other color as a distinguishing mark. The three most commonly found in northern gulf waters are the Bluefin, Yellowfin and Blackfin Tuna. The Bluefin is found offshore year around and is the largest of the three, reaching 1,000 pounds or more in gulf waters. It feeds almost constantly on fish and squid, and has been the target of heavy commercial fishing. The Yellowfin is another year-around offshore species. It is caught as close as 40 miles from shore in summer months, while is is most common more than 150 miles out in the winter. The Yellowfin ranges to 250 pounds or more, and is caught trolling as it feeds near the surfaces. The Blackfin is the tuna most frequently caught by northern gulf fishermen because it is the one found closest to shore, sometimes within just a few miles of shore. Once in a while one is even caught from a pier. It also is found offshore. The fish averages from 25 to 30 pounds, but can range to more than 60 pounds. The fish is found mostly in the summer as an incidental catch to mackerel fishing, and on rare occasions is brought up by bottom fishermen. It also is a fine food fish.

Wahoo – This fish has the same general shape of the King Mackerel, and may be confused with that fish. However the Wahoo can be identified by the longer nose and dark bars that run vertically on the body. They also are generally larger than King Mackerel, ranging to more than 100 pounds. The fish is found mostly in the summer inshore, but offshore year around. It is caught by trolling with mackerel-type and small versions of marlin-type lures. The Wahoo is an excellent food fish.

White Trout (Silver Trout) – This fish looks a bit like a small version of the Speckled Trout, but without the coloring or spots. It is white or silvery colored and generally runs from slightly less than a pound to about three pounds. It is common in bays and channels year around and can be caught in much the same way as Speckled Trout. Live or dead shrimp, sand fleas and fiddler crabs are favorite baits, as is a Sting Ray Grub artificial bait. The trout's soft meat is good when cooked fresh. It does not freeze well.

Whiting – Summer waders see the smallest of Whiting - little ghost-like minnows darting in and out of the surf. They grow to about three pounds, while they average a pound or less. The Whiting is a long, thin fish, mottled to silvery white, with an underslung mouth and a barbel on its chin. They are found in the surf and around channels leading into the gulf. They grub around the sand for bits of food. They are common and caught anywhere in the surf from the shoreline to beyond the breakers almost all year long. Light spinning tackle and smallish hooks baited with bits of shrimp, squid, cut bait or sand fleas is fine for Whiting fishing. Food value is excellent.

Rods and Reels

Fishermen, who at times have been known to stretch the truth, have for centuries told about days when the fish literally jump into the boat. Personally, I've never seen a fish jump in a boat, only out of them. That's why I own fishing tackle.

Fishing tackle is the bread-and-butter of fishing. An angler's rod and reel, or even a cane pole, is the single-most important piece of fishing equipment he owns. Fishing success is directly tied to that piece of equipment and how the angler makes it work.

A wide array of fishing tackle is used in Alabama. From a cane pole to a $100 graphite-composition rod tipped with a $100 reel, anglers have many tackle choices. The type fishing you plan to do and your budget should figure into the purchase of this type of equipment.

Here's the most commonly used tackle in Alabama:

Cane Poles

Fishing with a cane pole is fishing in its most simple form. A cane pole is simply a long pole which has been shellacked or lacquered to make it waterproof. A cane pole consists of the pole, a piece of line approximately as long as the pole, and the terminal tackle - usually a hook, float and a split shot.

An angler is severely limited in what he can do with a cane pole. Although it possible to outfit the pole with a small, inexpensive plastic reel, the line on a cane pole cannot be cast. The line rather must be swung out to the desired location, and naturally that location cannot be further away than twice the length of the pole.

Cane poles have other drawbacks, too. They are cumbersome and difficult to transport, even though some have ferrules that allow them to be broken into sections. Cane poles also are heavy. They can be tiresome during a long day of fishing.

Cane poles are not as common as they used to be, for spincast outfits have gotten so inexpensive they are now within the budget of almost all anglers.

Also, many anglers who still find the need of a pole have switched to an ultra-lightweight, fiberglass, telescoping pole. These inexpensive poles still have a drawback in that it is not possible to cast the bait.

Spincast Tackle

Spincast tackle, sometimes called a closed-faced or American reel, is the easiest to fish with, least expensive and most popular fishing reel on the market today.

Spincast tackle is almost always used in freshwater because its working parts are rarely stainless steel and they rust easily in saltwater. These parts also are contained within the reel housing and they are not easily accessible to be cleaned.

The inexpensive spincast outfit is perfect for panfish such as small bass, small catfish, crappie and bream. A spincast outfit is definitely the best outfit for a beginning or occasional freshwater angler because of its price and simplicity.

Spincast tackle is basic in that the line is held on a narrow, flat spool and is wound onto that spool with a pickup pin attached to a

Typical Spincast Reel

revolving disc. The entire retrieval apparatus is contained within a housing, with the line entering and exiting through the reel's nose cone. A push-button release that sets the line free and allows the lure to be cast can be found on the back of the reel.

Spincast reels are usually equipped with a simple drag system that allows the angler to fight and play bigger fish with the lessened liklihood of snapping the line. These drags usually consist of a star drag adjacent to the retrieval handle or a dial above the push button release.

Most of these reels are equipped with a anti-reverse button which prevents the handle from turning backward. This forces the drag system to absorb the pressure of an outgoing line when a fish makes a run. Another plus of the spincast outfit is that, unlike bait casting tackle, it's possible to fish a wide variety of weighted lures. The spincast is so versatile that either a tiny 8/32-ounce jig or a heavy topwater lure such as a Jitterbug can be cast equally well.

Baits fished with a spincast outfit usually consist of live baits such as worms, crickets, minnows or grubs, or artificial baits such as jigs, plastic worms or smaller crankbaits and topwater baits.

Spincast outfits are often neglected by the anglers which own them, but they take punishment remarkably well. A once-a-year cleaning (more often if the reel is ever submerged in water) and a twice-a-year line replacement is often all that is needed to keep the reel in top shape.

It should be noted that using too-heavy line (anything above 10-pound test is too heavy, 6-pound test to 8-pound test is perfect), allowing line to grow old and failure to keep the reel spool full are the most common maladies which make spincast reels inoperable.

Spinning tackle

Because of the availability of widely varying sizes of spinning tackle, it is the most versatile fishing tackle on the market. Ultra-light spinning tackle can be used to make a 10-ounce shellcracker feel like a fighting tarpon, or heavy-duty saltwater spinning tackle can be used to manhandle a feisty 35-pound king mackerel.

A spinning reel works on much the same principle as a spincast reel in that the weight of the lure is used to pull the coiled line from the reel. There are several major differences in these two reels, however. First, the spool isn't contained in a housing, hence it's common name of "open-faced" reel. Second, instead of sitting atop the rod as spincast and bait casting reels do, the spinning reels hangs below the rod. This makes the rod and reel combo well balanced.

The line is placed back onto the spool by being thread through a revolving bail, and this bail has a roller (to prevent line wear) on which the line rolls when it is retrieved. This bail flips open to

Typical Spinning Reel

disengage the line so the lure may be cast.

Unlike spincasting and bait casting reels which usually have handles permanently mounted on the right side, spinning reels usually have a handle that is interchangeable right or left. A spinning outfit is usually cast with the right hand and reeled with the left, but many anglers have a problem adjusting to that and choose to reel right-handed.

Spinning rods are usually limber, but their tell-tale giveaway is their abnormally large guides. These oversized guides allow the coiled monofilament to pass through them with ease.

As said before, spinning tackle comes in all sizes and can be used for almost any type fishing that is found in Alabama.

Ultra-light spinning tackle is a common sight when freshwater panfish such as bream and crappie are the quarry and the angler wants more action than simply winching the fish in with heavy tackle.

Medium-weight spinning tackle is common in the hot summer months when bass are suspended on ledges and a lightweight lure such as a grub or Sassy Shad is needed as a bait. Medium-weight spinning tackle is also common below Wheeler, Wilson and Pickwick dams in the fall when smallmouth make their move in the turbulent waters. Many anglers also opt for medium-weight spinning tackle when light line, a small bullet weight and a small plastic worm is needed for bass in clear water situations.

Heavy-duty spinning tackle is common along the Alabama Gulf Coast. This heavy tackle can usually be found being used by anglers fishing from Gulf Shores Pier, in the surf or sometimes trolling.

Bait casting tackle

Bait casting tackle is the tackle of choice for many bass fishermen. The lightweight construction, smooth retrieval and excellent drag system found on today's bait casting reel makes it a natural for this type of fishing.

The bait casting reels differs vastly from spincast and spinning reels in that the spool in this reel revolves as the lure is cast. This sometimes results in a spool overrun at the end of the cast. These overrruns are called "backlashes" or "bird nests". The difficulty in fishing with this type of reel has turned many anglers against it.

Many modern bait casting reels have integral devices designed to lessen the liklihood of these backlashes. A series of magnets inside the reel's left sideplate slow the spool's spin at the end of the cast. This "centrifugal" brake has made it possible for more anglers to use bait casting tackle.

The bait casting reel, which is nothing more than a winch, is equipped with a level wind system. The level wind system is a traveling guide for the line which puts the line onto the spool evenly. This level wind system disengages when the lure is cast.

The reels that are commonly used for bottom fishing and trolling in the Gulf are technically bait casting reels, but never is the bait cast with these reels. In bottom fishing, the spool is placed into the freespool position and the bait is simply lowered to the bottom. In trolling, the spool is placed in the freespool position and the bait is released to the proper distance behind the boat. In both cases, a thumb is usually placed on the revolving spool to prevent backlash.

These heavy-duty reels differ from their smaller counterparts in

Typical Bait Casting Reel

that most do not contain a level-wind system (you must use your thumb to direct the line onto the spool evenly), nor do they have, or need, magnetic cast control.

Fly fishing tackle

Fly fishing is considered by many modern day anglers as a type fishing best suited for pipe-smoking old stuffies and other elitists, but learning the art of "throwing line" can add an exciting new dimension to anyone's fishing.

Because the artificial flies used in fly fishing weigh virtually nothing, it is impossible to cast such a lure using its weight. That is why in fly fishing, the line, rather than the lure, is what is cast.

This makes fly casting dramatically different from other casting methods. Unlike in spincasting, spinning and bait casting tackle, the reel is a relatively unimportant part of the system. The fly reel is nothing more than a spool where extra line is stored.

To understand fly casting, you first must understand the basics of fly line. Modern fly line consists of a braided Dacron or cotton core covered with a PVC outer sheath. This line is extremely strong (30- to 40-pound test), waterproof and lightweight. Most fly lines are intended to float because the angler is attempting to lure a fish to the top of the water to catch an insect that has supposedly fallen there.

Floating lines come in many styles, including level lines, double tapers, weight forwards and "shooting heads".

Level lines are the same diameter throughout the length of the line. These lines are inexpensive, yet good enough for the beginning fly fisherman.

Double taper lines are standard thickness throughout their length, except for a taper at each end. This taper drops the line size down gradually except for the final feet, where the line is a small, standard diameter to the end. This configuration enables the fly to be dropped into the water with the most gentle of splashes and is designed not to spook fish.

Weight forward tapers have a thick bulge near the end of the line, with a pronounced taper with the final few feet being a standard diamter. This configuartion enables the angler to throw heavier lures such as bass popping bugs.

Another type of floating fly line is best known as "shooting head." Like weight forward lines, it is designed for long distance casting. Shooting heads are attached to long, low test-weight monofilament leaders.

Choosing fly line is simple. A universal code can be found on all fly line packaging to explain what is inside. It looks like this:

DT - double taper.

L - level.
ST - shooting taper
WF- weight forward
Numbers 3-12 - weight of line.
F - floating.
S - sinking.
F/S - floating/sinking.
A typical code may look like this:
L5F - level line, 5-weight, floating.
DT7F - double taper line, 7-weight, floating.

Although fly line is light, it is not small in diameter. It is for that reason that a length of monofilament leader (5 to 12 feet) must be attached to the fly line so that a fly may be tied to it. This leader may be attached to the fly line by either a knot or a a special eyelet which slides up into the line and will not back out.

Choosing line and the right fly rod and reel is easy. Learning to cast a tiny fly to a desired spot often proves to be much more difficult for some. Practice makes perfect and practice is needed to become a good fly fisherman. Start in an open field (water isn't needed at first) with a flyrod, line and a fly with the hook cut off.

Lay 10 to 15 yards of line directly out in front of the rod and grasp the rod in your right hand. Take the fly line in the left hand. Snap the line up and back over your right shoulder, stopping the rod at the 1 o'clock position. Pause to allow the line to pull tight, then snap the rod back to the front pulling the line with it.

Practice this maneveur until the line snaps smartly in both directions and the fly rolls out to the ground in a gentle touchdown. Once that is accomplished, you may begin to increase the length of the cast by pulling line out of the reel with your left hand.

Typical Fly Reel

Terminal Tackle

It's possible to own the most expensive rod and reel known to man, but as a fishing outfit, that expensive rig is no better than the terminal tackle that is affixed to it.

Terminal tackle is simply any of the tackle - hooks, weights, floats and swivels - that you attach to your line to aid in fishing.

Understanding the total terminal tackle picture can be a confusing nightmare. Literally thousands of options and variations in terminal tackle can be found as you circle the globe in search of bonefish, peacock bass, tuna, halibut, salmon, permit and the like. Fortunately for Alabamians, the options needed to catch the species of fish found in this state aren't nearly as complicated or numerous.

Hooks

Back up a bit. Hooks, a main component in fishing tackle, can be terribly complicated. If you were to make a point of trying to understand the seemingly endless variations in sizes, thicknesses, shank shapes and lengths, types of eyes and hook finishes, not to mention styles such as Aberdeen, Sprout, Kirby, Perfect,

O'Shaughnessy and Carlisle, you'd probably never have time to go fishing.

Understanding hook sizes is among the most confusing aspect of it all. Hook sizes range from size 22 to 1 (the larger number being the smallest hook), then once size 1 is reached, sizes run 1/0 to 16/0 (the largest number being the largest hook). Sizes 22 through 1 come in even numbers (22, 20, 18, 16, etc.), except, for some unexplainable reason, one odd number - size 1. To make matters more complicated, when hooks become larger than size 1, they are known as 1/0, 2/0, 3/0, etc., all the way to 16/0. These hooks sizes come in odd and even numbers.

Confused yet?

There are numerous styles of hooks on the market, each having a particular purpose. Each also has its own shank length, shank profile and shank thickness, not to mention point style.

There's no reason to cloud your mind with a complete understanding of hooks, however. Make a point of noticing what hook better anglers are using for your particular type of fishing. Apply that knowledge to your fishing.

Fish hook sizes commonly used in Alabama

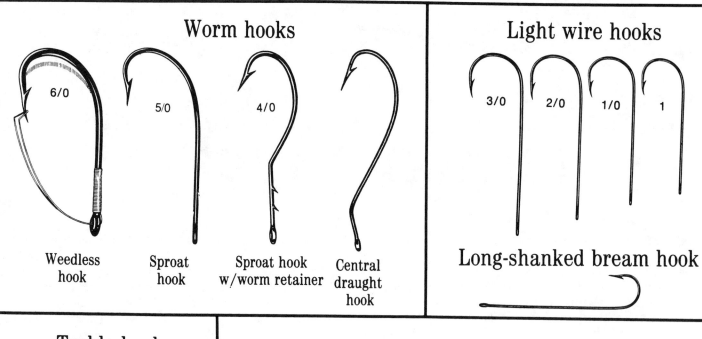

Worm hooks

Weedless hook

Sproat hook

Sproat hook w/worm retainer

Central draught hook

Light wire hooks

3/0 2/0 1/0 1

Long-shanked bream hook

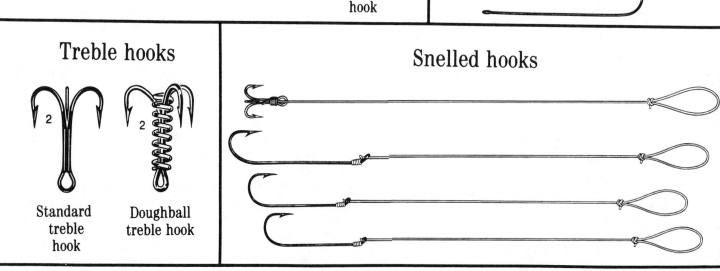

Treble hooks

Standard treble hook

Doughball treble hook

Snelled hooks

A few rules of thumb for hooks:

LARGEMOUTH, SMALLMOUTH, SPOTS

Hooks used to rig plastic worms usually range from 2/0 to 6/0, with 2/0 and 4/0 being the most common. These hooks may have an offset shank that allows the hook to be imbedded in the plastic worm without crimping the worm. A worm that doesn't hang straight on the hook will rotate when retrieved and will twist the line.

Some worm hooks may also have barbs along the shaft to make it difficult for the worm to slip off. Another option sometimes found on a worm hook includes a small wire loop that makes the worm weedless.

For live bait fishing for bass, a No. 2 to 2/0 wire hook causes little damage to live bait such as minnows and crawfish, but the smaller hooks could straighten under the weight of an extremely large bass. For larger live bait such as shad or water dogs, a 3/0 or 4/0 hook is needed.

HYBRIDS, STRIPED BASS

Hybrid and striped bass are, on the average, larger than largemouth, spotted and smallmouth bass. Live bait in the form of shad is normally used in Alabama for these species. If fishing exclusively for hybrids and small stripe, a 3/0 or 4/0 wire hook will suffice. For large stripe, a forged 5/0 hook may be needed. Striped bass that top 20 pounds are common in Alabama.

CRAPPIE

Minnows are the most common bait for crappie in Alabama. Gold-plated, extra fine wire hooks, No. 2 to No. 6, work well because they cause less damage to minnows than thicker shank hooks.

BREAM

The sunfish family has special hook needs. The mouths of these fish are extremely small, yet they have the ability to completely swallow most small hooks. The answer is a small throated hook with an extra-long shank. This extra-long shank makes hook removal easy. A No. 10 to No. 18 long-shanked, extra fine wire hook works well when crickets, worms and meal worms are used as bait.

CATFISH

Catfish in Alabama range from the half-pound cats found in farm ponds to the 50-pound-plus monsters found on the Tennessee River. Naturally, a wide range of hooks can be used for these fish.

Most cats you will fish for in Alabama will range from 1 to 5 pounds. A No. 2 to 2/0 wire hook works well on catfish this size. Catfish have extremely tough, spongy skin around their mouths and the thin wire hook penetrates easily. These hooks also work well with livers, gizzards, cut baits or other common catfish baits.

If custom-made catfish bait such as doughballs or stink baits are used, many anglers opt for treble hooks. No. 6 to No. 10 treble hooks work well, especially the hook is of the doughball-type hook. (see illustration).

Floats

Floats have been used for centuries for two purposes. They notify anglers when they are getting a bite, and to keep bait off the bottom and to present it at a level that fish can find it easily.

Floats come in many forms and are made from a wide variety of materials including cork, plastic, foam, balsa wood, balloons and porcupine quill. Floats can be used for any type of fishing that is done in Alabama.

Alabamians traditionally use corks too large for their needs. A cork should be chosen so it is large enough to ride upright in the water, but small enough that it can be pulled under easily and offer no real resistance to the fish. Fish that mouth a bait rather than swallowing it often spit it out when the feel the resistance of the cork. An easily sinkable float allows the fish to pull it under and swim away without detecting something is amiss.

Here are some float options available in Alabama:

PLASTIC FLOATS

The most common float used in Alabama is the red/white plastic bobber. This traditional float is inexpensive and its use is widespread. Bobbers are not the only float option available, however, and other type floats are often more effective in certain situations. The bobber's non-aerodynamic style makes it offer a lot of resistance to being pulled underwater.

Cylindrical-shaped plastic floats are much more effective than bobbers.

CORK FLOATS

Cork is naturally buoyant and thus makes for an excellent float. There are several drawbacks to cork floats, however.

Cork is a lightweight material and the result is a lightweight float. These cork floats are too lightweight to cast with most tackle. Most light cork floats may be cast on spinning tackle only.

Cork, in its natural color, is not very visible. Many cork floats are painted a bright color to increase their visibility.

PORCUPINE QUILLS

Porcupine quills, although a dying breed of float, make excellent floats for panfish. These floats stand on end easily, are slim enought to be easily pulled underwater and cast well.

BALLOONS

Small, round party balloons make excellent floats for stripe when live baits need to be drifted away from the boat in clear, shallow water in locations such as Smith Lake or Lake Martin.

FOAM FLOATS

Foam floats are probably the most popular floats used in Alabama. They are lightweight, but heavy enough to cast. They are also bright and inexpensive. Foam floats come in many shapes and sizes, including one that pops when retrieved. This float attracts some species of fish.

Balsa Floats

Balsa floats are durable and are used most often by the angler who takes his fishing for panfish seriously. Balsa floats are the most expensive type float found in Alabama, but they last longer and are the most sensitive to a fish's bite.

Weights

Weights, which are made of lead, have several purposes. Most importantly, they get the bait down where you want it and keep it there. They also, in some circumstances, provide weight to aid in casting.

A wide array of weights are used in Alabama. Some of the most popular include:

Bullet weights

These bullet-shaped weights are used when fishing for bass with plastic worms. The weight not only drops the worm to the bottom quickly, the tapered head guides the worm through underwater obstacles and helps avoid snags. These weights come in a variety of sizes.

Split shot

This is the most commonly used weight in Alabama. This easy-to-use weight simply clamps on to the line by squeezing it with pliers. One version, removable split shot, has ears that may be squeezed so that the split may be reopened and the weight removed from the line.

Split shot is used in all types of fishing in Alabama, but is most commonly used in bream, crappie and catfish angling.

Egg sinker

Eggs sinkers are commonly used when a large, heavy sinker is needed, as in catfish fishing. The egg shape allows the weight to be retrieved through rocks and other obstacles while minimizing the chance of snagging.

Bank sinker

Teardrop shaped bank sinkers are most commonly used in Alabama as weights for trotlines, and also by anglers fishing rock piles and jetties. This weight's shape allows it to be pulled through rocks easily. This weight shold not be used in current for its shape allows it to slide easily.

Casting sinker

A casting sinker is basically a bank sinker, but has a brass wire hanger rather than a cast-lead eye as the bank sinker. This weight casts better than the bank sinker because it doesn't wrap up in the line as easily as a bank sinker.

Clincher sinker

This long, thin sinker is basically an elongated split shot. The line is placed in the weight's slot and ears on each end are pressed down to keep the weight at the proper place on the line. Some versions have a rubber insert in the slot to keep the line from being damaged. This

Float options
These are the type floats most commonly used in Alabama

Peg float

Round plastic float

Natural cork ball

Quill float

Clear plastic float

Foam popping float

Cigar foam float

Balsa stick float

Clip-on stick float

Common float shapes

Heart body

Torpedo body

Round body

weight should be used when a heavy split shot is needed, or in trolling situations.

PYRAMID SINKER

Pyramid sinkers have sharp edges that dig into sand and mud, thus allowing the weight to hold to the bottom in current. Commonly used below dams when fishing for catfish, drum and hybrids.

Swivels

Swivels, like weights, come in many shapes and sizes. Most consist of two or three round metal eyes that rotate independently of each other to perform such functions as preventing line twist, attaching several components such as a bait and a sinker and to make for ease in switching lures.

The most commonly used swivels in Alabama are:

BARREL SWIVEL

Barrel swivels are used to connect fishing line to a leader. They are often used to keep a weight away from the bait. This is done by placing the weight on the line, attaching the barrel swivel and adding a length of leader.

BALL BEARING SWIVEL

These swivels are used when preventing line twist is a must, such as trolling with a lure such as a spoon that twists and rolls.

SNAP SWIVEL

The most common swivel used in Alabama. The safety pin-like snap on this swivel opens and closes easily to allow lures to be changed without having to cut line and re-tie knots. Inexpensive.

INTERLOCK SWIVEL

Similar to the snap swivel, this swivel is used for large fish when a stronger swivel is needed.

LOCK SWIVEL

The end of this wire snap hooks around itself and uses spring tension to keep the snap closed. This swivel is used in freshwater for big catfish and striped bass, but it's more common application is for bottom fishing in the Gulf.

THREE-WAY SWIVEL

This swivel is used to connect fishing line to two components. A common rig using this swivel consists of the line tied to one loop, a leader to one loop and a leader and weight attached to the other.

This rig can allow a weight to sit on bottom while a live bait or cut bait is held off the bottom. This rig is used for crappie fishing with minnows, catfishing in current with live or cut bait and bottom fishing in the Gulf with either live or cut bait.

Lead weights

Split shot: BB 3/0 7 6 5 4 2 1

Removable split shot

Bank sinker

Bullet weight

Egg sinker

Casting sinker

Swivels

barrel swivel

Ball-bearing swivel

Interlock swivel

snap swivel

Lock swivel

Three-way swivel

Other Tackle

Unfortunately for the ol' paycheck, there's more to fishing than rods and reels, terminal tackle and bait. Just as the accessories make the fashion-conscious female, they also make the fisherman.

Accessories can make or break a fishing trip. This author once went on a three-day deep sea fishing trip and left his polarized sunglasses hanging on the rearview mirror of his truck in the parking lot. When he returned, he was suffering snow blindness from looking at the bright white boat for three days.

Other trips have been hampered by spending time fashioning fish stringers out of coat hangars, building raincoats from Hefty bags and trying to tighten reel screws with dimes and the eyes of fish hooks. One especially memorable trip featured this author and two companions spraying down their bodies with WD-40 to repel biting gnats in the Mobile Delta. A new can of bug spray sat in the front seat of the car in the parking lot.

Before assembling a wide array of fishing accessories, sit down with a piece of paper and make a list of priorities. Having an electric hook sharpener or a set of electronic, digital, hand-held scales is nice, but not at the expense of not having a pair of needle-nosed pliers or a life jacket. The tendency is to go shopping and come away with neat gadgets, but that tendency can lead to some long, miserable days of fishing.

While putting together a list of accessories, these items should be at the top of your list:

Essential Items

PERSONAL SAFETY ITEMS

Personal safety items such as needle-nosed pliers, wire cutters, sunglasses, sunscreen, mosquito repellant, goggles (if you ride in a boat) and weather radio are covered in the section on personal fishing safety. Don't skimp here. Having these items with you can make the difference between a situation being minor and being trip-ruining or even life-threatening.

TACKLE BOX

A tackle box is an angler's purse. It's simple as that. In theory, a tackle box allows the angler to take the equipment necessary for a successful trip. Lures, terminal tackle, monofilament, stringers and a wide variety of other goodies can be carried with ease in a tackle box.

Modern boxes are wormproof, waterproof, durable and relatively inexpensive considering they can last a lifetime.

Many anglers opt for the smallest, cheapest box they can find, but many fishermen, including this one, believe the opposite route is the way to go.

An over-size tackle box, such as the Plano 797, can provide the angler with room to bring along all the things he really needs. The roomy top allows room for a pair of sunglasses, goggles (for boat riding), a neatly-folded rainsuit, mosquito repellant, sunscreen, weather radio, hand-held scales, fish attractant, wire cutters (for cutting hooks out of humans), needle nose pliers (for removing hooks from fish), jeweler's screwdriver (for reel repair), an extra drain plug for the boat and even an extra baseball cap (to replace the one that always blows out of the boat).

This large box also provides plenty of room for plugs, plastic worms, terminal tackle, extra line, reel oil and a few first-aid supplies.

This heavy, bulky box has caused this author some problems when a long-distance walk was needed from the car to the fishing hole, but its positives by far outweigh its negatives.

Not having to make several trips to the car is one plus, as is the peace of mind knowing that you always have everything with you.

Also, having a pair of wire cutters handy when someone gets hooked or having bug spray in reach when the mosquitos come calling makes the box worth its weight in gold. If nothing else, the box makes a wonderful seat when bank fishing.

What tackle box is right for you? You'll have to decide that. You may have $5 worth of tackle, or you may have enough to fill the back of a dump truck. Just be sure not to skimp and buy a box so small that it forces you to leave needed items - especially safety items - at home.

Many anglers who do different types of fishing have several different boxes, each loaded with the tackle they need for that type of fish.

An angler who bass fishes 90 percent of time and crappie fishes the remainder of the time may not see the need of having floats and crappie hooks with him 90 percent of time. Dividing the tackle up in different boxes makes sense.

Some anglers who do this have a tackle box or tote bag full of safety items that accompany them on every trip. That safety box or bag, along with the tackle box set up for the species that will be fished for that day, make a convenient fishing package.

If the amount of tackle you own is limited, a single box will usually suffice. A good, medium-size, inexpensive box with fold out lure trays makes an excellent selection.

LIFE JACKET

If you plan to fish from a boat, or if you fish from the bank and cannot swim well, a life jacket is a must.

This is a place not to skimp, but not for the reason you probably believe. In this day and time, any life jacket that can be found on the market can save your life. The secret is to purchase a jacket comfortable enough that you'll wear it, and of quality workmanship so it will be in once piece when you need it.

You'll find the old, orange, collar-type vest inexpensive and tempting to buy, but this is a life jacket you're probably not going to wear. Spend the money to purchase a fishing vest. You'll be glad you did.

STRINGER

If you fish from the bank, or from a boat that doesn't have a live well, you'll need a way to contain the fish you want to save and eat. A stringer is a must.

You can go two routes here, both of them inexpensive. A rope stringer usually sells for $2 or less, while a chain stringer costs only a little more.

If you have a choice, choose the chain stringer. On a rope stringer, fish are slid on top of one another, gill-to-gill, and they die easily. With a chain stringer, fish are connected individually to safety pin-like snaps. Used sensibly, this stringer allows fish to stay alive for a long time.

NAIL CLIPPERS

Probably no inexpensive item is worth more to the angler than a pair of nail clippers. These clippers easily handle the difficult chore of cutting monofilament fishing line.

Many anglers are quite adept at biting line in two with their teeth, but not only is this bad on the teeth, it also leaves a flattened end on the line which doesn't go through hook eyes or weights easily.

FISHING TOWEL

Of all the fishing items that can be found free, nothing is more valuable than a fishing towel. Keeping hands free of worm and fish slime can prevent an expensive rod and reel from being ripped from your hands when a fish strikes suddenly and unexpectedly. On more than one occasion, this angler has caught a fish, unhooked it, returned it to the water and on the very next cast thrown the rod and reel overboard because of slippery hands.

A fishing towel also serves as savior for clothes, for the natural reaction to dirty hands while fishing is to wipe them on clothes.

Towels have other uses, too. I keep several in the boat and use one to dip into the water to wash my face. A towel dipped into ice water and wrapped around your neck on a hot day not only prevents "redneck," it also rejuvenates you.

A towel may be nothing more than and old kitchen towel, or a rag out of the rag bag at home. An inexpensive, but wise investment is a golfer's towel. A golfer's towel has a brass eyelet stamped into it and a snap ring which lets you snap the towel to a belt loop or tackle box handle.

INSULATED ICE CHEST

If you eat the fish you catch, an insulated ice chest is a must. Too many anglers catch fish, do a good job of keeping them alive on a stringer, then throw them in the trunk or in the back of the truck for the ride home.

Fish have fragile meat which spoils easily. Fish should be kept in top-notch condition from the second they are caught until they are placed on the table.

If a fish can't be kept alive on a stringer, it should immediately be placed on ice. Fish being transported should always be kept on ice.

A few
non-essential items

As you get more involved with fishing, there will be items that you'll want to add to your fishing repertoire. Consider these:

HOOK SHARPENER

Fish hooks become dull with age. A sharp hook catches more fish.

RAIN SUIT

On a cold, rainy day, it can prevent the life-threateng situation of hypothermia.

CAMERA

There will be days you'll be proud of your catch and will like to show it off, but would also like to return that catch to the water. A camera is the only way that can happen.

FILET KNIFE

If you plan to dress the fish you catch, a good filet knife makes the task so much easier.

BINOCULARS

Binoculars may seem like a strange item to have on a boat, but many good fishermen use them religiously. During the spring and fall months, they'll help you locate schools of fish hitting shad on top of the water.

HAND-HELD SCALES

Have you ever kept a fish you would normally put back just bcause you want to know what it weighs? Scales help promote catch-and-release.

PLUG KNOCKER

Fishing lures are expensive. A plug knocker attaches to your line and slides down it to knock loose plugs that are hung up on stumps and other structure.

Lines and Knots

Line is one of the most easily damaged components in your tackle system. As excellent as present-day lines may be, all eventually wear out or need replacement for other reasons. Relying on it means you need to understand its strengths and vulnerabilities.

MODERN FISHING LINES

Fishing lines today are far better than those of 50 years ago. The best lines are made from synthetic materials, like nylon, which first appeared in the late 1930s. Natural fibers dominated line making for centuries. Synthetic lines gained acceptance because of their superiorities: greater strength relative to diameter, durability, freedom from rot and mildew and, in some cases, less visibility to the fish.

Over 90% of the fishing lines used today are nylon monofilament. "Mono," as it is often called, comes in several forms, referred to by chemists as "homopolymers," "copolymers" and "alloys" or "blends." Another kind of line looks like a mono, but isn't. Called a "cofilament," it consists of a polyester core sheathed by a polymer covering.

The different forms of nylon line start with a basic raw material called a "monomer." The monomer's structural unit is repeated in a chemical reaction to form what we know as a "polymer," of which there are various types.

A homopolymer is a resin consisting of a single polymerized monomer. A copolymer is formed by polymerizing two or more different monomers. And an alloy (blend) results from mixing two different polymers.

Although monofilaments are the most commonly used lines, other kinds of lines also enjoy some popularity. These include braided fly lines with poly-vinyl-chloride (PVC) coatings; wire and lead-core trolling lines; and braided nylon, Dacron or monofilament casting and trolling lines.

SELECTING THE CORRECT LINE

Line selection should be based on the type and size fish being sought, the fishing conditions and the type of rod and reel being used. For example, you need a tough, abrasion-resistant line for fishing around brush and underwater objects that might damage your line's surface. For ultralight spinning, you don't want a mono lacking a little "give"; line lacking any stretch won't withstand the shock of hook-set in really light-line tests. But these are only two qualities line manufacturers formulate to balance performance and durability. To varying degrees, these and other engineered qualities tend to affect how often you need to change line.

Line characteristics affecting your ability to cast, set the hook and see the line can be looked upon as control qualities. In this regard, it is important to consider limpness, stretch and visibility when choosing a line for a given kind of fishing.

For example, dead limp lines do not cast well from spinning reels because they do not easily spring free from underlying line coils on the spool. Resistance from this clinging shortens casting distance.

Similarly, lines that are too springy do not cast properly from revolving-spool reels, like baitcasting reels. When cast, such lines tend to fluff-up loosely over underlying line coils. Backlashes often result.

Some monos, cofilament and braided lines, by way of contrast, lie down smoothly on the spool. This helps them cast well from revolving-spool reels. But this very quality works against their best casting performance with spinning or closed-face spincast reels.

LINE STRETCH

The most popular nylon monofilament lines stretch enough to withstand the shocks and stresses of hook-set and long, sustained runs. For bass, some anglers prefer lines in which stretch is minimal, making hook-setting easier in such hard-mouthed species. Braided and cofilament lines have relatively little stretch compared with monos, making them great for hook-setting. They are also very strong. But one should respect their breakload ratings when battling heavy, fast-moving fish due to this lack of stretch.

VISIBILITY

Visibility refers to the color characteristics of line that allow you to see it while casting, retrieving and playing fish. Opinions vary among anglers and line scientists as to whether clear, color-dyed or flourescent lines are the least visible to the fish. One respected chemist feels there is little reason to believe a line's color frightens fish. He cites more trophy-class fish being caught on a colored flourescent line than on any other during a given year.

Many experienced anglers, on the other hand, believe there are justifiable reasons for using clear line in extremely clear water and flourescent line when poor light conditions or turbid water make watching clear lines difficult.

DURABILITY

How often you fish, the fishing conditions, and the strength and durability of your line influence how often you need to spool on fresh line. Most lines are damaged by coming into contact with fish teeth, gill plates, scaly skins and bills (in the case of sailfish, swordfish and marlin). They also are damaged when scuffed over underwater objects, like rocks and submerged stumps and trees. Severe line damage may occur when lines are cast through cracked or scored line guides. Additionally, the shock of hook-setting, pull of heavy fish and heat generated by the line moving rapidly under stress across guide surfaces also take their toll on a line's strength.

STRENGTH

Various kinds of strengths are formulated into lines to prevent breakage and prolong their life. Knot strength prevents a line from breaking when setting the hook or fighting fish heavy handedly.

The knots you use also are critical. So is how you tie them. Some knots are stronger than others. That's because they are designed to cushion the tough, synthetic lines to prevent their cutting into themselves.

Correct knot-tying techniques are needed to assure optimum knot strength. The twists or coils comprising a knot should be drawn up carefully. Lubricate monos with a little water to prevent their heating up while being drawn tight. Braided lines need no lubrication while knotting. The knot should be firmly and smoothly cinched up with a steady pull - never a quick jerk.

BREAKLOAD

Breakload is the pound-test rating of the line printed on the package label. Tensile strength often is confused with breakload. Tensile strength actually is a calculated value, rather than a lab-tested evaluation of breakload. Tensile strength expresses the mathematical relationship between breakload and line diameter.

ABRASION STRENGTH

This refers to a line's ability to withstand friction when coming into contact with objects above and below the surface. Much improvement has been made in nylon abrasion strength since the late 1970s. Despite this, all nylon lines (braid and cofilament too) eventually become worn enough to require replacement. Knots formed inadvertently in the line while fishing should be snipped off and the lure retied.

AGE

With synthetic lines, age is not the problem it was with lines made from natural materials. If synthetic line is protected from excess heat, sunlight, ozone and chemicals, it should retain its best qualities for at least a year, often longer.

Nylon, for example, is virtually ageless when stored properly, say the chemists.

THE REAL ENEMIES OF MONOFILAMENT LINE

Prolonged exposure to sunlight breaks down the chemical composition of nylon line. A clue to this is a bleached-out color. Excess heat literally cooks out nylon line strength. Trouble shoot this by looking for a chalky surface, excess stiffness and curl. Certain chemicals (like battery acid), chemical fumes and ozone either destroy or seriously weaken lines.

Prevent this by storing them away from chemicals and appliances with electric motors (like freezers and refrigerators) that generate ozone. Some anglers seal their bulk spools of line in large, zip-top plastic bags for fume and ozone protection.

FISHING DAMAGE

To detect line damage from fishing, inspect the line by sight and touch at least once an hour and after landing every fish.

Check the line from the lure's knot up through where it flexes against the rod tip while casting (two to three feet). If it feels rough or looks kinky and curly, snip off the suspect line and retie your lure.

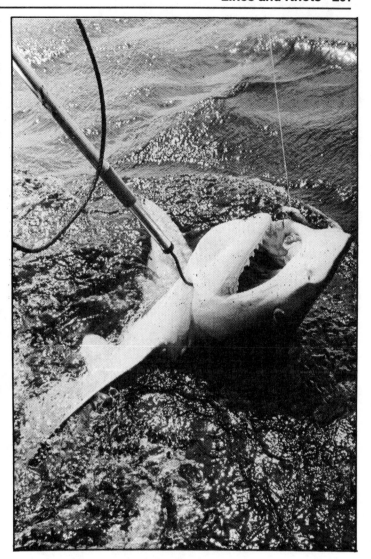

WHEN TO CHANGE LINE

Line-wise anglers usually change line on all their reels well before the start of each new fishing season. Select lines with qualities that dovetail with your tackle and methods, as well as the fishing conditions. Choose abrasion-resistant lines for fishing around brush and underwater objects. If you fish extremely light tackle, make sure your line has a little "give" to prevent break-offs when hook-setting. Use flexible lines for revolving-spool reels; those with slightly more springiness for closed-face spincast and spinning reels.

If you fish only a few days a year, then it is possible that changing line once a year will suffice. But if you fish frequently, such as one or more times a week, you may actually need to change line before every trip. Frequent anglers often examine the full casting length of the line after each day of fishing, changing line immediately if it appears the worst for wear.

Don't forget to store your reels and bulk spools of line as far as possible from heat, direct sunlight and chemical.

As one of your most important partners in fishing, your line deserves some mighty thoughtful attention

The Blood Knot is an excellent choice for splicing line. The know looks complicated but –with a little practice – lines can be spliced quickly and easily.

The Palomar Knot is one of the strongest knots available which will hold more than 90 percent of line strength. Notice the double line running through the hook eyes. Very seldom will the line break in the knot using this technique.

The Trilene Knot is another version of the double line used in the Palomar Knot. This know works equally well. The choice is which one is faster and easier for you to tie.

The Double Surgeons Loop Knot is another good knot to use on lures with no split ring. The only problem with the style is weving large lures in and out of the loop while making the tie.

The Improved Clinch Knot is one of the most popular and frequently used knots in all styles of fishing. This knot works well on live bair hooks and artificial lures.

Trilene Knot

1.   2.   3.   4.

Blood Knot

1.
2.
3.

Palomar Knot

1.   2.
3.   4.

Imporved Clinch Knot

1.
2.
3.
4.

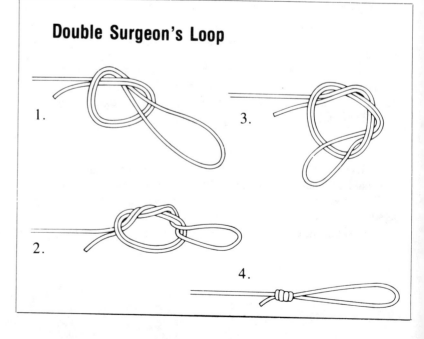

Double Surgeon's Loop

1.   3.
2.
4.

Artificial Lures

An angler may own the most expensive boat and tackle known to man, but if he isn't able to choose the bait appropriate for the moment and present it in an enticing manner, he may find catching fish an extremely difficult chore.

All too many anglers have favorite baits and stick with those baits come hell or high water. Those are the anglers who experience long hours of boredom sometimes interrupted by a moment of pleasure.

The well-rounded angler has a good understanding, as well as a good supply, of different lures. He may change lures several times a day, even several times an hour. He may fish one small stretch of bank during the late spring beginning with a buzzbait in the grass, switch to a medium-running crankbait on a stair-stepped dropoff, change to a topwater stick bait around shady pier pilings, then finish the bank with a plastic worm fished on the point.

All of the lures are capable of catching fish in the situations used, but a single one of those lures would have been ineffective most of the time.

Take time to learn about the vast number of lures available. Learn what lures work best in a given situation and why.

The lures listed below are most commonly used in Alabama.

Typical Plastic worm

Plastic worms

No lure has caught more bass through the years than the plastic worm. Several billion plastic worms are produced yearly in the U.S., with a major portion of them produced right here in Alabama. Mann's Bait Co., Southern Plastics and Fish World Lures, all based in Eufaula; Birmingham's Varnon Bait Co.; Sims Bait Co. in

Fairfield; and C&L Plastics in Pinson combine to produce more than 1 billion worms annually.

Plastic worms can be rigged hundreds of different ways and can be made to fish bottom structure, float on the surface over a weed bed, or anywhere in between. Plastic worms can be rigged weedless, or rigged with exposed hooks.

A plastic worm has produced almost every state record bass in Alabama, including the two most recent record catches.

Curly Tail Grub

Other plastics

Although the plastic worm is the most popular bait from plastics, a wide array of other baits also is available.

Plastic lizards are an effective bait in early spring when bass are protecting their beds, and also are good when flipping.

Plastic minnows, such as the Sassy Shad or Prissy Shad, are inexpensive, versatile baits that can be used for largemouth bass, spotted bass, smallmouth bass, white bass, hybrid bass, striped bass, crappie, catfish and drum in freshwater, and for flounder, speckled trout and other saltwater species.

Plastic grubs are similar to the imitation minnow and can be just as effective for the same species.

Other plastic baits include imitation frogs and crawfish for freshwater fishing, and imitation crabs, minnows, squid, mullet, eels and shrimp for saltwater fishing.

Lipped Crank Bait

Lipless Crank Bait

Crankbaits

The crankbait category of artificial lures is a wide-ranging one that lacks exact definition. Crankbaits, sometimes called "plugs," are almost any molded plastic or wood-bodied artificial bait that gets its action from the angler "cranking" it back to the rod. That excludes lures that fall into other categories such as topwater and spinner, etc.; even though those lures also derive their action from being retrieved.

Some crankbaits, called lipped crankbaits, have lightweight metal or molded plastic "lips." These lips are nothing more than a down-sloping hydrofoil that forces the lure to dive upon its return to the rod.

These lips come in many sizes, with the size and angle determining the lure's running depth. Some crankbaits are designed to run only 1 foot deep, while others are designed to run 30 feet and deeper. Water depth and depth of the fish should be taken into consideration when choosing a lipped crankbait.

Lipped crankbaits come in a variety of sizes, from 1/2-inch for crappie and bass, to those more than 1 foot long for stripes and saltwater species.

Crankbaits come in a wide variety of colors. All are designed to look like baitfish and are designed to wobble and put out erratic vibrations upon their return to the rod. This wobble is supposed to mimick an injured baitfish. Some lipped crankbaits contain BB's that rattle when they wobble.

In Alabama, lipped crankbaits are most commonly used for bass fishing. They work well whenever bass are suspended; these situations include those where weighted lures such as jig-and-pigs and worms would quickly go to the bottom and miss the fish. Lipped crankbaits work well in the spring and fall when bass are suspended on points, or during the summer when bass are suspended on ledges.

Lipped crankbaits may be used for other freshwater species such as striped and hybrid bass.

Lipless crankbaits are weighted, sinking baits that look much like lipped crankbaits, except for the lack of a lip. Rat-L-Traps, Cordell Spots, Kangaroo Shads, Pogo Shads and other such baits commonly used in Alabama fit into that category.

Lipless crankbaits are primarily used for largemouth and spotted bass fishing in Alabama. These baits are excellent for throwing into schooling fish that are chasing shad, for ripping past fish suspended on ledges and for buzzing over fish in underwater vegetation.

Lipless crankbaits are good for schooling hybrid bass. Smaller lipless crankbaits such as the minature Pogo Shad can be used for crappie fishing.

In saltwater, lipless crankbaits are excellent for speckled trout.

Spinnerbaits

Spinnerbaits have dramatically increased in popularity as a bass fishing bait in Alabama in recent years. The bass fisherman who doesn't have a spinnerbait in his tackle box is lacking one of the most effective bass baits available.

Spinnerbaits are effective on largemouth bass, spotted bass and smallmouth bass.

A spinnerbait is constructed on a wire frame and consists of a lead head, a hook molded into the head, a rubber skirt, and a single or double blade usually attached to the wire frame by a ball-bearing swivel.

Typical Single-blade Spinnerbait

Typical Bass Jig

Typical Crappie Jig

This sinking lure is normally allowed to go to the bottom before it is slowly retrieved, but it may also be fished at any depth from the bottom to the surface. The lure is almost snag-proof, capable of bouncing across logs, stumps, weeds and other structure.

Some of the state's better bass fishermen tip the spinnerbait with a pork frog. The pork frog not only gives the spinnerbait more weight for greater casting distance, it also also makes the lure more buoyant and makes it bounce better across bottom structure.

The skirts found on spinnerbaits most often come in white, black, brown, chartreuse, lime, orange and blue, or combinations thereof. The blades come in nickel, silver, copper and gold colors, as well as oval and willow leaf shapes.

Spinnerbaits are excellent for fishing vegetation, and are especially effective in murky, shallow water in early spring. They are also an excellent bait for night bass fishing.

is outfitted with a fringed rubber skirt, or a skirt made of feathers or hair. Rooster tails, horse hair, buck tails or squirrel hair are the most popular "natural" skirts. This type bait is normally used for bass fishing.

Another type of popular jig consists of a thin-wire hook molded into a smaller lead head. A plastic grub body is then added. This rig is normally used for panfish such as crappie. In salt water such jigs are used to catch flounder and, sometimes, speckled trout.

Jigs designed for bass fishing are often equipped with a plastic weed guard. These jigs are often tipped with a pork frog, creating the popular bass lure known as the "jig-and-pig."

Jigs come in a variety of weights and colors.

Typical Spinner

Spinners

Spinner are diminishing in polularity in Alabama, but are still effective nevertheless.

Spinners are a bait for small bass, sunfish, crappie, white bass and hybrids.

The spinner consists of a metal body, a main shaft, a hook attached to the shaft, and a small blade that rotates around the shaft when the lure is pulled through the water. Most spinners are tipped by feathers or a small rubber skirt.

The spinners found in Alabama are generally small and so lightweight that they can't be cast with bait-casting tackle. Most spinners are fished with spinning tackle.

Jigs

The jig is a versatile lure that can be used to take a variety of fish in fresh and salt water.

The traditional jig consists of a hook molded into a lead head and

Typical Spoon With a Single Hook

Spoons

Spoons once were just that, a lure built from the cupped portion of a spoon. The handle of the spoon was sawed off and holes were drilled fore and aft, one for the split ring for the line, another for the split ring to hold the hook.

Spoons of today are more advanced, as well as loaded with options. Some spoons are chrome-plated, hammered steel capable of excellent action that gives off flashes of light, thus mimicking an injured baitfish.

Other spoons are made of lead, and designed to be bumped in bottom structure for bass and crappie.

Still others are thin-walled in construction and outfitted with a single, fixed hook to be used for trolling.

Spoons are usually chrome or silver in color, but they sometimes are gold-plated or painted red or bright orange. Spoons come in a variety of shapes and weights, and may be outfitted with stationary or hanging single, double or treble hooks.

Topwater baits

A topwater bait is simply any bait, other than a buzzbait, used to entice fish to strike on the water's surface.

Topwater baits come in several varieties. They include:

Double-bladed Buzzbait

Buzzbait is constructed much like a spinnerbait, but the wire frame is equipped with a propeller rather than a blade. A buzzbait is designed to be fished on the surface where its propeller causes a disturbance that attracts bass.

Like the spinnerbait, a buzzbait is amazingly snagproof. It bounces across limbs, rocks, stumps and logs very well, but does poorly in vegetation. Weeds choke the propeller and inhibit its spinning, noisemaking motion.

Buzzbaits may have single or double propellers.

Hula Popper

Poppers are baits with a concave, or inwardly cupped mouth that gives out a loud "kerplunk" when yanked. The Fred Arbogast Hula Popper has long been the most popular popper for bass fishing, but other manufacturers make similar baits. Hula Popper is a registered trademark.

Jitterbug

Jitterbug is a torpedo-shaped bait with a spoon-like wing across its face that gives off surface disruptions that mimic an injured frog or baitfish. Jitterbug is a registered trademark.

Typical Torpedo Bait

Torpedo is a torpedo-shaped lure, usually made of plastic that sometimes has tiny propellers on each end. These propellers make ripples on the surface to attract fish.

Typical Stick Bait

Stick bait is a thin bait, usually made of wood, equipped with propellers on each end. It works on the same principle as the torpedo, but the bait is much thinner.

Typical Twitch Bait

Twitch bait is usually a shallow-running, floating, lipped crankbait. It is fished topwater by quickly twitching it forward 2 or 3 feet. This quick pull make the lure behave erratically by jumping side-to-side or diving.

Typical Bass or Bream Fly

Flies are used in fly fishing and come in a wide variety of shapes, sizes, forms and materials.

Flies are often tied to imitate insects, but some are tied to mimick everything from water rats to salmon eggs.

Materials used to construct flies include thread, feathers, fur, wool, nylon, tinsel and Mylar, but some are constructed from exotic materials such as peacock feathers and polar rabbit fur.

Most flies are intended for trout fishing, but in Alabama they are primarily used for bass and bream fishing. Bream and bass flies usually include waterproof cork bodies and are fished topwater.

Fishing for striped bass and hybrids with flies is becoming more popular. Many dedicated fly fishermen choose to tie their own flies, but commercially made flies are also available.

Live Bait

There's no question that something is special about fooling a trophy fish into taking an artificial bait. The challenge undoubtedly holds the fascination of many of Alabama's 500,000-plus licensed fishermen.

But never doubt that natural bait fishermen outnumber artificial bait fishermen. Crappie fishermen with their minnows, bream fishermen with their worms and crickets, stripe fishermen with their shad, catfishermen with their liver and other smelly baits and trotliners and jug fishermen with their cutbaits are in the majority in Alabama.

Fishing natural bait has its pros and cons, but mostly pros. There's no question it's easier to fool a fish with the real thing, and fish aren't as likely to spit out a natural taste such as worm or minnow as they are a painted piece of plastic or steel.

Also, most natural baits are easily available and inexpensive, often free. Red worms, wigglers, nightcrawlers, crickets, grasshoppers, grubs, wasp larvae, caterpillers, and catalpa worms often can be found right in the back yard.

RED WORMS, WIGGLERS, NIGHTCRAWLERS

Without question, worms are the most popular bait of any kind used in Alabama. Primarily used as a bait for bream and catfish, worms offer fish a natural-tasting food they love.

There are three types of worms primarily used in Alabama. Red worms are small, thin worms normally used for bream. Wigglers are slightly larger worms that have a lot of action. Wigglers are a versatile bait. They are used for bream, catfish and even bass.

Nightcrawlers are large, skinny worms with a flat head that are imported to Alabama from Canada, North Carolina and several northern states. They are usually 6 inches long or longer and have a tough body. They are expensive and usually are packed 16 to a box. Nightcrawlers are primarily used by commercial fishermen on trot lines.

Red worms and wigglers can be purchased from most lakeside tackle supply houses, or they can usually be dug wherever the angler can find damp, rich, loose soil. Shady hillsides with undergrowth and hardwoods are prime worm habitat, as are damp, shady agriculture areas left bare by animal traffic.

Shad and minnows can be netted or trapped in many lakes, and crawfish can be found in most small streams and water-filled ditches by anyone willing to turn over a few rocks. Mealy worms can be raised in a box at home.

For the angler in a hurry or the angler unwilling to hunt his own bait, most natural baits can be purchased rather inexpensively at tackle stores or marinas.

Natural baits do have a few drawbacks. They tend to be messy, and some carry odors. Natural baits also require special care and storage, and many require special containers. Unlike artificial baits, they can't be tossed into the tackle box and forgotten until the next fishing trip.

Here's a look at the most popular natural baits used in Alabama.

Many anglers construct their own worm beds or attractors by building up mounds of loose, black soil mixed with sawdust and peanut hulls and covering them with carpet or other heavy cloth. Perodic dousing of the carpet or cloth with a water hose insures the worms will stay close to the top of the bed where they can easily be dug.

The worm you choose should be based on what you plan to fish for. If bream are small enough to steal the worm and avoid the hook, go with red worms and stick the hook point into one of the worm's pointed ends and thread the worm onto the hook. This prohibits smaller fish from stealing bait and forces larger fish to inhale the hook when they take the bait.

For larger fish such as big bream, catfish and bass, a wiggler, or several wigglers, should be laced onto the hook by running the hook in and out of the worm along the length of its body. Unlike threading a worm on a hook, this juicy offering allows the worms to wiggle and further attract fish.

FIDDLE WORMS

Fiddle worms were once a staple for our grandfathers' fishing, but the inability to raise them in captivity and the difficulty in keeping the delicate worm alive has just about ended their use.

These worms, sometimes more than a foot long, derive their name from the age-old practice of "fiddling" them out of the ground. This is done by driving a stake into the ground and sawing through the stake with a hand saw. The resulting vibrations drive the worms from the ground.

Fiddle worms should be rigged like nightcrawlers.

CRICKETS, GRASSHOPPERS

Crickets are a wonderful bream bait, especially in spring when fish are bedding. A wiggling cricket floated over a bream bed is the safest bet in fishing that you'll get a strike.

Crickets are inexpensive to purchase - about two cents apiece. At that price, purchasing them makes more sense than chasing them around the backyard.

Only one method should be used to hook a cricket. Using a thin wire hook, enter the cricket at the rectum, pushing the hook up through the body and out directly behind the cricket's head. This allows the cricket to sit upright in its natural position.

Crickets are hardy and can be kept alive for up to three weeks by placing them in a plastic gallon milk jug and punching the top full of air holes. Crickets need to be fed and watered. A piece of raw potato and a damp paper towel dropped into the jug will provide the crickets with both food and water.

One good trick better bream fishermen use when bream are on bed is freezing crickets. Freezing will kill crickets, but will keep them fresh. Grasshoppers also make a good bait for bream, but grasshoppers are not sold commercially. If you want to save a few dollars, catching a few crickets out of the backyard beforehand isn't a bad way to go.

CATERPILLARS, GRUBS AND CATALPA WORMS

All three of these creatures are easy to find and make excellent bait.

Both caterpillars and catalpa (often pronounced ka-taw'-ba in Alabama) worms are the larva stage of butterfly-like insects and can be found in trees. Some build nests that are easily identifiable by a white, silky, opaque appearance.

These insects can be kept for long periods of time by placing them in glass jars (air holes should be punched in the lids) along with some of the leaves off of the tree from which they were taken. They can

be kept in the refrigerator or in a dark, cool basement.

They can also be frozen and used all times of the year.

The insects are messy, but worth the trouble. Both bream and catfish devour them.

The larger catalpa worms often are split down the middle with a knife or razor blade and turned wrongside out before being placed on the hook. This release their juices and gives fish a taste they won't let go of.

Grubs also make excellent bait, especially for bream. The white insects can be found in most backyards under rocks and at the base of shrubery.

WASP LARVAE

Were it possible to poll bream, wasp larvae might be their favorite snack, even outplacing the cricket. The tiny, white morsels stolen from wasp nests make for a delictable bait just the right size for hand-size bream.

Collecting wasp larvae can be a problem, however, and a painful one at that. Wasp larvae are present during the summer months, and because that is the wasps' young, they protect the nests with vigor.

The easiest, but most expensive solution is to use wasp spray, the kind that shoots a 20-foot stream of immediate death.

Another solution is to use a cane pole. The bait gatherer can quietly slip up on the nest, give it a long-distance whack and run like hell. A well-placed whack will knock the nest loose and let it fall to the ground. The nest can be retrieved later when the wasps decide to leave in search of a better neighborhood.

The nests can be kept in reclosable plastic bag until time for the fishing trip. The individual larva can be placed onto small bream hooks much like a worm or grub.

Wasp nests can be placed in resealable plastic bags and kept in the refrigerator until fishing time.

MINNOWS

Minnows have a natural place in the food chain of bass, bream, crappie, catfish, white bass and many other species found in Alabama. It's only natural that the small fish make excellent bait.

Two types of minnows are primarily used in Alabama – toughies and shiners. Toughies are a small, slick-skinned minnow sometimes called fatheads.

These minnows are hardy and take changes in temperature and rough handling well. Shiners are a larger, but softer and more delicate minnow. Sudden changes and temperature and rough handling will kill them.

A large variety of minnows can be found swimming across the state and all make good bait. They can be trapped in a minnow trap. The easy-to-use traps are available at many larger fishing supply houses.

Minnows may be hooked in one of two ways. If the minnow is going to be cast and retrieved, or trolled, it should be hooked through the lips. A thin wire hook should be forced through the lower lip and out the upper lip.

This allows the bait to be pulled through the water naturally.

If tight-line fishing, the minnow should be hooked through the fleshy portion of the back directly behind the dorsal fin, high enough to miss the backbone.

Piercing the backbone with a hook will result in immediate paralysis of the minnow and it will soon die.

CRAWFISH

Crawfish are an often overlooked bait, although they are naturally found in the food chain of largemouth bass, spotted bass, smallmouth bass, catfish, hybrid bass and striped bass.

As a bait, the crawfish's main drawback is availability. Rarely are they sold commercially, and collecting them can be time consuming. The smart angler sends the neighborhood kids on a mission into nearby creeks, streams and ditches with a 10-cent reward for every crawfish found.

Crawfish should be hooked through the fleshy tail and allowed to sink to the bottom. The pinching crustaceans will do your work for you as they crawl around the bottom and alert fish to their presence. Crawfish make an excellent bait on stumpy points and around underwater brushpiles.

SHAD

Shad, like minnows, are a natural part of the food chain for many Alabama fish, especially largemouth bass, spotted bass, smallmouth bass, striped bass and hybrid bass.

Two species of shad are predominant in Alabama: threadfin shad and gizzard shad.

Shad has some drawbacks because it is a less-than-hardy fish. Reduced oxygen, rough handling and sudden changes in water temperature can kill shad quickly.

A shad tank such as stripe fishermen use is a necessity for anyone fishing shad regularly. The tank should be white to reflect heat, round to prevent the shad from piling up in a corner and killing themselves and insulated to prevent sudden temperature changes.

The water should be kept cool (65-72 degrees) and should be treated with salt. Salt acts as a medicine and keeps the shad healthy and frisky. A good rule of thumb is to add one 32-ounce cup of salt

per 30 gallons of water.

Shad can be hooked in either of two ways. Many anglers hook shad through the lower lip and out the upper lip. This method is okay, but there is a better way.

The stripe guides on both Smith Lake and Lake Martin hook the shad through the nostrils. This location is free of vital organs and is tough. The shad can breath through its mouth and it stays alive and frisky.

Shad are plentiful and easy to catch on most bodies of water in the state. Shad school around dams, concrete walls near dams, in many sloughs and pockets, and along sea walls. A cast net will easily take shad schooling in shallow open water, while a shad dip net will take shad along concrete structures.

WATER DOGS

Many young fishermen probably believe water dogs are something new to fishing, but oldtimers have known for years that the large lizard-like creatures makes excellent fish bait.

The large salamander is a creature most fish despise. A water dog laid in an area where a bass is considering bedding will almost always result in a vicious attack. Country music star Tanya Tucker discovered this during a visit to the state in 1989. She dropped water dogs along the flats in Bibb County Lake during the spring and caught a 10 3/4-pound and 6-pound bass, the largest bass of her life.

Water dogs are difficult to locate and catch in streams, so buying them commercially (they firt appeared in Alabama tackle stores in 1989) makes more sense. They're expensive, however, usually costing $15 per dozen or more. Water dogs should be hooked through the lips or tail. They may be weighted to fish on bottom or floated under a bobber. They can be cast, or flipped like a jig-and-pig.

FROGS

Frogs are a natural bait often overlooked by fishermen. In lily-pad or grass infested lakes and ponds where frogs naturally appear, a kicking frog on top of the water in spring or fall is an explosion waiting to happen.

Frogs should be lip-hooked and cast gingerly around shallow-water structure when bass are hitting topwater.

Frogs aren't available commercially, so they have to be caught. Driveways and back porches near water tend to attract frogs at night during the summer. In early summer months, when frogs hatch, it is not uncommon to find hundreds of small hoppers.

The night before a fishing trip, a flashlight and a styrofoam cooler is about all you need. Shine the light in the frog's eyes to stun it, then capture by hand and place in the cooler.

SHRIMP

In the Mobile Delta, where brackish water results in the intermingling of both freshwater and saltwater species, shrimp are an excellent bait.

Shrimp should be hooked halfway up the fleshy portion of the tail, allowing the shrimp to swim freely. Shrimp may be Carolina-rigged and bottom fished, or hung from a bobber and floated off the bottom.

Shrimp make an excellent bait for largemouth bass, as well as saltwater species such as redfish, speckled trout and sheepshead.

Catching, Releasing Fish

People may claim to go fishing only to clear their minds, but never doubt that catching fish doesn't help the mind clear more quickly.

Catching fish is dependent on many factors. Anglers must first fish where the fish are, present a bait in an appealing manner, successfully detect the strike, hook the fish, fight the fish and land it. To catch a fish, the angler's mind, reflexes and tackle all must be in good working order.

Detecting the strike

One of the most difficult tasks for the novice angler is detecting the strike - the moment in which the fish takes the bait in its mouth. On rare occasions, a fish may inhale a bait and detecting the strike is unimportant. More often, however, a fish will carefully mouth a bait and if anything feels unnatural - hard plastic, steel, a strange taste or the feel of line pressure - it will spit it out. It's for that reason that detecting the strike is so important.

Reaction to a strike depends on the bait and type of fish. Live bait feels and tastes natural to fish so they are less likely to spit it out.

Different species of fish attack a bait differently, too. Catfish, buffalo, carp, drum and redhorse suckers often will lightly mouth a bait, spit it out and mouth it again. These fish will often swim off with the bait, feel line pressure, and spit out the bait again.

Small bream, meanwhile, will attack a bait and run, trying to keep other fish from getting it. Slab-size bream will often give an undetectable strike and the angler's first inkling a fish is on is seeing the line move.

Crappie also will often lightly inhale a jig or minnow, and the strike may be almost undetectable. Bass literally suck in a bait, giving an electric-feeling tap-tap on the line. They'll just as quickly

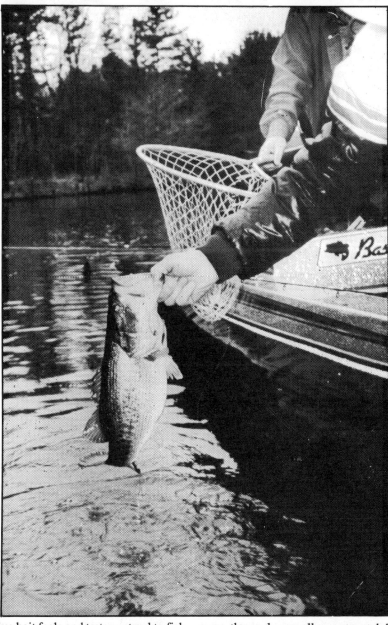

spit out the lure if it doesn't feel natural.

Striped bass and hybrid bass hit a lure on the run, never slower than 6 miles per hour, biologists say.

Setting the hook

The action of imbedding the hook in a fish's mouth is known as setting the hook. In trolling situations, or situations of a quickly retrieved lure, fish normally hook themselves and setting the hook isn't necessary. But in most situations, the angler must set the hook himself.

The type of fish, the type of hook and the strength of the line determine how the hook should be set.

In fishing for bream or crappie, the angler normally has to only watch a cork disappear, then lightly lift the rod tip to set the hook. The thin wire hooks used in this type of fishing penetrate the skin in the fish's mouth easily. The mouth of these fish tear easily and a strong hook set will pull the hook free.

In fishing for non-game species such as catfish and carp, the angler usually must watch his line and wait for the fish to swim off before setting the hook. To set the hook on these fish, the angler must give the rod tip a good pull from the 10 o'clock position to the noon position. Heavy wire hooks and treble hooks don't penetrate the rough mouths of the fish easily and a hard hook-set is needed.

In bass fishing with a worm, the angler must wait for the electric-feeling tap-tap before using a forceful snap of the rod, pulling up with both hands from the waist toward the face.

When bass fishing with crankbaits and other lures with multiple hooks, a lighter hook set is needed.

When tight-lining live bait for stripes and hybrids with rods mounted in holders on a boat, the fish swim away with a bait. These fish will mouth the bait from the rear, then turn the bait around head first before swallowing it. It is for this reason that a delay is needed before setting the hook.

Playing the fish

When it dawns on a fish that a hook is in its mouth and it is suddenly and unexplainably being pulled away from the direction it wants to go, its first reaction is understandably to escape.

The method of escape varies. Smaller largemouth and spotted bass may dive into cover, wrapping the line around stumps, pilings, brushtops or anything else that is handy. If that doesn't work, dazzling aerial displays often follow with the fish erupting from the water and trying to sling the lure by shaking their heads back and forth. Large bass rarely jump, choosing instead to break off the line in structure.

Smallmouth bass often try to sling a bait or lure by dramatic dives, followed by jumps of sometimes five and six feet into the air.

Catfish, drum, carp, striped bass and hybrid bass attempt to escape by trying to put enough pressure on the line to break it. Those species, when caught below dams in swift water, often run with the current and are successful in their escapes.

Smaller fish, such as bream and crappie, usually find today's modern tackle no match and can be reeled directly to the boat.

Some fish-fighting tips

1. Allow the action of the rod and the reel's drag system to absorb sudden runs by the fish. Never point the rod directly at the fish. This allows the line to absorb the shock, instead of the rod.

2. Adjust the drag on a reel every time you go fishing. Once a big fish is on, it's often too late.

3. It's best to set the drag too loose than too tight. When a big bass or striped bass makes a long run against the drag, the drag heats and expands, which tightens down on the drag.

4. Jumping fish are fun to watch, but the chances of losing a fish increase dramatically any time a fish leaves the water.

If the fish leaves the water, drop the rod tip and give it slack. This will make it more difficult for it to sling a lure by shaking his head back and forth. Better yet, discourage the fish from jumping by putting the rod tip down, even into the water, if necessary. This pulls down on the fish rather than pulling up on it.

4. Learn the technique known as "pumping." This age-old technique involves reeling the line tight, lifting the rod above the head to lift the fish up, then dropping the rod tip quickly as you crank in line. The rod tip is then lifted above the head again and the process begins again.

This procedure allows the angler to pull in a big fish when the big fish is putting up an extremely strong fight.

5. Never get a fish to the boat before it's ready. The shorter line it's on, the better its chance of escape. Wear a fish down, especially a big fish.

6. Once the fish is worn down and beside the boat, back off the drag considerably. Should the fish make an unexpected run on six inches of line, the loose drag will possibly contain it.

Landing fish

Which method to use in landing a fish is the choice of an angler. Smaller fish may be swung into the boat or onto the bank or dock, but larger fish need special landing procedures.

FISHING NETS

The net is the most common landing device, but landing a fish with a net isn't as simple as it looks. Many a well-meaning angler has lost his fishing buddy's fish-of-a-lifetime thanks to sloppy net work.

Never attempt to land a fish from the rear with a net, or make a swipe at a still-feisty fish as it makes a run at the boat. Wait until the fish is worn out and calm and lying on its side beside the boat.

Place the net into the water vertically, 3/4 of the way in. Use the fishing rod to slide the subdued fish into the net. Any sudden lunge the fish might make will drive it into the net.

Fish learn from birth to escape anything chasing it. A net coming at the fish from behind triggers that instinct. It's rare that you'll be able to net a fish from the rear.

LIPPING

Many anglers, and especially tournament bass anglers, prefer to land bass without a net.

How is that possible? Smaller bass are often simply swung into the boat to conserve time. Larger bass are "lipped."

Lipping requires a thumb to be placed inside the bass's mouth and an index finger to be placed under the lower lip. The fish can then be lifted out of the water.

When a fish is lifted in this manner, it is usually temporarily paralyzed and the hooks may be removed easily.

The drawback to this method, besides the fact the fish must really be worn down, is that the angler must handle the fish in close proximity to the hooks. A pair of needle-nose pliers should be used to remove the hooks to avoid a hook injury.

Safe release

If the fish is going to be released, it is often not necessary to put the fish into the boat or onto the bank or dock for hook removal. With the fish still in the water, a pair of needle-nose pliers can be used to take the hook out.

When using this method, wet your hands before handling the fish.

BEACHING

On occasion, the angler fishing from the bank will catch a large fish and find himself without a net.

The best method is play the fish in deeper water allowing the fish to tire itself out. The fish can then be led on its side into shallow water where it may be lipped. On medium-sized fish, it is often possible to lead the fish into shallow water and actually drag it onto the bank.

BRIDGE GAFFS

Anglers fishing from platforms below dams in Alabama, or anglers fishing from the piers on the Alabama Gulf Coast, are often faced with the predicament of having to land a big fish by pulling it up a great many feet. Monofilament fishing lines are often not up to the task.

These anglers often choose to use a bridge gaff. This device is made from either three or four large hooks welded together and weighted. This device hangs from a single rope.

The bridge gaff is lowered into the water, usually by a bystander, and the large fish is led over it. The bridge gaff is then lifted and the fish is impaled and raised to the platform.

Preserving tournament fish

Tournament fishing presents a different catch-and-release problem. Bass caught during a tournament cannot be released immediately. They must be kept alive until the end of the tournament so they can be weighed.

Fish can be kept alive in your boat with clean, cool water, oxygen, and chemical treatment to calm the fish and help them recover from injuries, including the touch of your hands.

How you handle the fish greatly increases or decreases the fish's chance of survival. If the fish is destined for release, use heavy enough tackle to bring the fish in without exhausting it. Then be careful handling the fish when you take the hook out. The use of nets isn't recommended because they can severely damage a fish.

The Bass Anglers Sportsman Society ran an experiment at major BASSmaster tournaments in 1988 using chemicals and ice in livewells and not a single fish was lost, BASS officials said.

Livewells in boats were treated with Catch and Release, made by Jungle Laboratories, and the livewell water was cooled with ice. Catch and Release is a tranquilizer and water conditioner. It also adds electrolytes to water to restore them to the fish. The water treatment also stimulates slime protection by fish. When a fish is stressed by being caught and handled, the cells which produce slime shut down. Taking off the slime has an effect similar to taking the skin off a human. There is a great likelihood of infection.

When adding ice to the livewell, try to lower the water temperature about 15 degrees from lake water temperature. Block ice works best, but bagged crushed ice will suffice. Loose crushed ice will not. A good rule of thumb is five to eight pounds of ice per livewell.

The best way to monitor water temperature is to put an aquarium thermometer in the livewell. The experiments with BASS disproved the old tale that you can't drop temperature on bass or it will kill them.

Finally, make sure the water in the livewell is clean. If you get your boat in shallow water and the pump sucks mud into the livewell, change the water, even if it means you have to dip it out. It's less harmful to the fish to change the water and leave them out of water for a minute or two than to leave them in dirty water.

New boats have aeration and recirculating systems in livewells. Older livewells circulate water from below the boat into the livewell. By keeping your fish alive, you can return to the water those you don't need for a tournament or don't want for dinner. They can grow and be caught another time.

Gaffs

The gaff is a standard feature on saltwater boats. A gaff is a barbless hook lashed to a long stick or pole.

Once a fish is brought beside the boat, the angler, or deckhand, uses the long-handled hook to impale the fish and lift it aboard.

Catch and release

One of the most important advances in sport fishing in Alabama is the advent of catch and release. Catch and release is a conservation tool in which fish are released back into the water unharmed rather than eaten or given away.

Unless the angler understands the art of catch and release, he may be defeating his purpose. Fish that are handled roughly are often returned to the water only to die later.

The largemouth bass is the most commonly released fish, and for good reason - it receives the most fishing pressure.

To release a bass, it's best to never remove the fish from the water. Handling the fish sometimes removes its protective coating of slime. While holding the fish in the water, use a pair of needle-nose pliers to remove the hook.

On occasion, it is necessary to bring a fish aboard the boat or onto the bank or dock to remove the hook. If that's the case, handle the fish by touching it only in the mouth area. Be careful not to allow the fish's body to brush against your clothing, the surface of the boat or dock, or the fishing rod or line.

Largemouth bass, spotted bass and smallmouth bass lend themselves to catch-and-release. Other species, such as bream, crappie, catfish, drum and carp, also can be released, but their release isn't as critical to an ongoing fishery as the release of the three bass species.

Striped bass and hybrid bass do not lend themselves well to catch-and-release, especially during Alabama's warmer months. Studies have shown these fish become heavily stressed during the long battle that is usually needed to subdue them. They often die after a long battle.

Cleaning Fish

Catch-and-release is a practice all anglers should implement into their fishing plans, but the angler who does not keep an occasional fish or two for his family's eating enjoyment is depriving them of one of the great joys of the fishing experience.

Approximately 240 species of fish and shellfish are fished for recreationally or harvested commercially across the United States, and approximately 65 of those species can be found in Alabama. Besides being a refreshing change in diet, fish are an inexpensive, healthy alternative to other foods. Fish are low in cholesterol, low in calories and when eaten regularly, have been proven to lessen heart disease.

But best of all, fish are tasty. Alabama boasts a large number of species of fish, both fresh and saltwater, that are excellent eating. If there is anything better than a mess of fried fish, hush puppies and french fries on a moonlit summer night in Alabama, the good Lord kept it for himself.

Alabama's fish are a valuable resource and a resource you should use wisely.

Cleaning Fish Is As Easy As 1-2-3

Panfish such as bluegill, bream, perch and crappie can be cleaned quickly and easily in five simple steps according to the fishing experts at Mariner Outboards.

Step #1: Hold fish upright on its belly or lay on its side and slice the head off at an angle, behind the gill covers.

Step #2: With the fish on one side, use fillet knife to cut along both sides of anal and dorsal fins.

Step #3: Using fish dressing pliers, pull out fins. Grasping them from the rear and pull forward. This should also remove entrails. If not, use finger to take out intestines, etc.

Step #4: Grasp skin at top corner and peel off with fish dressing pliers.

Step #5: Cut off tail! The fish is now ready for cooking your favorite way. Enjoy!

All you need to complete the job is a sharp fillet knife and a pair of fish dressing pliers. Follow these steps and refer to accompanying diagrams:

STEP #1

STEP #2

STEP #3

STEP #4

STEP #5

COURTESY OF **MARINER OUTBOARDS**

LIVE WELLS

One of the best innovations to keep fish alive and fresh is a boat's livewell. These aerated compartments circulate oxygen-rich water from the body of water into the boat to keep the fish alive.

The fish's chances of survival can be even further increased by the addition of certain chemicals into the livewell. These chemicals are designed to lessen stress on the fish, protect the fish's natural slime and lower the fish's metabolism. These chemicals are not harmful if the fish is destined for the dinner table.

During Alabama's warmer months, the addition of block ice, or bagged crush ice, can lower the water temperature in a live well and increase a fish's chance of survival.

STRINGERS

Stringers are an excellent way to corral fish and keep them for cooking, but many anglers use stringers incorrectly. Misuse of a stringer will often kill a fish rather than keep it alive.

Nylon string stringers are inexpensive and easy to use, but they are not conducive to keeping fish alive and in the best shape possible for the table. Anglers traditionally use these stringers by threading fish through the gills. Fish strung onto a stringer by this method don't survive long.

A metal stringer with numerous locking snaps is the best stringer. The sharp point of the snap should be inserted into the fish's mouth and forced through the fleshy portion of the fish's lower jaw before being locked. Not only is this method not painful to the fish, it also allows his gills to work. The fish will stay alive and healthy.

Many anglers choose to place their fish on a stringer, cut their throats, and allow them to bleed for several minutes before putting them on ice. Many anglers claim this produces a better tasting fish. It works exceptionally well on exceptionally bloody fish such as stripes and hybrids.

There is nothing wrong with keeping fish to eat, but don't overdo it. Keep only the limits set by Alabama law. Never continually keep fish just to give away to friends and neighbors to impress them of your fishing abilities. Instead, keep a camera in the boat and photograph the fish before you release them.

Pampering the catch

Unfortunately, fish need special attention above and beyond that of other meats. Fish begin spoiling the minute they perish. Anglers should make a special effort to either keep fish alive or get them onto ice where they will quickly cool.

COOLERS

Putting a fish on ice is an excellent way to keep it fresh. If the fish will be dressed in a matter of several hours, simply place the fish onto the ice whole. If it is not possible to dress the fish within a few hours, it is better to filet the fish or field dress it before placing it on the ice. To field dress a fish, insert a sharp knife into the fish's vent and split the fish toward the head, being careful not to puncture the intestines. Remove the entrails completely. It is not necessary to remove the head.

Coolers used for cooling fish should be filled with large crushed rather than small crushed ice, if possible. The water should be drained from the melting ice on a regular basis. Fish that are allowed to soak in icewater will ruin

FISH BASKETS

Anglers who want to keep fish captive and alive for long periods of time often use fish baskets. Fish baskets are made from wire and usually have a hinged top made of a material that allows the basket to float. Fish baskets are inexpensive and work well, often keeping fish alive up to 24 hours.

Fish cleaning methods

Just as there is more than one method to skin a cat, there's more than one method of cleaning fish.

Filleting, pan dressing and steaking are the most popular forms of fish cleaning in Alabama. Which is best? That is hard to say. It would be near impossible to fillet a 1/4-pound bream, and pan-frying a 20-pound catfish also would be impossible. Choose the method which best suits your taste and the size of the fish. It should be noted that experts at Auburn University estimate that 100 percent of a fillet is edible, 67 percent of a pan-dressed fish is edible and 84 percent of a steaked fish is edible.

FILLETING

Filleting has probably become the most popular form of cleaning fish in Alabama. Filleting produces a boneless piece of meat that can be fried, poached, baked or grilled. Filleting produces a piece of meat that can be eaten by all ages.

Not all fish can be filleted, and a general rule of thumb is that a fish larger than 1 pound is needed. It is also important to know that a cold fish or a semi-frozen fish fillets easier than a warm one.

Bass, catfish, large crappie, hybrid bass and striped bass and most saltwater species are prime candidates for filleting.

Fileting must be done with a sharp fillet knife. A fillet knife is long, thin and sharply tapered. Fillet knives are so thin that they are flexible.

To fillet a fish, it is not necessary to otherwise dress the fish. Simply follow these instructions for quick fish cleaning. It should be noted that an electric knife will work almost as well as a fillet knife on larger fish, and is much faster.

1. Lay the fish on its side on a cutting board. An old towel laid across the cutting board will prevent the fish from sliding.

2. Using a sharp fillet knife, make a vertical cut through the flesh just behind the gill plate.

3. Roll the knife so the sharp blade faces toward the rear of the fish.

Popular methods of dressing fish

Dressed or pan-dressed---whole fish with scales and entrails removed, usually with head, tail, and fins removed.

Steak-cross-section slices from large dressed fish.

Fillets--sides of the fish, cut lengthwise away from the backbone.

With a slight sawing motion, slide the blade close to the backbone, cutting through the ribs and continuing to the tail. Do not cut through the tail. Leave approximately 1/2 inch of skin intact.

4. Flip the fillet away from the fish, skin side down. The small piece of skin will keep the fillet connected to the fish. Using the fillet knife, grip the fish's tail and slide the knife between the meat and skin. With a sawing motion, cut the meat away from the skin.

5. Take the fillet and lay it on the cutting board. Use the fillet knife to remove the ribs for a boneless piece of meat.

6. Striped bass, hybrid bass and many saltwater species have a bloody streak in the filet. This streak has a strong fishy taste that many people dislike. This streak may be removed at this time.

Fillet option
If the fish is going to be cooked on the grill, begin the cleaning procedure by scaling the fish. Then, disregard step 4. Leaving the skin on the fillet holds the meat together when it is grilled.

Pan dressing
Pan dressing is another popular method of cleaning fish in Alabama. Pan dressing is the method normally used when fish are small and are destined for the frying pan or fish cooker.

All of the members of the sunfish family, as well as small bass and catfish can be pan dressed.

To pan dress a fish:

1. Lay the fish onto a cutting board. An old towel placed onto the board will keep the fish from sliding.

2. Using a fish scaler or a spoon, scrape the fish's scales off, being very careful to remove scales at the base of the fins. Scrape from the tail toward the head.

3. Insert a sharp knife into the fish's vent and slit the belly to the head, being careful not to rupture the intestines. Completely remove the entrails. Also remove the pelvic fins.

4. Make a vertical cut on both sides of the fish directly behind the gills. Don't dull the knife by cutting through the spine. Snap the head off.

5. Remove the dorsal fin by cutting along both sides of it. Grasp the rear of the fin and pull it forward and out of the fish.

6. Some people prefer their fish skinned, while others do not. To skin a pan-dressed fish, make a cut from the head to the tail the length of the fish. Roll the fish on its back and make a cut from the vent to the end of the tail.

Turn the fish back on its side, and insert your left thumb into body cavity from the front of the fish. Using a pair of pliers, grasp the fish's skin near where the back of the head was. The skin will peel off in a single piece. Flip the fish over and repeat the procedure.

Steaking
One of the best methods for preparing large fish for cooking is steaking. Steaking is simply taking a pan-dressed fish and cutting it vertically into manageable pieces.

Steaked fish lends itself well to grilling and baking, as well as both deep-fat and shallow-pan frying.

To steak a fish:

1. A chilled or semi-frozen pan-dressed fish steaks the best.

2. Using a sharp, strong knife, (not a fillet knife) begin cutting through the fish's back. Cut through the vertebrae and on through the fish. Cut the fish into pieces 3/4- to 1-inch thick. Cut these pieces from the tail toward the head.

3. Remove fat and all bones except the vertebrae.

Freezing fish

On most occasions, anglers find the need to freeze fish so they may be cooked at a later time. Freezing fish properly insures the fish will be fresh at cooking time.

Fish may be frozen by several methods. They include:

Freezing individually
One of the increasingly popular methods of freezing fish is to freeze each fish or filet individually. This is accomplished by coating a cookie sheet with a light coat of cooking oil and placing individual portions of fish on the cookie sheet. The cookie sheet is then placed in the freezer and the fish frozen.

The frozen fish is then removed and wrapped in freezing paper before being placed back into the freezer. This method allows small portions of fish to be prepared without thawing and wasting a large amount

Freezing in containers
Freezing fish in containers is another popular method in Alabama. Old milk jugs, paper milk cartoons, plastic containers and large, sealable bags are popular containers for freezing fish.

The fish is dropped into the container, the container is filled with water and frozen. Fish frozen by this method is good up to six months.

Sealable bags should only be used for fish without fins. Fins will puncture the bags and allow them to lose water.

Wrapping
Fish may be wrapped before being frozen. Freezer paper or aluminum foil work well. Fish wrapping should be of moisture-vapor-proof materials. Fish should be wrapped tightly with as little airspace between the fish and wrapping as possible.

Thawing Fish
Frozen fish should be thawed by placing it in the refrigerator, allowing 18 to 24 hours for a 1-pound package to thaw.

If quicker thawing is needed, place fish under cold running water. Never thaw fish by running it under hot or warm water or thaw at room temperature. Never refreeze fish.

Fishing Laws

This chapter is intended as a primer to Alabama's sport fishing laws and regulations. The Code of Alabama and the Alabama Regulation Book are the final authorities on laws and regulations relating to fishing and some laws may have changed since this printing. Contact the Game and Fish Division, District Game and Fish Offices or any Conservation Enforcement Officer if you have a question.

GENERAL INFORMATION

To qualify for a resident fishing license, a person must be a bona fide resident of Alabama for a minimum of 90 consecutive days immediately prior to purchasing the license. Resident annual fishing licenses are valid from August 1 through July 31 each year. Nonresident annual licenses are valid from October 1 through September 30. Licenses must be in possession while fishing.

It is illegal to kill or cripple any species of game fish without making a reasonable effort to retrieve same and include it in the creel limit. All live wells, boats, automobiles, etc. used in fishing shall be open for inspection by officers of the Department of Conservation and Natural Resources.

BUYING LICENSES

Alabama fishing licenses are available in all sections of the State at approximately 1,200 special license agents in many sporting goods stores, marinas, etc. and at all county courthouses. Nonresident licenses may also be purchased by mail from the Accounting Section, Alabama Department of Conservation and Natural Resources, 64 North Union Street, Montgomery, Alabama 36130.

Orders by mail must include applicant's address, driver's license number, proper payment, complete physical description including height, weight, hair and eye color and date of birth. Non-drivers must submit acceptable proof of current residence.

It is illegal to willfully or knowingly make a false statement to a licnese agent when purchasing a license. It is also illegal to lend, borrow, sell, buy, rent or use another person's license.

FISHING LICENSE REQUIREMENTS

Non-residents 16 years of age and older and most residents between 16 and 65 years of age must purchase an Alabama fishing license before fishing in Alabama. The following persons are exempt from the requirement of purchasing an Alabama sport fishing license:

1. Alabama residents fishing in saltwaters in Alabama.
2. Residents and nonresidents under 16 years of age.
3. Resident landowners or Alabama resident members of such landowners' immediate family who fish in a private pond on their own land.
4. Tenants or members of their immediate family who fish in a private pond on lands leased or rented by such tenants and who reside on such lands.
5. Residents fishing with ordinary hook and line (no rod and reel) in their county of residence. These fishermen must have reasonable proof of their county residency with them while fishing.
6. Residents over 65 years of age. They must have proof of age and permanent residence with them while fishing.
7. Residents and nonresidents fishing in Commercial Fee Fishing Ponds operating under permit from the Department of Conservation and Natural Resources.

FISHING LICENSE FEES

Resident Annual Fishing...$ 9.50
Resident Lifetime Fishing..$150.00
Resident Combination (Hunting & Fishing).........................$ 24.50
Resident Lifetime Combination (Hunting & Fishing) $450.00
Resident Disabled Fishing ....$ 1.25
Nonresident Annual Fishing ....$ 16.00
Nonresident Trip Fishing (7 day) ....$ 8.00

Prices listed include $1.00 issuance fee, except lifetime licenses.

Special license fees apply to residents of Georgia, Florida, Louisiana, Mississippi and Tennessee. Fees are the same prices as Alabama residents are charged to fish in those states.

Sport Fishing Laws and Regulations

SEASONS

All public streams, lakes and ponds in Alabama are open to fishing throughout the year except some State-Owned and Managed Public Fishing Lakes.

PRIVATE LANDS AND WATERS

It is illegal to fish in private waters without permission from the owners. It is also illegal to fish in public waters on or from posted private land without the owner's permission.

MEANS OF CATCHING GAME FISH

It is illegal to take, catch or kill or attempt to take, catch or kill any game fish by any means other than ordinary hook and line, artificial lure, live bait, troll or spinner in any of the public waters of this State. It is unlawful to use electrical devices, explosives, poisons or firearms to take fish of any species from these waters.

GAME FISH

The following species are game fish in Alabama: rainbow trout, all members of the sunfish family, including largemouth, smallmouth, redeye and spotted bass (commonly called trout or green trout), white and black crappie (commonly called white perch), rock bass, flier, warmouth, redbreast, bluegill, longear and shellcracker (commonly called bream). All members of the bass family including white bass, yellow bass, saltwater striped bass (commonly called rockfish) and hybrid striped bass (a cross between the white bass and the saltwater striped bass). All members of the pike family including redfin, grass and chain pickerel. The following members of the perch family: the sauger, walleye (commonly called jack salmon) and yellow perch.

Creel and Possession Limits

SPECIES DAILY LIMITS

Black Bass, All Species or Combinations 10
Walleye or Sauger 15
White Bass, Yellow Bass, Saltwater Striped Bass, and Hybrids or Combinations (no more than 6 of the 30 can exceed 16 inches in total length) 30
Crappie 30
Bream 50
Rainbow Trout 5

Limits, laws and regulations may differ on certain waters shared by Alabama and adjacent state. Please check the Reciprocal Agreement Section of the Alabama Regulation Book when fishing border waters. Limits may differ on state-owned or managed lakes. Size and creel limits will be as posted at each lake.

LENGTH LIMITS

At time of publication, a 16-inch minimum length limit on black bass was in effect at West Point Reservoir. Several State or Federally Owned and Managed Public Fishing Lakes also have bass length limits in effect. These are posted at each lake where they apply. No more than 6 of the 30 daily creel limit of white bass, yellow bass, saltwater striped bass and hybrid bass, or combinations of these may exceed 16 inches in total length.

USE OF SUNFISH FOR BAIT

The following species of the sunfish family may be used for bait in the streams and waters of Alabama: bluegill, redear sunfish, green sunfish and/or any other species of bream provided that no person has in his possession any sunfish or bream in excess of the daily creel limit, regardless of size. Other native game fish may not be used for bait.

SALE OF GAME FISH

It is unlawful to sell any game fish from Alabama or in Alabama from another state except (1) game fish raised in hatcheries and sold for stocking ponds and lakes; (2) non-native game fish (trout, salmon, etc.) raised for human consumption; or (3) largemouth bass, shellcracker and bluegill bream raised in farm ponds. Such game fish may only be sold under permit from the Commissioner of Conservation and Natural Resources.

TROTLINES

It is illegal to fish a trotline or snag line unless the end or ends of such line tied within twenty-five feet of the bank are made of at least six feet of cotton line and such line shall be attached to the bank or anchors with said cotton line only. All other anchors within twenty-five feet of the bank shall be attached to said line only with cotton line and any setline (bush hook) must be made of 100 percent cotton line. It is illegal to fish by means of any trotlines, setlines, snag line, commercial fishing nets, slat boxes, or wire baskets within one-half mile below any lock, dam or powerhouse.

WIRE BASKETS

Wire baskets may be used in certain counties to harvest nongame fish for personal consumption only. Persons holding a commercial fishing license may not fish with wire baskets. No fish taken in wire baskets may be sold or offered for sale. All game fish taken in the baskets must be immediately returned to the water. All baskets must be clearly marked with the license number and name of the person using and owning the basket. It is illegal for any person to fish with more than four wire baskets. Consult the Alabama Regulation Book or local Conservation Enforcement Officer to determine counties where wire baskets are legal.

GIGS OR GRABBLING

Commercial or nongame fish may be legally taken by gigs or by grabbling by hand by persons possessing a valid sport fishing license.

SPEARFISHING

The spearing of nongame or commercial fish solely for the purpose of sport in all waters of this State, both fresh and salt, shall be legal provided that the person engaged in the act of spearing shall be completely submerged and possesses a spearfishing license. This license is issued only by the Accounting Section, Department of Conservation and Natural Resources, Montgomery, Ala. 36130.

BOWFISHING EQUIPMENT

Any longbow, straight or recurve, or compound bow may be used for bowfishing (no crossbows); only solid fiberglass or solid metal arrows may be used or in possession. Barbed bowfishing heads shall not have sharpened cutting surfaces. Heads shall be designed so that the barbs may be reversed or removed to permit removal of the arrow from the fish. One end of a line having a minimum breaking strength of forty (40) pounds, and a minimum length of forty (40) feet must be attached to the arrow being used, and the other end of the line must be attached to the bow or some type of reel which is attached to the bow.

Licensed sport fishermen may take any of the following fish at any time by bowfishing: (a) shad, (b) white amur, (c) shark, (d) mullet, or (e) any fish designated as commercial or nongame except sturgeon, paddlefish or other protected species.

Consult the Alabama Regulation Book for special bowfishing regulations and exceptions.

Taking Minnows and Shad for Bait

It is legal to take minnows and shad by the use of a cast net, dip net, minnow jug, minnow basket, not to exceed 24 inches in length, 12 inches in diameter, with funnel entrance not more than one inch in diameter, minnow seine, the length of which shall not exceed 25 feet and the width or depth of which shall not exceed 4 feet for the purpose of taking shad or minnows for the exclusive use as fish bait. All game fish and all commercial or nongame fish taken by nets or seines must be immediately returned to the water from whence they came with the least possibly injury. Dip nets may be used to land legally caught fish.

Mussel Harvest for Bait

Licensed fishermen may use their hands, a rake or dip net no wider than 24 inches to collect Asiatic Clam Corbicula for fish bait. Harvest of any other species of freshwater bivalved mollusca with such equipment or sale of Corbicula harvested with a rake or dip net is illegal. Clams and freshwater mussels picked up by hand may be used for bait.

Life Jacket Requirement Below Dams

It is unlawful for any person to operate any vessel on the waters of this State within 800 feet below a hydroelectric dam and/or navigation lock and dam unless each person aboard, including the operator, is wearing a U.S. Coast Guard approved personal flotation device Type I, II or III.

Public Access Areas

Public access areas include state-owned, leased and/or operated boat launching ramps, associated parking lot, pier, and any real or personal property within the boundaries of said area. Such public access areas are for the use of the pleasure boating, hunting and fishing public in general only. The following is a synopsis of regulations for use of such areas:

1. Picnicking is allowed only where tables are provided.

2. It is unlawful to litter. Where trash receptacles are provided, only trash directly incidental to use of the access area may be deposited.

3. No camping, building of fires or loitering is permitted on access areas.

4. It is unlawful to discharge firearms on all public access areas.

5. It is unlawful to swim, dive or jump from any pier or ramp at any public access area. Any activity that interferes with the intended use of the access area by the public is forbidden.

6. No commercial, industrial or construction equipment such as barges, dredges, etc., are to be loaded or unloaded on public access areas without prior written authorization of the Commissioner of Conservation and Natural Resources.

7. It is unlawful to park vehicles or boat trailers where they will block use of the ramp or pier, or the approach, or interfere with the use of the access area by other persons.

8. Only licensed vehicles are allowed on public access area roads and parking lots. No off-road traffic and no all-terrain vehicles are permitted.

9. It is unlawful to solicit, sell, advertise or install any signs without prior written authorization of the Commissioner of Conservation and Natural Resources.

10. It is unlawful to willfully destroy, damage, cut or remove any tree, bush, shrub, plant or flower growing on any public access area.

11. All other state laws apply and are enforced on State Public Access Areas.

Public Fishing Lakes

State-Owned Public Fishing Lakes include all waters and land under the direct supervision of the Fisheries Section of the Game and Fish Division. The lakes are as follows:

Barbour County Public Lake
Bibb County Public Lake
Chambers County Public Lake
Clay County Public Lake
Coffee County Public Lake
Crenshaw County Public Lake
Dale County Public Lake
Dallas County Public Lake
DeKalb County Public Lake
Fayette County Public Lake
Geneva County Public Lake
Lamar County Public Lake
Lee County Public Lake
Leon Brooks Hines Public Lake (Escambia County)
Madison County Public Lake
Marion County Public Lake
Monroe County Public Lake
Pike County Public Lake
Walker County Public Lake
Washington County Public Lake (J. Emmett Wood)

Regulations and limits that apply at the above listed State-Owned and Managed Public Lakes are posted at each lake.

Commercial Fishing

This chapter covers only freshwater sport fishing laws and regulations. For information on freshwater commercial fishing, contact the Game and Fish Division, Alabama Department of Conservation and Natural Resources, Montgomery, Ala. 36130.

Violators

To report game and fish violators, call 1-800-272-GAME.

Alabama Boating Laws

This chapter is not intended to be a complete summary of the Alabama Boating Safety Law. It is, rather, an attempt to answer in simplified language, some of the frequently asked questions.

For a complete copy of the Alabama Boating Safety Law, write to: Department of Conservation and Natural Resources, Marine Police Division, 64 North Union St., Administrative Building, Montgomery, Ala. 36130.

LICENSING

Alabama law requires all boat operators under age 40 to take a written test to receive a boating license.

The operator can take the test and receive the license when he renews his driver's license. A "V" — for vessel — will be stamped on the driver's license. There is a one-time $5 charge. The license must be renewed, at no charge, when the driver's license is renewed.

People over 40 do not have to take the test but still must get a license.

Violation carries a minium fine of $100.

DUI

Alabama's drunken driving laws also apply to boating. There are fines and license suspensions on the first offense; fines, suspensions and jail on later offenses.

YOUTH LIFE JACKETS

Children under 8 must wear a life jacket whenever on a boat, unless inside an enclosed cabin.

PERSONAL WATERCRAFT

State law requires all boaters to wear life jackets on personal watercraft. Operators of such craft (and all motorized boats) must be at least age 12 and licensed.

OBSTRUCTED VIEW

State law prohibits boat operators from operating a vessel while their view is obstructed by people or equipment.

MAXIMUM HORSEPOWER

Beginning in 1998, no boats can be operated with horsepower over the vessel's maximum horsepower rating.

POINT SYSTEM

Alabama law provides a point system, much like the highway system, that allows for revocation of licenses for people convicted of multiple offenses such as speeding, DUI or reckless driving.

WHAT BOATS MUST BE REGISTERED?

1. All mechanically propelled vessels
2. All sailboats - regardless of size
3. All Livery (rental) boats The Boating Safety Law requires that no person shall operate or give permission for the operation of any vessel unless such vessel is registered in accordance with regulations established by the Commissioner of the Department of Conservation and Natural Resources and such certificate of registration shall be on the vessel at all times during operation for inspection.

WHERE TO REGISTER?

All boat owners may register, re-register or accomplish transfer of ownership of their vessel at the Marine Police Division, Montgomery, or at the office of County Judge of Probate and/or License Commissioner. Dealers and Livery operators must register with the Marine Police Division, Montgomery.

Boat owners must register their boats in the same months that they register their automobiles.

WHAT IF I BUY A USED BOAT?

If you buy a used boat that is currently registered with this State, you must make application for a transfer certificate to your name within 15 days.

NOTE: If you buy a used boat with an expired registration, you must currently register the boat before it is used.

WHAT ARE THE CLASSES OF BOATS?

Class 1 - Less than sixteen (16) feet in length.
Class 2 - Sixteen (16) feet or over and less than twenty-six (26) feet in length.
Class 3 - Twenty-six (26) feet or over and less than forty (40) feet in length.
Class 4 - Forty (40) feet or over.
Class 5 - Dealers or Manufacturer's registration.

WHAT IF I LOSE MY REGISTRATION?

A duplicate certificate for the one lost or destroyed may be obtained by application to the Marine Police Division, Department of Conservation and Natural Resources, Administrative Building, Montgomery, Ala., 36130.

Data required: (a) registration number; (b) name and address of applicant; (c) year last registered; and (d) correct fee. The office of County Judge of Probate and/or License Commissioner also may

---

Note: These are Alabama's boating laws as of May 1995. These laws are subject to change.

issue a duplicate certificate for the one lost or destroyed, provided the boat is currently registered and the boat's last registration record is in the county where application is being made.

What If I Sell My Boat?

The seller is required to notify the Marine Police Division within 15 days of sale of a vessel, if ever having been assigned a Certificate of Number in Alabama, specifying the name and address of the new owner and the number assigned to the vessel.

What If My Boat is Destroyed?

Notification within 15 days must be made to the Marine Police Division when a registered boat is abandoned, lost, destroyed or stolen.

What About The Registration Number?

Your permanent registration number appears in the top center of your certificate. This number remains with the boat regardless of change of ownership.

Where And How Do I Affix My Registration (Permanent) Number?

The registration number must be placed on each side of the bow of the vessel for which it was purchased, in such position as will make it clearly visible at all times.

The registration number must be displayed in three parts with a hyphen or equivalent space separating each part: AL-1234-AA; and be of a color that contrasts with the background - dark on light, or light on dark.

Numbers shall be block characters, not less than three inches in height excluding borders and must be of good proportion.

Characters of varying thickness, slanted characters, and scroll-type characters are not acceptable.

No other number awarded shall be displayed on a bow.

What Is My Validation (Decal) Number?

This is your Decal Emblem. Do not re-register your boat under the serial number on this decal - it is not your registration number.

The emblem must be affixed before or after, and in line with registration number on port and starboard bow.

How Do I Report An Accident?

Any operator of a boat involved in an accident causing loss of life, injury or damage in excess of $50 must, within 10 days, submit an accident report to the Marine Police Division, Department of Conservation and Natural Resources on forms provided by Marine Police Officers, Marine Police Division, or County Sheriff's Office.

What About Lights?

All vessels must be equipped with prescribed navigational lights when operated at night in accordance with the Boating Safety Law. Operators of all vessels must comply with the requirements for the type and use of lights when anchored or underway from sunset to sunrise.

What Are the Rules About Personal Flotation Devices (Life Preservers)?

Vessels less than 16 feet in length will have aboard a type 1, 2, 3, 4, or 5 personal flotation device for each person. Vessels 16 feet and over in length shall have aboard a type 1, 2, 3 or 5 personal flotation device for each person and at least one type 4 on board as a throwable device.

CAUTION: Personal flotation devices must be accessible and of the proper size.

CAUTION: A type V flotation device is a PFD approved for restricted uses.

Type V PFD's must be worn in open boats and when on deck of larger boats in order to be classified as U.S. Coast Guard approved. (See the chapter on Boating Safety for more details.)

What About Fire Extinguishers?

All vessels, as herein designated, must be equipped with a serviceable U.S. Coast Guard approved fire extinguisher of the type and capacity indicated.

1. All inboard and inboard/outboard vessels, regardless of size, and all motor vessels having closed compartments wherein portable fuel tanks are stored or having permanently installed fuel tanks shall have a hand portable or semi-portable fire extinguisher using carbon dioxide ($CO2$) foam, or other chemical ingredient such as is commonly used for extinguishing gasoline fires or petroleum fires.

Such fire extinguisher shall be approved by the Coast Guard.

2. All vessels equipped with any butane gas, propane gas, kerosene, gasoline or petroleum product consuming device except outboard motors, such as a stove or lantern shall have a hand portable or semi-portable fire extinguisher using carbon dioxide ($CO2$), foam, or other chemical ingredient such as is commonly used for extinguishing a fire produced by the use of such device. Such fire extinguisher shall be approved by the U.S. Coast Guard.

3. All motor vessels having closed or semi-closed cabins and any vessel with sleeping accommodations shall have a hand portable fire extinguisher or semi-portable fire extinguisher using carbon dioxide (CO_2), foam, or other chemical such as is commonly used for extinguishing fires.

Must My Boat Have A Flame Arrestor?

Every motorboat using gasoline as fuel except outboard motors shall have the carburetor or carburetors of every engine therein equipped with a U.S. Coast Guard approved flame arrestor.

Does My Boat Need An Emergency Engine Cut-Off Switch?

No person shall operate or give permission to operate any vessel less than eighteen (18) feet in length, having an open cockpit and having more than fifty (50) horsepower, unless said vessel is equipped with an emergency engine or motor shut-off switch.

What About A Sound Device?

All vessels sixteen (16) feet or more in length, must have onboard, the proper signal device for use during nighttime operation or inclement weather where visibility is greatly reduced.

Boating Safety

For the angler who keeps safety foremost in his mind, fishing from a boat isn't a dangerous experience. For the angler who doesn't, a boat can be an accident waiting to happen. Alabama's boating record through the years is horrendous. Since the state started keeping records in 1959, 1,137 Alabamians have lost their lives in boating accidents. That averages 37.9 fatalities per year. The biggest black mark was 1972 when 55 boaters were killed.

Driving a boat is a serious matter. Unfortunately, too few Alabamians approach it as such. Although a boating course isn't required by Alabama law, the smart boater takes one. The Alabama Marine Police Enforcement division offers boating courses year around, and they also offer a home study course. To find out about either, write the Alabama Marine Police Division, 64 N. Union St., Montgomery, Ala. 36130 or by calling 242-3673.

The Boat U.S. Foundation, a nationwide non-profit organization, has a toll-free number (1-800-336-BOAT) that you may call to find when other boating courses will be offered in your area.

Boating Hazards in Alabama

DROWNING

Drowning is the No. 1 cause of boating fatalities in Alabama. Almost all of those fatalities could have been prevented if the drowning victim had been wearing a personal floatation device (PFD).

Years ago, life jackets were bulky and uncomfortable. For that reason, few anglers chose to wear them. Today's PFD is lightweight, trim and comfortable to wear.

More and more anglers are wearing their PFDs at all times while in the boat.

Most modern bass boats are stable enough in the water that the angler can walk front-to-back and side-to-side without fear of capsizing.

Clutter in the form of tackle boxes, nets, trolling motor cables, etc., can cause an angler to trip and fall overboard, however.

Smaller aluminum jon boats are less stable than wide bass boats. Standing up in a jon boat can be dangerous.

If you need to reposition yourself in a jon boat, hold onto both sides and move with your weight low.

WEATHER

It's been said that the weather in Alabama can become violent without warning, but that is rarely true. The National Weather Service stays on top of weather by the minute and it's rare that a dangerous storm approaches without the NWS first broadcasting information about it. For that reason, a weather radio is important to boaters in Alabama.

It's not unusual for fishermen to take off on an early morning fishing trip dependent on weather information they received from the 6 o'clock news the day before.

In Alabama, the weather picture can change in a 12-hour period. The angler may head for the lake expecting the 30 percent chance of rain that was forecast the night before. Once on the water, he may find the dangerous thunderstorm that was forecast earlier that morning – a forecast the angler missed.

A weather radio also comes in handy once the angler gets on the water and begins fishing. A threatening looking cloud can turn into a lightning-laced thunderstorm, or even tornadic winds. A weather radio will give information regarding these storms, almost always in time for the angler to make his way to shore.

Storms cause several problems that can be trouble for boaters, including lightning, high winds, rough water, blinding rain and flying debris.

If you're caught in a lightning storm, immediately place all rods in the bottom of the boat.

If possible, head for land. Once there, lie on the ground away from trees and other tall objects. If possible lie in a ditch or other low spot.

If you're caught in a thunderstorm and the water is too rough, or you lack goggles that will enable you to make a fast run, lie flat in the boat until the storm passes.

If you're caught in high waves that begin to swamp the boat, immediately turn on the bilge pump and begin a quartering course that will keep water out of the boat. Head into the waves at an angle, riding over each wave.

Hitting the wave head on is rough on the boat and its riders and can put the boat under with one big wave. Heading directly away from the waves can be just as dangerous. Any hesitation on the driver's part can allow a wave to crash over the transom, thus flooding or stalling the boat.

A boat without power is a sitting duck. Waves can crash over the boat's side filling it with water, or can wash it to shore where it can be thrashed on the rocks.

HYPOTHERMIA

A person falling overboard in warm spring weather while wearing a life vest may not think his life in danger, but he can be fatally wrong. He may quickly find himself suffering from hyptothermia.

Hypothermia is the loss of body heat faster than the body can warm itself. It doesn't take a freezing January day for this to happen. It can happen any time the water temperature is below 70 degrees.

Hypothermia results from exposure to wetness and/or wind. A hypothermia victim may become blue/gray in color. Violent shivering develops before giving way to muscle spasms. Confusion and a drunken-like behavior also indicate a person may be hypothermic.

To protect yourself from hypothermia, dress warmly and stay dry. Put on rain gear and a jacket in cool or cold, rainy weather. Understand that it may be 50 degrees outside, but during a 40 mph boat ride in rainy weather, the temperature seems like 10 degrees.

When a person falls overboard in water less than 70 degrees, life expectancy time falls rapidly. Get the person out of water as quickly as possible. If the weather is cold, don't subject the person to a long ride. Get to the bank and find a house where the person can get warm.

If that's not possible, build a fire on the bank. Remove the victim's outer clothing and dry over the fire. Leave the victim's underwear and inner clothing on. Once the outer clothing is dry, remove the inner clothing and replace with the dry clothing and go get help.

If matches aren't available to start a fire, a fire can be started with a bit of gasoline from the tank and a spark from a battery.

COLLISIONS

Unlike an automobile driver, the driver of a boat must expect traffic from 360 degrees. Boat collisions are common in Alabama. Most are caused by excessive speed and driver inattention. Many of the fatal collision accidents are caused by drivers failing to stay on their side of the "road," choosing instead short cuts on blind curves.

WATER HAZARDS

Boating on Alabama's waterways requires a driver who can adjust. On Aliceville Lake, for instance, a boater in five foot of water may suddenly have his motor's lower unit ripped off by a stump. Boaters on Smith Lake at night may be cruising along in 95 feet of water - just before they crash head-on into a solid rock wall.

Every body of water in Alabama is different in its underwater makeup. Keep in mind that many of these lakes, reservoirs and rivers weren't designed for boaters. Before they were flooded, they were acres of land full of trees, boulders and hills. Almost all of that original terrain remains.

Before venturing out on a new body of water, talk with anglers and other boaters about the lake's makeup. Better yet, ride the lake with another boater before you try. Get a topographic map of the lake.

TAILRACES

Fishing below locks and dams is common in Alabama, but such fishing can be dangerous.

Swift current, whirlpools, boulders and sudden releases of turbulent water are a few of the hazards that anglers sometimes face.

Different laws apply to different locks and dams in the state. It is illegal to fish within 500 feet of a lock or dam operated by the U.S. Army Corps of Engineers and that is strictly enforced.

It is legal to fish below dams operated by Alabama Power Company and the Tennessee Valley Authority, but, by law, anglers must wear a PFD within 500 feet of them.

Most boating accidents below dams are caused by problems in the swift water. Always anchor with the nose of the boat heading upstream, and a long anchor rope.

Use the boat's motor to hold the boat steady in the current while the anchor is being readied, then allow the boat to drift backward while you throw the anchor way in front of the boat. Let the anchor hit bottom before you feed out line. If too much line is fed out beforehand, it may wash underneath the boat and tangle in the propeller. The anchor will then grab, the boat will spin around backward and it will swamp immediately.

Too many anglers anchor too well in tailraces. When a turbine is cut on, a wall of water sometimes five feet tall is released. Anglers need to be able to quickly get away from this wall of water, and boats anchored too well can't escape.

The best idea is to tie the end of the anchor rope to a foam block or a 5-gallon jug. Then, approximately 50 feet above the anchor, fasten a steel ring to the rope. A 3-foot length of cotton cord with a snap should then be tied to the front eye of the boat.

Use the snap on the cotton cord to snap onto the steel ring of the anchor rope. This cotton cord should be heavy enough to hold the boat in the current. If a turbine is cut on and a wall of water released, simply use a pocket knife to cut the cotton cord. The boat will float away from the anchor and when it gets to the end of the anchor rope, it will snatch the foam block or jug out of the boat. The foam block or jug will float the anchor line so the anchor isn't lost.

Rules of the Road

The water traffic "Rules of the Road" in the State of Alabama are:

1) Vessels passing head-on shall keep to the right.

2) Vessels overtaking another vessel may do so on either side, but must grant the right-of-way to the vessel being overtaken.

3) When vessels are passing at right angles, the vessel on the left will yield the right-of-way to vessel on the right.

4) Motor boats shall yield right-of-way to non-motor powered boats except as follows:

a) When being overtaken by non-powered vessels.

b) For deep draft vessels that have to remain in narrow channels.

c) When vessel is towing another vessel.

5) Motor boats must maintain a direct course when passing sailboats.

6) Any vessel approaching a landing dock or pier shall yield the right-of-way to any departing vessel.

7) Any vessel departing shoreline or tributary shall yield right-of-way to through traffic and vessels approaching shoreline or tributary.

8) Vessels will not abruptly change course without first determining that it can be safely done without risk of collision.

9) If an operator fails to fully understand course of an approaching vessel he must slow down immediately to a speed barely sufficient for steerageway until the other vessel has passed.

10) Vessels yielding right-of-way shall reduce speed, stop, reverse, or alter course to avoid collision. Vessel with right-of-way shall hold course and speed. If there is danger of collision, all vessels will slow down, stop, or reverse until danger is averted.

11) Vessels will issue warning signals in fog or thick weather.

12) No mechanically propelled vessel shall be operated in a circular course around any other vessel or any person swimming.

13) In narrow channel vessels will keep to the right.

14) Vessels approaching or passing another vessel shall be operated in such manner and at such rate of speed as will not create a hazardous wash or wake.

15) No vessel shall obstruct or interfere with take-off, landing, or taxiing of aircraft.

16) All vessels shall be operated at reasonable speeds for given situations and must be under the complete control of the operator.

17) No vessel or person shall obstruct or block navigation channel, entrance to channel, mooring slip, landing dock, launching ramp, pier or tributary.

18) Vessels shall keep at least 100 feet clearance of displayed diver's flag.